DOCUMENT PREPARATION SYSTEMS

Document Preparation Systems

A Collection of Survey Articles

Edited by

Jurg NIEVERGELT
Giovanni CORAY
Jean-Daniel NICOUD
Alan C. SHAW

1982

NORTH-HOLLAND PUBLISHING COMPANY
AMSTERDAM • NEW YORK • OXFORD

ISBN: 0 444 86493 8

Publishers:
NORTH-HOLLAND PUBLISHING COMPANY
AMSTERDAM • NEW YORK • OXFORD

Sole distributors for the U.S.A. and Canada:
ELSEVIER SCIENCE PUBLISHING COMPANY, INC.
52 VANDERBILT AVENUE
NEW YORK, N.Y. 10017

Cover: © L. Strik, 1982 c/o Beeldrecht Amsterdam

Library of Congress Cataloging in Publication Data
Main entry under title:

Document preparation systems.

1. Printing, Practical. I. Nievergelt, Jurg.
Z244.D63 1982   686.2'24   82-14310
ISBN 0-444-86493-8 (U.S.)

PRINTED IN THE NETHERLANDS

PREFACE

We are witnessing yet another revolution caused by the introduction of computer techniques into an established commercial field. The rapid spread of computer aids to the preparation, dissemination, storage and retrieval of documents of all kinds is having a profound impact on personal and business activities that had remained unchanged for decades. Professionals turn into their own typists, even an amateur working with advanced tools can produce documents of high standard typographic appearance all by himself: the work 'typesetter' denotes a machine rather than a craftsman.

Document preparation started as a cottage industry when books had to be copied by longhand, turned into a publishing industry with the invention of the printing press, and may well be on its way back to an activity confined to the individual's desk, as it was in the good old days of the handwritten manuscript. The break-through that makes this possible is the recent development of 'computerized desks' that are exceptionally adept at supporting the author in all phases of document preparation: organizing large collections of text fragments, merging them in different ways, prompting the writer with spelling checks, producing indices, drawing diagrams, attempting page layouts, and even mailing the electronic document over computer networks.

The purpose of this book is to select for the reader a snapshot of representative developments in the rapidly changing field of computer aids to document preparation, dissemination, storage and retrieval. Our plan to produce a collection of survey articles originated in conjunction with the Lausanne Conference on Research and Trends in DOCUMENT PREPARATION SYSTEMS held at the Swiss Federal Institute of Technology in February 1981: it demonstrated the vivid interest of researchers and practitioners in this budding field, and emphasized the lack of comprehensive surveys. The organizers and several participants felt that a joint effort by a number of authors could succeed in producing a timely survey of this field that is as yet not treated in book form.

This collection thus consists of six independently written chapters that are reasonably disjoint and attempt to cover the key areas in this emerging field. First comes a case study of a widely used and completely developed **document preparation environment.** Brian W. Kernighan and Michael E. Lesk present the various text processing, editing, and line-graphics features embedded in the UNIX operating system.

The **editor,** a frequently used interactive tool in the context of computer based document handling, deserves particular attention. A detailed survey of editing systems is reported and a classification of their functional capabilities is presented by Andries van Dam and Norman Meyrowitz. Generalizing from line-oriented text editors to interactive graphics, from menu oriented dialogue to syntax driven interaction, their synthesis accounts for the state of the art in the field, whose impact has become relevant in most computer applications.

Another important class of tools are the **formatters.** They provide the modern writer with layout facilities such as needed for hard-copy printing, video displays or photo-setting. Their integration with editing and operating systems facilities is first discussed on the ground of examples which are either commercially available or under the focus of present day research. The authors of this chapter, R.R. Furuta, J. Scofield and A. Shaw, also present the concepts and mathematical models which have evolved from the study of a document as a concrete object, to be handled according to its abstract properties. New programming **languages** are referenced, as they are needed to describe both the formatting process and the structure of a document in terms of its constituant classes of objects.

The development of text processing aids gives rise to **algorithmic problems** of an entirely new kind. As just one example, Donald E. Knuth and Michael F. Plass present their way of breaking paragraphs into lines; a problem encountered, and treated by ad hoc means in any justification or page layout technique.

The impact of the new technology on the world of **commercial typesetting** is described by John W. Seybold, early first generation phototypesetting systems up to present developments are traced to give a consistent, overall picture of the modern Gutenberg's art.

From the user's point of view, the common aspect of all the utilities described is that he uses them interactively; in the last chapter, Jurg Nievergelt presents recent insights into the systematic **design of man-machine dialogs:** an overview and a 'check-list' to those who take the responsibility of building a new computer tool.

What is not to be found in the book? Being written by computer specialists and researchers, the focus of the book is the computer as a tool in a new field of application. There has been no attempt to analyse the social and ethic implications of the human activity which is being automated away! Critical aspects, such as the increased ease to propagate redundant paper, information and errors, or the reduced quality of typographed material, would certainly find their adequate place in such a survey.

However, the discussion of these aspects is likely to be untimely in this fast moving field and we prefer to let the reader build his own opinion, from the information that he will find in this survey.

ADDRESSES OF EDITORS

Giovanni Coray
Dépt. Mathématiques, EPFL
61, avenue de Cour
CH-1007 Lausanne, Switzerland

Jurg Nievergelt
Informatik, ETH
Clausiusstrasse 55
CH-8006 Zuerich, Switzerland

Jean-Daniel Nicoud
Dépt. d'Electricité, EPFL
16, chemin de Bellerive
CH-1007 Lausanne, Switzerland

Alan C. Shaw
Dept. of Computer Science FR-35
University of Washington
Seattle, WA 98195, USA

ADDRESSES OF AUTHORS

Andries van Dam, Dept. of Computer Science, Box 1910, Brown University, Providence, Rhode Island 02912, USA

Richard Furuta, Dept. of Computer Science, University of Washington, Seattle, Washington 98195, USA

Brian W. Kernighan, Bell Laboratories, MH 2C-572, Murray Hill, New Jersey 07974, USA

Donald E. Knuth, Dept. of Computer Science, Stanford University, Stanford, California 94305, USA

Michael E. Lesk, Bell Laboratories, MH 2C-572, Murray Hill, New Jersey 07974, USA

Norman Meyrowitz, Dept. of Computer Science, Box 1910, Brown University, Providence, Rhode Island 02912, USA

Jurg Nievergelt, Informatik, ETH, Clausiusstrasse 55, CH-8006 Zürich, Switzerland

Michael F. Plass, Xerox PARC, 3333 Coyote Hill Road, Palo Alto, California 94304, USA

Jeffrey Scofield, Dept. of Computer Science, University of Washington, Seattle, Washington 98195, USA

John W. Seybold, Seybold Publications, Inc., Box 644, Media, Pennsylvania 19063, USA

Alan C. Shaw, Dept. of Computer Science, University of Washington, Seattle, Washington 98195, USA

LIST OF CONTENTS

Document Formatting Systems: Survey, Concepts, and Issues
  Richard Furuta, Jeffrey Scofield, and Alan Shaw **133**

KEYWORDS AND PHRASES

Document preparation, text processing, typesetting editors, formatting, interactive systems, man-machine dialog.

DOCUMENT PREPARATION SYSTEMS
J. Nievergelt, G. Coray, J.D. Nicoud, A.C. Shaw (eds.)
© North-Holland Publishing Company, 1982

UNIX Document Preparation*

Brian W. Kernighan and Michael E. Lesk

Bell Laboratories
Murray Hill, New Jersey 07974

ABSTRACT

The UNIX† operating system provides programs for sophisticated document preparation within the framework of a general-purpose operating system. The document preparation software includes text editors, programmable text formatters, macro-definition packages for a variety of page layout styles, special processors for mathematical expressions, tabular material, bibliographic references, and line drawing, and numerous supporting programs, such as a spelling-mistake detector.

In practice, this collection of facilities has proven to be easy to learn and use, even by secretaries, typists, and other non-specialists. Experiments have shown that preparation of complicated documents is about twice as fast as on completely manual systems. There are many benefits to using a general-purpose operating system instead of specialized stand-alone terminals or a system dedicated to "word processing." On the UNIX system, these include an excellent software development facility and the ability to share computing and data resources among a community of users.

1. INTRODUCTION

We use the term *document preparation* to mean the creation, modification, and display of textual material, such as manuals, reports, papers, and books. "Document preparation" seems preferable to "text processing" (which is not precise), or "word processing" (which has connotations of stand-alone specialized terminals).

A variety of comparatively elegant output devices has become available, supplementing the traditional typewriters, terminals, and line printers; this has led to a much increased interest in automated document preparation. Computerized systems are no longer limited to straight text printed in unattractive constant-width characters, but can produce a full range of documents in attractive fonts and page layouts. The major example of an output device with significant capabilities is the phototypesetter, which produces high quality printed output on photographic paper or film. Other devices include typewriter-like terminals capable of high-resolution motion, dot matrix printer-plotters, microfilm recorders, and xerographic printers.

Some of the benefits of computer-aided document preparation are familiar. Text is only entered once, and editing is only needed where changes are being made. There are many other benefits, however. Special languages can be used to simplify the entry of complex material such as tables and mathematical expressions. The format of a document can be decoupled from its content;

---

† UNIX is a Trademark of Bell Laboratories.

* This is a revised version of a paper entitled "Document Preparation" that appeared in the Bell System Technical Journal, vol. 57, no. 6. pp. 2115-2135, August 1978. Reprinted by permission.

the only format-control information that need be embedded is that describing textual categories and boundaries, such as titles, section headings, and paragraphs. Alternative document styles are then possible through the use of different formatting programs and different interpretations applied to the embedded format controls. Furthermore, programs can examine text to detect spelling mistakes, compare versions of documents, and prepare indexes automatically. Machine-generated data can be incorporated in documents; excerpts from documents can be fed to programs without transcription.

Further advantages accrue when document preparation is done on a general-purpose computer system. One is the sharing of programs and data bases among users; programs originally written for some other purpose may be useful to the document preparer. Having a broad range of users, from typists to scientists, on the same system leads to an unusual degree of cooperation in the preparation of documents. In addition, the existence of electronic mail and inter-machine networks makes possible the transmission of documents in machine-readable form at electronic speed.

The UNIX document preparation software includes several text editors. All can be used on documents, data files, or programs. The most often used are the original editor, **ed**, which is a line-oriented command-driven editor, and **vi**, a cursor-driven video editor. Two programmable text formatters, **nroff** and **troff**, provide paginated formatting and allow unusual freedom and flexibility in determining the style of documents. Augmented by various macro-definition packages, **nroff** and **troff** provide footnote processing, multiple-column output, column-length balancing, and automatic figure placement. A preprocessor called **eqn** translates a simple language for describing mathematical expressions into formatter input; a table-construction preprocessor, **tbl**, provides an analogous facility for input of data and text that is to be arranged into tables. Similarly **refer** extracts bibliographic references from a common data base and inserts them, in various formats, into documents. Most recently, the **pic** and **ideal** languages permit the typesetting of line drawings.

Besides describing these tools in some detail, we will also mention some supporting software useful to the document preparer, and summarize some comparisons between manual methods of document preparation and methods using UNIX.

2. TEXT EDITING

The original UNIX text editor was **ed**. We will not try to give a complete description of **ed** here; details may be found in Ref. 1. Rather, we will try to mention those attributes that are most interesting and unusual.

The **ed** editor is not specialized to any kind or style of text; it is used for programs, data, and documents alike. It is based on editing commands such as "print" and "substitute," rather than on special function keys, and provides convenient facilities for selecting the text lines to be operated on and altering their contents. Since it does not use special function keys or cursor controls, it does not require a particular kind of input device. It has a relatively restricted command set, with no macros or programming capabilities.

A text editor is often the primary interface between a user and the system, and the program with which most user time is spent. Accordingly, an editor has to be easy to use, and efficient of the user's time—editing commands have to "flow off the fingertips." In accordance with this principle, **ed** is quite terse. Each editor command is a single letter, e.g., **p** for "print," and **d** for "delete." Most commands may be preceded by zero, one, or two "line addresses" to affect, respectively, the "current line" (i.e., the line most recently referenced), the addressed line, or the range of contiguous lines between and including the pair of addresses. There are also shorthands for the current line and the last line of the file. Arithmetic expressions involving line numbers are also permitted:

```
-5,+5p
```

prints from five lines before the current line to five lines after, while

```
$-5,$p
```

prints the last six lines. In both cases, the last line printed becomes the current line, so that subsequent editing operations may begin from there.

Most often, the lines to be affected are specified not by line number, but by context, that is, by naming some text pattern that occurs in them. The "line address"

```
/abc/
```

refers to the first line after the current line that contains the pattern **abc**. This line address standing by itself will find and print the next line that contains **abc**, while

```
/abc/d
```

finds it and deletes it. Context searches begin with the line immediately after the current line, and wrap around from the end of the file to the beginning if necessary. It is also possible to scan the file in the reverse direction by enclosing the pattern in question marks: **?abc?** finds the previous **abc**.

The substitute command **s** can replace any pattern by any literal string of characters in any group of lines. The command

```
s/ofrmat/format/
```

changes **ofrmat** to **format** on the current line, while

```
1,$s/ofrmat/format/
```

changes it on every line. In both searches and substitute commands, the pattern // is an abbreviation for the most recently used pattern, and **&** stands for the most recently matched text. Both can be used to avoid repetitive typing. The "undo" command **u** undoes the most recent substitution.

In all cases, the trailing delimiter ("/", for instance) may be omitted if it is the last thing in the command.

Text can be added before or after any line, and any group of contiguous lines may be replaced by new lines. "Cut and paste" operations are also possible—any group of lines may be either moved or copied elsewhere. Individual lines may be split or joined together; text within a line may be rearranged.

The editor does not work on a file directly, but on a copy. Any file may be read into the working text at any point; any contiguous lines may be written or appended to any file. And any UNIX command may be executed from within the editor, even another instance of the editor.

So far, we have described the basic editor features: this is all that the beginning user needs to know, and about as much as most of our clerical users need. More sophisticated users can include in their search patterns "metacharacters" that specify character classes, repetition of characters or classes, the beginning or end of a line, and so on. For example, the pattern

```
/^[0-9]/
```

searches for the next line that begins with a digit.

Any set of editing commands may be done under control of a "global" command: the editing commands are performed starting at each line that matches a pattern specified in the global command. As the simplest example,

```
g/interesting/p
```

prints all lines that contain **interesting**.

Finally, given the UNIX software for input-output redirection, it is easy to make a "script" of editing commands in advance, then run it on a sequence of files.

The basic pattern-searching and editing capabilities of **ed** have been co-opted into other, more specialized programs as well. The program **grep** ("global regular expression print") prints all input lines that contain a specified pattern; this program is particularly useful for finding the location of an item in a set of files, or for culling items from larger inputs. The program **sed** is a variant of **ed** that performs a set of editing operations on each line of an input stream

Some users prefer more complex editors. The **vi** editor, written by Bill Joy at Berkeley, depends on cursor motion and so runs only on video terminals. It maintains a current screen display of the file at all times. The 'undo' feature of this editor is very attractive for learning; it can back up across any command and restore the previous version of the text. **vi** is not nearly as heavily used as **ed**, partly because it simply is not as familiar, and partly because it places a significantly greater load on the system.

The **emacs** editor, originated by Richard Stallman of MIT, is another screen editor in limited use, but it is too complex for the typical typist, at least as normally presented. **emacs** is programmable, however, so users can define their own editing interfaces if they wish.

As an operating system, UNIX provides sufficient facilities for these editors and indeed a variety of others; the system does not foreclose any options. The choice of which one to use is thus made according to personal taste, although there is some pressure to mimimize the number of different editors so as to avoid problems of maintenance and training. It is easier for users to help each other if they are all using basically the same tools.

3. TROFF AND NROFF — BASIC TEXT FORMATTERS

Once a user has entered a document into the file system, it can be formatted and printed by **troff** or **nroff**.[2] These are programmable text formatters that accommodate a wide variety of formatting tasks by providing flexible fundamental tools rather than specific features. **troff** supports phototypesetting on any typesetter; we use equipment from Wang, Mergenthaler, and Autologic today. **nroff** produces formatted output for a variety of terminals and line printers, using the full capabilities and resolution of each. **troff** and **nroff** accept the same input language. Except for device description tables, device-oriented routines, and a small amount of conditionally-compiled code, the source code for these programs is also identical. Both programs are driven by device description tables, so that **troff** can drive a variety of typesetters and **nroff** can understand the entire typesetter character set, printing non-ASCII characters where available or where they can be constructed (by overstriking) on a particular device. The remaining discussion in this section focuses on **troff**; the behavior of **nroff** is identical within device capability.

troff is intended to permit unusual freedom in user-designed document styles, at the price of being somewhat hard to use for basic formatting tasks. The fundamental operations that **troff** provides are sufficient for programming complicated formatting tasks. For example, footnote processing, multi-column layout with column balancing, and automatic figure placement are not built-in operations, but are programmed in **troff** macros when needed. To program in **troff**, the user writes a set of macro definitions, which expand into the command sequences needed for each formatting task. **troff** may also be instructed to invoke specified macros automatically at particular page positions, such as at the top and near the bottom of the page; other commands are invoked by the user by placing macro calls at paragraphs, section headings, and other relevant boundaries. Once a macro package has been written for some particular style of document, users preparing a document in that style need only prepare their text with macro calls at the appropriate points, as described in the next section.

Complex formatting tasks require complex macro packages designed by competent programmers. A well-designed package can be easy to use, and usually permits convenient choice between several related styles. At the simple end of the style spectrum, a newspaper-style galley may not require any embedded format control except paragraphing. A simple paginated style might use only three macros, defining the nature of the top-of-page margin, the bottom-of-page margin, and paragraph breaks.

Input consists of text lines, which are destined to be printed, interspersed with control lines, which set parameters or otherwise control subsequent processing. Control lines begin with a control character—normally a period—followed by a one- or two-character name that specifies either a built-in request or the substitution of a user-defined macro in place of the control line. This form is reminiscent of earlier text formatters.[3,4] A typical sequence of requests is

```
.pl 8.5i
.ll 5i
.ps 10
.ft R
.sp 2
```

which sets the page length to 8.5 inches, the line length to 5 inches, the type size to 10 points, the font to Roman, and then spaces down two lines.

Formatting functions may also be introduced anywhere in the input by an in-line command, which consists of an escape character, normally \, a command, and perhaps parameters. For example, \f specifies a font change, so \fB causes a change to bold font when it appears, and \fP reverts to the previous font. Similarly, \l´3i´ draws a three-inch line.

There are about eighty built-in control-line requests that implement the fundamental operations, allow the setting of parameters, and otherwise affect format control. In addition, more than forty in-line commands may appear anywhere to specify certain characters, to set indicators, and to introduce various functions. Automatic services available include filling and adjusting of text, hyphenation with user control over exceptions, user-settable left, right, and centering tabs, and output line numbering.

User-settable parameters include font, point size, page length, page number, line spacing, line length, indent, and tabs. Functions are available for building brackets, overstriking, drawing lines, circles, ellipses, arcs and splines, generating vertical and horizontal motions, and calculating the width and height of a string. In addition to the parameters that are defined by the formatter, users may define their own, stored in **troff** variables called "number registers" (for numeric parameters) and "strings" (for character data). These variables may be used in arithmetic and logical expressions to set parameters or to control the invocation of macros or requests.

A *macro* is a user-named set of lines of arbitrary text and format control information. It is interpolated into the input stream either by invoking it by name, or by specifying that it is to be invoked when a particular vertical position on a page is reached. Arguments may be passed to a macro invoked by name. A *string* is a named string of characters that may be interpolated at any point. Macros and strings may be created, redefined, appended to, renamed, and removed. Macros may be nested to an arbitrary depth, limited only by the memory available.

Processed text may be diverted into a macro instead of being output, for footnote collection or to determine the horizontal or vertical size of a block of text before final placement on a page. When reread, diverted text retains its character fonts and sizes and overall dimensions.

A *trap* mechanism provides for action when certain conditions occur. The conditions available are position on the current output page, length of a diversion, and input line count. A macro associated with a vertical page position is automatically invoked when a line of output falls on or after the trap position. For example, reaching a specified place near the bottom of the page could invoke a macro that describes the bottom margin area. Similarly, a vertical position trap may be specified for diverted output. An input line count trap causes a macro to be invoked after a specified number of input text lines have been read.

Some parameters are available to the user in predefined number registers; these include the day, month, year, page number, input line number, etc. In addition, users may define their own registers. Except for certain predefined read-only registers, a number register can be read, written, automatically incremented or decremented, and interpolated into the input in decimal, alphabetic, or roman numeral format. One common use of user-defined registers is to automatically number sections, paragraphs, lines, etc. A number register may be used any time numerical input is expected or desired. In most circumstances, numerical input may have appended scale factors representing inches, points, ems, etc. Numerical input may be provided by expressions involving a variety of arithmetic and logical operators.

A mechanism is provided for conditionally accepting a group of lines as input. The conditions that may be tested are the value of a numerical expression, the equality of two strings, and the truth of built-in conditions such as page number parity or whether the formatter is **troff** or **nroff**.

Certain of the parameters that control text processing constitute an *environment*, which may be switched by the user. It is convenient, for example, to process footnotes in a separate environment from the main text. Environment parameters include line length, line spacing, indent, and character size and font. In addition, any collected but not yet output lines or words are a part of the environment. Parameters that are global and not switched with the environment include, for example, page length, page position, and macro, string and number register values.

It is not possible to give any substantial examples of **troff** macro definitions, but we will sketch a few to indicate the general style of use.

The simplest example is to provide pagination—an extra space at the top and bottom of each page. Two macros are usually defined—a *header* macro containing the top-of-page text and spacings, and a *footer* macro containing the bottom-of-page text and spacings. A trap must be placed at vertical position zero to cause the header macro to be invoked and a second trap must be placed at the desired distance from the bottom for the footer. Simple macros merely providing space for the margins could be defined as follows.

```
.de hd          \"  begin header definition
'sp 1i          \"  space 1 inch
. .             \"  end of header definition
.de fo          \"  footer
'bp             \"  space to beginning of next page
. .             \"  end of footer definition
.wh 0 hd        \"  set trap to invoke hd when at top of page
.wh -1i fo      \"  set trap to invoke fo 1 inch from bottom
```

Normally the **.sp** and **.bp** commands cause a *break*, that is, the current output line is flushed and a new one begun. A command that begins with a quote (as in **'bp**) does not cause a break when it is invoked. The sequence \" introduces a **troff** comment.

A more complicated header might print the current page number at the top right or left, being sure to preserve the proper size and font:

```
.de hd
'sp 0.5i
.if o .tl '''\\s10\\fR- \n% -\\s0\\fP' \"  odd page
.if e .tl '\\s10\\fR- \n% -\\s0\\fP''' \"  even page
'sp 0.5i
..
```

The backslashes are necessary inside a macro to delay evaluation until the macro is invoked.

The production of multi-column pages requires still more complicated macros. The basic idea is that the header macro records the vertical position of the column top in a register and initializes a column counter. The footer macro is invoked at the bottom of each column. Normally it increments the column counter, increments the page offset by the column width plus the column separation, and generates a reverse vertical motion to the top of the next column (the place recorded by the header macro). After the last column, however, the page offset is restored and the bottom margin functions for the complete page occur.

Footnote processing is even more involved; only the general strategy will be summarized here. A pair of macros is defined that allows the user to indicate the beginning and end of the footnote text. The footnote-start macro changes to the footnote environment and begins a diversion that appends to a macro in which footnotes are being collected. The footnote-end macro terminates the diversion, resets the environment, and moves the footer trap up the page an amount equal to the size of the diverted footnote text. The footer eventually invokes and then removes the macro containing the accumulated footnotes and resets its own trap position. Footnotes that don't fit have their overflow rediverted and are treated as the beginning footnote on the next page.

The use of preprocessors to convert special input languages for equations and tables into **troff** input means that many documents reach **troff** containing large amounts of program-generated input. For example, a simple equation might produce dozens of **troff** input lines and require many string definitions, redefinitions, and detailed numerical computations for proper character position-ing. The **troff** string that finally contains the equation contains many font and size changes and local motions, and so can become very long. All of this demands substantial string storage, effi-cient storage allocation, larger text buffers than would otherwise be necessary, and the accommoda-tion of large numbers of strings and number registers. Input generated by programs instead of peo-ple severely tests program robustness.

Regardless of the input, the output of **troff** is a simple, typesetter-independent language that basically tells where to put each character on the page, and in what size and font. A post-processor interprets this language and generates the necessary commands to drive a particular output device. There is generally one post-processor per typesetter.

4. MACROS—DECOUPLING CONTENT AND FORMAT

Although **troff** provides full control over typesetter (or terminal) features, few users exercise this control directly. Just as programmers have learned to use problem-oriented languages rather than assembly languages, it has proven better for people who prepare documents to describe them in terms of content, rather than specifying point sizes, fonts, etc., in a typesetter-oriented way. This is done by avoiding the detailed commands of **troff**, and instead embedding in the text only macro commands that expand into **troff** commands to implement a desired format.

For example, the title of a document might be prefaced by

```
.TL
```

which would expand, for this paper, into "Times Roman bold, 11 point type, centered at top of new page," but for a journal might be "Helvetica Bold, 14 point, left adjusted, preceded by copy-right notice and a one-inch space," or whatever is desired. In a similar way, there would be macros for other common features of a document, such as author's name, abstract, section, paragraph, and footnote.

This document actually begins

```
.TL
UNIX Document Preparation*
.AU
Brian W. Kernighan and Michael E. Lesk
.AI
.MH
.AB
.PP
The
.UX
operating system provides programs
for sophisticated document preparation ...
.PP
In practice, this collection of facilities has proven to be
easy to learn and use ...
.AE
.FS
* This is a revised version of a paper ...
.FE
```

Some of these macros are obviously specialized to our environment. For instance, **.MH** expands into the company name and address, and **.UX** becomes UNIX, with a footnote about trademark on the first occurrence.

Macro packages have been prepared for a variety of document styles. Locally, these include formal and informal internal memoranda; technical reports for external distribution; the Association for Computing Machinery journals; some American Physical Society journals; *Software—Practice and Experience*; and *The Bell System Technical Journal*. All of these macro packages recognize standard macro names for titles, paragraphs, and other document features, so the same input can be made to appear in many different forms, without changing it at all. Authors can prepare camera-ready copy for any of these journals, merely by naming the journal type when **troff** is invoked.

An important advantage of this system is the ease with which new users learn document preparation. It is necessary only to learn the correct way to describe document content and boundaries, not how to control the typesetter at a detailed level. A typist can easily learn the dozen or so most common macros in a few minutes, and another dozen as needed. This entire article uses only about 30 distinct macro calls, rather more than the norm.

Although **nroff** is used for typewriter-like output, and **troff** for photocomposition, they accept exactly the same input language, and thus hide details of particular devices from users. Macro packages also provide a degree of independence: they permit a uniformity of *input*, so that input documents look the same regardless of the output format or device they eventually appear in. This means that to find the title of a document, for example, it is not necessary to know what format is being used to print it. Finally, macros also enforce a uniformity of *output*. Since each output format is defined in appearance by the macro package that generates it, all documents prepared in that format will look the same.

5. EQN—A PREPROCESSOR FOR MATHEMATICAL EXPRESSIONS

Much of the work of Bell Laboratories is described in technical reports and papers containing significant amounts of mathematics. Mathematical material is difficult to type and expensive to typeset by traditional methods. Because of positioning requirements and the multiplicity of characters, sizes, and fonts, it is not feasible for a human to typeset mathematics directly with **troff** commands. **troff** has the facilities needed for preparing mathematical expressions, such as arbitrary horizontal and vertical motions, line-drawing, size changing, etc., but it is not easy to use them directly because of the difficulty of deciding the degree of size change and motion suitable in every circumstance. For this reason, a language for describing mathematical expressions was designed; this language is translated into **troff** input by a program called **eqn**.

An important requirement is that the language should be easy to learn and use by people who don't know mathematics, computing, or typesetting. This implies that normal mathematical conventions about operator precedence, parentheses, and the like cannot be used, for otherwise the user would have to understand what was being typed. Further, there should be few rules, keywords, and special symbols, and few exceptions to the rules. Finally, standard actions should take place automatically—size and font changes should follow normal mathematical usage without user intervention.

When a document is typed, mathematical expressions are entered as part of the text, but are marked by user-settable delimiters. **eqn** reads the entire input and passes through untouched those parts that are not mathematics. At the same time, it converts the mathematical parts into the necessary **troff** commands. The result is passed to **troff**. UNIX makes it easy to direct the output of one program into the input of another, with a mechanism called a "pipe." Thus normal usage is a pipeline of the form

        eqn files | troff

The two programs run concurrently, with scheduling and input-output synchronization handled by the operating system.

The **eqn** language is defined by a grammar, written in a compiler-compiler language called Yacc,[5] to insure regularity and ease of change. We will not describe **eqn** in detail; see Refs. 6 and 7. Nonetheless, it is worth showing a few examples to give a feeling for the language. Throughout this section we write expressions exactly as they are typed by the user, except that in general we will omit the delimiters that mark the beginning and end of each expression.

eqn is an oral (or perhaps aural) language. To produce

$$2\pi \int \sin(\omega t)dt$$

one writes

```
.EQ
2 pi int sin ( omega t)dt
.EN
```

The markers **.EQ** and **.EN** delimit the expression. They are passed through to **troff**; most macro packages provide definitions for them that cause the equation to be displayed, as it is here, perhaps with a number in the margin.

Each "word" within the expression is looked up in a table. In this case, **pi** and **omega** are recognized as Greek letters, **int** is a special character, and **sin** is to be placed in Roman font instead of italic, following conventional practice. Parentheses and digits are also made Roman, and spacing is adjusted around characters to give a more pleasing appearance.

Subscripts, superscripts, fractions, radicals, and the like are introduced by words used as operators:

$$\frac{x^2}{a^2} = \sqrt{pz^2 + qz + r}$$

is produced by

```
x sup 2 over a sup 2 ~=~ sqrt {pz sup 2 + qz + r}
```

Braces { and } are used to group items that are to be treated as a unit, such as all the terms to go under the radical. The precedence of **sup** is higher than that of **over** so braces are not needed for the left side of this expression. **eqn** input is free-form, so blanks and new lines can be used freely to make the input easier to type, read, and subsequently edit. The tilde ~ forces extra space into the output; **eqn** does not automatically add the extra space that would normally appear around the = sign.

The operator **sub** produces a subscript in the same manner as **sup** produces a superscript; if **sub** and **sup** occur together they are treated specially to keep the subscript and superscript nearly vertical, so that

```
x sub i sup 2
```

is printed as x_i^2, not $x_i{}^2$.

```
roman erf (z) ~=~ 2 over sqrt pi int sub 0 sup z e sup -t sup 2 dt
```

produces

$$\mathrm{erf}(z) = \frac{2}{\sqrt{\pi}} \int_0^z e^{-t^2} dt$$

"**roman**" forces the next object into Roman font; it would otherwise be italicized.

Limits may be placed below and above a construct with **from** and **to**:

```
zeta (s) ~=~ sum from k=1 to inf k sup -s ~~~ ( Re ~ s > 1)
```

is

$$\zeta(s) = \sum_{k=1}^{\infty} k^{-s} \quad (\mathrm{Re}\ s > 1)$$

and

```
lim from {x -> pi /2} ( tan~x) sup {sin~2x} ~=~ 1
```

yields

$$\lim_{x \to \pi/2} (\tan x)^{\sin 2x} = 1$$

Built-up brackets, braces, etc., are available:

```
lim from {x -> inf} left ( 1 + 1 over x right ) sup x ~=~ e
```

produces

$$\lim_{x \to \infty} \left(1 + \frac{1}{x}\right)^{x} = e$$

In such expressions, the character following the keywords `left` or `right` can be any of a family of characters that stretch vertically, such as braces, brackets, bars, floor and ceiling. The character will be stretched enough to cover the enclosed construction.

eqn also provides for matrices; in fact, "matrix" is used in more situations than might be supposed from the name:

$$A = \tfrac{1}{2}\,ab\,\sin\theta$$
$$c^2 = a^2 + b^2 - 2ab\,\cos\theta$$
$$S = \pi r \sqrt{r^2 + h^2}$$
$$V = \frac{\pi}{3}r^2 h$$

is produced by a matrix of three columns and four rows:

```
matrix {
    rcol { A above c sup 2 above S above V }
    ccol { = above = above = above = }
    lcol { half ~ ab ~ sin ~ theta
        above a sup 2 + b sup 2 - 2ab ~ cos ~ theta
        above pi r sqrt {r sup 2 + h sup 2}
        above pi over 3 r sup 2 h
    }
}
```

Matrices are specified by columns, each of which may be independently centered or left or right justified.

eqn also provides for diacritical marks such as dots and bars:

```
x dotdot ~=~ y bar
```

produces

$$\ddot{x} = \bar{y}$$

Font and size changes are available to override defaults, as are facilities for lining up equations and a rudimentary macro substitution process.

Because not all potential users have access to a typesetter, there is also a compatible version of **eqn** that interfaces to **nroff** for producing output on terminals capable of half-line motions and printing special characters. The quality of terminal output leaves something to be desired, but it is often adequate for proofreading and some internal uses.

The **eqn** language has proven to be easy to learn and use; at the present time, several hundred typists and secretaries use it at Bell Laboratories. Most are either self-taught, or have learned it as part of a UNIX course taught by other secretaries and typists. Empirically, mathematically trained users (mathematicians, physicists, etc.) can learn enough **eqn** in a few minutes to begin useful work, for its syntax and rules are similar to the way that mathematics is actually spoken. Persons not trained in mathematics take longer to get started, because the language is less familiar, but it is still true that an hour or two of instruction is enough to begin doing useful work.

By intent, **eqn** does not know much about typesetting; in general, it lets **troff** do as much of the job as possible, including all character-width computations. In this way, **eqn** can be relatively independent of the particular character set, and even of the typesetter being used.

The basic design decision to make a separate language and program distinct from **troff** does have some drawbacks, because it is not easy for **eqn** to make a decision based on the way that **troff** will produce the output. Nonetheless, these drawbacks seem unimportant compared to the benefits of having a language that is easily mastered, and a program that is separate from the main typesetting program. Changes in one program generally do not affect the other; both programs are smaller than they would be if they were combined. And, of course if one doesn't use **eqn**, there is no cost, since **troff** doesn't contain any code for it.

6. TBL—A PREPROCESSOR FOR TABLES

Tables also present typographic difficulties. The primary difficulty is deciding where columns should be placed to accommodate the range of widths of the various table entries. It is even harder to arrange for various lines or boxes to be drawn within the table in a suitable way. **tbl**[8] is a table construction program that is also an independent preprocessor, quite analogous to **eqn**.

tbl simplifies entering tabular data, which may be tedious to type or may be generated by a program, by separating the table format from its contents. Each table specification contains three parts: a set of options affecting the whole table, such as "center" or "box"; then a set of commands describing the format of each line of the table; and finally the table data. Each specification describes the alignment of the fields on a line, so that the description

```
L R R
```

indicates a line with three fields, one left adjusted and two right adjusted. Other kinds of fields are "C" (centered) and "N" (numerical adjustment), with "S" (spanned) used to continue a field across more than one column. For example,

```
C S S
L N N
```

describes a table whose first line is a centered heading spanning three columns; the three columns are left-adjusted, numerically adjusted, and numerically adjusted respectively. If there are more lines of data than of specifications (the normal case), the last specification applies to all remaining data lines.

A sample table in the format above might be

Position of Major Cities		
Tokyo	35°45' N	139°46' E
New York	40°43' N	74°01' W
London	51°30' N	0°10' W
Singapore	1°17' N	103°51' E

The input to produce the above table, with tab characters shown by the symbol ⓣ, is as follows:

```
.TS
center, box;
C S S
L N N.
Position of Major Cities
Tokyo ⓣ 35°45' N ⓣ 139°46' E
New York ⓣ 40°43' N ⓣ 74°01' W
London ⓣ 51°30' N ⓣ 0°10' W
Singapore ⓣ 1°17' N ⓣ 103°51' E
.TE
```

Just as in **eqn**, the delimiters **.TS** and **.TE** set off the table specification; they are passed through to **troff** where they may well be interpreted as macros that will perform such operations as keeping the table together on a page, centering it, leaving space around it, etc.

tbl also provides facilities for including blocks of text within a table. A block of text may contain any normal typesetting commands, and may be adjusted and filled as usual. **tbl** will arrange for adequate space to be left for it and will position it correctly. Extensive glossaries and other items that would often not be thought of as tables are produced this way with our software, to take advantage of **tbl**'s ability to adjust positioning and draw boxes more easily than a typist can. For example, the table on the next page uses text blocks, line and box drawing, size and font changes, and the facility for centering vertical placement of the headings (compare the heading of column 3 with that of columns 1 and 2).

Functional Systems		
Function Number	Function Type	Solution
1	LINEAR	Systems of equations all of which are linear can be solved by Gaussian elimination.
2	POLYNOMIAL	Depending on the initial guess, Newton's method $(f_{i+1}=f_i-\dfrac{f_i'}{f_i})$ will often converge on such systems.
3	ALGEBRAIC	The program ZONE by J. L. Blue will solve systems for which an accurate initial guess is not known.

The input for this table is as follows:

```
.TS
center, box;
cB s s
cBp9 | cBp9 | cBp9w(2.2i)
cBp9 | cBp9 | ^
n | ap8 | lp8.
Functional Systems
.sp 3p
=
.sp 3p
Function  Function  Solution
Number    Type
_
.sp 3p
1    LINEAR     T{
.fi
Systems of equations all of which are linear ...
T}
2    POLYNOMIAL    T{
Depending on the initial guess, Newton's method
($f sub i+1 = f sub i - {f sub i '} over {f sub i}$) ...
T}
3    ALGEBRAIC  T{
The program ZONE by J. L. Blue will solve ...
T}
.sp 3p
.TE
```

Note that there is no difficulty with equations in tables. In fact, there is sometimes a choice between writing a matrix with the matrix commands of **eqn** or making a table of equations. Typically, the typist picks whichever program is more familiar.

The **tbl** program writes **troff** code as output, just as **eqn** does. This code computes the width of each table entry, decides where to place the columns and lines separating them, and prints the table. **tbl** itself does not understand typesetting: it does not know the widths of characters, and may (in the case of equations in tables) have no knowledge of the height, either. However, it writes **troff** output that computes these sizes, and adjusts the table accordingly. Thus tables can be printed on any device and in any font without additional work.

As with **eqn**, **tbl** is normally run in a pipeline, perhaps with **eqn** as well:

```
tbl files | eqn | troff
```

Most of the comments about using **eqn** apply to **tbl** as well: it is easy to learn and is in wide use at Bell Laboratories. Since it is a program separate from **troff**, it need not be learned, used, or paid for if no tables are present. Comparatively few users need to know all of the tools: typically, the workload in one area may be mathematical, in another area tabular, and in another only ordinary text.

7. BIBLIOGRAPHIC REFERENCES

Another preprocessor, **refer**, finds and formats bibliographic references. It can be used with a public data base of citations to avoid the need for each author to keep track of precise citations. We have, for example, a list of 5,000 papers in computer science and related areas, any of which can be inserted at any point. To cite the report "Some Applications of Inverted Indexes on UNIX", which describes **refer** in detail, writing

```
.[
lesk inverted indexes
.]
```

produces the citation,[9] suitably formatted, in the text. A few words chosen from author names, title words, or journal names are usually enough to select the correct paper.

The index of citations is maintained using hashed inverted files for fast retrieval. The indexing program extracts the words from the citations and truncates them to six characters (this avoids requiring the retriever to type the exact spelling out to the end). The words are then converted to hash codes, and a conventional inverted file index is made on the hash codes. The size of the hash table is chosen to fit in **refer**'s memory, so that for each word in the citation request (bracketed by .[and .]) only one seek is made to the disk. The lists of citations for each word in the request are then merged, and the text of the citations retrieved. The program then checks for false drops (relatively rare if several search terms are given) and formats the output for typesetting.

In line with the general **troff** philosophy, **refer** itself delivers a set of string definitions containing the information in the citation: who the author is, what the title is, etc. The formatting macro packages define what the style of a reference is in the particular format being printed. Thus, the reference for the original version of this paper is in the data base as

```
%T UNIX Time-Sharing System: Document Preparation
%K unix bstj
%A B. W. Kernighan
%A M. E. Lesk
%A J. F. Ossanna
%J Bell Sys. Tech. J.
%V 57
%N 6
%P 2115-2135
%D 1978
```

and the final macro package decides whether this will be printed with the article title in quotes or italics, for example. Each macro package for a particular journal style needs as a part, therefore, the description of the bibliographic reference style imposed by that journal.

In addition, the **refer** program can sort the references in an article into alphabetical order by author or title and number them sequentially or by author name and date or other styles. The same data base of papers can also be used to prepare bibliographies and publication lists for individuals. Any number of private and public data bases can be used with **refer**; many of our users maintain private bibliographies for this purpose. In addition, if a reference is not likely to be needed again, the entry can be typed into the text at the appropriate point, and **refer** can be used to format and sort it, without making use of the data base.

Experience with **refer** has been mixed. The use of the program to format and sort citations is welcomed. The public data base, however, is difficult to maintain because different users have different, and strongly held, ideas about what should be in it. Although these differences are often trivial (should authors' first names be given or only initials; should the *Bell System Technical Journal* be abbreviated as above or as *BSTJ*) they nevertheless often require people to make private bibliography lists rather than using the public list.

8. GRAPHICS – LINE DRAWINGS

When we acquired our first CRT typesetter, it became possible to make line drawings as well as typeset text. The **troff** program now accepts commands to draw lines at arbitrary angles, instead of just horizontal and vertical lines. For those authors who have slipped from the straight and narrow, there are also commands to draw circular arcs and spline curves.

There are two programs to draw pictures: **pic** and **ideal**. Both are language-based: they use an ordinary terminal as input device, with the picture description spelled out as a sequence of statements in a language. **pic** is like a conventional algorithmic language: the user asks the typesetter to draw this, then to draw that, and so on until the picture is finished. The **ideal** program is analogous to an applicative language: the user states a set of constraints sufficient to define the picture, and **ideal** determines the details and prints the picture. In practice **pic** is more heavily used by typists, since it is easier to understand and somewhat more specialized to the kinds of line drawings customary in our work. We will discuss only **pic** and refer those interested in **ideal** to Chris Van Wyk's paper.[10]

The basic objects in **pic** are boxes, lines, arrows, circles, ellipses, arcs and splines, which may be placed anywhere and labeled with arbitrary text. Normally, these objects can be placed relative to one another, rather than needing absolute coordinates for location.

As a simple example, the figure

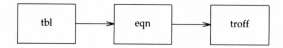

is entered as

```
.PS
box "tbl"; arrow; box "eqn"; arrow; box "troff"
.PE
```

The **pic** program is implemented as another preprocessor; as with **eqn**, the language is defined by a Yacc grammar. With a preprocessor, it is much easier to include text, perhaps containing mathematics or tables, inside figures than it would be using a separate co-routine followed by electronic cut-and-paste. Since our local environment until recently had no good graphics input devices, it is natural that **pic** uses ordinary terminals for input; a textual representation also fits naturally with the other components of the system.

The basic elements of **pic** are the objects: box, circle, ellipse, line, spline, ..., and the motions left, right, up, down, ..., which may be combined using conventional programming concepts of nesting and labeling. In addition, there are modifiers of the objects, such as the text inside a box, or the direction of an arrow. Saying

```
box "word"
```

puts the word inside the box, and

```
arrow right 1i
```

draws an arrow right 1 inch. Normally, a simple list of items is turned into a set of drawings, lined up left to right as in the first example above. However, lines may be drawn between specific points. Labels can be placed on pieces of a picture, and the corners of these pieces specified with modifiers such as "ne" or "e". Thus, for example,

```
A: box "start"
move
B: box "finish"
arc from A.ne to B.nw
arc from A.se to B.sw
```

draws

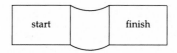

pic also provides the notion of an ordinal name to supplement conventional labels. This example can also be written as

```
box "start"; move; box "finish"
arc from 1st box.ne to last box.nw
arc from 1st box.se to 2nd box.sw
```

The "last" object of a given type is of course the most recent, as illustrated here:

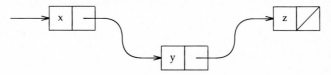

The input for this figure is

```
boxht = 0.3i; boxwid = boxht
arrow
box "x"; box
spline -> from center of last box right then down then right
box "y"; box
spline -> from center of last box right then up then right
box "z"; box
line from last box.sw to last box.ne    # diagonal line
```

The default sizes of objects may be overridden either locally or (as here) by setting the values of standard variables that control them. The curves are quadratic B-splines; the notation -> calls for an arrowhead.

The **pic** language also contains macro expansion, location by x,y position, and invisible objects (used to locate other, visible objects). For further details, see Ref. 11.

As a final, more complex example, here is a chained-overflow hash table:

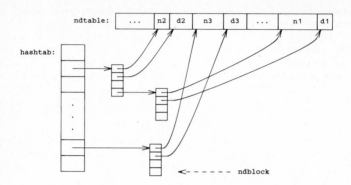

The problem of creating **pic** input is being addressed with still other preprocessors. Programs exist, for example, to generate **pic** input from the output of a graphics terminal, permitting those with better hardware to take advantage of it. Another program abstracts numerical data from a report and generates the **pic** input to draw a histogram from it. As is typical in the UNIX environment, existing software is used in new ways in preference to writing new packages.

9. OTHER SUPPORTING SOFTWARE

One advantage of doing document preparation in a general-purpose computing environment instead of with a specialized word processing system is that programs not directly related to document preparation may often be used to make the job easier. In this section, we discuss some examples from our experience.

One of the most tedious tasks in document preparation is detection of spelling and typographical errors. Existing data bases originally obtained for other purposes are used by a program called **spell**, which detects potential spelling mistakes. Machine-readable dictionaries (more precisely, word lists) have been available for some time. Ours was originally used for testing hyphenation algorithms and for checking voice synthesizer programs. It was realized, however, that a rudimentary program for detecting spelling mistakes could be made simply by comparing each word in a document with each word in the dictionary; any word in the document but not in the dictionary is a potential misspelling.

The first program for this approach was developed in a few minutes by combining existing UNIX utilities for sorting, comparing, etc. This was sufficiently promising that additional small programs were written to handle inflected forms like plurals and past participles. The resulting program was quite useful, for it provided a good match of computer capabilities to human ones. The machine can reduce a large document to a tractable list of suspicious words that a human can rapidly scan to detect the genuine errors.

Naturally, normal output from **spell** contains not only legitimate errors, but a fair amount of technical jargon and some proper names. The next step is to use that output to refine the dictionary. In fact, we have carried this step to its logical conclusion, by creating a brand new dictionary that contains only words culled from documents. This new dictionary is about one-third the size of the original, and produces better results.

Further checking of documents is possible with the **style** and **diction** programs of Lorinda Cherry.[12] These have been popularized through their inclusion in the Writer's Workbench software package. The **style** program uses a part-of-speech analyzer to determine sentence categories. It measures properties of documents related to readability: Flesch and other readability indices, the number of complex and compound sentences, and so forth. Authors can use this information to revise documents to make them simpler and easier to read. For example, this paper is at 12th grade reading level and contains 41% simple sentences, 27% complex sentences, 16% compound sentences and 15% compound-complex sentences. If the authors of this paper were less stubborn about taking advice from a computer on how to write, we might revise it to include more short and simple sentences and thus make it easier to read (there is a 55-word sentence in this paper).

Similarly, the **diction** program looks for hackneyed or commonly misused phrases, marking occurrences such as "in the case that" or "sophisticated" in the text, since revision to eliminate these phrases often improves the style of the document. These programs obviously do not represent an alternative to editing and revising, but they do call the attention of authors to things that might be improved. **style** and **diction** have become quite popular, since most authors are interested in writing better.

One of the more interesting peripheral devices supported by the UNIX system is an inexpensive voice synthesizer.[13] The program **speak**[14] uses this synthesizer to pronounce arbitrary text. Speaking text has proven especially handy for proofreading tedious data like lists of numbers: the machine speaks the numbers, while a person reads a list in parallel.

Another example of a borrowed program is **diff**,[15] which compares two inputs and prepares a list of all the places in which they differ. Normally, **diff** is used for comparing two versions of a program, as a check on the changes that have been made. But of course it can also be used on two versions of a document as well. In fact, the **diff** output can be captured and used to produce a set of **troff** commands that will print the new version with marginal bars indicating the places where the document has been changed.

We have already mentioned several major preprocessors for **troff** and **nroff**. The same approach, of writing a separate program instead of cluttering up an existing one, has been applied to *post*processors as well. Typically, these postprocessors are concerned with matching **troff** or **nroff** output with the characteristics of some different output device. One example is a processor called **col** that converts **nroff** output containing reverse motions (e.g., multi-column output) into page images suitable for printing on devices incapable of reverse motion. An analogous program sorts the output of **troff** into vertical order for typesetters that are incapable of reverse paper motion. There are also programs that interpret **troff** output intended for a phototypesetter for display on a terminal. This permits a view of the formatted document without actually printing it, which is convenient for checking page layout.

One final area worth mentioning concerns the problem of training new users. Since there seems to be no substitute for hands-on experience, a program called **learn** was written to walk new users through sets of lessons.[16] Lesson scripts are available for fundamentals of UNIX file handling commands, the editor **ed**, **eqn**, and a standard macro package, as well as for topics not related to document preparation. **learn** has been heavily used in the courses taught by secretaries and typists for their colleagues.

10. EXPERIENCE

UNIX document preparation software has now been used for several years within Bell Laboratories, with many secretaries and typists in technical organizations routinely preparing technical memoranda and papers. Several books[17, 18, 19, 20, 21, 22, 23] printed with this software have been published directly from camera-ready copy. Technical articles have been prepared in camera-ready form for periodicals ranging from the *Journal of the ACM* to *Science*.

The longest-running use of the UNIX system for document preparation is in the Bell Laboratories Legal and Patent Division, where patent applications have been prepared on a UNIX system for a decade. Computer program documentation has been produced for several years by clerks using UNIX facilities at the Business Information Systems Programs area of Bell Laboratories. More recently, the "word processing" centers at Bell Laboratories have begun significant use of the UNIX system because of its ability to handle complicated material effectively.

It can be difficult to evaluate the cost-effectiveness of computer-aided versus manual documentation preparation. We took advantage of the interest of the American Physical Society in the UNIX system to make a systematic comparison of costs of their traditional typewriter composition and a UNIX document preparation system. Five manuscripts submitted to *Physical Review Letters* were typeset at Bell Laboratories, using the programs described above to handle the text, equations, tables, and special layout of the journal.

On the basis of these experiments, it appears that computerized typesetting of difficult material is substantially cheaper than typewriter composition. The primary cost of page composition is keyboarding, and the aids provided by UNIX software for input of complex mathematical and tabular material reduce input time significantly. Typing and correcting articles on the UNIX system, with an experienced typist, was between 1.5 and 3.3 times as fast as typewriter composition. Over the trial set of manuscripts, input using the UNIX system was 2.4 times as fast. These documents were extremely complicated, with many difficult equations. Typists at *Physical Review* averaged less than four pages per day, whereas our (admittedly proficient) UNIX system typist could type a page in 30 minutes. We estimate a substantial saving in production cost for camera-ready pages using a UNIX system instead of conventional composition or typewriting. A typical UNIX system for photocomposition of *Physical Review* style pages might produce 200 finished pages per day on a capital investment of about $200,000 and with 20 typists. Further details of this comparison can be found in Ref. 24. The American Physical Society in fact has been using a UNIX system for some years now to produce approximately 35000 pages per year of *Physical Review*, a family of heavily mathematical journals. Their staff of typists has been reduced from 38 to 20.

11. CONCLUSIONS

It is important to note that these document preparation programs are simply application programs running on a general-purpose system. Any document preparation user can exercise any command whenever desired.

As mentioned above, a surprising number of the programming utilities are directly or indirectly useful in document preparation. For example, the program that makes cross-reference listings of computer programs is largely identical with the one that makes keyword-in-context indexes of natural language text. It is also easy to use the programming facilities to generate small utilities, such as one that checks the consistency of equation usage.

Besides applying programming utilities to text processing, we also apply document processors to programs and numerical data. Statistical data are often extracted from program output and inserted into documents. Computer programs are often printed in papers and books; because the programs are tested and typeset from the same source file, transcription errors are eliminated.

In addition to the technical advantages of having programming and word processing on the same machine, there can be personnel advantages. The fact that secretaries and typists work on the same system as the authors allows both to share the document preparation job. A document may be typed originally by a secretary, with the author doing the corrections; in the case of an author who types rough drafts but doesn't like editing after proofreading, the reverse may occur. We have observed the full spectrum, from authors who give hand-written material to typists in the traditional manner to those who compose at the terminal and do their own typesetting. Most authors, however, seem to operate somewhere in between.

The availability of the system for electronic mail, calendar service, and other facilities also helps a great deal. It is more convenient to use one system for all these functions than to learn separate command languages for each function, let alone have to use separate terminals and devices. The presence of the secretaries on the same system, for example, makes it easy to send mail back and forth, and most people do this routinely.

The UNIX system provides a convenient and cost-effective environment for document preparation. A first-class program development facility encourages the development of good tools. The ability to use preprocessors has enabled us to write separate languages for mathematics, tables, and several other formatting tasks. The separate programs are easier to learn than if they were all jammed into one package, and are vastly easier to maintain as well. And since all of this takes place within a general-purpose operating system, programs and data can be used as convenient, whether they are intended for document preparation or not.

Acknowledgements

We are indebted to Rich Graveman for his careful reading of the manuscript.

References

1. K. Thompson and D. M. Ritchie, UNIX *Programmer's Manual*, Bell Laboratories (1978). See ED (I).

2. J. F. Ossanna, "NROFF/TROFF User's Manual," *UNIX Programmer's Manual* **2**, Section 22 (January 1979).

3. J. E. Saltzer, "Runoff," in *The Compatible Time-Sharing System*, ed. P. A. Crisman, M.I.T. Press, Cambridge, Mass. (1965).

4. M. D. McIlroy, "The Roff Text Formatter," Computer Center Report MHCC-005, Bell Laboratories, Murray Hill, New Jersey (October 1972).

5. S. C. Johnson, "Yacc — Yet Another Compiler-Compiler," *UNIX Programmer's Manual* **2**, Section 19 (January 1979).

6. Brian W. Kernighan and Lorinda L. Cherry, "A System for Typesetting Mathematics," *Communications of the ACM* **18**(3), pp. 151-157 (1975).

7. B. W. Kernighan and L. L. Cherry, "A System for Typesetting Mathematics," Comp. Sci. Tech. Rep. No. 17, Bell Laboratories, Murray Hill, N.J. (April 1977).

8. M. E. Lesk, "Tbl — A Program to Format Tables," *UNIX Programmer's Manual* **2**, Section 10 (January 1979).

9. M. E. Lesk, "Some Applications of Inverted Indexes on the UNIX System," *UNIX Programmer's Manual* **2**, Section 11 (January 1979).

10. C. J. Van Wyk, "A Graphics Typesetting Language," *Proc. ACM SIGOA/SIGPLAN Conference on Text Manipulation*, Portland, Oregon (1981).

11. B. W. Kernighan, "PIC — A Language for Typesetting Graphics," *Software — Practice & Experience* (January, 1982).

12. L. L. Cherry, "Writing Tools - The STYLE & Diction Programs," Comp. Sci. Tech. Rep. No. 91 (February 1981).

13. Federal Screw Works, *Votrax ML-1 Multi-Lingual Voice System*.

14. M. D. McIlroy, "Synthetic English Speech by Rule," Comp. Sci. Tech. Rep. No. 14, Bell Laboratories, Murray Hill, New Jersey (March 1974).

15. J. W. Hunt and M. D. McIlroy, "An Algorithm for Differential File Comparison," Comp. Sci. Tech. Rep. No. 41, Bell Laboratories, Murray Hill, New Jersey (June 1976).

16. B. W. Kernighan and M. E. Lesk, *Computer Aided Instruction on UNIX*, Bell Laboratories internal memorandum (1976).

17. B. W. Kernighan and P. J. Plauger, *The Elements of Programming Style, 2nd Edition*, McGraw Hill, New York, New York (1978).

18. C. H. Sequin and M. F. Tompsett, *Charge Transfer Devices*, Academic Press, New York (1975).

19. B. W. Kernighan and P. J. Plauger, *Software Tools in Pascal*, Addison-Wesley, Reading, Mass. (1981).

20. T. A. Dolotta et al., *Data Processing in 1980-1985: A Study of Potential Limitations to Progress*, Wiley-Interscience, New York (1976).

21. Alfred V. Aho and Jeffery D. Ullman, *Principles of Compiler Design*, Addison-Wesley (1977).

22. Committee on Impacts of Stratospheric Change, *Halocarbons: Environmental Effects of Chlorofluoromethane Release*, National Academy of Sciences, Washington, D. C. (1977).

23. W. H. Williams, *A Sampler on Sampling*, John Wiley & Sons, New York (March 27, 1978).

24. M. E. Lesk and B. W. Kernighan, "Computer Typesetting of Technical Journals on UNIX," *Proc. AFIPS NCC* **46**, pp. 879-888 (1977).

DOCUMENT PREPARATION SYSTEMS
J. Nievergelt, G. Coray, J.D. Nicoud, A.C. Shaw (eds.)
North-Holland Publishing Company, 1982

21

Interactive Editing Systems

Norman Meyrowitz
Andries van Dam

Department of Computer Science
Box 1910
Brown University
Providence, Rhode Island 02912

ABSTRACT

Many daily tasks, whether done with conventional tools or with computers, can be viewed as **editing** tasks: tasks in which the state of some target entity is changed by the user. This article examines computer-based **interactive editing systems**, which allow users to change the state of targets such as manuscripts and programs.

We present the material in two parts: a tutorial and a survey. The tutorial defines terms and introduces issues for the novice, and provides a reference for the more knowledgeable reader. Our aim is to provide a comprehensive and systematic view of the features of typical systems, highlighting substantive similarities and differences. We provide user and system views of the editing process, present an historical perspective, and cover the functional capabilities of editors, emphasizing user-level rather than implementation-level considerations.

The survey is intended for a more general audience: the more experienced user and the editor-designer as well as the curious novice. It presents numerous examples of the state-of-the-art in both the academic and commercial arenas, covering line editors, screen editors, interactive editor/formatters, structure editors, syntax-directed editors, and commercial word processing editors. We discuss pertinent issues in the field, and conclude with some observations about the future of interactive editing.

CR Categories and Subject Descriptors: I.7.1 [**Text Processing**]: Text Editing—*languages, spelling*; I.7.0 [**Text Processing**]: General; I.7.2 [**Text Processing**]: Document Preparation—*format and notation, languages, photocomposition*; I.7.4 [**Text Processing**]: Miscellaneous; H.4.1 [**Information Systems Applications**]: Office Automation—*equipment, word processing*; D.2.2 [**Software Engineering**]: Tools and Techniques—*user interfaces*; D.2.3 [**Software Engineering**]: Coding—*program editors, pretty printers*.

General Terms: Human Factors, Languages, Design.

Additional Keywords and Phrases: editing, editors, text editing, text editors, program editors, syntax-directed editors, structure editors, user interface design, text formatting, text processing, word processing.

INTRODUCTION

The interactive editor[1] has become an essential component of any computing environment. It uses the power of the computer for the creation, addition, deletion, and modification of text material such as program statements, manuscript text, and numeric data. The editor allows text to be modified and corrected many orders of magnitude faster and easier than would manual correction.

Though editors have always been deemed important tools in computing systems, they have only recently become a fashionable topic of research, as they become key components in the office of the future. No longer are editors thought of as tools only for programmers, or for secretaries transcribing from marked-up hardcopy generated by authors. It is now increasingly realized that the editor should be considered the primary interface to the computer for all types of **knowledge workers**, as they compose, organize, study, and manipulate computer-based information. Unlike the literature in areas such as programming languages or operating systems (with rich collections of written materials, from basic definitions and tutorials to complex formalisms, analyses, and implementation strategies), the literature in the field of editing consists primarily of functional descriptions of particular editors. Little work has been done to standardize terminology or to create a framework for comparing, contrasting, and analyzing editing systems.

This article is designed as a starting point for developing such a framework. Our intended audience is composed of two distinct groups: those with only limited experience with an interactive editor and those with a broader background in the field. Part I of the paper is tutorial in nature and is meant for those with only superficial experience in using an editor to create program or document text. It is a reasonably comprehensive introduction to text editing. As such, it is not meant to be read in its entirety by the editor designer, but rather to be used as a reference. It is here that we present our definitions and overview of the field, making explicit what has previously been largely implicit or passed on as "oral tradition." We look at document editing from a user and system standpoint, at some of the major historical developments, and at the functional capabilities of editors.

Part II presents technical details of specific editors, using the terminology·and concepts laid out in Part I. It is intended for a broader audience, including those quite familiar with the concepts covered in the first half as well as those comfortable with the editors in their own computing environments but not necessarily familiar with the range of editors available. This part surveys editors available in the academic and commercial realms, providing points of departure for further investigation rather than an exhaustive point-by-point comparison. We discuss unresolved issues in the field, and examine the future of editing. A bibliography provides a list of materials for further reading.

Several topics directly related to interactive editing will **not** be covered here; instead, we supply references to surveys in those fields. In particular, text formatting techniques are left to Furuta et al. [FURU82], implementation of editors is covered by Rice and van Dam [RICE71] and Finseth [FINS80], editor evaluation is surveyed by Embley and Nagy [EMBL81], and graphics editors are described in Newman and Sproull [NEWM79] and Foley and van Dam [FOLE82].

---

[1] "Editor" throughout refers to an interactive editing program, not to an author/user correcting a document.

PART I: TUTORIAL

---

1. GENERAL OVERVIEW

1.1 The Editing Process

An **interactive editor**[2] is a computer program that allows a user to create and revise a target **document**. We use the term "document" to include targets such as computer programs, text, equations, tables, diagrams, line art, and halftone or color photographs – anything one might find on a printed page. In this paper, we restrict our discussion to **text editors** (in which the primary elements being manipulated are character strings of the target text) used for manuscript and program production, and to **structure editors** (in which the primary elements being manipulated are portions of some generic structure such as a tree).

The document-editing process is an interactive user-computer dialogue 1) to select what part of the target is to be viewed and manipulated, 2) to determine how to format this view online and then to display it, 3) to specify and execute operations that modify the target document, and 4) to update the view appropriately.

Selection of the part of the document to be viewed and edited involves first **traveling** through the document to locate the area of interest with operations such as next screenful, bottom, and find pattern. Next, having specified *where* the area of interest is, the selection of *what* is to be viewed and manipulated there is controlled by **filtering**. Filtering extracts the relevant subset of the target document at the point of interest, such as the next screen's worth of text or the next statement. **Formatting** then determines *how* the result of the filtering will be seen as a visible representation, the **view**, on a display screen or hardcopy device.

Only in the actual **editing** phase is the target document created or altered per a set of operations, commonly including insert, delete, replace, move, and copy. The editing functions are often specialized to operate on **elements** meaningful to the type of editor, such as single characters, words, lines, sentences and paragraphs for manuscript-oriented editors, and keywords and source language statements for program-oriented editors.

In a simple scenario, then, the user might **travel** to the end of a document. A screen's worth of text would be **filtered**, and this subset would be **formatted** and the **view** displayed on an output device. The user could then, for example, delete the first three words of this view.

1.2 The Editor: A User Viewpoint

The user of an interactive editor is presented with a **conceptual model** of the system, which is the designer's abstract framework on which the editor and the "world" in which it operates are based, and with a **user interface**, the collection of tools and techniques with which the user communicates with the editor.

The conceptual model, in essence, provides an easily understood abstraction of the target document and its elements, and a set of guidelines with which to anticipate the effects of operations on these elements. Conceptual models range from those that are hardly visible to the user and not very cohesive or thorough, to those that are well-articulated and provide a consistent and complete framework both for using and implementing the system. In others, the conceptual model is incomplete; it is insufficient to describe more than a very cursory notion of the system. Some of the early **line editors** simulated the world of the keypunch, allowing

---

[2]In this paper, Bold type is used to introduce concepts and terms. Typewriter type is used to set off editor commands. Italic type is used for emphasis.

operations upon numbered sequences of 80-character card-image lines, either within a single line or upon an integral number of lines. Some more modern **screen editors** define a world in which a document is represented as a quarter-plane of text lines, unbounded both downward and to the right. The user sees through a cutout only a rectangular subset of this plane at any time on a multi-line display screen, but can move the cutout both left and right and up and down to see other portions of a document. Operations manipulate portions of this quarter-plane without regard to line boundaries.

The user interface contains the **input devices**, the **output devices**, and the **interaction language** of the system. Examples of each of these will be discussed in the following subsections. Along with the user interface, the user is often given documentation that may include a description of the conceptual model, a high-level description of the system architecture in user-level terminology, a user's guide detailing the syntax and semantics of the interaction language, and a tutorial that provides operational definitions and demonstrates typical situations with examples.

Each individual forms a personal **user model** of an editing system, partly extrapolated from information provided in the recorded documentation or passed on by "experts" and partly based on repeated use of the system. The user model may differ from the conceptual model in several ways. First, it can be thought of as a subset of the conceptual model. For example, a user experienced in document preparation may have no notion of the language-specific commands for correct program indentation; similarly, a programmer may have no notion about the features provided for online table manipulation. Second, when the user consistently uses combinations of primitives to perform common operations in ways not originally encompassed by the conceptual model, the user model can be thought of as an extension of the conceptual model. Third, the user model can be thought of as an operationally equivalent but logically different form of the conceptual model. For example, rather than considering his/her actions to be moving a cutout over various parts of a document as described above, the user may consider the cutout as stationary and the *document* as scrollable horizontally and vertically past this cutout.

The user model is a personalized, high-level understanding of the conceptual model provided, of the manipulable entities and their interrelationships, of the set of operations allowed on the entities, and of the interaction language used to invoke these operations. The user model is not simply descriptive but prescriptive as well: to perform editing tasks, the user employs the user interface based on his/her user model.

1.2.1 User Interface

1.2.1.1 Input Devices

Input devices are used for three main purposes: 1) to enter elements; 2) to enter commands; and 3) to designate editable elements. These devices, as used with editors, can be divided into three categories: **text** devices, **button** devices, and **locator** devices [GSPC79, FOLE82].

Text or **string** devices are typically typewriter-like keyboards on which a user presses and releases a key to send to the CPU or to an I/O controller a unique code for each key. Essentially all present computer keyboards are of the QWERTY variety. This variety of keyboard, named for the first six letters in the second row of the keyboard, was invented by Christopher Latham Sholes in the 1860's. The strange key layout was done for purely mechanical reasons – letters most commonly used together were placed as far apart as possible so mechanical typewriter keys would not clash. As surveyed in MONT82, several experimental text input devices have been constructed. The Dvorak Simplified Keyboard rearranges the keys to reduce fatigue and increase typing speed; despite experimental evidence showing its superiority, it has not caught on strongly. The Montgomery "wipe-activated" keyboard requires the user not to press keys, but rather to "wipe" a stylus across the keyboard surface. Letters comprising common digrams and trigrams, such as TH and ING are placed next to one another on the keyboard; the user simply wipes the wand from left to right across the letters, rather than typing two or three separate keystrokes. NLS's keyset [ENGE68] consists of a pad of five long keys, similar in shape to white piano keys, and provides a method for entering small text additions or corrections. Each key corresponds to a position in a 5-bit binary word called a "chord"; by depressing the proper combination, the user can represent $2^5 - 1 = 31$ numbers or ASCII codes (binary "00000" is not counted, as this means no keys are being pressed).

An alternative to direct keyboard input is **optical character recognition (OCR)**. Typically a standard electric typewriter, (inexpensively) equipped with an OCR typeface, is used for typing the text on normal paper. This paper is then fed through an optical character reader, an electromechanical device which scans the page and translates each character into the proper digital representation for that computer system. This technique allows the continued use of pre-existing facilities: the typewriters become offline "links" to the computer facilities. Although many OCR systems also allow rudimentary editing of the raw text stream via character- and line-delete control characters inserted in the text, this cannot compete with the convenience and essentially instant editing facility of online input. While OCR is often seen as an inexpensive way to begin "computerization," it is contrary to the spirit of online authoring, in which the author is able to express his/her thoughts and experiment with a composition from its inception.

Button or **choice** devices generate an interrupt or set a system flag, usually causing invocation of an associated application program action. They typically are grouped as a set of special function keys on the alphanumeric keyboard or on the display itself. Alternatively, buttons are often simulated in software by having the user choose text strings or symbols displayed on a screen.

Locator devices are x-y analog-to-digital transducers that position a cursor symbol on the screen by continually sampling the analog values produced by the user's movement of the device. They include **joysticks, trackballs, touch screen panels, data tablets**, and **mice**. The latter two are the most common locator devices for editing applications. The data tablet is a flat, rectangular, electromagnetically sensitive panel. Either a ballpoint-pen-like **stylus** or a **puck**, a small (approximately 3" square x 1" high) device which fits in the palm of the hand, is moved over the tablet surface. The tablet returns to a system program the coordinates of the point on the data tablet on which the puck or stylus is currently located. The program can then map these data tablet coordinates to screen coordinates and move the cursor to the corresponding screen position. The mouse is another hand-held device about the same size as the puck. As it is moved on a flat surface, the motion of the mouse causes relative changes in x and y to be sampled by a system program. These mouse coordinates are again mapped to screen coordinates to move a cursor on the screen.

A locator device coupled with a button device allows the user to specify either a particular point on the screen at which text should be inserted or deleted, or the start and end points of a string of characters to be operated upon. In fact, the mouse and puck usually have built-in buttons for the user to signal a selection. When the cursor has been positioned over an element, the user presses a button to indicate the selection; the system correlates the cursor position with the element it covers and performs the appropriate action.

Text devices with arrow (cursor) keys are often used to simulate locator devices. These keys each show a pictured arrow, pointing up, down, left, or right, respectively. Pressing an arrow key typically generates an appropriate character which the program then translates to update the cursor position in the direction of the arrow on the key pressed. Up, down, left, and right keys must be used sequentially to position the cursor a character at a time, aided typically by continuous movement in "repeat mode," which the device enters if a key is held down for more than, say, a second.

Still in the research stage, **voice input devices**, which translate spoken words – both literal text and commands – to their textual equivalents, may prove to be the text devices of the future. While currently restricted to a small vocabulary (typically fewer than 1000 words), voice recognizers may soon be commercially viable for command recognition.

1.2.1.2 Output Devices

Formerly limited in range, output devices for editing are diversifying. The output device serves to let the user view the elements being edited and the results of the editing operations. The first generation output devices were the (now largely obsolete) teletypewriters and other character-printing terminals, which generated output on paper. Next, "glass teletypes" based on **cathode ray tube (CRT)** technology used the CRT screen essentially to simulate a hardcopy teletypewriter, though a few operations, such as backspace, were performed more elegantly. Today's advanced CRT terminals use hardware assistance for such features as moving the cursor, inserting and deleting characters and lines, and scrolling lines and pages. The new generation of professional workstations, based on personal computers with high-resolution raster displays, support multiple proportionally-spaced character fonts to produce realistic facsimiles of hardcopy documents. Thus, the user can see the document portrayed essentially as it would look when printed on paper.

While many editors, especially traditional ones, have interfaces that allow them to run on both CRT and hardcopy terminals, we concentrate on the more sophisticated capabilities that can readily be implemented only on CRT terminals with user-manipulable cursors. Much of the discussion does, however, apply to both hardcopy and CRT output devices.

1.2.1.3 Interaction Language

The interaction language of a text editor can be divided into three parts: the **semantic component**, the **syntactic component**, and the **lexical component** [FOLE82]. The semantic component of the language specifies functionality: what operations are valid for each element, what information is needed for the manipulation of each element, what the results of the operations are, and what errors may occur. The semantic component defines meanings of the specified operations, not particular data structures or dialogues to implement those operations.

The syntactic component specifies the input and output rules by which **tokens**, as the atomic elements, are put together to form sentences in the **grammar** of the language. In terms of editor input, the set of tokens might include character strings, commands, and screen positions. In terms of output, the set of tokens might include character strings, lines, and formatted paragraphs. The syntax must be easy for the user to learn and remember, and must follow naturally from the conceptual model of the system. The syntax of interaction languages is generally one of three sorts: **prefix, postfix,** or **infix**. A prefix (verb/noun) command specifies the operation desired, followed by the element(s) which that operation will affect. A postfix (noun/verb) command specifies just the opposite: the element to be operated upon is specified first, followed by the operation. An infix (noun/verb/noun) command is a cross between the two former types: the operation is surrounded by its operands. Infix typically only is needed when there exists more than one operand. Many languages are basically postfix, but rely on infix in the cases where more than one operand is needed. In a **cross-product** interface, the user can match a noun from a list of nouns with a verb from a list of verbs to form the appropriate command. In other types of interfaces, the verb/noun distinction is not always clear-cut; a single editor command, such as **delete-word**, can be composed of both a verb and noun. Here the user specifies the command **delete** and the element is particularized to the nearest unit of the corresponding type **word**.

The lexical component specifies the way in which **lexemes**, information from the input devices or for the output devices, are combined to form the tokens used by the syntactic component. Thus typing the lexemes D, -, ₩ followed by a carriage return would result in the **delete-word** token.

The interaction language is generally one of several common types, based on the manner of specifying lexemes. The **typing-** or **text command-oriented** interface is the oldest of the major editor interfaces. Here, the user communicates with the editor by typing text strings both for command names and operands. These strings are sent to the editor and are usually echoed on the output device.

Typed specification often requires the user to remember the exact form of all commands, or at least of their abbreviations. (Some systems will prompt the user with valid choices if an ambiguous command abbreviation is typed.) If the interaction syntax is complex, the user must continually refer to a manual or an online "help" command for a description of less frequently used commands. Additionally, typing is time-consuming, especially for the beginner. The **function-key** interface addresses these deficiencies. Here each command has associated with it a marked key on the user's keyboard. For example, the **insert character** command might have associated with it a key marked IC. Forgetting the commands is unlikely, since they are literally at the user's fingertips. For the common functions, usually only a single key need be pressed. Function-key syntax is typically coupled with cursor-key movement for specifying operands, thereby eliminating much typing. Advocates cite "muscle memory" of key location as a prime advantage of function key interfaces.

For less frequently invoked commands or options in a many-function editor, an optional textual syntax may be used. More commonly, special keys "shift" the standard function key interpretations, just as the shift key on a typewriter shifts the standard interpretation of a key from being lowercase to being uppercase. As an alternative to shifting function keys, the alphanumeric keyboard is often **overloaded** to simulate function keys. The user again uses special shift keys – the most common being the **control**[3] key depressed simultaneously with normal keys to generate new characters that are interpreted like function keys. Generally, functions are assigned to alphanumeric keys in two ways: topologically and mnemonically. In topological layout, functionally similar keys are grouped in close proximity; for example, in Brown's bb [REIS81], the control key coupled with the **Q, ₩, E,**or **R** keys correspond to **delete word, delete to end of line, delete to blank line,** and **delete paragraph,** respectively, while the keys directly below, **A, S, D, F,** coupled with the control key, correspond to **insert word, insert to end of line, insert to blank line, insert paragraph.** Another topological layout is seen in Wordstar [MICR81], in which the cursor commands, **up, down, left, and right** are bound to the **CTRL-E, CTRL-X, CTRL-A,** and **CTRL-F** keys to make use of their relative directions on the keyboard. Mnemonic layout binds commands to keys whose letters or symbols invoke some type of mental image or connection. For instance, in the EMACS [STAL80] default key bindings, **CTRL-B, CTRL-E, CTRL-F, CTRL-R,** and **CTRL-K** stand for **Backward character, End of line, Forward character, Reverse search,** and **Kill line,** respectively.

---

[3]In examples, the control key will be abbreviated CTRL- and the escape key ESC.

Typing-oriented systems require familiarity with the system and language, as well as some expertise in typing. Function-key-oriented systems often have either too few keys, thus requiring keyboard-overloading by binding single keys to several interpretations and necessitating multiple keystroke commands, or have too many unique keys, resulting in an unwieldy keyboard. In either case, even more agility is demanded of the user than by a standard keyboard. The **menu-oriented** user interface is an attempt to address these problems. A **menu** is a multiple-choice set of text strings or **icons** (graphical symbols which represent objects or operations) from which the user can select items to perform actions [GOLD79]. The editor prompts the user with a menu of only those actions that may be taken at the current state of the system. The user knows that if a command appears in the menu, it can be selected, and the typical "you can't do that operation in this *(x)* mode" error messages that occur with other types of interfaces are eliminated.

One problem with a menu-oriented system can arise when there are many possible actions and multiple choices required to complete an action. Since the display area for the menu is usually rather limited, the user might be presented with several consecutive menus in a hierarchy before the appropriate command and its options appear. Since this can be annoying and detrimental to the efficiency of a seasoned user, some menu-oriented systems allow the user to turn off menu control, leaving a language- or function-key-oriented editor as a base. Others have the most-used functions on a main command menu and have secondary menus to handle the less frequently used functions. Still others display the menu only when the user specifically asks for it. For instance, in more modern editors based on a Smalltalk-80*-like interface [TESL81, GOLD82] (see Figure 1), **pop-up** menus, in response to the user's button-push, instantly appear on some part of the screen near the cursor (perhaps temporarily overlapping some existing information) to give the user the full choice of applicable commands. The user selects the appropriate command with a mouse; the system executes the command and the menu disappears instantly. Interfaces like this, in which prompting and menu information are given to the user at little added cost and little degradation in response time, are becoming increasingly popular.

While the semantic component of the language is similar from system to system (at least for simple operations), the lexical and syntactic specification of commands vary widely. For example, to delete the word "**bazinga**" in an editor using typed commands from a keyboard without cursor keys, one might search for an occurrence of the pattern "**bazinga**" and then type **delete/bazinga**; in another, using typed commands with cursor keys, one might type **dw** after driving a cursor to point at any character in the word "**bazinga**"; in a function-key driven system, one might press the **del word** key (or keys) after pointing at "**bazinga**"; and in a menu-oriented system, one might point to and then **select** the 'b' in "**bazinga**," adjust the selection to the entire word by pushing the **adjust** button, and then select the **delete** icon from the displayed menu. The interaction language can be viewed as a layered architecture: similar semantics can be reflected in a variety of syntaxes, while similar syntaxes can be reflected in a variety of lexical styles. For example, given semantic routines that perform insertion and deletion in an unbounded stream of characters, designers could provide a prefix or postfix syntax for specifying **insert** or **delete** commands. Similarly, given either the prefix or postfix syntax, designers could provide typing-oriented, function-key-oriented, or menu-oriented lexical input styles. This layering invites device-independence, since differing lexical forms can be mapped into the same syntax. The layering also allows syntax-independence, since differing syntactical styles can be mapped into the same semantic operations.

---

* Smalltak-80 is a registered trademark of Xerox Corporation.

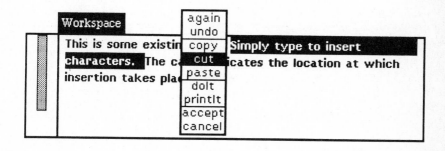

Figure 1. *A Smalltalk-80 Pop-up menu.*

Here the arrow cursor, driven by the mouse, points to the cut item in the pop-up menu temporarily overlapping the text window. When the proper mouse button is pressed, the command is executed and the menu, no longer needed, disappears.

1.3 The Editor: A System Viewpoint

Editors in general follow an architecture similar to that in Figure 2, regardless of the particular computers on which they are implemented and the features they offer.

The **command language processor** accepts input from the user's input devices, lexically analyzes and tokenizes the input stream, syntactically analyzes the accumulated stream of tokens, and, upon finding a legal composition of tokens, invokes the appropriate semantic routines.

At the syntactic level, the command language processor, like a programming language processor, may generate an intermediate representation of the desired editing operations instead of explicitly invoking the semantic routines. This intermediate representation is decoded by an interpreter that invokes the proper semantic routines. This allows the use of multiple interaction syntaxes with a single set of semantic routines that are driven from a common intermediate representation.

The semantic routines invoke traveling, editing, viewing, and display. While editing operations are always specified explicitly by the user, and the display operations implicitly by the other three categories of operations, traveling and viewing operations may be either explicitly specified or implicitly invoked by the editing operations. In fact, the relationship between these classes of operations may be considerably more complicated than the simple model of Section 1.1 (travel to determine *where* the selection should take place, filter to select *what* is to be viewed and manipulated, format to determine *how* the view is to appear, then edit and reformat) might

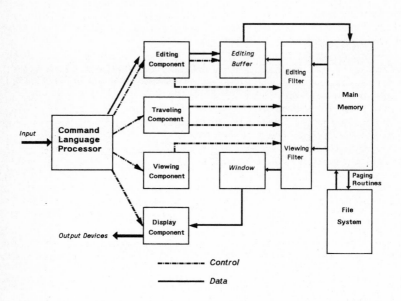

Figure 2. *The Editor – A System Architecture*

suggest. In particular, there need not be a simple one-to-one relationship between what is "in view," i.e., what is displayed on the screen currently, and what can be edited. To illustrate this, we take a closer look at the *conceptual* components of Figure 2 below.

In editing a document, the start of the area to be edited is determined by the **current editing pointer** maintained by the **editing component** of the editor, the collection of modules dealing with editing tasks. The current editing pointer can be set or reset explicitly by the user with a traveling command such as **next paragraph** and **next screen**, or implicitly by the system as a side effect of the previous editing operation, such as **delete paragraph**. (The **traveling component** of the editor actually performs the setting of the current editing and viewing pointers, and thus the point at which the viewing and/or editing filtering begins.) When the user issues an editing command, the editing component invokes the **editing filter**. The editing filter filters the document to generate a new **editing buffer** based on the current editing pointer as well as the editing filter parameters. These parameters are specified both by the user and the system, and provide such information as the range of text that can be affected by the operation, for example the "current line" in a line editor or the "current screen" in a display editor. Filtering in both the case of editing and viewing may be defaulted to the selection of contiguous characters at the current point or depend on more complex user specifications pertaining to content and structure of the document to gather not-necessarily contiguous portions of the document, as discussed in Section 3.1. The semantic routines of the editing component then operate on the editing buffer, which is essentially a filtered subset of the document data structure. (Note that this explanation is at the conceptual level – in a given editor, filtering and editing may be interleaved, and no explicit editing buffer created.)

Similarly, in viewing a document, the start of the area to be viewed is determined by the **current viewing pointer** maintained by the **viewing component** of the editor, the collection of modules responsible for determining the next view. The current viewing pointer can be set or reset explicitly by the user with a traveling command or implicitly by the system as a side effect of the previous editing operation. When the display needs to be updated, the viewing component invokes the **viewing filter**. The viewing filter filters the document to generate a new **viewing buffer** based on the current viewing pointer as well as the viewing filter parameters. These parameters, again, are specified both by the user and the system, and provide such information as the number of characters needed to fill the display and how to select them from the document. The viewing buffer may contain the "current line" or the null string (for "silent" feedback) in line editors, while in screen editors it may contain a rectangular cutout of the quarter plane of text. This viewing buffer, is then passed to the **display component** of the editor, which maps it to a **window** or **viewport**, a rectangular subset of the screen, to produce a display.[5]

The editing and viewing buffers, while independent, can be related in many ways. In the simple case they are *identical*, as in the case of screen editors, in which the user edits the material directly in view on the screen, rather than specifying material with typed commands (see Figure 3).

The editing and viewing buffers can also be *disjoint*. For example, in the Berkeley UNIX* editor *ex* [JOY80a], a user might travel to line 75, and after viewing it, decide to change all occurrences of "ugly duckling" to "swan" in lines 1 through 50 of the file by using the substitute command:

    1,50s/ugly duckling/swan/

As part of this editing command, there is implicit travel to the first line of the file, lines 1 through 50 are filtered from the document to become the editing buffer, and successive substitutions take place in the editing buffer without corresponding updates of the view. If the pattern is found, the current pointers are moved to the last line on which it was found, and that line becomes the default contents of both the editing and viewing buffers, while if the pattern is not found, line 75 remains as the default editing and viewing buffers.

The editing and viewing buffers can be *partially overlapping* on a screen when the user specifies a search to the end-of-document starting at a character position in the middle of the screen. Here the editing filter creates an editing buffer that contains the document from the

---

[5]The term "viewport" is standard for "visible representation on the screen" in computer graphics terminology, while in editing terminology, the term "window" is used loosely to mean both the viewing buffer and the mapped representation of the viewing buffer on the screen. Unfortunately the term "window" in graphics terminology is analogous to our "viewing buffer," lending more confusion to the definitions. We have tried to limit the use of the term "window" to reduce confusion, but when we do, we use it in the editing sense of the "mapped representation of the viewing buffer on the screen." We use the term "view" to mean a "display of a filtered subset of a document in a window."

* UNIX is a trademark of Bell Laboratories.

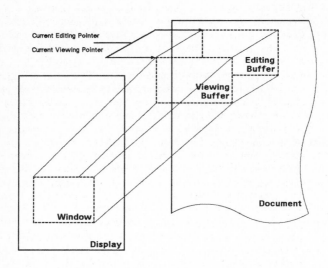

Figure 3. *Elements of the Editing Component*
The diagram above shows the relationship of the current operating pointer in a document file
to the editing buffer and the viewing buffer. In this diagram, the file is indicated as a quarter
plane of text. The current editing pointer points to the start of the editing buffer. The current
viewing pointer points to the start of the viewing buffer. The two point to the same place, since
the viewing buffer coincides with the editing buffer in this example.

selected character to the end of the document, while the viewing buffer contains the part of the
document that is visible on the screen (only the last part of which will be in the editing buffer).

Finally, the editing and viewing buffers may be *properly contained* in one another. As an
example of the editing buffer contained in a larger viewing buffer, the CPT word processing
editor [SEYP79] allows full 8-1/2-x-11-inch page views. The user must scroll a page to put a
line to be edited at the **typing bar**, analogous to rolling the platen of a typewriter to align the
desired line with the typing element. Here the editing buffer corresponds to the one-line subset of
the document which is in the middle of the viewing buffer. Conversely, a number of traditional
editors, limited by low-speed, line-oriented output devices, provide a large editing buffer. The
viewing buffer is a a small initial subset of the editing buffer to allow quick regeneration of
the view; the entire scope of the editing operation is need not be in view. The FRESS editor
[VAND71a, PRUS79] allows the user to select the number of lines and the number of characters
per line for the viewing buffer (the default being a single line the width of the display device
for alphanumeric terminals) and also allows the user to select the size of the editing buffer (the
default being 2000 characters); the viewing filter selects as many characters as necessary, starting
at the beginning of the editing buffer, to provide the viewing buffer for the necessary display.

Windows typically cover either the entire screen or a rectangular portion of it. Mapping to windows that cover only part of the screen is especially useful for editors on modern, high-resolution raster-graphics-based workstations, as they allow the user to view and to interact with multiple views, allowing inter- and intra-file editing and "cutting and pasting." The notion of multiple viewing buffers and multiple windows showing differing portions of the same or multiple files at the same time on the screen is designed into such editors. Alternatively, on graphics-based workstations with multi-window **display managers** or **window managers** that allow the user to manipulate the placement of windows on a screen [LRG76, TEIW77, LANT79, MEYR81, SYMB81, TESL81], the user can run a one-viewing-buffer editor in each of the many windows. It is through the support of the display manager, not of the editor, that the user can cut and paste text between multiple windows containing portions of the same file or portions of multiple files.

As a comment on slow progress in the editing field, we note that in the database and graphics fields, the notion of multiple simultaneous views of the same or related data is well understood and commonly accepted. Though the facility for multiple views of documents at varying levels of detail and appearance has been available in the NLS editor since the mid-1960's [ENGE68] (see Section 2 and Part II, Section 4.5), this powerful organizational mechanism is only now beginning to gain acceptance in the editing community.

The viewing buffer-to-window mapping is accomplished by two components of the system. First, the viewing component formats an ideal view, often expressed in a device-independent intermediate representation. This ideal view can range from simply a window's worth of text, arranged so that lines are not broken in the middle of words ("ragged right" justification), to a facsimile of a page of fully formatted/typeset text with equations, tables, and figures.

Second, the **display component** takes this idealized view from the viewing component and simply maps it to a physical output device in the most efficient manner possible. If a view that has been computed by the viewing component cannot be fully displayed because the window is partly obscured by another window, this mapping becomes somewhat more complicated.

Updating of a full-screen display connected over low-speed lines (1200 baud or less) is slow if every modification requires a full rewrite of the display surface. Much research is concerned with optimal screen-updating algorithms that compare the current version of the screen with the following version and, using the innate capabilities of the terminal, write only those characters needed to generate a correct display. Typical algorithms for this intelligent screen update are described in ARNO80, BARA81, GOSL81, and STAL81.

Device-independent output, like device-independent input, promotes interaction language-portability. This decoupling of editing and viewing operations from display functions for output is important for purposes of portability: it is unwieldy to have a different version of the editor for every particular output device. Many editors make use of a **terminal control database** [JOY81]. Instead of having explicit terminal-control sequences in display routines, these editors simply call terminal-independent library routines, such as `scroll down` or `read cursor position`, that look up the appropriate control sequences for the host terminal. Consequently, adding a new terminal merely entails adding a database description of that terminal.

In addition to the interrelated traveling, viewing, editing and displaying components, special **utility components** may exist to provide a variety of services to aid the user in document production such as spelling checkers/correctors and word-count analyzers.

The components "communicate" with a user document on two levels: in main memory and in the disk file system. At the beginning of an editing session the editor first asks the file system to open the appropriate file and then reads the entire file or files, or portions thereof, into main memory. Loading an entire document into main memory may be infeasible. Yet if only a portion of the document were resident in main memory and if many user-specified operations entailed a disk-read by the editor to load the affected portion, editing would be unacceptably slow. In many modern systems this problem is solved by mapping the entire file into virtual memory and letting the operating system perform efficient demand-paging. Alternatively, in systems without virtual memory or with limited virtual memory per user, **editor paging routines** are required. These read in one or more logical chunks of a document, called pages (though there is typically no correspondence between these pages and hardcopy document pages or virtual memory pages), into main memory, where they reside until a user operation requires another piece of the document. In either case, documents are often represented not as sequential strings of characters, but as an **editor data structure** that allows addition, deletion, and modification with a minimum of I/O and character movement. When stored on disk, the file may be stored in terms of this data structure or in an editor-independent, general-purpose format (e.g., as character strings with imbedded control characters such as linefeed and tab).

1.3.1 Configurations

Editors function in the three basic types of computing environments: **timesharing, standalone**, and **distributed**. Each type of environment imposes some constraints on the design of an editor. The timesharing editor must function swiftly within the context of the load on the computer's processor, primary memory, and secondary memory. The editor on a standalone system must have access to the functions that the timesharing editor obtains from its host operating system; these may be provided in part by a small local operating system or may be built into the editor itself if the standalone system is dedicated to editing. The editor operating in a distributed resource-sharing local network must, like a standalone editor, run independently on each user's machine, and must, like a timesharing editor, contend for shared resources.

Some timesharing-based editing systems take advantage of local (terminal-based) hardware to perform editing tasks. These **intelligent terminals** have their own microprocessors and local buffer memories in which editing manipulations can be done, thus saving the time needed to read and write main computer memory, but adding tricky data structure synchronization problems. Small actions are not controlled by the CPU of the host processor but are handled by the local terminal itself. In a system using an IBM 3270 series terminal, for example, the editor sends a full screen of material from the mainframe computer to the terminal. The user is free to add and delete characters and lines; when the buffer has been edited, its updated contents are transmitted back to the mainframe. The advantage of this scheme, that the host need not be concerned with each minor change or keystroke, is also the major disadvantage. With a non-intelligent terminal the CPU "sees" every character as it is typed in and can react immediately to perform error checking, to prompt, to update the data structure and to record or "journal" the keystrokes for undoing editing operations (see Section 3.4). With an intelligent terminal, the lack of constant CPU intervention often means that the functionality provided to the user is more limited. Also, local work on the intelligent terminal is lost in the event of a system crash. Conversely, systems which allow each character to interrupt the CPU may not use the full hardware editing capabilities of the terminal because the CPU needs to see every keystroke and provide character-by-character feedback.

As the local-area network of largely self-sufficient workstations becomes the dominant architecture, we can expect that the problem of synchronizing intelligent terminals with timeshared hosts will disappear and that character-by-character feedback will become the norm.

2. HISTORICAL DEVELOPMENT OF EDITORS

The history of editing is one of many complementary development efforts proceeding in parallel. Editors are so numerous and their relationships so cloudy, that it is very difficult to provide an accurate chronology. Rather, we briefly overview some of the important concepts, citing familiar and representative examples. (For a survey of specific editors through 1971, see VAND71b.)

Non-interactive computerized editing began with the manipulation of "unit record" punched cards. The basic unit of information was the 80-column line; the user made corrections on a line-by-line basis, retyping mistyped cards. Compared to toggling in bits at the system console, the card gave the programmer new freedom. One could store information in both human- and machine-readable form and one could "travel" through this information, changing its order, discovering and fixing errors, recognizing color-coded groups of cards, or simply browsing through the deck.

Punched card decks had many disadvantages, such as the "rearrangement" that resulted when a box was accidentally dropped. More seriously, editing a small part of a large document required feeding the entire document, often thousands of cards, into the reader for every change. To correct small errors such as single character errors or double-character transpositions, the user had to retype the offending characters and to replicate the other characters with the duplication facilities of the keypunch. Replacing a word with a word of a different size necessitated duplicating all characters prior to the word and retyping all the characters from the new word forward. If the incorrect card was almost completely filled with characters, inserting a new word might result overflow of the contents, causing the insertion of one or more new cards to handle the overflow. Performing a global change required manually finding every occurrence of the old pattern and again manually replacing it with the new pattern; if the new pattern were larger than the old pattern, multiple overflows could easily occur.

To address the problems of the punched card in the still predominantly batch environments of the 1960's, **card** or **batch editors** were created. Here the programmer's initial deck of cards was stored as a card-image tape or disk file. Each card was referenced by a unique sequence number. Changes were made by creating an **edit deck** composed of cards containing editing requests, and running the deck through the batch editor program. For example, the request "in card 35, correctly spell the word 'rate'," would be made by simply typing the desired sequence number 35 on one card followed by a card containing the new contents of line 35, or more simply, by composing a card with a sequence number and an editing command, as in

    35 CHANGE/RATA/RATE/

Batch editors removed the problems of dropped cards and of retyping (in many cases), and, in some versions, provided new operations such as global replacement of a pattern. There were several disadvantages, however. Programmers needed to have a lineprinter listing of the entire card deck before making any change. Also, some of the organizational characteristics offered by cards, such as the easy visual inspection of a properly sequenced, color-coded, and well-labeled card box, were lost.

Systems like IBM's MTST [IBM67], which used a Selectric typewriter as an input device and small magnetic tapes and/or cards as storage media, were the forerunners of today's word processing systems. Because these primitive interactive editors relied on sequential storage media such as magnetic tape or magnetic cards, the user could only step through card images linearly, stopping at lines which needed correction and retyping them. To go backward, the user had to "rewind" and then "fast-forward" the file to the desired place. In addition, the utility of these initial line editors was limited by the typewriters, which supported the viewing of only one line at a time and had very slow printing speeds.

With the advent of timesharing in the mid-1960s, interactive **line editors** were designed that allowed the user to create and modify disk files from terminals. These editors attached either fixed or varying ("varying" meaning "sequential relative to the top of the file") line numbers to lines of limited length (initially 80 characters), allowing the user to reference a unit of information. Early examples of these include ATS [IBM70] and VIPcom [VIP69]. Simple command languages allowed the user to make corrections within a line or even within a group of contiguous lines, using much the same syntax as batch editors. Some early timesharing editors still restricted the user to forward access; later, this restriction was lifted and the user could scroll both forward and backward through a file. Typically, line editors with bounded-length lines shared the unfortunate property of **truncation**: if an insert or change of characters would force the line to exceed the maximum length, characters were dropped off the end of the line as needed. This implementation "feature," stemming from a conceptual model of the editing process based on simulating punched cards and line printer listings, was only marginally acceptable for program editing and unacceptable for serious manuscript preparation. (In the latter case, automatic creation of a new line upon overflow would have been a trivial fix.)

Another advance was the creation of the **context-driven line editor**, which allowed the user to identify the line containing the target of an operation by specifying a character context pattern for the editor to match, rather than by giving an explicit line number. One of the first examples of the context-driven line editor was the trendsetting editor running on the IBM 7090 as part of Project MAC's CTSS [CRIS65]. Other classic examples include IBM's CMS editor [IBM69] (see Part II, Section 4) and Stanford's WYLBUR [FAJM73]. At this point in the history of editing, users were still forced to think about multi-line entities, such as paragraphs and program blocks, as groups of integral lines, usually in card-image format; no interline commands were available that would, for example, delete text spanning from the middle of one line to the middle of the next line.

The first break from the 80-column card image came in the form of **variable-length line editors**, typified by Com-Share's Quick Editor (QED) [DEUT67, COMS67]. The main element of operation was still the line, but now each line could be of "arbitrary" length. Initially, these lines were actually limited to some maximum. QED popularized the notion of a "superline" (limited to 500 characters in length), which the online display process broke into viewable lines of 80 characters each until the superline was exhausted. While editing across superline boundaries was still impossible in these editors, the probability that a full phrase or sentence that needed editing would fall within a single superline was much greater than with an 80-character limit. Later, true variable-length line editors removed the restriction. By removing the card-image orientation of the editor, the variable-length line editor had strong and beneficial impact on the versatility of text processing. Another far-reaching result of the invention of variable-length line editors was that displayed text was no longer considered to be a one-to-one mapping of the internal representation, but rather a tailored, more abstract view of the editable elements.

Even with superline editors, three basic problems in manuscript editing remained: truncation when the line length was exceeded, inability to edit a string crossing line boundaries, and inability to search for a pattern crossing line boundaries. This last problem is an especially pesky one when transcribing editing changes from formatted hardcopy in that even a short phrase which appears on one line within the paper may be spread across two lines in the document's source file, unbeknownst to the user. Consider, for example, the familiar "the the" typo problem. If a document being edited on a line editor contained the lines:

```
...The power of the
the stream editor...
```

a search command:

```
locate/the the
```

would not find the pattern "the the," since it appears on two separate lines. The **stream editor** concept solved all three problems by eliminating line boundaries altogether: the entire text was considered a single stream or string that was broken into screen lines by display routines. An arbitrary string between any two characters could be defined for searching and editing. HES [CARM69], and FRESS are examples of stream editors. Although the TECO stream editor left the carriage returns and line feeds in the text stream, these could be edited like any other character; they did not serve to isolate one line from the next in editing. In fact, the generality of the TECO stream model has made possible the construction of several sophisticated editors using TECO as a nucleus (see Part II, Section 4).

Another way of dealing with the limitations of line/superline editors was to use the power of multi-line display screens, which provided cursor addressability and (possibly) local buffers, to create what are called synonomously **full-screen, display,** or **cursor editors**. These editors work either with variable-length lines or with streams, offering the user an entire screenful of text to view and edit without regard to line boundaries. An early example of a time-shared display editor is Stanford University's TVEDIT [TOLL65, McCA67]. Commands, represented by control character sequences, could be interspersed with the input of "normal" text. Users were able to move the cursor to point to the text they wished to manipulate rather than having to describe text arguments in some awkward syntax. Characters could be replaced by simply typing over them. Characters could be deleted by placing the cursor on the character and pressing the delete control character; characters to the right of the cursor moved left so that the cursor seemed to "swallow" characters. Similarly, for insertions, the characters to the right of the pointer moved to the right, "making room" for the new characters. The TVEDIT concepts and similar work by Ned Irons [IRON72] form the basis of many screen editors in use today.

A major new way of thinking about editing was introduced as early as 1959 by Douglas Engelbart at Stanford Research Institute. His NLS (oNLine System), implemented in the 1960s to create an environment for online thinking and authoring, showed the power of display terminals, multi-context viewing, flexible file-viewing, and a consistent user interface [ENGE63, ENGE68, ENGE73]. One of the NLS project's many important contributions was the mouse, an input device which is only now being integrated into commercial products. NLS was the first structure editor in that it provided support for text structure and hierarchy, not just for manipulating raw strings of text: the user could manipulate documents in terms of their structure, not only their content. NLS and other related systems, such as HES, FRESS, and Xanadu* [NELS74, NELS81], were particularly important because they view the editor as an *author's tool*, an interactive means for organizing and browsing through information, rather than simply as a mundane tool for altering characters in a single file.

Hansen's EMILY [HANS71] extended the concept of the structure editor and developed the **syntax-directed editor**, in which the structure imposed on a program being edited was the structure of the programming language itself. Users were able to manipulate logical constructs, such as do-while loops and their nested contents, as single units.

---

* Xanadu is a registered trademark.

In the late 1960's, general-purpose timesharing facilities typically supported only simple interactive line-editing and batch-formatting facilities for lineprinter output. These "value-added" facilities were barely adequate enough to create and modify programs and rudimentary documentation. By the early 1970's, text processing had become sufficiently important that it became the single dedicated application on both standalone and timeshared ("shared-logic") minicomputers. Since these minis did not need to support general-purpose computing facilities, manufacturers were able to offer comprehensive editing and formatting/typesetting capabilities as well as features oriented towards document production such as database management, information retrieval, workflow management, and print- and job-queue management that were usually unavailable on general-purpose systems. For a time, owners of these systems often had more text-processing power than those with much more expensive and much larger general-purpose computers. Examples of dedicated word processing systems include CPT, Lanier, QUIP, DEC Word/11, NBI, and Wang.

An important milestone in text editing and text processing was the early-70's development and mid-70's acceptance of the UNIX* timesharing system, the first general-purpose computing environment in which text utilities were given as much weight as programming utilities. In UNIX, a suite of utilities (the *ed* text editor, the *troff* text formatter, the *eqn* equation formatter, the *tbl* table formatter, the *refer* bibliographic database and formatter, the *spell* spelling corrector, and the *style* and *diction* text analyzers [KERN82]) introduced and popularized an extensive set of text tools in the general-purpose computing community. At the same time the publishing industries – newspapers, magazines, wire services, the graphi:s arts – converted wholesale to electronic typesetting and layout of pages, borrowing ideas from traditional computer-based text processing, and also channeling ideas in typesetting and page-layout back to the computing community.

In the then-separate area of computer graphics, picture editors were being designed to allow the user to manipulate graphical elements. Interactive drawing techniques from Sutherland's pioneering Sketchpad system [SUTH63] were later incorporated into editor interfaces. The Carnegie-Mellon tablet editor [COLE69] is an example of the use of this technology. In this experimental editor, hand-drawn proofreader's symbols were used to edit displayed text. The symbols were drawn on a data tablet and were recognized by the program by passing various characteristics for a given symbol through a decision tree. For a **delete** or **substitute** operation, for instance, the user drew a line through the text to be deleted. The system deleted this line, blinked the indicated text for verification, separated the text by opening a blank line, and inserted a cursor, enabling new text to be typed in from the keyboard. For a **transpose** operation, the user simply used the familiar transposition mark. With the existence of data tablets with built-in microprocessors dedicated to this recognition task [IMAG81], we may expect to see †his technique used in commercial editing products in the near future.

The major innovations of the 1970's in text handling and the user interface, specifically the Bravo editor [LAMP78] and the Smalltalk environment, took place at Xerox's Palo Alto Research Center (Xerox PARC). These systems demonstrated the expressive power of blending text and graphics on a high-resolution, bitmapped, raster graphics screen, using a dynamic graphical interface provided by a dedicated personal computer. Editing was done by selecting items on the screen, using the mouse as a pointing device. These systems were also the first **interactive editor/formatters**, in which the user's text was displayed on the bitmapped screen in a facsimile of the typography and layout of the final document *as* the document was being input

---

*UNIX is a trademark of Bell Laboratories.

or modified. For the first time, the user was given a notion of not only the up-to-date content, but also of the up-to-date form of the document.

Current research in the field of editing is focused upon several overlapping areas. One is that of providing a consistent, editor-based interface throughout a computer system [GOLD79, LANT80, FRAS80, APOL81, STAL81, TESL81, GOLD82]. This allows many common functions, such as renaming files, searching through directories, and debugging programs, to be performed as editing operations. For instance, to rename a file, one would type over the old filename in a listing of available files that would appear on the screen; in debugging a program, one would be able to edit the values of displayed variables. Other research topics include generalized structure editors, powerful syntax-directed editors with program-tracing capability, and interactive editor/formatters. Research in these and other areas is discussed more fully in Part II.

3. FUNCTIONAL CAPABILITIES

In this section, we take a more detailed look at interactive editors, examining their functional capabilities from a user perspective.

3.1 Traveling

User-specified traveling commands cause the **current editing and viewing pointers** of the editing and viewing components to be moved, resetting the filters that extract the editing and viewing buffers.[9] Traveling ranges from simple motion such as moving to a subsequent screenful of data, to more complicated movement such as pattern search and tree or directed-graph traversal.

Early systems, and even many of today's word processing systems, are oriented toward transcription of editing changes from hardcopy. They therefore provide relatively unsophisticated traveling mechanisms. For online authoring, however, a system should be oriented to browsing, studying, and organizing as well as to composition and revision. In such a system, traveling flexibility and power are mandatory, as the NLS experience has shown [ENGE68].

3.1.1 Simple movement

Editors commonly support two types of **intrafile motion**: **absolute** and **relative**. An absolute specification indicates a destination independent of the current position, while a relative specification indicates the destination relative to the current position. Generally, the current pointer is maintained internally to point to the corresponding current position in the data structure; in editors with pointing devices, the cursor usually points at this position in the visible text with the current pointer in lockstep. The user can move the editing buffer and viewing buffer from this position by issuing simple commands. In IBM's line-oriented CMS editor, moving the editing buffer and the viewing buffer five lines ahead in the document would be accomplished by typing:

    next 5

In line-oriented editors, line numbers can be **fixed** or **varying**. In editors with fixed line numbers, numeric labels provided by the user or the system, the user can easily specify an absolute goto to that number. As an example, the editor portions of BASIC interpreters use fixed line numbers specified some interval apart, such as:

```
00010 FOR I = 1 TO 10
00020     J = I * I
00030 NEXT I
```

To add a print statement after the increment statement, one could simply type

```
00025     PRINT I,J
```

and the editor would put the new line between lines 20 and 30, as indicated by its numeric label.

In contrast, editors with varying line numbers keep track of a line's position internally as an offset from the top of the file. When a new line is added, the internal line numbers of all lines beneath the new line are incremented by one. Since the line numbers change dynamically, the deletion (insertion) of a line near the top of the file causes all the line numbers below it to be decremented (incremented) by one. Because of this, editing by specification of line number is best done from the bottom of the file upwards, since insertions or deletions will typically only

---

[9] To simplify the remainder of our discussions, we will group both pointers together under the term "current pointer."

affect the lines at and below the current pointer. This is a restriction palatable (if at all) only for transcription from hardcopy, not for online revisions.

As we have seen, the user of a display editor travels by pushing function keys such as

```
+LINE or -LINE
+WORD or -WORD
+PAGE or -PAGE
+1/2 PAGE or -1/2 PAGE
```

that effectively change the contents of both the editing and viewing buffers. Additionally, the editing and viewing buffers can be moved left or right by a specified number of character positions (columns) to allow editing of wide lines, as in the following command:

```
50 LEFT
```

Top and bottom (of file) are two very common, highly functional traveling commands.

Many editors have **mark** or **saved-position stacks** or **rings** that record locations in the file. Some maintain an implicit mark ring, automatically storing the location each time the user makes a selection for a command, and allowing the user to retrace his/her steps. Others have explicit mark buffers; the user uses the save position command to store the current location in any number of buffers. Additions or deletions in the file will throw off the exact location if the editor only saves a character- or line-pointer or other varying index, but will typically leave the user in a location close to the original marked location.

Systems like NLS and FRESS allow character string **labels** to be inserted in the text; these move as the adjacent text is moved. The user need not know of the location of a piece of text, whether relative or absolute, in this system, but, for example, can travel instantly to the text labeled "casestudy" with the command goto-label casestudy. In the case of program editors, identifiers in procedure declaration statements can be used as implicit labels, as in the EMACS **tags** facility explained in Part II, Section 4.

Of course, many target-dependent traveling operations exist. In document editors, for example, simple movements are provided to bring a user to the beginning of a section or chapter. In a program editor, a traveling command might take the user to the next syntactic element. More specific examples are provided in Part II, Section 4.

3.1.2 Pattern searching

The above methods of traveling are *position*-dependent: goto line 7, go-back 15 lines, or goto-label "sec5". Almost all modern text editing systems additionally allow a *content*-dependent specification of location: **pattern searching**. A pattern searching command (usually called find or locate) generally changes the editing and viewing buffers so that they contain the pattern that was being sought.

Since typing an entire pattern is a tiresome operation, specification aids have been developed. The familiar "..." (**ellipsis**) construct can be specified to abbreviate a long pattern by indicating simply a few characters of context at the beginning and end of the pattern. Thus, one can locate the text string:

```
Now is the date for some good men
```

with the command:

```
locate /Now...men
```

Regular expression context patterns extend the ellipsis concept to more powerful pattern-matching capabilities, for instance, matching a pattern that does or does not contain a particular set of characters, matching a pattern only if it occurs at the beginning of the line, or matching a pattern regardless of the case of the characters (known as **case-insensitive pattern matching**).

3.1.3 Interfile Motion

The ability to travel between two or more files is extremely useful in online authoring. At the least, the user must be provided with commands to switch between two files. (This is much more useful, of course, if the two files can be displayed in two windows on the screen.) More advanced editors maintain a circular list of the files visited; the user can travel from one to the next or the previous in an ordered fashion, or in some cases choose any of the files from a display of the circular list.

Interfile travel generates several new problems. An editor may need a more intricate internal data structure and associated editing and viewing buffers for each open file to allow multiple files to be active at once. If the editor has the ability to map file viewing buffers to multiple windows, but can only keep track of one file at a time, a file must be saved each time the user switches windows; this discourages online browsing. As well, attributes might be kept for each file so that when a user is editing a LISP program the editor matches parentheses and automatically indents lines. When the user returns to a textual document, the editor would no longer do so.

3.1.4 Hypertext and Trails

The above types of travel are usually employed by the user *during* the editing of a document, typically to get to the next place in the file where an edit is to be performed; the paths of travel are not stored from one editing session to the next. Occasions do arise when the user wants to set up (semi-) permanent paths or links within a document or between documents. The motivation for such text links is well-stated in a seminal article by Vannevar Bush [BUSH45], who envisioned the "memex" device for authors and readers in 1945:

> The human mind. . .operates by association. With one item in its grasp, it snaps instantly to the next that is suggested by the association of thoughts, in accordance with some intricate web of trails carried by the cells of the brain. It has other characteristics, of course; trails that are not frequently followed are prone to fade, items are not fully permanent, memory is transitory. Yet the speed of action, the intricacy of trails, the detail of mental pictures, is awe-inspiring beyond all else in nature. . . . Consider a future device for individual use, which is a sort of mechanized private file and library. It needs a name, and, to coin one at random, "memex" will do. A memex is a device in which an individual stores all his books, records, and communications, and which is mechanized so that it may be consulted with exceeding speed and flexibility. . . .when numerous items have been thus joined together to form a trail, they can be reviewed in turn, rapidly or slowly, by deflecting a lever like that used for turning the pages of a book. . . .It is exactly as though the physical items had been gathered together from widely separated sources and bound together to form a new book. It is more than this, for any item can be joined into numerous trails.

Hypertext editing systems are the modern-day incarnation of Bush's pre-computer memex. Hypertext, a term coined by Ted Nelson [NELS67], is "the combination of natural language text with the computer's capacities for interactive branching, or dynamic display...a nonlinear text...which cannot be printed conveniently...on a conventional page." Simply, hypertext is defined as non-sequential writing. Hypertext systems allow the user to construct arbitrary links from any chosen point in a document to any other point in that document or in any other document in the user's domain. Menus of such links can be set up to provide a branching text that constantly evolves to provide a "dynamic and plastic structure" [ENGE68]. A batch

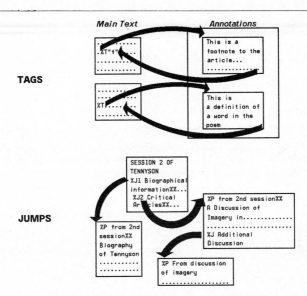

Figure 4. *An example of hypertext in FRESS.*

Tags and **jumps** are two of FRESS's hypertext elements. A tag T points to a single element (such as a footnote) in an "annotation space"; the user views the annotation but remains in the main text. A jump J indicates a path to another part of the current document or to another document. By taking a jump, one travels, changing the editing and viewing buffers of the document. In the new context, one can edit, take another jump, or take the reverse of a jump (labeled P for **pmuj**, jump spelled backwards), which returns to the unique source of the J that brought the user to the P in the first place. Multiple jumps to the same text would have multiple P labels so the user could distinguish the sources. Other system commands allow the user to retrace steps on a session basis, i.e. to return from all previous jumps with explicit **return** commands.

formatter can follow keyword-specified links to compile the text needed to produce a document. An interactive user can select links by keyword-specification or by menu-selection to lead to desired text, typically displayed in a separate window. In NLS, links can also be accessed via complex specifications of structure and/or content. One can specify, for example, "follow the first link containing the string '**edit**' in any third-level statement in the hierarchy, starting the search at the current first-level statement in view."

In the simplest sense, a hypertext document can consist of a "table of contents" with online links to files containing each chapter, each of which can link to sections. More advanced forms of hypertext include the use of links, rather than the online equivalent of standard footnotes, to point to the actual material referenced, allowing instantaneous access to cited material. Thus a document can be browsed online and predesigned but optional diversions can be set up along trails that readers may find interesting. Of course, authors and readers are free to create links to new files or to **annotation spaces** in which they may comment on what they are reading, thereby enriching the trails for others. A hypertext system may allow the user not only to see links to other places *from* the current position, but also to see that there are links from other places *to* the current position [VAND71a] (see Figure 4). The browser is then free to jump backward to see from what document this link was issued. A hypertext document is a bidirectional network of associative trails, a constantly evolving directed graph structure of text nodes that readers and authors can traverse. Catano [CATA79], Robertson et al. [ROBG79], and Herot et al. [HERO80] provide examples of the use of this arbitrary directed-graph structure for documents. Feiner et al. [FEIN82] use the hypertext concept in the context of graphics-oriented "electronic books" (see Figure 5).

3.2 Viewing

To provide a basis for editing and browsing, and to provide feedback after an editing command is executed, the viewing component creates an up-to-date view on the display. The viewing operations are of three sorts: 1) filtering operations in which appropriate portions of the raw data structure of the file are selected for the viewing buffer; 2) operations that format this

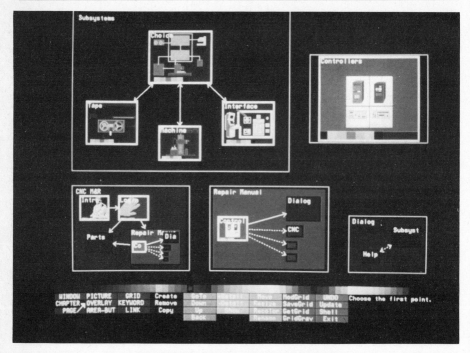

Figure 5. *Electronic Book Layout [FEIN82].*

A multiple-window display in the document layout system. The author may traverse the document's structure independently in each window and make links between chapters and pages in different windows. The author may also create, resize, and remove windows as needed, and revise the level of detail of the pages and chapters shown to control the amount of information presented.

filtered data to produce an ideal view; and 3) operations that map this ideal view to a window or page on a physical output-device.

3.2.1 Filtering

Editors that are especially oriented towards browsing (for example, NLS and FRESS), usually provide facilities to alter the **viewing specifications (viewspecs)**, allowing the user to control the filtering operations. Viewspecs can be used to control any number of selection and viewing parameters (parameters controlling what is to be displayed and how, respectively) to effect **information hiding** and online formatting. NLS, for instance, allows the user to indicate what levels of detail in a hierarchy are to be displayed, as well as how many characters per statement and even which statements, on the basis of content specification (for example, "fill the window with the first 50 characters of as many of the statements that lie between section 1.3 and 1.9 as possible, up to and including the third decimal level"). Additionally, the viewspecs control whether the selected text is to be shown normally or in indented outline form, with or without section numbers, with or without format codes, or in ragged-right or right-justified format. **Display keyword** or **password viewspecs** allow the user to see pieces of text only upon the presentation of the proper key; this facility can be used to protect sensitive materials and to reduce the clutter of online presentation by presenting only (potentially) relevant information. Similarly, a syntax-directed editor can allow the user to turn off the display of declarations or comments in a program.

Since the view is a mapping of the internal data structure onto the user's display, external factors such as noise on the communications line or a received system message can corrupt the displayed view, while the internal data structure remains intact. A system often supplies a `refresh display` function to restore the appropriate view from the internal data structure.

3.2.2 Formatting[10]

The simplest method of formatting the filtered viewing buffer contents is the "null" formatting: the text is shown exactly as it is stored in the internal data structure. Typically this is not sufficient for the user. In simple editors, text is stored essentially as consecutive characters on disk, with special characters indicating tabs and physical end-of-lines. A simple formatting routine is needed to map stored lines to a screen image, inserting logical carriage returns and/or linefeeds where appropriate. In many editing systems, especially stream editors, the formatting routines must make on-the-fly decisions about where to break lines that do not fit on one screen line [KNUT79, ACHU81]. For program editors, an intelligent formatting routine might include automatic indentation of program constructs.

In early text processors, **formatting codes** (such as .pp for paragraph, .in 5 for indent 5 spaces, .ce for center) were typed in as literal text and subsequently compiled in a batch formatting pass to produce formatted pages; no online feedback was available. Later **softcopy** or **proof copy** facilities were made available to display (but not to allow editing of) monospace (line-printer quality) output on the alphanumeric terminal. With high-resolution point plotting and raster displays, even proportionally spaced typeset text could be previewed outside the editor as the result of a separate batch formatting pass. The next major step in the formatting field was the creation of the interactive editor/formatter. Today most editors, especially commercial word processors, instantaneously display the results at least of commands with local effect (such as `indent`, `tab`, `embolden`, and `center`) as they are entered or changed. In the newest

---

[10]We do not attempt to cover the entire field of formatting here, but simply point out salient features of formatting directly tied to the editing task. We refer readers to Furuta et al. [FURU82] for a thorough survey.

generations of word processing systems the idea of on-the-fly formatting has been taken to the next logical step: they allow essentially all formatting, including hyphenation and pagination to be done on-the-fly. Interactive editor/formatters make possible an especially useful view in which all operations on the document take place immediately on a displayed facsimile of the printed page, thus giving instant user feedback. Other optional views may include the facsimile document along with ancillary windows in which the typesetting codes controlling the formatting are displayed (see the description of the Xerox Star in Part II, Section 4), or with inline "tags" describing the various document elements that appear on the screen (see the description of Etude in Part II, Section 4).

With hardware such as the personal workstation becoming prevalent, users will be less patient with traditional, tiresome, monospace characters on 80 x 24 CRTs, and will demand that display output make use of the many traditional, hardcopy information-coding techniques that improve reading efficiency. These include proportionally spaced text, font changes, high-lighting, complex page layout, and even imbedded equations and graphics. Thus online for-matting for display (softcopy) and offline formatting for paper (hardcopy) will become more similar, especially when bitmap raster displays approaching the 200-points-per-inch resolution of inexpensive (less than $10,000) electrostatic or laser printers become commonplace. (Even before this becomes a reality, we see that computerized typesetting, once reserved for special documents or for final copies only of a document whose drafts were produced on line printers or typewriter terminals, is now within the reach of many commercial or academic installations for routine work.) Editors must therefore make it possible for the user to specify sophisticated formatting effects shown online during the editing phase. Good examples of systems providing interactive typesetting can be found in several works in the literature [LAMP78, HAMM81, SEYJ81, SMIT82, and XERO82].

3.2.2.1 Formatting Commands

Approaches to the specification of formatting are numerous. In some systems, primitives provided as part of the interaction language allow the user to specify formatting operations on designated elements. For instance, the use of the center command in the editor might actually insert the appropriate spacing for centering and alter the internal representation of the document. Alternatively, this type of specification may be used to generate a low-level representation such as a formatting (typesetting) code that is stored in the file. In some systems these are invisible to the user and a mechanism must be provided to change these low-level representations using high-level editing commands. For example, many word processors provide a **tab rack**, an on-screen simulation of a typewriter's margin and tab controls, that contains the current margin settings, font styles, tab stops, and so on. The user can change these settings by simply moving the cursor into the tab rack and editing the attributes. In Xerox's Star, alternatively, every element (from a single character up to the entire document as a whole) has associated with it an optionally displayable **property sheet**, which simulates a pre-printed form or checklist. The user can examine the property sheet at any time and fill in or change the stored formatting options for any element (see Fig. 6).

In other editors, the formatting specification is entered as a formatting code in the same manner as "normal" (literal) text. In some systems, these codes must be entered on separate lines to distinguish them from literal text; in other systems a special character is used as a delimiter so that the codes can be imbedded in the normal text stream; two delimiters in a row then designate a literal delimiter character.

Regardless of how they are indicated, the specifications are one of two types: **procedural** or

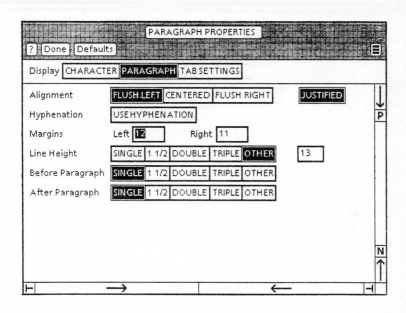

Figure 6. *Xerox STAR Property Sheet.*
The Xerox Star property sheet allows the user to edit attributes of various elements. The paragraph property sheet lets the user change alignment, spacing, and hyphenation by pointing at graphical buttons on the screen. Selected attributes are shown in reverse video.

declarative (markup). In a procedural specification, the author indicates the exact operations to be done to effect the formatting choices (e.g., skip 2 lines and indent 3 spaces). Conversely, in a declarative system, **tags** are used to identify elements of the document, such as items in a numbered list, paragraphs, chapter headings, and running heads. A separate facility stores the actual formatting attributes for the particular elements, and the formatter recognizes the tags and uses the tag facility (usually a set of formatting macros or a database of formatting information) to determine *how* to format any part of the document. These tags allow the same document to be formatted in different styles or for different output devices by simple parameterization: for instance, the user could format a *Computing Surveys* document by specifying the tag <Style=Surveys> at the beginning of the document and for *Communications of the ACM* by specifying the tag <Style=CACM>. Similarly, the user could format a document for the lineprinter by specifying the device tag <Device=1pr> and on a high-quality typesetter by specifying the tag Device=typesetter>. **Style sheets** containing a skeleton of tags for a particular document, for example, an online corporate memo that can be filled in by users, allows standardization of documents for a community, much like preprinted stationery or pads. Declarative languages provide less complicated user specifications, and often less complicated editor interfaces for online formatting; the user need not supply detailed formatting commands, and need use only high-level structural indicators as tags. Reid's SCRIBE [REID80a, REID80b, REID80c] is a popular declarative language and document compiler. IBM's GML [GOLC81] is a formatter-independent declarative language. Hammer et al. [HAMM81], Walker [WALK81b], and Chamberlin et al. [CHAM81] discuss editors that make use of the declarative technique (see Part II, Section 4).

3.2.3 Window Manipulation

In editors with multiple windows, the user must be able to specify and alter the placement of the windows on the display. The system can allocate windows: a single window would occupy the entire screen, two windows, half the screen each, and so on. The system can allow the user to specify the windows, either by typing coordinates or, more likely, by defining the bounds with a pointing device.

3.3 Editing

Our discussion of the editing component focuses on two major concerns: specifying the operands of an editing command and the commands themselves.

3.3.1 Specification of Scope

The range of a document used as an operand for an editing operation is called its **scope**. The user typically thinks of the scope not in terms of "raw" text, but rather in terms of logical elements that can be both edited and traversed. These elements are also known as units, nouns, objects, and structures, and are often a function of the internal representation of the target data. In line editors, for example, manuscript text may be stored as sequential lines and edited and traversed on a line basis. In stream editors, the text may be stored as a one-dimensional, indefinitely long stream of characters, broken into discrete lines by formatting routines for viewing purposes. Programs may be stored in textual form or in some intermediate form such as a parse tree or abstract syntax tree.

In addition to logical elements that match the internal representation, editors provide a variety of elements corresponding to user-level abstractions, often grouped in order of increasing scope: characters, words, lines, sentences, paragraphs and sections are typical for text. In addition to these standard system-provided elements, users can also define arbitrary **regions** or **blocks** that exist only for the duration of a given operation. A third class of elements may be a (partially overlapping) set of abstract document components such as sections, headings, titles, running headers, footers, and numbered lists. These are typically defined just in terms of formatting conventions and are available for explicit manipulation only in the most recent editors.

The goal of scope specification for all these elements is to approximate within the limitations of the computer interface the ways users would manually gesture ("delete *this*, move *that* over *there*"). As we have seen, in line editors the user establishes the current line (by specifying its line number or by traveling to it via scrolling or pattern searching) and then specifies the scope (by typing either a context pattern within that line or an integer to indicate a group of one or more discrete lines whose first line is the current one). In the UNIX *ed* editor the command

    s/Julius/Brute/

substitutes the word "Brute" for the scope "Julius" when the user is at the line

    Et tu Julius!

In stream editors, of course, the pattern matching is not limited to a current line but has potentially the entire file as its domain. In display editors, the user specifies the scope by driving a cursor with a locator device to define the appropriate element(s), in a manner more directly analogous to the manual technique of pointing.

There are several techniques for specifying a scope, some applicable to a typing-oriented interface, some applicable to a pointing-oriented interface, and some applicable to both.

In the first technique, the user simply selects an element – a character, word, line, or paragraph, for example. The user may **extend** this selection by selecting another element of this same type; all elements between the starting point and the other selected point (inclusive) would be selected. This is typically done using the ellipsis or regular expression facilities in a textual interface, and direct cursor positioning in a pointing interface.

In the second technique, the user adds modifiers to the commands. For example, having established a location in the text with context or cursor specification, the user can complete or modify the scope of a **delete** operation with **word** to form **delete word** or with a numeric parameter to form **delete 3 words**.

In the third technique, the user again establishes a starting selection at the smallest element (for example, a character) and then **adjusts** the selection. For instance, by using the mouse in Xerox's Star, a character can be selected as an initial scope and this scope adjusted to include successively the word, the line, the sentence and the paragraph containing that character (see Figure 7).

In a hierarchical structure editor, selection and adjustment can be easily used to traverse the hierarchy, as in **select node** and **extend to left child**.

3.3.2 Editing Operations

3.3.2.1 Creating

Text is inserted into a computer-based document with a text input device. To enrich this hardware, special software is frequently supplied. Editors often provide automatic **wordwrap**, which eliminates the need for typing a carriage returns at the end of each line. When the editor senses that the word currently being typed has exceeded the right margin, it breaks the line at the first blank space before the overflowing word and automatically pushes it, followed by the cursor, to the next display line.

Display editors generally offer one of two kinds of input styles: **typeover mode** or **insert mode**. In typeover mode, each typed character replaces the character at which the cursor is pointing. For adding characters, such editors supply **insert character** or **insert line** functions that open a blank character or a blank line at the cursor position. In insert mode, each time a user types a character, the character at the cursor position and all those to its right are shifted right one character and the typed character is inserted at the cursor position. Thus insertion can always be done without any commands, while replacement requires a command such as **delete character** or **delete line** before or after the insertion. Many editors allow the user to toggle between typeover mode and insert mode.

Other creation techniques include the capability of **imbedding** files or parts of files into the document being edited, thus making it possible to recycle previously created material. The user can create **boilerplate** documents, as is often done with proposals, contracts, and specifications, by using bits and pieces from the entire domain of user files on the computer. Form letters may be created by imbedding consecutive addresses from an address file at the top of a generic letter file.

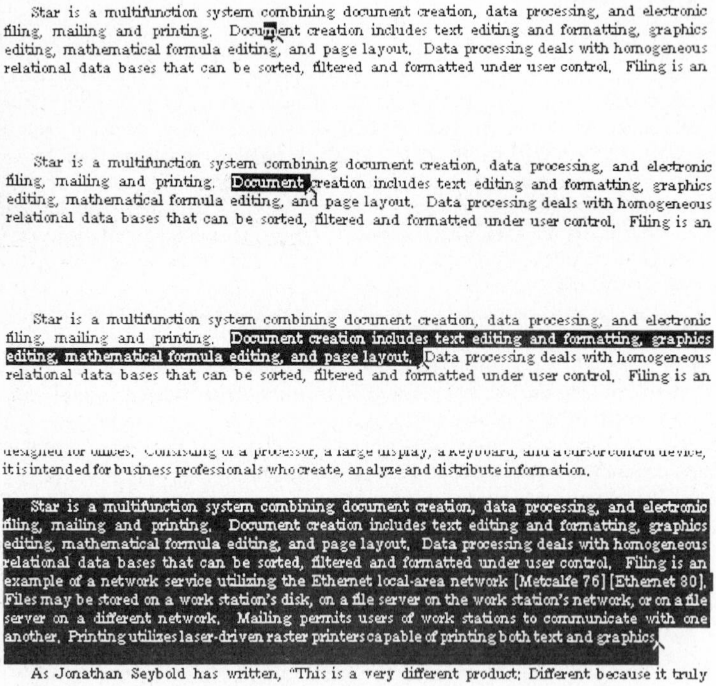

Star is a multifunction system combining document creation, data processing, and electronic filing, mailing and printing. Document creation includes text editing and formatting, graphics editing, mathematical formula editing, and page layout. Data processing deals with homogeneous relational data bases that can be sorted, filtered and formatted under user control. Filing is an

Star is a multifunction system combining document creation, data processing, and electronic filing, mailing and printing. **Document** creation includes text editing and formatting, graphics editing, mathematical formula editing, and page layout. Data processing deals with homogeneous relational data bases that can be sorted, filtered and formatted under user control. Filing is an

Star is a multifunction system combining document creation, data processing, and electronic filing, mailing and printing. **Document creation includes text editing and formatting, graphics editing, mathematical formula editing, and page layout.** Data processing deals with homogeneous relational data bases that can be sorted, filtered and formatted under user control. Filing is an

designed for offices. Consisting of a processor, a large display, a keyboard, and a cursor control device, it is intended for business professionals who create, analyze and distribute information.

Star is a multifunction system combining document creation, data processing, and electronic filing, mailing and printing. Document creation includes text editing and formatting, graphics editing, mathematical formula editing, and page layout. Data processing deals with homogeneous relational data bases that can be sorted, filtered and formatted under user control. Filing is an example of a network service utilizing the Ethernet local-area network [Metcalfe 76] [Ethernet 80]. Files may be stored on a work station's disk, on a file server on the work station's network, or on a file server on a different network. Mailing permits users of work stations to communicate with one another. Printing utilizes laser-driven raster printers capable of printing both text and graphics.

As Jonathan Seybold has written, "This is a very different product; Different because it truly

Figure 7. *Selection in Star.*
One click of a mouse button selects a character, the second click, as shown on the left, adjusts the selection to be the word containing that character, and the third click, as shown on the right, adjusts to the sentence containing that word.

3.3.3 Deleting

The `delete` command requires the user only to select the scope of the operation. Since `deletes` are obviously dangerous commands, some systems require confirmation before actually completing the operation. Other systems allow the user to `undo` commands, making the deletion operation reversible. For the `delete` command, as well as the `copy` and `move` commands described below, many systems provide `delete buffers`. This allows the deleted elements to be placed in "limbo" so that they can be used later as the objects of `put` (also called `insert`) operations, which put the elements from the delete buffer back into the text. To move a paragraph, for instance, the user first selects it and specifies the delete operation; the editor then deletes the paragraph and places it in the delete buffer. To put the paragraph back in somewhere else, the user indicates the desired destination and specifies the put operation. Often, systems provide multiple, named delete buffers for more complex manipulations. Berkeley's vi editor [JOY80b], for instance, has a **buffer stack**, which keeps track of the last nine pieces of text that have been deleted. EMACS [STAL80, STAL81] has a **kill ring**, a circular list containing the last eight blocks of text that were deleted. The user can "walk around" the previous kills in this ring until the desired text is found, with the walk always leading back to the starting point. Usually delete buffers and kill rings are saved while performing inter-file editing, so that text deleted from one file can be inserted into another easily.

3.3.4 Changing

Many of the changes made to a document are corrections of typographical and other minor errors. The simplest change is the replacement of one letter with another. In typeover mode of a display editor, the correction is made by simply typing the new character over the erroneous one. In insert mode of a display editor, the correction is made by typing the new character and then using a delete-char-forward command to delete the old character, which has been pushed to the right by the insertion of the new character. Similarly, changing a word in typeover mode simply involves typing over the erroneous word. However, since the replacement word may be shorter (longer) than the original word, a delete (insert) character function may also be needed. In insert mode, changing a word would be done entirely with the implicit insertion combined with delete-word functions.

In editors without cursor keys, the user needs a method of specifying what character(s) to replace. These editors have a change or substitute command, as shown previously, that takes as arguments both the scope of the change and the replacement string.

Because of its speed, the computer naturally offers the facility of global operations – operations that take place uniformly throughout a document. The global change command allows the user to specify a pattern to be found throughout a document and a replacement string to replace that pattern wherever it appears. In some systems, this command may do its work but not indicate what changes have been made. In others, a count of the number of changes is given. In others the pattern string is highlighted each time it is found, and the user is prompted to indicate whether or not the change is desired. Column-dependent changes are useful for editing programs or tables.

The transpose command is a special-purpose change command. In EMACS for example, the CTRL-T command will exchange the character at which the cursor points with the one directly to its left, and similarly, the META-T command will do so for words.

3.3.5 Moving

The ease with which blocks of text can be rearranged is one of the great advantages of interactive editors. To move a block of text the user specifies a source (the scope of text to be copied) and destination (the place where the text is to be copied). In an editor in which the scope is specified by pointing, the user defines the source by selecting the beginning and end of the text to be moved, and then defines the destination by pointing to the location at which it should be placed.

In line editors and context editors, where such a physical sequence of steps is impossible, the user must resort to textual specification. For example, the misordered poem by Frost

```
Two roads diverged in a yellow wood,
And looked down one as far as I could
To where it bent in the undergrowth;
```

```
And sorry I could not travel both
And be one traveler, long I stood
```

could be ordered properly with a typical line editor by traveling to the line "And looked down one as far as I could" and specifying

```
move 2 down 2
```

This would temporarily delete the following two lines, including the one currently being pointed to, move the current pointer to the line following the last line deleted, move it down 2 more lines, and insert the temporarily deleted lines below where the current pointer now points.

Note that with most line editors, the user is severely limited to moving integral numbers of lines, rather than arbitrary regions. In a context-driven stream editor this specification is a bit easier:

```
move/And looked...undergrowth;/stood/
```

Rather than specifying relative line numbers, the user now specifies context patterns.

Note that systems with delete buffer facilities may have no need for a special-purpose move command, since, as discussed in the previous section, one can delete the desired text and re-insert it in the appropriate place with a put command.

3.3.6 Copying

A copy command is simply a move command in which the source text is not removed after the destination text is in place.

An alternate strategy for the copy command is to have a pick command that stores a selection of text in a pick buffer. This is analogous to using the delete buffer described above, with the important exception that the picked text is not deleted. Now a copy of the picked text is in limbo in the pick buffer and can be reinserted in the text with the put command. If the put command does not erase the contents of the pick buffer, this facility can be used to make multiple copies of some selected text quickly.

3.4 Miscellaneous Capabilities

Commands grouped under this heading are not directly involved with manipulating text, but rather with assuring the integrity of user's work and with making the user interface more powerful and helpful.

3.4.1 Reliability

3.4.1.1 Backup Capability

To minimize the possibility of the accidental erasure or destruction of a document, editors often have **backup** capabilities. One strategy is to give the user **workfiles**, copies of the actual files, to work with, saving them as the actual files only when the user exits or when an **autosave** feature copies the workfiles as the actual files after a (user-specifiable) number of keystrokes or command executions. A similar strategy is to make automatically a backup copy of the files as they exist when the editor is invoked; the user is given the actual files to edit, but can always make the backup copy become the actual file in the case of a system crash or editing mishap while editing the actual file. An **abort** command allows the user to scrap an editing session and return to the backup copy that contains the state of the file when the editing session began.

3.4.1.2 Undo Facility

The **undo** facility is a critically important, time-saving, and unfortunately not yet universal feature. The most basic version allows the user to undo the last command entered. More useful systems have an *n*-level undo stack that allows the user to undo commands *n* levels back (sometimes to the beginning of the session or even back to previous sessions). The undo feature frees the user from the burden of making sure that each command does exactly what is wanted by guaranteeing that any result can be undone. The general undo facilitates risk-free experimentation, especially important for online composition and organization. Some systems [ARCH81] provide an undo-redo facility, which allows the user to undo operations and then redo them at the push of a button. Another way of presenting undo, rather than as a complete backtracking of a session, is simply as a command that performs the inverse of the last specified command. For instance, after one performs a delete, the undo command would essentially perform a put. Issuing undo again would then perform a delete. Smalltalk-80's cancel/accept pair allows the user to accept the editing state at a point in time and experiment freely, knowing that a single cancel command will return the document to the accepted state.

3.4.1.3 Cancel Facilities

The cancel command allows the user simply to cancel the command that is currently in progress. This is of great importance if time-consuming operations such as pattern searching have been specified erroneously. When commands are not queued and typeahead is not in effect, specifying a new command while a previous command is still executing often implicitly cancels the executing command. Alternatively, especially when an operation is simply a traveling command rather than a command that makes extensive changes to the internal data structure, specifying a command while one is executing could cause feedback from the first command to be cancelled. For example, if the user presses the + PAGE key in a screen editor, and, while the new page is being displayed, the user presses + PAGE again, an intelligent system would not first complete the display of the first page and then replace that completely with the second page, but would cancel the display of the first page and proceed to display the second page.

3.4.1.4 Keystroke History

The **keystroke history** is a powerful reliability mechanism that keeps a copy of every keystroke (both command and text) that the user has specified since the current editing session started. If the system crashes, the user is provided with mechanisms to run the keystroke history file against the old copy of the edit files as if the commands were being typed in. This history file can also provide the basis for the undo command.

3.4.1.5 Context Saving

A useful feature provided by some systems is the ability to save editor attributes and parameters from session to session. In *bb*, for example, a control file (see Fig. 8) saves information about the initial cursor position when the editor is invoked, the file to use, and enough other information that the user can simply invoke the editor, without any parameters, and continue a session exactly where it ended five minutes or five days ago. In more advanced systems, a **checkpoint/restart**, **snapshot** or **workspace** facility allows the recording and subsequent restarting of the entire editing environment, including complete internal data structures. This is common in programming languages like LISP, APL, and Smalltalk-80.

3.4.2 Ergonomics

3.4.2.1 Repetition

A **repeat** command, which re-executes the command last executed, is a simple and convenient facility. Another alternative is to have the user apply a new selection and then reissue the command. Another is to "bring back" the last command and allow the user to edit it before re-executing it.

```
savetemp=1                      Pscreen=7
bufinfile=.bbbuf                Pmargin=0
bufoutfile=.bbbuf               Pwindow=0
filename=macrofig.me            Preadonly=0
curcrypt=0                      Planguage=
curstream=1                     Pfileid=10
curtabin=0                      Qfilename=/usr/info/b.help
curtabout=0                     Qcrypt=0
curindent=1                     Qstream=0
curline=19                      Qtabin=0
curchar=43                      Qtabout=1
curscreen=0                     Qindent=1
curmargin=0                     Qline=0
curwindow=0                     Qchar=0
curreadonly=0                   Qscreen=0
curlanguage=roff                Qmargin=0
fileid=10                       Qwindow=0
Pfilename=dopstitle.tex         Qreadonly=0
Pcrypt=0                        Qlanguage=
Pstream=1                       Qfileid=2
Ptabin=0                        Asearch=shar
Ptabout=0                       Arsearch=^[WM]
Pindent=1                       Afsearch=
Pline=17                        Aexit=
Pchar=6                         Abfsave=
```

Figure 8. *A bb Control File.*

The control file saves information from one editing session to another. Here, for example, the **bufinfile** and **bufoutfile** variables indicate where the pick and delete buffers are to be saved from session to session. **Curline** and **curchar** indicate where in the document the cursor was pointing when the session was ended. **Curscreen** indicates which line is at the top of the screen. **Filename** indicates what file was being edited at the time the session was ended. The variables beginning with **P** and **Q** keep track of the same information for multiple files.

3.4.2.2 Online Documentation/Help Facility

An online **help facility** is extremely important to new and occasional users, as well as dedicated users who do not use all parts of the system regularly. The help facility can provide an expanded explanation of an error message, a short summary of a command syntax, or perhaps complete access to an online version of the manual. Some systems create a separate help window, allowing the user to have access simultaneously to both the help information and to the document being edited, rather than forcing the user to leave the document and lose the information on which the user sought help in the first place.

3.4.2.3 User Feedback

Feedback is a vital part of the editing process; it is necessary for specifying operations, for specifying scopes, and for showing the results of an operation in the updated view. The last kind of feedback is provided out of necessity, but the first two categories are not always given due consideration by editor designers.

In editors with typing-oriented interfaces, echoing the typed command provides immediate feedback on both operation and scope. In function-key interfaces, a button push provides no inherent feedback. If no supplementary feedback were supplied, the user would have to rely on examining the results of the operation to see if the specification was correct; by this time, it would often be too late to reverse the results. Thus feedback techniques, such as highlighting a selection in progress (with such hardware-supported techniques as brightening, underlining, or reverse video) in display editors, or highlighting the menu items as they are browsed through in menu-oriented interfaces, are vitally important. In non-display-oriented systems, a summary of the command that is to be executed or has been executed is useful. This feedback might consist of displaying a condensed English-language message such as "**move 'red fox...dog' after 'The quick'**." If an editor has undo facilities, this type of condensed feedback of results is useful but not necessary, since the user can afford to make mistakes or experiment.

Other audio and visual cues aid the user at a little cost in efficiency or in implementation. Beeping to signal errors usually ensures that a user does not miss the occurrence of an error. Programmable cursors allow the cursor to take on different symbolic forms depending upon what the user is doing. Time-consuming operations require intermittent feedback so that the user can be satisfied that the system is still working. Newshole [TILB76] uses a Buddah to remind the user to be patient while the Xerox Star uses an hourglass icon to indicate that it is busy. A status line at the top or at the bottom of the screen, indicating the current position in the document, the name of the file, any modes that might be set, and other such information, is an easily implemented method providing positive feedback.

3.4.3 Customization

3.4.3.1 Profiling

A **profiling** facility allows the user to "tune" the editor environment at invocation time. This allows important or preferred environment settings to be handled automatically and removes the need for all users to accept a common default. Some editors allow the setting of simple state variables such as number of backup versions and number of modifications before saving the file on disk. Others allow each user to reconfigure major parts of the interface, such as redefining function key bindings.

3.4.3.2 User-Defined Commands (Macros)

Editing systems often allow the user to define **macros** or **editing scripts** (super-instructions) based upon the system operation repertoire using an editor **macro language**. The user can thus package under one name sequences of commands that are often executed as groups (see Figure 9). In some systems, these commands prompt for or simply accept parameters (operands) and even provide conditional execution, for maximum power and flexibility. Function-key editors often have **keystroke macros**; the system "captures" a set of keystrokes typed in by the user and can then repeatedly execute those keystrokes as if they were one command. Some keystroke macro systems even allow the user a form of parameterization, temporarily stopping the execution of the keystroke macro, allowing the user to type in the "parameter," and then finishing the execution.

3.4.3.3 Extensibility

Some editors allow the user to extend the command set, in the same language in which the editor is written. Thus the user is not limited to designing macros made up of editor primitives, but can design operations using the same lowest-level primitives as the nucleus of the editor uses itself. The fact that the extension is being done in an actual programming language, rather than a special-purpose editor macro language, implies greater efficiency and ease of expression of new functions. In EMACS, for instance, the editor can be used to modify or to create a function and this function can be "linked" into the editor without ever leaving the editing environment. Of course, such a feature is not targeted to the general public but to more advanced users or programmers who are willing to learn the internals of the editor to modify or to add code.

Suppose a user has mailbox file which contains all the headers and text of messages received for a period of time and would like to create a shorter version of this file for quick reference containing only the headers. A macro to do this might look like this:

```
DEFINE MACRO mail_to_headers
deluntil /From /
skip 2
insert ----------------------------------------------
next
DEFINE MACRO END
```

In this hypothetical editor, the user defines a macro called *mail_to_headers* by bracketing typical editor statements between a *DEFINE MACRO* and a *DEFINE MACRO END* bracket. The statements in this macro indicate to delete everything until the first line with the characters "From ", to skip 2 more lines (the "To" line and the "Subject" line in the mail message), to insert a line of underscores, and to go to the line after these new underscores.

Given, with the current line pointer pointing to a line preceeding the line "From wcs...":

```
From wcs Thu Mar  5 02:49:41 1981
To: nkm
Subject: (un)natural language processing
Cc: wcs

hi nrmn.

ths is a tst of th nw unix* cmnd avd. it mr  or is
bindy strps vwls frm stndd inpt & pics th rslt
on stndd otpt.
              .
              .
              .


From avd Fri Mar  6 20:17:16 1981
To: nkm
Subject: Another lost cause
Cc: skf wp

Do you know where the excess fress resource manuals are, or the master
for that matter? Do you know how to copy it off the C-disk so someone
could take a look at it? Where the source is kept these days?

From skf Fri Mar  6 18:47:14 1981
To: fac grad graphics ugrad
Subject: The ACM Lecture Series: Judson Rosebush

On Thu Mar 12 @ 4pm in Pembroke Hall 210, the ACM will be sponsoring a
lecture by Judson Rosebush, president of Digital Effects, a NY-based
company doing commercial computer animation.
will be shown on film/videotape. The talk should be
```

successive invocations of the macro *mail_to_headers* would result in the file being changed to:

```
From wcs Thu Mar  5 02:49:41 1981
To: nkm
Subject: (un)natural language processing
-----------------------------------------------
From avd Fri Mar  6 20:17:16 1981
To: nkm
Subject: Another lost cause
-----------------------------------------------
From skf Fri Mar  6 18:47:14 1981
To: fac grad graphics ugrad
Subject: The ACM Lecture Series: Judson Rosebush
-------------------------------------------
```

Figure 9. *Example of Macro Facility.*

3.4.4 Target-Specific Operations

Target-specific operations are those not common to all editors but specific to the target application area for which the editor is designed. A LISP program editor, for example, might have routines to locate matching parentheses. The target-specific operations are the most marked distinguishing characteristics between editors. These operations go further than manipulating elements as simply neutral parts of some larger whole; rather, they operate on these objects with some "knowledge" of what they are, for example, a `capitalize` command would need to know that a capital a was represented as an A. In syntax-directed program editors, for example, compilation of a syntactic entity is a target-specific operation. A more thorough description of these will be found in the next section in the discussion of actual editors.

PART II: SURVEY

4. IMPLEMENTATIONS

This survey discusses a wide variety of editors used in academic and commercial circles. Our purpose is not to provide a detailed point-by-point comparison; our coverage from editor to editor is not necessarily consistent in either subject matter or depth. Rather, using the terminology of our tutorial, "Interactive Editing Systems: Part I," we attempt to illustrate the capabilities outlined in Part I, Section 3 of that tutorial by briefly describing the distinctive features of each editor or class of editors. While a taxonomy of the interactive editor – one in which we could compare the genealogy, purposes, and features of various systems – would be useful, it is difficult to construct. Terminology for categorizing editors is far from standard, a fact that often leads to identical labels for less than identical software and hardware. The history of editing contains many parallel developments and much cross-fertilization of ideas; a strict ordering or categorization is thus impossible. Informally, then, we will be looking at editors from the viewpoint of the target applications for which they were designed, the elements and their operations, the nature of the interface, and the system configuration. These categories do not form strictly independent axes; the choice of one frequently influences the choice of another.

"Target applications" are the high-level entities that the editor manipulates, for example, manuscripts, programs, or pictures. "Elements" are the units of target data that may be manipulated by the user. For example, a user may manipulate a program in the units of single lines of text, of individual programming language constructs, or of individual nodes in a parse tree. User "operations" fall into several subcategories. Editing operations allow the user to manipulate the target elements. Traveling operations allow the user to browse through a document. Viewing operations allow the user to control what subset of target data is presented to the user and how it is formatted: for example, text may be viewed as single lines, as full-screen pages, as a prettyprinted program, or as a facsimile of a typeset document. "Interface" defines the interaction language, input devices, and output devices with which the user performs these operations. "Configuration" describes the architecture of the systems on which the editor can run.

For compatability with popular terminology, we review some of the most common terms that will be used in the discussions in this section. A **text editor**[11] is one of the basic components of a **text processing system**, which is concerned not only with creation and maintenance but also with formatting and interactive presentation of text. In addition to a text editor, a text processing system includes a **text formatter**, concerned with the layout and typography of the text, and various **text utilities** such as spelling correctors that aid in analyzing and preparing the text. **Word processing** is a commercial synonym for text processing. An **office automation system** typically combines a word processing system with utilities such as database management, information retrieval, electronic mail, and calendar management. **Program editors** operate on programs, whether represented in textual form or in another canonical form, such as a parse tree or abstract syntax tree. **Picture** or **graphics editors** facilitate the creation and revision of computer-based graphics. A new development in the text processing field is the **document preparation system**, which integrates text editing, picture editing, and formatting. A **voice editor** is a specialized interactive editor in which the target is digitally-encoded voice.

---

[11]In this paper, Bold type is used to introduce concepts and terms. Typewriter type is used to set off editor commands. Italic type is used for emphasis.

A **forms editor** is an interactive editor that allows users to create and to fill in business forms conveniently. An **interactive editor/formatter,** often called a "what-you-see-is-what-you get" editor/formatter, allows the user to edit a facsimile of the printed page such that the changed text is reformatted instantaneously. On standard alphanumeric terminals, the facsimile represents a monospaced, typewriter page. On high-resolution raster graphics displays, the facsimile represents a proportionally-spaced, typeset page, with a variety of typefaces, sizes, and weights, and such non-textual material as equations, line drawings and even photographs. The goal of the **universal** or **virtual** editor, a current topic of research, is to generalize and integrate previously target-dependent software, providing a uniform way to manipulate seemingly dissimilar targets such as manuscript text, program text, pictures, and digitized voice. A **structure editor** is a special type of virtual editor that gains its generality by imposing the same structure on different targets. For example, a structure editor based on hierarchy may allow the user to impose this tree structure on diverse targets and edit them with the same tree-editing primitives (e.g., `delete subtree`, `move current subtree up 1 level`, `display all siblings of` node). A **syntax-directed editor** is based on the same principles as a structure editor but imposes the syntactic structure of a particular language, rather than a general-purpose structure, on the target.

4.1 Line-Oriented Editors

Line-oriented editors are covered here simply to round out our treatment of common editors. We do not, however, advocate the continued production or use of these editors. The conceptual model presented with line editors is that of editing virtual card images; the line editor constantly visits the limitations of this outdated representation of data on the user. Notable drawbacks are pattern searches and edits that do not cross line boundaries, and overflow and subsequent truncation of fixed-length lines. The continued dependence on the card analogy illustrates an important design flaw in many editors: they adhere to outmoded conventions even though those conventions unnecessarily limit the technology of the day. Unlike the TECO model below, where lines are simply an optional filtering presented to the user as a service, line editors force this limited view on the user.

IBM's CMS Editor

IBM's CMS editor (c. 1967) is a classic example of a fixed-length line-oriented editor with a textual interface, designed for a timesharing system whose terminals lack cursor motion keys and function keys. It presents the user with a one-line editing buffer (the amount of the document that can be edited at a given time), though this is extended for some operations. Similarly, it presents a corresponding one-line viewing buffer (the amount of the document that is used to construct the display). The display is a simple mapping of the one-line viewing buffer to a one-line window; it is typically updated after the execution of each command. (A more thorough explanation of the editing buffer, viewing buffer, and window model is presented in Part I, Section 1). Traveling is done with line granularity using absolute and relative `gotos` to varying internal line numbers and context pattern-matching. The input language is textual with two major modes: input mode and edit mode. Typically the user spends most time in edit mode, with input mode reserved for bulk input of text. The prefix syntax is generally consistent across commands:

command/scope/optional destination/optional parameters

The commands are full English words; the user does not have to remember abbreviations, though the system will accept the smallest possible unambiguous abbreviation. Most commands operate upon the line units, and across lines, as well, if so specified by the scope.

We now show some simple editing using the CMS editor. Assume we are in edit mode and that the following section of a program, which computes the sum of two matrices, is to be modified to compute the difference of the two matrices:

```
ADD: PROCEDURE;
FOR ROW = 1 TO N DO;
  FOR COLUMN = 1 TO M DO;
    C(ROW,COLUMN) = A(ROW,COLUMN) + B(ROW,COLUMN);
  END;
END;
```

The following sequence of interactions with the editor would provide the necessary changes (the user's requests are preceded by the system prompt character ">".

```
>find/add:
ADD: PROCEDURE;
>change/add/subtract
SUBTRACT: PROCEDURE;
>next 3
    C(ROW,COLUMN) = A(ROW,COLUMN) + B(ROW,COLUMN);
>change/+/-
    C(ROW,COLUMN) = A(ROW,COLUMN) - B(ROW,COLUMN);
>top
>change/add/subtract/ * *
```

The routine ADD is first located by using the column-dependent find command that searches for the string "ADD:" beginning in the first position of a line. (The locate commands, after searching for a pattern that does not exist, travel to and leave the buffer either at the beginning or end of the file, frustrating the user who has erroneously specified a search pattern and must manually grope back to the former location.) The current line pointer now points to the line "ADD: PROCEDURE"; this line is echoed on the screen. The next user command, change/add/subtract, affects only the contents of the buffer: the first occurrence of "ADD" is replaced by "SUBTRACT." For appropriate types of files, the editor does automatic lower-case to upper-case translation. If the maximum line length of 132 characters is exceeded, the editor will truncate the line. Line numbers in the CMS editor are varying. Travel is specified relatively, with next (next 3 moves the current pointer and hence the editing and viewing buffers 3 lines down from the current location), or absolutely, with goto (goto 276 moves the current pointer to the 276th line of the document). The change/+/- command changes the "+" to a "-". The top command moves the current line pointer to the first line of the file. The "* *" operand of the final change specifies the replacement of all occurrences of "ADD" in all lines – this is a global change that will affect the entire file.

The CMS editor provides the ability to set up logical tab stops – tabs implemented in the editor software rather than in terminal hardware – so that tabs may be specified by typing a user-chosen logical tab character in the input stream. Certain installation-specific enhancements of the basic CMS editor allow the user to undo the most recent command, shorten the scope specification by using ellipses (. . .), and do automatic indentation tailored to language-dependent needs [BROW81].

One of the most confusing attributes of the CMS editor are its two modes. Edit mode gives the user access to all the functional capabilities of the editor, including the capability to switch to input mode. Input mode, though, only gives the user two options: typing in text, which is simply inserted into the file at the current line pointer, or pressing dual carriage returns, which returns the user to edit mode. (A blank line is entered by typing at least one space). Even if the text that the user types in input mode is a command, it is not executed. To get into input mode, the user types the command input while in edit mode (if the file is new, the user is automatically placed in input mode on invocation of the editor). Often, a user might type a sequence like

```
locate/bull
next 3
type
```

only to discover, after some pondering, that the system is in input mode and that these commands were not executed but were actually inserted into the file as text. The "fix" is to get into edit mode, move the current pointer up n lines to the first erroneous line, delete n lines, move up 1 to reposition the pointer to the location from which the erroneous commands were first issued, and finally reissue the commands as commands.

SOS

SOS [DIGI78], like the CMS editor, is a line editor designed for editing on "glass teletypes" – display terminals underutilized as hardcopy terminal emulators – on a timesharing system, specifically a wide range of Digital Equipment Corporation computers. The input language is textual and is very similar to the CMS editor. The commands, as shown in Figure 10, are typed in prefix notation (verb/noun). The major unit of manipulation is the line.

Unlike the CMS editor, SOS attaches fixed, visible line numbers to each line in a file being edited. Typically a file is stored with these numbers, but special commands allow it to be stored without numbers and enable the numbers to be regenerated at the beginning of the next editing session. The editing buffer defaults to one line, though for most SOS commands a user can specify a line number or range of line numbers to expand this editing buffer. The default viewing buffer is a line; the window is simply a mapping of this line to the output device.

For selection and organization purposes, SOS goes one step further and allows the user to create logical pages within a file, using the page mark command. This essentially divides the file into subfiles that are independently sequence-numbered. SOS maintains a current position pointer made up of the current page number and the current line number.

SOS is a highly modal editor, with the following seven different modes of operation (see Figure 11):

- *Input mode*, in which SOS accepts the text being typed and inserts it into the file;
- *Read-only mode*, in which a user can travel through a file but not modify it;
- *Edit mode*, in which the user spends much of the editing session, performing editing, traveling, and viewing operations;
- *Copy-file mode*, in which the user can copy part or all of ai file into another one;
- *Alter mode*, in which a user can perform character-by-character intraline editing without pressing carriage return to execute the command; it is a textual approximation to display editing without cursor keys;
- *Alter/insert mode*, in which the user can insert characters such asiii control characters that have special meaning to the editor; and
- *Decide mode*, in which the user can make case-by-case decisions for substitute commands. In fact, decide mode has two submodes, *decide alter* and *decide alter/insert*. These two modes

Command	Page	Form	Arguments
Alter[1]	2-27	A	[range]
Copy[2]	2-40	C	position[=file-spec] ,range[,increment1 [,increment2]]
			position=file-spec/C
Delete	2-43	D	[range]
End	2-44	E	[B] [Q] [S] [T] [:file-spec]
Overwrite input file		EB	
No output file		EQ	
Strip line numbers		ES	
No numbers, no pages		ET	
Find[3]	2-46	F	[[string] (ESC)[range]] [,A] [,N] [,E] [,n] [,-]
Help	2-51	H	[:n]
Input[4]	2-52	I	[position] [,increment]
			[position] [;increment]
			[position] [;!n]
Join	2-55	J	[position]
Kill page mark	2-56	K	/page
List:LP or file	2-57	L	[range[,S] [,P[:file-spec]]]
			[range] [,[S] [,F:file-spec]]
Mark	2-58	M	[position]
reNumber	2-59	N	[increment] [,[range] [,start]]
Print: terminal	2-61	P	[range] [,S]
Replace[4]	2-63	R	[range] [,increment]
			[range] [;increment]
			[range] [;!n]
Substitute[5]	2-65	S	[[oldstring(ESC)newstring] (ESC)[range] [,D] [,N] [,E]]
Transfer	2-69	T	position,range[,increment1 [,increment2]]
Save World	2-73	W	[B] [:file-spec]
eXtend[6]	2-74	X	[range] [,N]
Move Position	2-76	.	position
Give Parameter	2-77	=	parameter
Set Parameter	2-78	/	parameter[:n]
Command File	2-79	@	file-spec
Print next line		(RET)	
Print previous line		(ESC)	

[1] Enter Alter mode.   [4] Enter Input mode.
[2] Enter Copy-file mode (if /C).   [5] Enter Decide mode (if ,D).
[3] Enter Alter mode (if ,A).   [6] Enter Alter/insert mode.

Figure 10. *SOS Commands [DIGI78].*

differ from *alter mode* and *alter/insert mode* primarily in that they, upon returning from the submodes, leave the user in *decide* mode rather than *edit mode*.

Alter mode is the most unusual of the modes. It simulates the intraline editing that is easily provided on display editors, and provides access to elements other than lines. The command syntax is postfix (noun/verb) and infix (noun/verb/noun), not prefix. Commands allow the user to skip forward and backward by characters and words, delete characters and words, capitalize

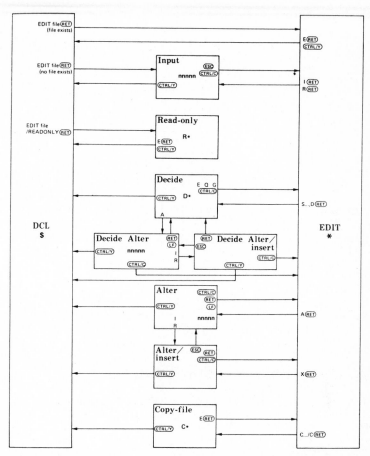

The paths among the various SOS modes and submodes of operation are marked by arrows. Prompts are shown in boldface type.

Figure 11. *SOS Modes [DIGI78].*

nd uncapitalize characters, delete all characters until the occurrence of a particular character, nd so on. Unfortunately, the user must explicitly enter *alter mode* to take advantage of these acilities.

As Figure 11 shows, the transitions from mode to mode are almost mazelike; the user can asily become trapped in a remote area of the system. For instance, in *decide alter/insert mode* ЗC brings one to *decide alter mode*, typing carriage return brings one to *decide mode*, typing

Con- struct	Internal represen- tation	Meaning
Find-string constructs:		
?/	(CTRL/T)	Match any character
?:	⎮	Match any separator
?<	(CTRL)	Match a space or tab
?%x	(CTRL/E)	Match any character except x
?)x	(CTRL/N)	Match 0 or more of the character x
?1x	(CTRL/Y)	Match 1 or more of the character x
?9	(CTRL/X)	Match any alphanumeric character
?!	(CTRL/A)	Match any letter (A-Z, a-z)
?&	(CTRL/F)	Match any uppercase letter (A-Z)
?2	(CTRL/W)	Match any lowercase letter (a-z)
?+	(CTRL/P)	Match any decimal digit (0-9)
?>	(CTRL/])	Match beginning or end of line
?7c	(CTRL/^)	Match internal representation of c
Substitute-string constructs:		
?"	(CTRL/B)	Substitute next string matched
?*n?*	(CTRL/O)	Substitute nth string matched

Figure 12. *SOS Regular Expression Meta-notation [DIGI78].*

CTRL-C brings one to *edit mode*, and typing CTRL-Y brings one to *DCL*, the operating system command interpreter. In *decide alter mode*, these command bindings change. While CTRL-C and CTRL-Y remain the same, now carriage return or linefeed bring the user to *decide mode*, and both I and R bring the user to *decide alter/insert mode*. In decide mode CTRL-C and CTRL-Y still perform the same, but E, Q, and G also bring the user to *edit mode*. This time A, as opposed to ESC, will bring the user to *decide alter mode*. The remaining transitions, as shown in Figure 11, are no less inconsistent and confusing.

Not only are the mode transitions difficult, but the actual command mnemonics for similar commands differ substantially from mode to mode. For example, in *edit mode*, the f (find) command allows the user to search for and move the editing buffer to the first line that contains a specified pattern; the s (substitute) command allows the user to replace an occurrence of an old pattern with a newly specified pattern. In *alter mode* the s now stands for skip and allows the user to find the next occurrence of a specified character; c (change) allows the user to change the next *n* characters in the line; f no longer exists.

SOS has some interesting concepts: powerful scope specification as a suffix to commands; a regular-expression pattern-searching facility as shown in Figure 12; a query-replace user-dialogue set up by *decide mode*; user-selectable toggles to indicate the level of experience of the user and to control the verbosity of prompts, and more. Yet the sheer complexity of the user interface often makes the system undesirable for even the most dedicated of users. We feel that SOS is a classic example of a powerful nucleus crippled by a poor user interface.

UNIX ed

The UNIX text editor, *ed* [KERN78a, KERN78b], is a variable-length line editor similar to both the CMS editor and SOS. *Ed*'s commands, like those in SOS, are only one or two characters long. It has a single-line viewing buffer but, like SOS, *ed* allows the user to expand the editing buffer for a command by specifying a range of line numbers in the form starting,ending as an optional prefix to each command. Thus, to perform the above change from ADD to SUBTRACT on the first 50 lines of a file, we use the *ed* **substitute** command:

    1,50s/add/subtract/

The special **metacharacter** "$" indicates the last line of the file. Thus prepending a "1,$" to a command causes the buffer for that command to be the entire file. To move a number of lines, we simply say

    1,10m/insert after this/

This will move lines 1 through 10 to follow the first line in the document that contains the string "insert after this". Lines in *ed* are variable-length so that truncation problems are solved.

A powerful feature of *ed* is its facility for user-specified regular expressions in patterns defining the scopes of operations (as opposed to other editors which use regular expressions simply for **search** commands). (This feature has been available since NLS, but has become more common in other editors since its implementation in *ed* and SOS.) The user is supplied with the metacharacters

    * $ ^ .   [ ] \

with which to form regular expressions specifying the content of the pattern. The "*" is a repetition character. Thus, a character "n" followed by a "*" tells the editor to match the first character string containing an "n" followed by zero or more occurrences of "n". The "$" metacharacter in this use matches the end of the line while the "^" caret companion matches the beginning of the line. A "." matches any character. The "\" escape character allows one of the metacharacters to be used as an actual character. Finally, the "[ ]" pair allows the user to specify a range of characters to be matched: [a-j] would match the first string (a single character) containing one of the letters lower-case "a" through lower-case " j"; [nkm] would match the first string with either an n or a k or an m. If the user wanted to find the first line beginning with a capital letter followed by a vowel in the text of the Ogden Nash poem

    I think that I shall never see
    A billboard lovely as a tree
    Perhaps unless the billboards fall,
    I'll never see a tree at all.

the user would specify the search (using / as the find command)

    /^[A-Z][aeiou]/

The ^ requires the pattern to be matched to start at the beginning of the line; the [A-Z] requires the first character of the pattern to be matched to be a capital letter; the [aeiou] requires the next character of the pattern to be matched to be a lowercase vowel. Upon executing this command from the top of the file, *ed* would find (and move the current pointer to)

    Perhaps unless the billboards fall,

One interesting feature in *ed* is the ability to reference the scope of an operation indirectly in another operand of that operation. For instance, to parenthesize the entire line above, one would type

s/.*/(&)/

The ".*" is metanotation that means "match all characters on the current line." The "**&**" is metanotation that is shorthand for "all that were matched."

As in the CMS editor, lines in *ed* have varying internal numbers. Thus traveling is done as in the CMS editor, with both absolute or relative specifications (as well as context pattern specification). A timesaving feature is the use of a simple carriage return in edit mode (with nothing else on that line) as an implicit **next** 1 command. The user is given an explicit symbol called the **dot** to reference the current line pointer that can be used in arithmetic expressions to change the scope of an operation. For example,

.-10,.+7p

tells *ed* to print the 10 lines before the current position, the line at the current position, and the 7 lines after the current position. *ed* also allows the user to mark a specific line with a single lowercase character for later reference. The user simply types the **save position** command (abbreviated **k**) followed by a single character label, as in

kx

and the current line is now referenced with "**x**." To travel to that line, the user simply types " ' ", the **goto saved-position** command, followed by the label:

'x

and immediately is returned to that saved position. Like the CMS editor, *ed* has two main modes, edit mode and append mode, and the associated problems of two modes. In fact, these problems are compounded by the fact that *ed* is, as characterized by Norman [NORM81], "shy":

> Ed's major property is his shyness; he doesn't like to talk. You invoke Ed by saying, reasonably enough, "ed." The result is silence: no response, no prompt, no message, just silence. Novices are never sure what that silence means. Ed would be a bit more likeable if he answered "thank you, here I am," or at least produced a prompt character, but in UNIX, silence is golden. No response means that everything is okay; if something had gone wrong, it would have told you.

In the edit/append mode dichotomy, this silence causes major confusion. To add text to the file, the user issues the "a" command to **append**, followed by a carriage return. Unlike the CMS editor, *ed* gives no indication that it is now in append mode; it just waits for the user to input text, like the CMS editor. To return to edit mode, the user types a line with only a "." on it and follows it with a carriage return. As Norman points out, this is not an oversight, but in fact is acknowledged, rather flippantly, in the documentation [KERN78a]:

> Even experienced users forget that terminating "." sometimes. If ed seems to be ignoring you, type an extra line with just "." on it. You may then find you've added some garbage lines to your text, which you'll have to take out later.

One of the designers of UNIX system software defends the terseness of UNIX commands by citing their contribution to an important capability of UNIX: the ability to easily use the output of one program as the input to another [LESK81]. But silencing a user-oriented interactive program so that its output may be used by another program seems to us a large price to pay. In fact, UNIX easily allows the user to select just which output should be passed on to another program as standard input; careful programming can ensure that user prompts and status information can be interspersed with standard output without interfering with it.

While *ed* is a powerful line editor, it is questionable whether the interface, which requires the user to memorize small, non-mnemonic, and often obscure command names and, more critically, to "guess" the status of the system, is proper for a general-purpose audience. In fact, this editor was developed not for a large community, but for a group of a half-dozen computer science researchers familiar with the notions of regular expressions and file organization who were designing the operating system and file system in which the editor would run; they wanted maximum keystroke efficiency and minimum distraction. While the *ed* line editor has illuminated several important concepts in editing, it nevertheless represents a decreasingly popular breed of editors.

4.2 Stream Editors

Stream editors act upon a document as a single, continuous chain of characters, as if the entire document were a single, indefinitely long character string, rather than as fixed-length or variable-length lines. By doing so, they avoid line editor problems such as truncation and inability to perform interline searching or editing. TECO, described below, is the most popular editor of this category.

TECO

TECO, the Text Editor and COrrector, (c. 1970) is an interpreter for a string processing language. TECO can be used interactively as a stream-oriented editor; its basic commands can also be used as building blocks to provide quite elaborate editing operations. Many variations exist (DEC TECO and TENEX TECO are two), with varying capabilities and syntax. The conceptual model considers a document to be a sequence of characters, possibly broken into variable-length virtual pages by form-feed characters, and into virtual lines by line-end characters. Pages may be combined in an in-core editing buffer considered to be simply a varying-length string whose length may grow up to the in-core memory available.

The interface is based on typed input, typically consisting of single-character command syntax of the form:

[argument][single character command]

Commands can be combined to form sequences. Regardless of whether the user specifies a single command or combined command, TECO does not interpret the command string until the user presses the ESC key. In the ensuing examples, the terminating ESC is implied. The editing buffer is the amount of the file in memory. The viewing buffer on the document defaults to the null viewing buffer. The document is displayed only upon explicit command; the user can specify a viewing buffer of any size as explained below.

TECO maintains the current position as a value called **point** (symbolized by ".," which simply contains the number of characters in the buffer to the left of it. This pointer can be positioned absolutely (by a numeric value), relatively (by a positive or negative character or line displacement), or by pattern searches. For example, in TENEX TECO [BBN73], 0J or BJ jumps the pointer to the top of the buffer, ZJ jumps the pointer to the end of the buffer, 43J jumps to the 43rd character of the buffer, .-9 or -9C moves the pointer backwards nine characters, and 17;BJ jumps to the top of page 17. The symbols Z, B and . are not simply command modifiers but are registers that contain the point for the end of the buffer, the point for the beginning of the buffer, and the current point respectively; thus, the above commands using these registers resolve to an absolute character address.

Though TECO is character-oriented, special commands allow the user to edit a document in terms of a line model. Again, using appropriate register values, L moves the pointer to the beginning of the next line, -L moves the pointer to the beginning of the previous line, 0L moves the pointer to the beginning of the current line. Similarly, :L moves to the end of the current line while -:L moves to the end of the previous line. Line-oriented printing commands are provided as well; 7T prints the characters from the pointer until the beginning of the seventh line after the pointer, T prints the segment of the current line after the pointer. We stress that lines are an abstraction provided to the user; the text is stored not as lines, but simply as sequences of characters that are interpreted as lines by a filter that understands special line-end delimiters. A more complicated filter, for instance, might be able to extract programming language constructs from the stream.

Fundamental commands such as insert, delete and context search are supplied. INow is the time(CTRL-D) inserts the string "Now is the time" before the current pointer. 5D deletes the five characters after the pointer. Sgood(CTRL-D) finds the first match for "good" after the current pointer and moves the pointer there; similarly, Rgood(CTRL-D)bad(CTRL-D) replaces the first occurrence of "good" with "bad."

Importantly, TECO also supports commands for conditional execution to aid in creating more complex commands. Q-registers are available for holding any numeric or string value. Simple uses include performing arithmetic and moving or copying strings. To move a string of text, for example, the string is first saved in a Q-register and then deleted from the buffer (in some versions, the deletion is automatic). Next, the character pointer is moved to a new location and the contents of the Q-register are copied into the buffer at this new point.

If a Q-register contains text, the text may be interpreted as a command string. Thus, TECO can be used as a programming language to build editing commands. Higher-level commands are created by joining together many lower-level operations. Consider the pseudo-code for a global change operation with query and replace prompting:

```
WHILE (pattern is found in source)
    IF user response = "Y" THEN
        substitute newstring for pattern
END
```

With this pseudo-code in mind, to query and replace "good" with "bad," one could write the TECO code:

```
J<Sgood(CTRL-D); V↑T-↑↑Y"E-4CRgood(CTRL-D)bad(CTRL-D)'>
```

J puts the pointer at the beginning of the buffer. The < > pair are loop delimiters, indicating that the commands inside the loop should be executed repeatedly. Sgood(CTRL-D) is the search command we have seen previously. Upon failure of the search, ; V skips to the end of the loop construct. The ↑T is a "variable" that is assigned the value of a character typed by the user, while the ↑↑Y is the value of a capital Y. The subtraction expression, ↑T-↑↑Y, equals zero only when a Y is typed in. Thus, if the preceding expression is equal to zero, then the commands following the "E are run; otherwise everything until a delimiting ' is skipped. The -4C moves the pointer to just before the beginning of good. Finally, the Rgood(CTRL-D)bad(CTRL-D) performs the appropriate replacement. The loop then repeats until failure.

The raw power of TECO is evident from the above example. The abstraction of text (a continuous stream of text with a pointer) is simple, especially for the programmer, as it parallels the abstraction of computer memory with associated program counter. Continuing this analogy,

TECO is to a text stream what assembly language is to sequential computer memory. The TECO language provides a powerful base for a trained systems programmer or for a compiler's code generator; however, it does not provide a reasonable high-level interface for the average user, just as assembly language does not provide a reasonable interface for the casual (and even proficient) programmer. The syntax is cryptic. While all commands operate at the point, user misconceptions of the exact point location often results in off-by-one errors. TECO has been used effectively as an implementation language in several editors, most notably in EMACS described below. However, we believe that it is not a proper tool for either knowledge workers or competent programmers because of its low-level orientation.

4.3 Display Editors

This category includes several editors based on work done by Deutsch [DEUT67] and on the work of Irons and Djorup [IRON72], as well as several editors with an Irons-like model. The simple Irons outline for a CRT editing system has been the backbone of many editors: NED [BILO77, KELL77], bb [REIS81], PEN [BARA81], Z [WOOD81] and sds [FRAS81]. We present a general overview of the standard functions available in this kind of editor and then describe in more detail the unique features of several specific instances.[12]

In the Irons conceptual model, text is conceived of as a quarter-plane extending indefinitely in width and length, with the topmost, leftmost character the origin of the file. The user travels through this plane by using cursor keys and changes characters by overtyping. At any time, the user sees an accurate portrayal of the portion of the file displayed. Text is input on the screen at the position of the cursor. The environment is "modeless"; since all typing on the screen is considered text, commands must be entered either through function keys, control characters, and escape sequences, or by moving the cursor to and typing in a special command line at the bottom of the screen.

The command syntax is typically single-operand postfix. Basic traveling and editing primitives are provided, such as +/- pages, +/- lines, +/- words, insert character, delete word, and back word. Some of these may be preceded by an optional modifier. Thus, + page scrolls forward to the next page, while 3 + page scrolls three pages. Additionally, the editing and viewing buffers can be moved left and right and multiple windows support easy interfile editing. These editors make use of pick and delete buffers; hence deleted text is not discarded but is put in a buffer for possible subsequent use for moving or copying text. Functions such as delete, pick, and put may be combined with element modifiers such as character, word, line, and paragraph to allow more familiar specification of deletes, copies, and moves. A marking facility allows the user to select with the cursor two arbitrary points in the text to define a scope not easily specified with the element modifiers.

For display, most of the Irons derivatives use special algorithms to minimize the amount of screen updating necessary.

Brown's bb

Brown's bb [REIS81] is a typical example of the Irons model editor. Running under the UNIX operating system on a VAX 11/780, it makes use of a wide range of function keys for interaction.

One of bb's extensions of the model is the maintenance of an up-to-date temporary file on disk along with a linked list of changes that have been made to the old file. This change history

---

[12]In this general overview, the syntax used does not reflect that of any given system, nor does an example of a general operation imply that each system contains that operation.

serves as the backbone of the undo command, which is capable of reverting changes back to the beginning of the editing session.

For travel, as well as providing the standard +/- keys, *bb* allows the user to save positions in named buffers and to jump to these positions with a **goto** command.

bb provides user-manipulation of the instructions with the **do** facility. Rather than providing a macro language, **do** provides a mechanism for capturing and naming a group of keystrokes. In general, a **programming-by-example** facility is an extremely elegant, powerful tool for both the novice and the experienced user. The user does not have to think in terms of a macro language syntax (with associated variables, flow-of-control constructs, and textual verbosity), but defines the new operations in terms of the same syntax that is used for editing. Complex operations that are hard to specify in a a procedural macro are almost trivial in terms of keystroke macros where the user simply executes the commands while the system captures them. For example, to find all instances of a *troff/me* italic formatting command, a separate line of the form:

```
.i "this will be italicized"
```

and change them to the TEX form:

```
{\sl this will be italicized}
```

one could use the following keystroke macro (all capitalized words are commands implemented as function keys or control sequences):

TOF	[goes to top of file]
DOBEG	[begins capturing keystrokes]
ENTER ^.i +REG-EXPR-SEARCH	[search forward for an occurrence of ".i" which starts on a newline]
{\sl	[type over existing ".i "»]
INSERT-SPACE	[inserts needed space]
+EOL	[goes to end of line, 1 char past the quote]
BACKSPACE	[put cursor at end quote]
}	[types right bracket over quote]
DOEND	[finishes capturing keystrokes]

Now every time the user presses the DO key, *bb* will perform all the keystrokes entered between the DOBEG and DOEND keys. *bb* does not support parameterized keystroke macros or macros that prompt for particular input and subsequently continue executing; hence, one could not design a general-purpose keystroke macro similar to the special-purpose one above.

bb examines the file extension (file type) of the current file and loads an internal table with target-dependent information. This allows *bb* to perform automatic indenting for various programming languages and to recognize structural entities such as paragraphs in documents. Like many of the editors in this category, *bb* supports multiple viewing buffers and windows, though it only maintains a single editing buffer.

bb allows users to bind their own personal keyboards to the standard commands by modifying a control file. *bb* also supports an invocation-time profile, allowing personalized defaults on startup. This is coupled with a state-save facility that maintains necessary parameters from session to session. A **help** facility allows easy access to a complete online manual. Screen manipulation is performed by looking up terminal capabilities in the UNIX *termcap* database [JOY81] to determine output device characteristics, and by using specialized screen-optimization algorithms.

Yale's Z Editor

Yale's Z editor [WOOD81] extends the general Irons functionality by providing facilities that aid in program creation while maintaining the general-purpose functionality of the editor.

Editor commands are entered using control characters coupled with cursor keys. Function keys are not used; the developers dislike the fact that the user's hand must be moved from the typewriter keyboard to use them. Software allows overloading of the standard ASCII character set by using certain keys as shift keys. The interaction language also supports the overloading of each editor command. Here, as in most of the Irons derivatives, one command may be made to do slightly different things by prefacing it with optional arguments. For example,

  arg *string* fSearch

searches forward for the next instance of the pattern *string* and moves the cursor there if successful. Each command may be prefixed with the special command **meta**, slightly altering the function of the command to which it is attached. For instance, **meta fSearch** causes case-insensitive searching.

For travel, Z remembers the last seven buffer positions, allowing the user to review previous contexts while the current one retains the status quo. Like *bb*, Z allows the user to put a "bookmark" on a certain spot in the file for later return.

The unique features of Z are its solutions to the program-editing task. Rather than using the structure-oriented approach, in which the editor has specific knowledge of the syntax (and possibly the semantics) of a target programming language, the Z editor represents programs as text, offering visual cues and a tight interface with existing compilers and debuggers to take the place of the innate knowledge of syntax-directed editors.

The designers of Z contend that "existing structure-oriented program editors have several disadvantages, such as increased complexity in the implementation, a restrictive user interface, and poor support for editing." Their solution is to represent the program as a text while equipping the editor with knowledge of program elements such as quoted strings, end-of-line delimiters, and matching tokens (such as **begin/end**) that signal indentation, as well as with indentation rules.

This representation allows Z to perform many functions normally associated with structure editors. Prettyprinting for block-structured languages is done by examining the last token on a line when the newline key is pressed. If that token is in a table that lists it as a token requiring subsequent indentation or exdentation relative to the previous line, the next line will be appropriately indented or exdented. This algorithm gives the desired result most of the time; a manual mode is offered to correct any mistakes made by the automatic mode. The matching token table also drives commands that close off the most-recently-begun matching unit, that find the end of the nearest unit if already closed, and that skip over the matching expressions as single units. This is particularly useful in LISP programming, where levels of parenthesization are hard to manipulate. Again, this facility does not require the editor to have syntactic knowledge of the target language, but simply to maintain a table of matching tokens.

Syntax-directed structure editors allow the user to manipulate syntactic units as single entities, as well as to view levels of syntactic detail. Z provides analogous features based on indentation level, which the designers claim work because "all the important information about the block structure of a program is contained in the indentation, provided the programmer is consistent."

The designers of Z chose to do neither the syntactic checking nor the incremental compilation often associated with syntax-directed editors, as the philosophy is *not* to integrate the compiler directly into the editor. Feeling that "the programmer is the person best able to decide when his program is in a state ready for compilation" and that "existing compilers are perfectly able to locate errors" [WOOD81], the designers of Z attempted to enhance communications between editor and compiler. The user can execute the compile command from the editor; this communicates with an asynchronous process that formats the compiler request per the target language, puts the request on the processor queue, appends error messages in a special file, and returns a completion message to the editor when done. The user can continue editing while this is being done.

Z also provides a link to Multiple User Forks, a program that maintains multiple user contexts in parallel. This allows the user to exit from Z into any of the other forks (perhaps to read documentation or check on the state of some running program) and to return to Z without loss of state.

EMACS

MIT's EMACS [STAL80, STAL81] is an "extensible, customizable, and self-documenting" display editor. Several versions and dialects exist, most notably the Stallman version for the Tops-20 operating system (from which our examples are derived), the Honeywell Multics version [GREE80], and the UNIX version by James Gosling of Carnegie-Mellon. Some versions of this full-screen editor for timesharing systems are written in TECO, others in the high-level language LISP. To extend or customize the functionality, users write routines in the same language as that in which the standard editor functions are written, rather than using an editor macro language. Richard Stallman, the designer of the first EMACS, feels that this capability allows the user to transcend any limitations imposed by the editor's implementors. The basis of the successful EMACS strategy is that defining the extensions or changes in the source language "is the only method of extension which is practical to use"; it is unwise to maintain a "real" implementation language for the implementors and a "toy" one for the users. The user is able to bind many extensions or changes in a library, which can be loaded at invocation time. In fact, many of the core facilities that exist today were originally user-written extensions and were later adopted into the production system, thereby encouraging arbitrary growth rather than design. EMACS does offer a keystroke macro facility with prompts, so that non-programming users do have an alternative to a programming language at their disposal.

In EMACS, every typed character is considered a command. The keys for printing characters are bound, by default, to a command called self insert that causes that character to be inserted into the text at the cursor location. Generally, non-printing characters (control and escape sequences) invoke commands to modify the document. The editing language accepts single-character commands and finds the current binding between command key and function in a table. EMACS and other display editors offer a quote facility that allows characters typically used as commands to be inserted as characters into a document. A few of its many interesting features include a query replace facility, transposition functions for lines and words, and an automatic balanced parenthesis viewer.

The windowing facilities are extensive as well. The system supports multiple open files and hence multiple editing buffers[13] with associated viewing buffers and windows. The CTRL-X 2 command divides the screen into two windows containing the viewing buffers designated by the user. The cursor is in one window at a time; CTRL-X O switches between windows. Special "narrowing" commands serve to change the size of the viewing buffer and editing buffer while

---

[13]Note that our use of the term "editing buffer" here, while consistent with our previous usage, differs slightly from Stallman's terminology in describing EMACS [STAL80, STAL81].

leaving the window intact. The user marks one end of a region, moves the cursor to the other end and issues the command CTRL-X N. This range now defines the maximum range of the editing buffer. If it is larger than a window's worth of text, the viewing buffer is set to a full window's size; otherwise it is set to the size of the editing buffer.

The fact that all keys (including alphanumerics) are bound to actions is very important, as the self insert action can be extended to effect more complex results. For example, one can extend the definition of the space character to insert itself and to check to see if an automatic wordwrap is necessary. A more detailed use of the key redefinition facility is the EMACS abbreviation package. Here, all the punctuation characters are redefined to look at the previous word, to check for its existence in an abbreviation table, and if it exists, to substitute the expanded word for the abbreviation as the user types.

EMACS offers *major modes*, editing environments tailored for editing a particular kind of file. For example, *text mode* treats the hyphen as a word separator; LISP mode distinguishes between lists and s-expressions. The major mode can automatically define different key bindings for a particular application. For example, in many programming language major modes, the tab key is redefined to provide automatic indentation.

EMACS can keep a record of all keystrokes typed in a session in a **journal file**. If a system crash destroys a current editing session, the user can instruct EMACS to bring up an old version of the file and replay the keystrokes from the journal file. The user watches the changes being made, and can stop the process at any time. (This allows a primitive undo facility: the user can replay up to a desired point and then discard the rest of the changes that are no longer wanted.)

Another interesting facility for program editing is the TAGS package. The separate program TAGS builds a TAGS table containing the filename and position in that file in which each application program function is defined. This table is loaded into EMACS; specifying the command Meta . *function-name* causes EMACS to select the appropriate file and go to the proper function definition within that file. Other special libraries incude DIRED, a subsystem for editing a file system directory using the full-screen display capabilities, and BABYL, a complete message-handling subsystem. INFO reads tree-structured documentation files, performing the necessary operations to travel from one node to the next.

EMACS has a very large and faithful following in the academic research community. While the basic editor is not vastly different in functionality from Irons model editors, the customized, application-specific packages have "sold" the system. To obtain a distribution of EMACS, one must agree to redistribute all extensions that one develops. By now, these extensions are quite numerous and powerful. Thus, it is not the raw editor, but the editor and its extensions that far exceed the capabilities of most other editors. While the programming language certainly cannot be used competently by the average user, the availability of extensibility features for programmers has manifested itself in many powerful facilities.

Extensibility, however, has negative points. Though the major new packages are distributed to all EMACS installations, many customizations are personal ones. This leads to situations in which two people using EMACS have different syntax and functionality. One set of keyboard bindings might be different from the next (e.g., one CTRL-D moves down 1 line while another deletes a line) or, alternatively, an identical keyboard arrangement and apparently identical functionality may have fine distinctions that confuse a user from a different microcosm trying to use someone else's EMACS (e.g., one GOTO END-OF-WORD command might go to the last character in a word, preceding punctuation, while another may go to the first white space following the word). Thus, with extensibility in any editor comes the price of widespread divergence over various installations and even over the same installation. The tradeoff between a large number of divergent but customized dialects and a single, standard language is unclear.

IBM's XEDIT

XEDIT [IBM80] is IBM's screen editor for their VM/CMS timesharing system. Unlike the Irons model editors just described, XEDIT uses local terminal intelligence to perform screen editing operations. The high-level conceptual model is the unbounded quarter-plane of text in which the user views a rectangular region, yet XEDIT still relies on the sequential card model in some of its operations.

The display editing functions of XEDIT only work on IBM 3270 or 3270-compatible terminals. These terminals have a local screen buffer memory and a special keyboard with keys that support editing on the local buffer, such as **add char, delete char,** and **delete to end of line.**

The user has several methods of command specification. The first is changing the screen image by driving a cursor and using the local editing capabilities. The user is able to edit both the displayed text and a status line that displays file name, record length, and several other options. The user changes the text and the status line by simply inserting, deleting, or changing the options field of each line. Pressing the ENTER key causes the contents of the editing buffer to be sent to the host computer, which determines the difference between the terminal's local editing buffer and the host's internal data structure, and updates its internal data accordingly. This synchronization between the screen buffer and the internal data structure is an important component of an editor using a terminal with local intelligence. Note that throughout this editing process, the host processor is not signalled of any changes, regardless of how long the user has been editing a screenful of text, until the user presses the ENTER key to transmit that screen.

Besides the display-editor-style commands, XEDIT accepts typed commands that are almost identical to those of the CMS line editor; in fact on non-3270 series terminals, XEDIT operates essentially like the CMS line editor. These commands, typed in on a special command line, control those operations that cannot be done using the local editing buffer, including control functions, such as reorganizing viewing buffer-window mappings and ending a session, search commands, and some types of insert, move, and copy commands. Any of these commands can be bound to the 10 function keys on the keyboard. XEDIT cannot support selection by marking with a cursor because the current position of the cursor cannot be read by the CPU. While it does allow textual specification of region commands, it also provides the user with a *prefix* field before each line on the screen (see Figure 13), to give additional functionality.

As we see in Figure 13a, the D on the line beginning "THE HIPPOPOTAMUS" marks this line for subsequent deletion. The **2a** is an instruction to add two blank lines after this line. The DD is a grouping marker that delimits the beginning and end of a region of text to be deleted (the two DDs need not be on the same screen of text). The single A again stands for adding a blank line. When the user presses ENTER, the screen buffer is transmitted, and the host computer interprets the prefix fields (as well as any local editing), updates the internal data structure appropriately, and redisplays the updated text, as shown in Figure 13b.

Figure 14 shows a similar move command using the prefix fields. The **mm** is a grouping marker, much like the DD above, to delimit the beginning and end of a multi-line region of text to be moved, and the **f** is a marker signaling the line after which the moved text should be inserted.

XEDIT's local editing style offers both advantages and disadvantages. The use of the local

```
ANIMALS  FACTS    A1  F 80  TRUNC=80 SIZE=14 LINE=9 COLUMN=1

===== * * * TOP OF FILE * * *
D==== THE HIPPOPOTAMUS IS DISTANTLY RELATED TO THE PIG.
===== ELEPHANT TUSKS CAN WEIGH MORE THAN 300 POUNDS.
===== LAND CRABS FOUND IN CUBA CAN RUN FASTER THAN A DEER.
===== ELECTRIC EELS CAN DISCHARGE BURSTS OF 625 VOLTS,
=2a== 40 TIMES A SECOND.
===== THE ANCIENT ROMANS AND GREEKS BELIEVED THAT BEDBUGS HAD MEDICINAL
===== PROPERTIES WHEN TAKEN IN A DRAFT OF WATER OR WINE.
==DD= STURGEON IS THE LARGEST FRESHWATER FISH AND CAN WEIGH 2250 POUNDS.
===== ANTS HAVE FIVE DIFFERENT NOSES.  EACH ONE IS DESIGNED TO
      |...+....1....+....2....+....3....+....4....+....5....+....6....+....7...
=DD== ACCOMPLISH A DIFFERENT TASK.
==A== ALL OSTRICHES ARE POLYGAMOUS.
===== SNAKES LAY EGGS WITH NONBRITTLE SHELLS.
===== THE PLATYPUS HAS A DUCK BILL, OTTER FUR, WEBBED FEET, LAYS
===== EGGS, AND EATS ITS OWN WEIGHT IN WORMS EVERY DAY.
===== * * * END OF FILE * * *



===>                                                    X E D I T  1 FILE
```

```
ANIMALS  FACTS    A1  F 80  TRUNC=80 SIZE=13 LINE=9 COLUMN=1

===== * * * TOP OF FILE * * *
===== ELEPHANT TUSKS CAN WEIGH MORE THAN 300 POUNDS.
===== LAND CRABS FOUND IN CUBA CAN RUN FASTER THAN A DEER.
===== ELECTRIC EELS CAN DISCHARGE BURSTS OF 625 VOLTS,
===== 40 TIMES A SECOND.
=====
=====
===== THE ANCIENT ROMANS AND GREEKS BELIEVED THAT BEDBUGS HAD MEDICINAL
===== PROPERTIES WHEN TAKEN IN A DRAFT OF WATER OR WINE.
===== ALL OSTRICHES ARE POLYGAMOUS.
      |...+....1....+....2....+....3....+....4....+....5....+....6....+....7...
=====
===== SNAKES LAY EGGS WITH NONBRITTLE SHELLS.
===== THE PLATYPUS HAS A DUCK BILL, OTTER FUR, WEBBED FEET, LAYS
===== EGGS, AND EATS ITS OWN WEIGHT IN WORMS EVERY DAY.
===== * * * END OF FILE * * *



===>                                                    X E D I T  1 FILE
```

Figure 13. *Add and Delete with XEDIT prefix commands [IBM80].*

```
ANIMALS  FACTS     A1   V 132   TRUNC=132 SIZE=22 LINE=10 COLUMN=1

===== CHAMELEONS, REPTILES THAT LIVE IN TREES, CHANGE THEIR COLOR WHEN
===== EMOTIONALLY AROUSED.
===== THE GUPPY IS NAMED AFTER THE REVEREND ROBERT GUPPY, WHO FOUND THE FISH
===== ON TRINIDAD IN 1866.
===== AN AFRICAN ANTELOPE CALLED THE SITATUNGA HAS THE RARE ABILITY TO
===== SLEEP UNDER WATER.
==mm= THE KILLER WHALE EATS DOLPHINS, PORPOISES, SEALS, PENGUINS, AND
===== SQUID.
===== ALTHOUGH PORCUPINE FISHES BLOW THEMSELVES UP AND ERECT THEIR SPINES,
===== THEY ARE SOMETIMES EATEN BY SHARKS.   NO ONE KNOWS WHAT EFFECT THIS
      |...+....1....+....2....+....3....+....4....+....5....+....6....+....7...
===mm HAS ON THE SHARKS.
===== A LIZARD OF CENTRAL AMERICA CALLED THE BASILISK CAN RUN
===== ACROSS WATER.
===== OCTOPI HAVE LARGE BRAINS AND SHOW CONSIDERABLE CAPACITY FOR
===== LEARNING.
f==== THE LION ROARS TO ANNOUNCE POSSESSION OF A PROPERTY.
===== A FISH CALLED THE NORTHERN SEA ROBIN MAKES NOISES LIKE A WET
===== FINGER DRAWN ACROSS AN INFLATED BALLOON.
===== STINGAREES, FISH FOUND IN AUSTRALIA, CAN WEIGH UP TO 800 POUNDS.
===>
                                                        X E D I T   1 FILE
```

```
ANIMALS  FACTS     A1   V 132   TRUNC=132 SIZE=22 LINE=7 COLUMN=1


===== * * * TOP OF FILE * * *
===== CHAMELEONS, REPTILES THAT LIVE IN TREES, CHANGE THEIR COLOR WHEN
===== EMOTIONALLY AROUSED.
===== THE GUPPY IS NAMED AFTER THE REVEREND ROBERT GUPPY, WHO FOUND THE FISH
===== ON TRINIDAD IN 1866.
===== AN AFRICAN ANTELOPE CALLED THE SITATUNGA HAS THE RARE ABILITY TO
===== SLEEP UNDER WATER.
===== A LIZARD OF CENTRAL AMERICA CALLED THE BASILISK CAN RUN
      |...+....1....+....2....+....3....+....4....+....5....+....6....+....7...
===== ACROSS WATER.
===== OCTOPI HAVE LARGE BRAINS AND SHOW CONSIDERABLE CAPACITY FOR
===== LEARNING.
===== THE LION ROARS TO ANNOUNCE POSSESSION OF A PROPERTY.
===== THE KILLER WHALE EATS DOLPHINS, PORPOISES, SEALS, PENGUINS, AND
===== SQUID.
===== ALTHOUGH PORCUPINE FISHES BLOW THEMSELVES UP AND ERECT THEIR SPINES,
===== THEY ARE SOMETIMES EATEN BY SHARKS.   NO ONE KNOWS WHAT EFFECT THIS
===== HAS ON THE SHARKS.
===>
                                                        X E D I T   1 FILE
```

Figure 14. Move with XEDIT prefix commands [IBM80].

3270-series editing capabilities implies that users need not worry about an overloaded host system most of the time; most of the intraline editing, and even some of the block moving, as above, can be done without intervention of the host CPU. The editor is dependent upon the host system only when a screenful of text must be transmitted or a textual command (like search) must be executed. On the other hand, the local buffer offers no safety; if the host system crashes while a user is screen editing, all modifications on the local buffer are lost. More specific to XEDIT, the inability to do region selection within lines (because marking without CPU intervention is impossible on the 3270), reduces the generality of the editor. Additionally, the several styles of commands (typed, cursor-driven, prefix field) can confuse a novice user.

4.4 Graphics-Based Interactive Editor/Formatters

Xerox PARC's Bravo

Xerox PARC's Bravo (c. 1975) is one of the first of the interactive editor/formatters based on the display of high-resolution, proportionally-spaced text. Bravo allows the creation and revision of a document containing soft-typeset text with justification performed instantly by the system. The conceptual model is of a continuous scroll of typeset text that can be paginated when desired.

Bravo runs on Xerox's Alto, a 16-bit minicomputer with a raster graphics "portrait" display (roughly 8-1/2-x-11 aspect ratio) of 606-x-808-pixel resolution. This high-resolution pixel-addressable display allows more complex visual cues (overlapping windows, typeset facsimile text, graphics) than does the normal CRT terminal. A mouse drives a cursor and offers three buttons (called left, middle and right) that can be read independent of the cursor.

Bravo offers a mix of graphical and keyboard user interfaces. By moving the mouse, the user drags the cursor across the screen. The cursor addresses characters, special "menu" items, and other selectable elements on the screen. The interaction language is modal: the user can be in either **command mode**, in which text elements can be selected and commands initiated, or **typing mode**, in which keyboard text is entered into the document. Because of the modes, the user can specify commands with single alphanumeric characters; unlike many display editors, alphanumeric characters are not entered into the document unless the user is in typing mode. Commands not invoked with single alphanumeric keys are invoked with control characters.

As shown in Figure 15, the Bravo screen is divided into several areas. The **system window** contains information concerning what the user has just done and what can presently be done. The **document window** contains a viewing-buffer's worth of the document text scroll. The **line bar** and **scroll bar** are graphical entities that help the user travel through the document.

To travel in Bravo, the mouse is used to move a double-headed arrow cursor along the scroll bar, a vertical strip at the left side of the document. Pressing the left button on the mouse while the arrow is pointing to a line in the document's window causes that line to become the top line in the window; pressing the right button causes the top line in the window to move to the line the cursor is at. For more extensive traveling, one is supplied with a graphical **thumbnail** that moves along the scroll bar, and a **bookmark** that indicates on a graphically-displayed linear continuum from "front cover" to "back cover" the proportional current position in the document. If the user is half-way through the document, for instance, the bookmark indicates a point half-way across the continuum. To travel to a part of the document preceding what is being viewed, the user simply places the thumbnail somewhere before the bookmark on the continuum and presses the middle button; the document will "fall open" at the corresponding position in the text. By placing the thumbnail after the bookmark on the continuum, the user can similarly travel through the remainder of the document.

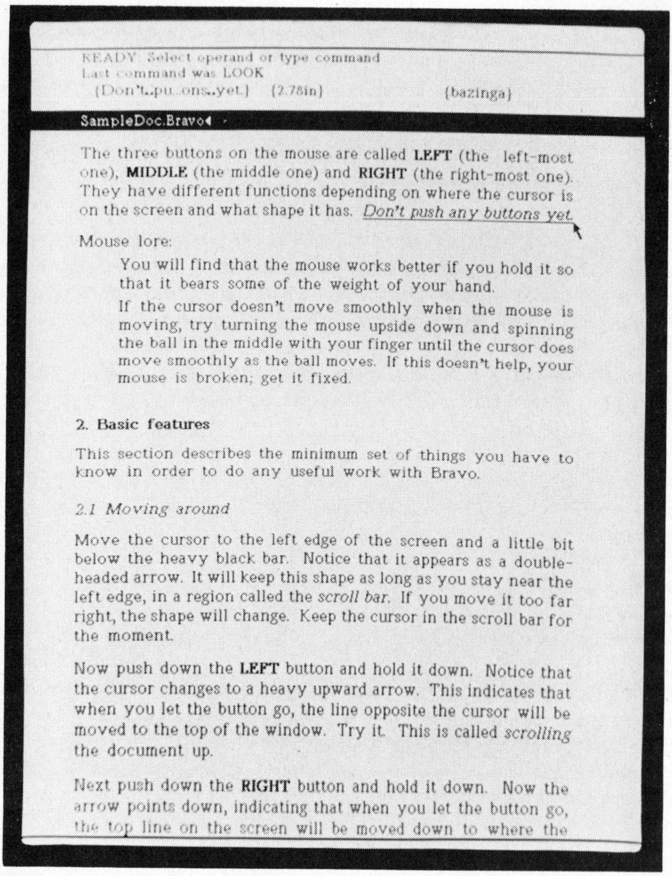

The three buttons on the mouse are called **LEFT** (the left-most one), **MIDDLE** (the middle one) and **RIGHT** (the right-most one). They have different functions depending on where the cursor is on the screen and what shape it has. *Don't push any buttons yet.*

Mouse lore:

You will find that the mouse works better if you hold it so that it bears some of the weight of your hand.

If the cursor doesn't move smoothly when the mouse is moving, try turning the mouse upside down and spinning the ball in the middle with your finger until the cursor does move smoothly as the ball moves. If this doesn't help, your mouse is broken; get it fixed.

2. Basic features

This section describes the minimum set of things you have to know in order to do any useful work with Bravo.

2.1 Moving around

Move the cursor to the left edge of the screen and a little bit below the heavy black bar. Notice that it appears as a double-headed arrow. It will keep this shape as long as you stay near the left edge, in a region called the *scroll bar*. If you move it too far right, the shape will change. Keep the cursor in the scroll bar for the moment.

Now push down the **LEFT** button and hold it down. Notice that the cursor changes to a heavy upward arrow. This indicates that when you let the button go, the line opposite the cursor will be moved to the top of the window. Try it. This is called *scrolling* the document up.

Next push down the **RIGHT** button and hold it down. Now the arrow points down, indicating that when you let the button go, the top line on the screen will be moved down to where the

Figure 15. *Bravo Display*

Bravo uses a postfix/infix interaction syntax: a selection is followed by the **command**, followed by an optional **argument**. For example, deletion works by selecting the scope and pressing the D key, while insertion works by selecting the scope, pressing the I key, typing the desired text, and finally pressing the ESC key. Unlike the Irons model editors, Bravo is modal: characters are only inserted into the document during special modes, and are interpreted as commands in others.

Selection operates on four main elements: characters, words, lines, and paragraphs. The left and middle buttons of the mouse are used to select items, while the right button is used to extend those selections. With the cursor in the text area, the left button would cause the addressed character to be selected as the scope, while the middle button would cause the addressed word to be selected. To select the large elements, the user moves the cursor into the line bar. In the line bar, the left button selects a line and the middle button selects a paragraph. Extending the selection allows the user to specify a scope that lies between two of the entities addressed. Thus, clicking left in the text area would cause a single character to be selected; clicking right at some other character would cause all the text between (and including) the two selected characters to be selected. Similarly, a middle right sequence would select all the text between and including two words. In the line bar, a left right sequence selects all the text between and including two lines; a middle right sequence selects all the text between and including two paragraphs.

Operations are typically performed on the current selection. To delete a word, the user simply selects a word by clicking the middle button and then types D to execute the delete command. Similarly, to delete all the text between and including two paragraphs, the user clicks middle right in the line bar and types D. Changes are done analogously. To replace a word, the user clicks middle and types R. Bravo deletes the selected word and puts the user into insert mode; everything the user types until the escape key is pressed is inserted in place of the old word. The Append and Insert commands allow the user to add text in a similar manner without first deleting a selection. Bravo supplies an undo facility that undoes only the last operation.

Files are never saved until the user explicitly saves them. However, Bravo keeps a transcript of the operations that have occurred in the editing session. One can run BravoBug with the transcript against the old version of the file to interactively replay the editing session. The user is given the choice of single-stepping through each change or running the entire transcript, stopping whenever desired.

At the time of its introduction, the most innovative features of Bravo were its interactive formatting facilities. Bravo's unit for specifying the formatting attributes of text is the **look**. Each character in the document has associated with it particular looks; the looks of any character can be displayed by selecting that character and typing L ?. The looks specify a large assortment of type attributes: font style, point size, subscripting, superscripting, centering, justification, nested indenting, and leading (interline spacing), to name a few, are attributes that the user can change by typing L followed by a one-character operand. Other look attributes cannot be changed directly by command but are constrained by previous formatting attributes. As soon as a look command is executed, the document is dynamically reformatted to effect the revision – the document is up-to-date in both format *and* content at all times. A special page-format mode allows the user to see the document paginated as it will be printed.

Bravo does not allow integrated graphics, but provides output that can be postprocessed to add figures from the PARC interactive picture-editing systems [BAUD78, NEWM78, BOWM81].

Xerox Star

Star [SEYJ81, XERO82, SMIT82], Xerox's commercial successor to the Bravo, is, in terms of its user interface, the most advanced commercial product for office automation on the market at the time of this writing.

Like the Alto, the 8010 workstation on which Star runs is a personal computer with access to shared resources such as file- and printer-servers via an Ethernet network. It has a "landscape"

13-1/2-x-10-1/2 inch screen with a resolution of 1024 x 809 pixels, capable of displaying both a full page of a document and a large menu area.

Several design goals are important to the understanding of Star's interface and functionality:

- The designers determined that users should simply point to specify the task they want to invoke, rather than remember commands and type key sequences. They believed that the user should not need to remember anything (of consequence) to use the system.
- An important consideration was the development of an orthogonal set of commands across all user domains: the copy command in the text formatter, for example, should have similar semantics to one in the statistical graphing package.
- The system was designed to operate by "progressive disclosure." Star strives to present the user with only those command choices that are reasonable at any given juncture.
- Finally, Star is an interactive editor/typesetter; the screen is, for the most part, a facsimile of what the final document will look like.

The Star development team, which considered possible models for several years, remarks [SMIT82]:

> The designer of a computer system can choose to pursue familiar analogies and metaphors or to introduce entirely new functions requiring new approaches. Each option has advantages and disadvantages. We decided to create electronic counterparts to the physical objects in an office: paper, folders, file cabinets, mail boxes, and so on – an electronic metaphor for the office. We hoped this would make the electronic "world" seem more familiar, less alien, and require less training. (Our initial experiences with users have confirmed this.) We further decided to make the electronic analogues be concrete objects. Documents would be more than file names on a disk; they would also be represented by pictures on the display screen.

The high-level conceptual model of the environment is that of a desktop in which multiple documents can be operated upon simultaneously. Star uses a two-button mouse and a postfix interaction syntax. Rather than presenting the user with a simple textual menu or a list of available options and files, Star presents the user with graphical icons that resemble the entity to which the user is referring (see Figure 16).

To open a file for editing, the user simply points to the iconic file drawer that symbolically holds the document (noun selection) and issues the **open** command (verb selection). Choosing **open** causes a file drawer directory, containing identifiers for file folders and individual documents, to fill part of the screen. The user can open, copy, move or delete any of these folders or documents; touching **copy**, for example, causes a new document icon to be placed on the user's "desktop" area on the screen. Selecting this icon and **opening** it causes the editor to open a window that is large enough to hold a facsimile of an 8-1/2-x-11 inch page (see Figure 17). Editing operations similar to those provided by Bravo can be performed in this window. The interface, however, does not use control characters. Mouse buttons and function keys provide the most frequently used commands; a menu of window-specific commands appears in the window banner at the top of the window for selecting with the cursor, and a menu of infrequently used system commands is always available by selecting a menu icon in the upper right corner of the screen.

Traveling buttons located on the bottom and right borders of each window, as shown in Figure 17, are selected with the mouse. The |— on the bottom makes sure that the left margin

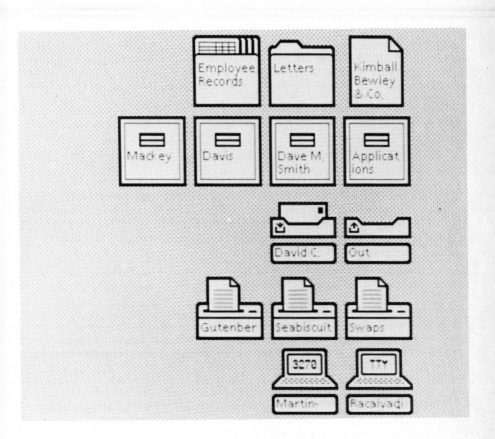

Figure 16. *Star Icons*

of the document is in view while the ⊣ makes sure the right half of the document is in view. The → scrolls the document to the right, the ← scrolls the document to the left, the ↓ scrolls the document downwards, and the ↑ scrolls the document upwards. P goes to the previous document page, while N goes to the next document page.

Other icons include a printer icon, a floppy disk icon, and an in/out box icon. To print a file one simply selects the appropriate document icon and places it on top of the printer icon. The programmable cursor changes to an hourglass to indicate that processing is taking place. Similarly, electronic mail is sent by placing a document on the **out box** and is received by selecting the **in box**.

As in Bravo, the mouse is used to drive the cursor and select elements. Selections are performed with the left mouse button and can be adjusted with the right mouse button. To select a character in the text, the user clicks the left button. Subsequently, when the right mouse button is held down, all the characters between the selected point and the current position of the cursor will be highlighted in reverse video; when the right button is released the highlighted area becomes the selection. Two left button clicks select the word containing the cursor; holding down the right mouse button extends the selection to include full words between the selection points and the cursor. Three left button clicks select the sentence containing the cursor; holding down the right mouse button extends this selection by sentences. Four left mouse button clicks select the paragraph containing the cursor; holding down the right mouse button extends the selection by paragraphs. A fifth left button click returns to the original character selection.

Most commands are postfix, requiring simply the selection of an icon or a region of text

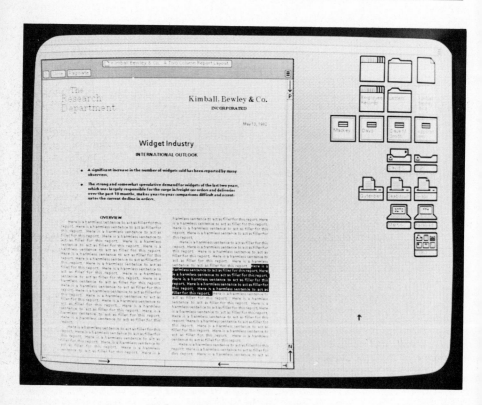

Figure 17. *Star Document in Window*

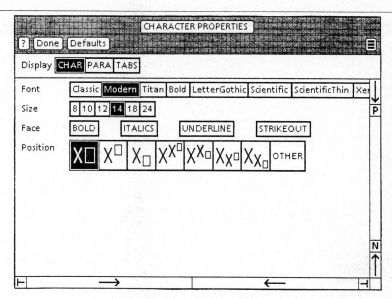

Figure 19. *Character Property Sheets*

followed by the issuance of a command using a function key or menu selection. Commands such as find, move and copy that need multiple operands are specified in infix or prefix, as appropriate. To perform a find, the user presses the find function key and is given a find property sheet to fill out, as shown in Figure 18a. The user fills in the Search for box by typing a search pattern and specifies other attributes of the search by selecting various options on the property sheet with the mouse. (Here TEXT, IGNORE CASE, and ENTIRE DOCUMENT are selected). The options that are selected remain selected from search to search until the user explicitly alters them. To perform the search, the user selects the Start button in the window menu. While Star is searching, it displays the message "Searching..." as feedback for the user. The ? and Cancel button provide help and abort the search, respectively.

The search and replace operation uses the same property sheet. Picking the CHANGE IT button on the find property sheet brings into view a second set of properties. The user can now type in the pattern to Change to and specify what should be altered and whether the replacement should be done with confirmation. When performing these operations, the message "Substituting..." provides needed feedback.

Like Bravo, Star performs instant formatting and justification in the proper type size and style. Associated with each element (element being any entity from a character to the entire document itself) are property sheets that contain status information for that element (see Figure 19). Initially, attributes in property sheets have system-assigned default values. To change the typeface of a particular character, the user selects the character, presses the props key, points to the desired typeface in the property sheet and closes it. The change takes effect immediately.

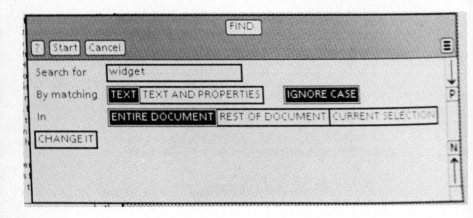

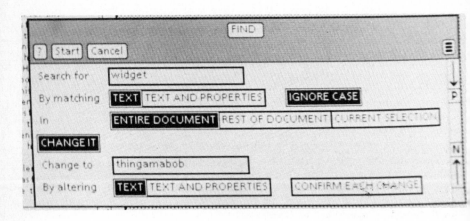

Figure 18. *Search, Search and Replace Operations*

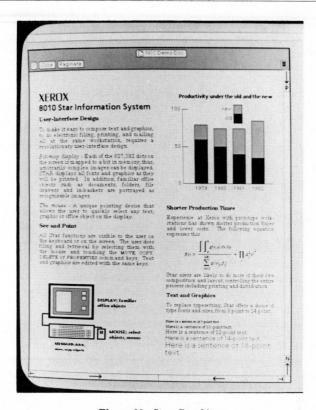

Figure 20. *Star Graphics*

(Note that the property sheet is presented in the same kind of window as a normal document. In fact, to see all the available typefaces in this example, the user would have to scroll the document to the left with one of the scroll symbols.) Star enables the user to define a standard collection of property sheets to provide document templates (style sheets), as in a database-driven formatter such as Scribe. The user simply copies the template and enters the new text, assured that the basic format is properly defined. The designers compare this to tearing off a standard form from a preprinted pad [SMIT82].

Star provides a drawing package, the results of which can be integrated into a document (see Figure 20). The user selects lines, boxes, shading patterns, and other primitives from a menu and uses these to draw on a user-determined grid. Just as selections can be extended, several graphic items can be selected at once by holding down the appropriate mouse buttons. Users are also allowed to define clusters of graphical items to form new "primitives." Graphics can be scaled up or down to fit in a fixed space in a document. Star also provides packages for making and editing bar charts and spread sheets, and for retrieving information through a relational database system. The designers have stressed what we believe to be a vitally important concern: that all the packages have consistent interfaces, as users especially want a particular command to behave in a consistent way in the provided multi-view environment. Whether in the text editor, the graphics editor, or the chartmaker, the user issues commands by selecting the object of the operation and issuing the appropriate command through function keys or menu buttons. To delete a word, one selects the word and presses the `delete` key; to delete a rectangle, one selects the rectangle and presses the `delete` key.

Besides its carefully-crafted user interface, Star provides some interesting solutions to typical online manuscript-preparation problems. Mathematical and foreign-language typesetting in most systems involves using escape/control sequences or long English-language mnemonics to represent the special characters. Star presents the **virtual keyboard**, a graphical representation of the keyboard on the screen. To use a key, one simply points at it or presses the corresponding physical key. Star has knowledge of mathematical symbols and can construct complex equations and formulas as they are typed, changing the size of the symbols used as equations get larger or smaller. Editing continually adjusts the horizontal and vertical spacing and placement of subscripts and superscripts.

ETUDE

ETUDE [HAMM81] is a document production system designed with twin goals: "to *extend* the functionality of conventional word processing systems while *reducing* the complexity of the user interface." Unlike Bravo or Star, ETUDE uses prefix syntax:

action modifier element

where an *action* might be **move** or **delete**, a modifier might be a number or a word like **start-of** or **next**, and an element might be **paragraph**, **word**, **document**. The designers feel that the prefix syntax, as in "**delete 3 words**," more closely approximates natural language, and thus is preferable.

Like Bravo and Star, ETUDE is an interactive editor/formatter, providing typeset, formatted text on a standalone workstation with a bitmapped screen. ETUDE has adopted a Scribe-like method for describing formatting, switching the burden of complex formatting from the user to a document database that contains standard formats for a range of documents and document components. In a letter, for example, the ETUDE system will do special formatting for the **returnaddress, address, salutation, body,** and **signature**. While ETUDE always keeps the up-to-date formatted document on the screen, it uses the left margin of the screen as a **format window** to place formatting descriptor tags that indicate the type of high-level action that has been taken on a particular section of text (see Figure 21). This technique attempts to bridge the gap between the unformatted but explicitly expressed formatting code, and the displayed facsimile page that, once formatted, often does not contain information about the act that caused the formatting to occur. (A more detailed discussion of the interactive vs. batch formatting question is presented in Section 5).

The user interface is designed for various levels of expertise. The user can call a menu to the screen at any time and select a command with cursor keys or a pointing device. Alternatively, the user can type a command to perform the same action – or use specialized function keys provided for the most widely used commands.

The system provides a `cancel` command to abort the current operation, an **again** command to execute the current command again, and an indefinitely deep **undo** facility. The same tree

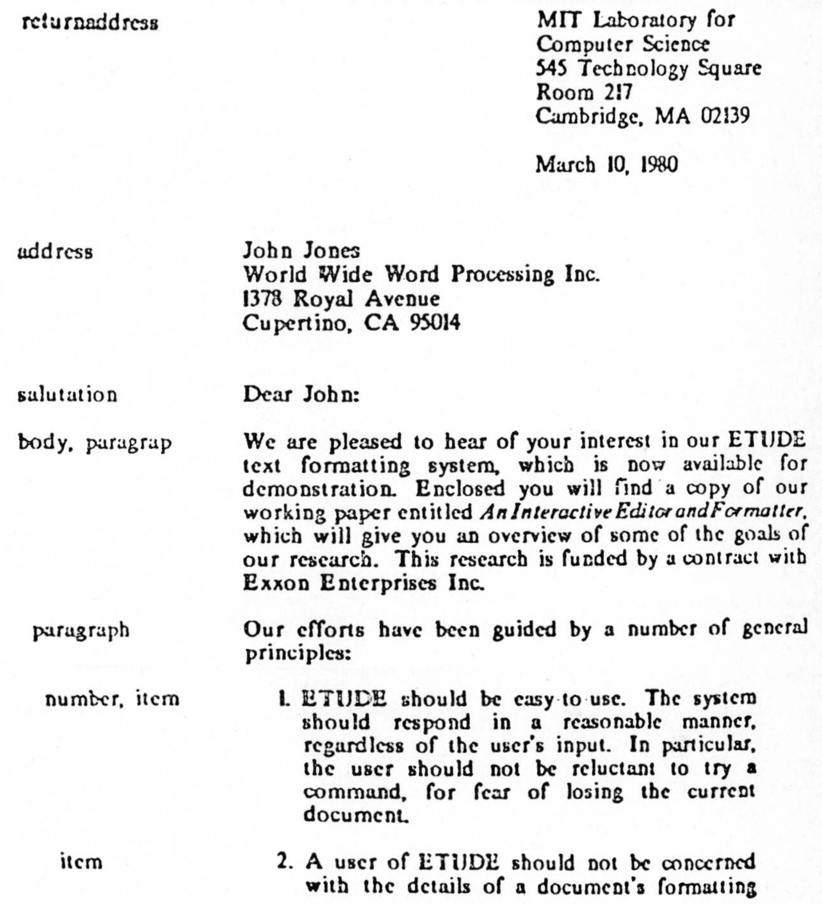

returnaddress

MIT Laboratory for
Computer Science
545 Technology Square
Room 217
Cambridge, MA 02139

March 10, 1980

address

John Jones
World Wide Word Processing Inc.
1378 Royal Avenue
Cupertino, CA 95014

salutation

Dear John:

body, paragrap

We are pleased to hear of your interest in our ETUDE
text formatting system, which is now available for
demonstration. Enclosed you will find a copy of our
working paper entitled *An Interactive Editor and Formatter*,
which will give you an overview of some of the goals of
our research. This research is funded by a contract with
Exxon Enterprises Inc.

paragraph

Our efforts have been guided by a number of general
principles:

number, item

1. ETUDE should be easy to use. The system
should respond in a reasonable manner,
regardless of the user's input. In particular,
the user should not be reluctant to try a
command, for fear of losing the current
document.

item

2. A user of ETUDE should not be concerned
with the details of a document's formatting

Figure 21. *ETUDE Screen*

structure that keeps track of the undo history is used in a `help` command that creates windows
to show the user the session's history and what options are currently available. When the `help`
command is invoked the user is presented with descriptions of a few past operations plus what
is currently being done.

4.5 General-Purpose Structure Editors
Structure editing, pioneered by Englebart with NLS, has been "rediscovered" as an alterna-

Operation	Effect on Tree
INSERT	Insert a new site (with empty data collection) into a specified gap
DELETE	Delete a subtree (nodes and data)
COPY	Copy a subtree to a specified gap
MOVE	Move a subtree to a specified gap
SPLIT	Split a node and its data into two
MERGE	Merge two nodes and their data
EXPAND	Insert an intermediate level in the tree
SHRINK	Delete an intermediate level of the tree
ORDER	Permute the nodes on a tree level

Figure 22. *Tree Editor Functions of a Structure Editor [BURK80]*

tive to standard character-oriented methods of editing. Since most target applications have some innate structure (manuscripts, for example, are composed of chapters, sections, paragraphs), the philosophy of structure editors is to exploit this "natural" ordering to simplify editing. The most common representation is a hierarchy of elements. Standard operations on this tree structure, as taken from XS-1[BURK80], are shown in Figure 22.

NLS/AUGMENT

NLS was a product of research at the Stanford Research Institute (now renamed SRI, International) between the early 1960s and late 1970s. Renamed AUGMENT and marketed by Tymshare, Inc., NLS is one of the seminal efforts in the field of text editing and office automation; indeed, many of its features are being reexamined and reimplemented today – almost 20 years since the inception of the NLS project. For example, NLS introduced the notion of conceptual models for the editing and authoring processes, (tree-) structured editing, element modifiers for the editing and viewing operations, device-independent interaction syntax, the mouse as a cursor-manipulation device, sophisticated browsing and viewing mechanisms, intermixed text and graphics, and even multi-person, distributed editing. At a spectacular, landmark demonstration of the system at the 1968 Fall Joint Computer Conference in San Francisco, text, graphics, and live video of Doug Engelbart in San Francisco and colleagues twenty miles away in Menlo Park were superimposed on multiple viewports on the (video projected) screen, as they were working together and explaining what they were doing. "Chalk-passing" protocols were demonstrated for synchronizing multiple users. This demo was a forerunner of graphics- and sound-based teleconferencing.

NLS/AUGMENT clearly embodies much more than just a text editor. Its aim is to provide a new way of thinking and working by utilizing the power of the computer in all aspects of one's work [ENGE68]:

> We are concentrating fully upon reaching the point where we can do all of our work on line
> – placing in computer store all of our specifications, plans, designs, programs, documentation,
> reports, memos, bibliography and reference notes, etc., and doing all of our scratch work, planning,
> designing, debugging, etc. and a good deal of our intercommunication, via consoles.

Regardless of the subject matter, all NLS information is stored in a hierarchical outline structure of the form:

```
1 ...
   1a ...
   1b ...
      1b1 ...
         1b1a ...
      1b2 ...
      1b3 ...
      1b4 ...
      1b5 ...
2 ...
   2a ...
3 ...
4 ...
   4a ...
      4a1 ...
      4a2 ...
```

Statements can be nested an arbitrary number of levels. Each statement has associated with it a statement number of the form shown above; these are the main means of referencing the statements from other parts of the text. One statement may be a **substatement** of another statement (1a1 is a substatement of 1a), one may be the **source** of another (1a is the source of 1a1), one may be the **predecessor** of another (4a1 is the predecessor of 4a2), or one may be the **successor** of another (4a2 is the successor of 4a1). NLS provides modifiers to reference not only text elements but structure elements as well. A **statement** is a text node of up to 2000 characters. A **branch** is a statement and all its substatements. A **plex** is a branch plus all the other branches with the same source. The plex of 4a1 is 4a1 and 4a2; the plex of 4a2 is the same. A **group** is a subset of a plex; it consists of all the branches of a plex that lie between and include two branches. The group of 1b2 and 1b4 includes 1b2,1b3, and 1b4.

The hierarchy is useful for programs as well as for documents since it can be used to model the block structure of the program. Viewspecs allow levels of detail in the outline structure to be made invisible; the viewspecs effect **information hiding**, the selective display or non-display of existing material based on attributes provided by the user.

NLS/AUGMENT allows the user to create a hypertext by superimposing on the structure a network of links that point to various discrete statements in this document. In general, these links are specified by the identifier

<host,owner,file,statement>

which allows linking of documents over multiple computers.

Commands in NLS/AUGMENT can be executed by using a mouse to select from a menu on the screen, by using the keyboard, or by using both the keyset (described in Part I, Section 2) with one hand to enter the command, and the mouse with the other to make a selection.

The editing commands are quite extensive, providing the first attempt at an orthogonal command syntax with element modifiers. For instance, the insert command can be modified, with nouns such as word, sentence, and branch. As in most structure editors, the commands are divided into those which operate on the structure (such as move) and those which operate on the text. NLS/AUGMENT provides a very large repertoire of both. Most standard tree manipulations are allowed, such as locating or deleting the next node or the previous one, locating the first subnode, and rearranging neighboring nodes. The move and copy structure commands provide dynamic renumbering of sections and updating of links throughout the document if necessary.

The system provides the ability to imbed control codes in special delimiters within the text both for formatting options such as font changes and for travelling information (links, annotations). These codes can be edited like regular text until they are invoked by special commands (a link is not operable until the jump command is invoked). Viewspec parameters allow one to turn off viewing of these special codes as desired.

A journaling facility provides extensive archiving power for past online conversations and teleconferences. TYMSHARE's commercial version of AUGMENT makes use of TYMNET, a transcontinental satellite network, to satisfy one of the original goals of the project: the sharing of knowledge across great distances. In fact, it is not uncommon for someone in New York to compose a document by making several links to an existing document belonging to a colleague in California.

At its time of introduction, NLS was unusual not only in terms of its functionality but also because of the software engineering environment in which it was produced. This environment included compiler-compilers, systems-implementation languages, and command language interpreters.

Burkhart/Nievergelt Structure Editor

Burkhart and Nievergelt at the Institute for Information in Zurich have designed a family of structure-oriented editors called XS-1 [BURK80]. The designers contend that the basic set of editing operations, regardless of the target being manipulated, are similar, and that "a universal structure defined on all data within a system" exploits that similarity to its greatest advantage. As in NLS, the structure of data of all types in XS-1 is represented as a tree, with the nodes ("sites") representing subsets of data. Like many structure editors of its kind, the core of the XS-1 system is a flexible tree editor that allows the user to manipulate the elements at the site (node) level. Fundamental to the XS-1 philosophy is the belief that the user works only on a restricted set of data and with a restricted set of commands at any one time. Therefore, the system supports progressive disclosure, explicity showing the user the valid command repertoire and operation targets at any given moment. The user always has the familiar tree operations available at all times.

XS-1 provides the user with standard structure editor methods of travel through the **explore** command. Here, the user can use relative motion to traverse up, down, left, or right in the tree. As well, absolute motion allows the user to move explicitly to something by specification of an identifier such as a name.

The tree editor follows several basic principles. After completion of any operation, the integrity of the tree structure is guaranteed. (This may be accomplished by attaching target-specific syntax rules to operations, making a syntax-directed editor.) XS-1 provides the ability to specify different views of the same targets, such as a tree structure of a program or an indented view of the same program.

An important aspect of XS-1 is the combination of the same target-independent tree editor with target-dependent back ends to create multiple editors. One such combination is a document editing/formatting system. Here, the author sees on the screen a rectangular window into the text and a text cursor. All high-level operations (**move**, **copy**, etc.) are handled by the target-independent tree editor; only a small set of text editing primitives, at the character, word, or sentence levels, are provided. The command set is consistent between targets; operations provided by the universal editor are also provided for specific, target-dependent modes, enabling the user to deal with a relatively small set of operations which do "obvious" things. For example, a **move** command in a text editor would move the selected text from source to destination while a **move** command in a graphics editor would move the selected graphics object from source to destination. Text formatting is done by appending a formatting descriptor to each site; these can be edited by the tree editor as well.

Fraser's s

Fraser's *s* [FRAS80] is an attempt to provide standard editing primitives which can be used to build a variety of editors. *s* allows the programmer quickly to create different front ends for a text editor so that various targets can be modified using existing editing routines.

The philosophy behind *s* is that many computer utilities – interactive debuggers, file system utilities, even tic-tac-toe games – are simply editors, in that they accept a particular input syntax and modify the existing representation and or state of their particular data. Rather than producing languages and scanners for each application, *s* attempts to use a generalized structure and a generalized text editor nucleus for editing all applications.

One application allows the user to edit UNIX **i-nodes**, complex (18-field) data structures containing pointers and information about a file block from the UNIX file system. When the system crashes or a disk block becomes unusable, the systems programmer occasionally has to go into the file system and manually change pointer values from a dump-type format. *s* provides a screen-based view of the file descriptor, allowing the user to edit each of the fields, which are represented one per line. An overstrike, for example, is translated into a call to the nucleus routine **fetch** to retrieve the appropriate field and a call to the nucleus routine **change**, to update the field. The deletion of a field would be performed with a call to the nucleus routine **delete**.

Another interesting use of *s* is as a UNIX file directory editor. The UNIX **ls -l** command provides a listing of file attributes:

```
drwxr-xr-x 2 nkm       224 May  9 15:27 bBACKUP
-rw-r--r-- 1 nkm     36585 May  2 16:42 section1.tex
-rwxrwxrwx 1 nkm     16714 Apr 25 17:11 section2.tex
-rw-r--r-- 1 nkm     48414 May  2 16:44 section3.tex
-rw-r--r-- 1 nkm     55282 May  6 00:23 section4a.tex
```

```
-rw-r--r-- 1 nkm    20113 May  6 00:49 section4a2.tex
-rw-r--r-- 1 nkm     9209 May  9 14:50 section4b.tex
-rw-r--r-- 1 nkm    22049 May  9 14:20 section4c.tex
-rw-r--r-- 1 nkm    26958 May  6 02:24 section4d.tex
-rw-rw---- 1 nkm     3362 May  9 15:10 section4e.tex
-rw-rw---- 1 nkm    18541 May  7 11:13 section5.tex
```

The first field contains a d if that entry is a directory; this field is not editable. The next nine fields contain r, w, x for read, write, and execute privileges for the owner, the group, and for all others, respectively, with a - indicating no access. The next field, the link count, is not editable. The next field contains the owner of the file. The rest of the fields are not editable, except for the last entry, the actual filename.

Rather than forcing the user to use the UNIX shell commands for performing renaming (mv oldname newname), deleting (rm filename), changing ownership (chown filename), and changing access rights (chmod a+rwx filename to allow all to read, write, and execute the file), the s directory editor allows the user to edit the listing directly, barring protected fields. Deleting the characters r, w or x removes read, write, and execute access for the corresponding parties; overstriking a - with r, w or x adds access. Typing over the owner name changes the owner, typing over the filename changes the filename. Deleting an entire line deletes that file.

A different front end allows the user to edit the state of a simple pedagogical computer. Rather than having the student submit punched cards in batch mode and easier and cheaper than having a physical laboratory machine, an s front end was written representing the machine data structure as editable lines and allowing the students to modify the appropriate fields. While the goals of the i-node and machine applications are different, the primitives to edit them, at least from a system view, are the same.

While the s editor was a limited experiment, its ramifications are wide-ranging. Many applications, especially ones that are computer-based, have some aspect which requires editing. We feel that Fraser's basic premise – that when changing a filename in a filesystem, when adding a user to a mailing list, or when editing a UNIX *i-node* as above, there is no reason why the user should have to resort to special maintenance programs – will be an important goal in the future of editing. As Fraser's s has shown, a general-purpose editor can be used to give the user a far more common interface across diverse applications than typically exists today. Moreover, with an appropriate interface, one can perform editing on a graphical representation of the target rather than on an unfamiliar, textual representation.

Walker's Document Editor

Walker's Document Editor is an attempt to design an editor for the preparation of complex documents such as technical manuals. An initial goal of the system [WALK81b] was to "develop a structured description for documents...distinct from any particular commands in the document source." The Document Editor uses EMACS as a base text editor and Scribe as a document-description database and compiler.

The Document Editor operates on a "document" as a collection of files in Scribe manuscript file form; it infers the structure of the document from the tags in the file being edited. The specialized functions for technical writing provided by the Document Editor are actually extensions to EMACS in the form of a user library.

The Document Editor provides four major categories of document structure editing commands: **locators, selectors, mutators,** and **constructors**. Locator commands allow the user to specify places in the document; these include commands to go up and down a structural level (e.g., from section to subsection), to go to the next or previous item at the same structural level, and to go the next structural element of any type. Selector commands allow the user to determine the current makeup of the document by checking the status of the parts and the structure of the document at various (user-specified) levels. Mutators revise the structural makeup of the document, providing functions such as **change structural level** (make a chapter a section). Constructors allow the user to create and copy structural elements.

The Document Editor uses Scribe's commands for cross-referencing for maintaining cross-references for section numbers, table numbers, and other document information. This facility provides a **follow CREF (cross-reference) pointer** function to allow the user to view the target of the cross-reference. More interestingly, it contains the **find all fingers** function, which allows the user to see which cross-reference pointers in the document point *to* a particular spot in a document. This forms a rudimentary hypertext capability [NELS67, VAND71a], but requires the high computational overhead of being extrapolated from Scribe, rather than being an editor primitive.

The Document Editor uses the cross reference capabilities to provide functions that manage the task of creating an index for a document. For traveling, the user can follow an index pointer and examine all the fingers pointing to a location, as well as make an index entry, show index symbols, and find all the index symbols containing a particular word.

The Document Editor runs Scribe as an underlying formatting process. The editor itself, EMACS, does not present the formatted text for the user to edit. As discussed in more detail in Section 5, Walker contends that for large documents, one has little interest in anything but the content and the formatting abstractions (as opposed to the actual formatting) during most of the life of the document. However, the Document Editor does provide the functions for compiling those parts of the document that have actually changed, while conforming to the formatting constraints of the entire document (proper page numbers, indentation levels, margins, typefaces). This alleviates the cost of recompiling an entire document because of minor editing changes.

4.6 Syntax-directed Editors

Syntax-directed editors attempt to increase the productivity of the programmer by removing the time-consuming process of eliminating syntax errors. Syntax editors are structure editors that insure that the structure always is constrained to preserve syntactical integrity. Often syntax-directed editors do not merely recognize the syntax and translate the user's actions into linear text, but instead parse the input into an intermediate form that can be used to generate code. Here the editor is both a tool for the programmer and a tool for the compiler/interpreter. We give some prototypical examples below.

Hansen's EMILY

Hansen's EMILY [HANS71] is one of the earliest syntax-directed editors. Rather than typing in arbitrary text, the user creates and modifies text by graphically selecting units of text (templates) that are constructs in a programming language. Text is created with a sequence of selections. The screen is divided into three areas: text, menu, and message. The text area in the upper two-thirds of the screen displays the text under construction as a string that contains the nonterminals (non-atomic entities) of the program, highlighted by underlining. The current non-terminal is enclosed in a rectangle. The menu in the lower third of the screen displays a set of possible replacements for the current nonterminal. The user selects a replacement rule and the system makes the substitution, locates a new current nonterminal, and displays a new set of choices. The message area is used for entering identifiers and also displays status and error messages. Assuming a partial PL/I-type grammar like the following:

```
<STMT>  ::= <VAR> = <EXPR>; | IF <EXPR> THEN <STMT> | DO; <STMT*> END;
<STMT*> ::= <STMT> | <STMT> <STMT*>
<EXPR>  ::= <EXPR> + <EXPR> | <VAR>
<VAR>   ::= id
```

where symbols surrounded by "<" and ">" are nonterminals, an IF statement might be created in the following manner:

The current (boxed) nonterminal is <STMT> and the menu displays the three choices:

```
<VAR> = <EXPR>;
IF <EXPR> THEN <STMT>
DO; <STMT*> END;
```

The user selects the second with a lightpen and gets the expansion:

```
IF  <EXPR> THEN
      <STMT>
```

The current nonterminal is now <EXPR>, and the menu displays the possible expansions for this. Subsequent derivations to arrive at the appropriate IF clause are:

```
IF  <VAR> THEN
      <STMT>
IF FIRSTTIME THEN
      <STMT>
IF FIRSTTIME THEN DO;
      <STMT*>
END;
      .
      .
      .
IF FIRSTTIME THEN DO;
      FIRSTTIME = FALSE;
      SYMBOLS = NULL;
      ENDTIME = DAYMINUTES + 10;
END;
```

Since a syntax imposes a hierarchical structure on text, EMILY can be used for any hierarchical text structure. Each selection from the menu generates a node with space for one pointer for each nonterminal in the replacement string. When a nonterminal is replaced, the corresponding space is filled in with a pointer to the node generated for the replacement. Each nonterminal thus generates a subtree of nodes that is presented on the display, through a tree-walking display routine, as a string of text.

As in NLS, the user can change the view of the text, so that the string generated by any nonterminal is represented by a single identifier called a **holophrast**. For example, the IF statement above could be displayed with all text generated from the <STMT*> represented by a holophrast. In larger programs, this feature means that the user can view the structure of the text without viewing the details. Alternatively, the user can descend into the structure and view the details in full.

Text is also modified in terms of its structure. The text represented by any holophrast can be deleted, moved, or copied. When text is deleted, it is not destroyed immediately, but is automatically moved to a special system fragment called *DUMP*. If a mistake is discovered before the next text modification is made the deleted text can be retrieved from this dump.

EMILY is a pure syntax-directed editor. Statements are derived by the menu-picking scenario down to the lowest level, for example, the identifier. This makes the editing awkward, since the user must often traverse long derivations to type in a simple identifier or assignment statement.

Cornell Program Synthesizer

Much work in individual areas was done after EMILY, most notably the Mentor [DONZ75, DONZ80] tree-manipulation and programming environment, the CAPS diagnostic programming system [WILC76], and the INTERLISP Programmer's Assistant [TEIW77]. The Cornell Program Synthesizer [TEIT81a, TEIT81b], running on both the Terak (LSI-11 based) personal computer and the VAX family of computers, combines many of the ideas from these and other projects into a syntax-directed editor and programming environment for PL/CS, and more recently, PASCAL.

In the Synthesizer, designed for simple terminals which use cursor keys as the only locator device, the user types textual commands that represent the set of possible expansions of the current nonterminal. The set of possible commands can be displayed in an optional window so that the user need not memorize the command sequences. The synthesizer differs markedly from EMILY in that it is not a pure derivational syntax-directed editor. Rather, the synthesizer is a hybrid between the traditional structure editor and the character-string text editor. Thus, common elements such as identifiers, expressions, and assignment statements do not have to be considered as elements of a tree structure, nor do they have to be edited and stored as such.

The user is presented with three types of high-level entities. **Templates** are program constructs which need to be filled in. **Placeholders** are tags in the template describing the parts that need to be completed, and these are the only parts of templates that can be altered. **Phrases** are pieces of text, not structure, that are typed in to replace placeholders.

To start a PL/CS program editing session, the user types •main followed by a carriage return to obtain the template for a PL/CS main program.[14] This template is of the form:

```
/* comment */
file-name: PROCEDURE OPTIONS ( MAIN );
   {declaration}
   {statement}
   END file-name;
```

The user can position the cursor at the placeholder comment and type a phrase containing the text of a comment. Now the user positions the cursor at the placeholder for the nonterminal declaration. Since this is a nonterminal (indicated by the braces), the user must select an applicable template for further derivation. At this point, the user can type •fx for a fixed variable, •fl for a float variable, •bt for a bit variable, •ch for a character variable, or •c for a comment. For our example we will choose •fx. This expands to the template:

```
DECLARE ( list-of-variables ) FIXED [attributes];
```

The cursor is moved to the list-of-variables placeholder and a phrase containing the name of the variable is typed in. This name, typed in as text, not as structure, is parsed for syntactic correctness upon pressing carriage return, and is stored and manipulated as text. If an illegal variable name had been typed, this phrase would be highlighted in reverse video and flagged

---

[14] •, long, clip, delete, left, right, up, down, and diagonal are function keys on the synthesizer keyboard.

internally. If the attributes are not inserted, the square brackets indicate that default values will be used. The declaration nonterminal is now completely defined, and the user moves on to expand the statement nonterminal, for which there are 13 possible templates. Typing •ie would generate the template

```
IF ( condition )
   THEN  statement
   ELSE statement
```

(The box here indicates the current cursor position.) Typing •p at this position would generate the PUT template, giving

```
IF (condition)
   THEN PUT SKIP LIST (  list-of-expressions );
   ELSE statement
```

The user could then type a phrase like "'min = ',beta " to fill in the placeholder.

The user uses the left, right, up, and down cursor keys to traverse the structure. In fact, the key names do not represent the true functions attached to those keys. Right and down both move the cursor forwards through the program; left and up move it backwards through the program. Rather than moving character by character, these keys move the cursor one program element (template beginning, placeholder, or phrase) at a time. Left and right, additionally, stop at each individual character in a phrase. In the expanded template like the one above, the cursor would stop at the underscored places when using up and down:

```
IF ( alpha < beta)
   THEN  PUT SKIP LIST ( 'min = ',beta );
   ELSE statement
```

and at these underscored places when using left and right:

```
IF ( alpha < beta)
   THEN  PUT SKIP LIST ( 'min = ',beta );
   ELSE statement
```

The two-key sequence long down (up) moves the cursor to the next (previous) structural element of the same level. Other keys move the cursor to the nearest enclosing structure template and to the beginning of the program.

Insertion and deletion are based on the pick, put, and delete buffer concepts. The user positions the cursor at an appropriate template or phrase, and then issues the delete command to delete that template (including, of course, all sub-templates) or phrase and store it in the delete buffer. Similarly, clip will store a copy of the selected entity in the clip buffer, but not delete the original. The insert command allows the reinsertion of the deleted or clipped text at the current cursor position. In the above example, if the cursor were positioned at the P in "PUT," the sequence delete, down, insert would result in the program segment

```
IF ( alpha < beta )
   THEN statement
   ELSE PUT SKIP LIST ( 'min = ', beta );
```

Correcting mistakes can only be done by preserving structural integrity. Assume the following incorrect code segment:

```
/* compute factorials from 1 to 10 non-recursively */
a = 0;
DO WHILE ( a < 10 );
  a = a + 1;
  fact = 1;
  PUT SKIP LIST ( a,' Factorial =' );
  temp = a;
  END;
DO UNTIL ( temp = 1 );
  fact = fact * temp;
  temp = temp - 1;
  END;
PUT SKIP LIST ( fact );
```

The traditional programmer, realizing that the END of the DO-WHILE loop should properly come at the end of all of this code (nesting the DO-UNTIL and the PUT SKIP LIST), would move the END statement to the end of the code with a single **move** command or a **delete/put** sequence to achieve:

```
/* compute factorials from 1 to 10 non-recursively */
a = 0;
DO WHILE ( a < 10 );
  a = a + 1;
  fact = 1;
  PUT SKIP LIST ( a,' Factorial =' );
  temp = a;
  DO UNTIL ( temp = 1 );
    fact = fact * temp;
    temp = temp - 1;
    END;
  PUT SKIP LIST ( fact );
  END;
```

In a syntax-directed editor, since the END is part of the DO-WHILE template, it cannot be separately moved. Instead of moving the END forwards, the equivalent backward move of the two following statements must be done. To perform the desired alteration, the user would have to position the cursor at the start of the DO-UNTIL template, press **long delete**, move the cursor to the last element in the list of structures to be moved (the PUT SKIP LIST (fact) statement), signal completion of the selection by typing •, move the cursor to the structural element after which the new part should be inserted (the temp = a; phrase), press carriage return to open a **statement** placeholder, and issue •ins DELETED to position the desired text in the desired spot. While this is certainly more complicated than the traditional method, the interface is partially to blame. A pointing device that would easily allow selection of elements and extension by structural or contiguous units would eliminate many of the keystrokes above. Even without the pointing device, one could imagine extending the starting or ending portions of a template to encompass contiguous statements.

Even if many syntax-directed editing techniques are nominally longer than traditional techniques, the excess time must be weighed against the time saved by ensuring that a program is syntactically correct every step of the way. One major time-wasting operation that is avoided is the backmapping of frequently inscrutable syntax-error messages to the source lines, all too often a heuristic and frustrating process. Indeed, an important contribution of the Synthesizer project was the concept of the syntax-directed editor as an integral part of a programming environment. The synthesizer is not typically used to create text files which will later be passed to a standard compiler, but rather as an editor which will create a representation of a program suitable for online interpretation. The Synthesizer allows the user to run a program and watch the cursor step through the lines of code as they are being executed, much like the "bouncing ball" familiar to cartoon watchers. Information hiding (such as seeing only the comments or top-level templates) still allows single-step viewing of the program in which the cursor jumps from one visible high-level unit to the next; the user does not have to watch the low-level details, for example, the inner workings of a loop. Uninitialized variables are flagged, type checking is enforced interactively, and duplicate declarations are prohibited, all at edit time, rather than compile time. Invalid phrases are highlighted as soon as the user types them in. A syntax-directed approach avoids the time-consuming backmapping error messages from a batch compiler to the proper lines in the source file by generating the error messages interactively, with the offending program components highlighted. Programs are incrementally compiled, allowing the user to re-edit and experiment with small parts of a program without waiting for an extensive recompilation. In fact, the approach taken with the Synthesizer allows the suspension of program state, the correction and incremental compilation of a portion of the program, and the resumption of the program.

Templates can be input only in a structurally sound manner, while phrases, typed textually, are allowed to be erroneous. When editing, the user does not need to expand all nonterminals or remove all errors in phrases. An incomplete or erroneous program can be run at any time. However, these irregularities are highlighted from the moment they are input until the moment they are corrected; the synthesizer relaxes some of its constraints, but warns the user accordingly. In both cases, the program will run normally until the error or unfinished program construct is encountered. When this is encountered, the user is free to correct or insert the code and continue the execution.

The program is stored as a combination of a parse tree for the templates, and as actual text for the phrases. The prettyprinted code that the user sees is actually an interactively generated view of the internal data structure.

Currently, a Synthesizer Generator is being developed which will allow a complete syntax-directed editor to be generated from a formal description of the syntax. We point the reader to the GANDALF project at Carnegie-Mellon University [HABE79, NOTK79, FEIL80, MEDI81], for a description of a similar syntax-directed editor and editor-generator project.

Frasers's *sds*

Fraser's *sds* is a general structure editor driven by a grammar that describes a hierarchical data structure. Our interest in it is due to the stress that has been put upon imposing a syntax on targets that are not necessarily programs, and upon the generation of the editor from a procedural description.

The user-viewable part of *sds* is a screen editor which displays a current record of some tree structure. The cursor keys **down, up, left, right** and **home** allow the user to move down to a node field, back up, left or right to adjacent fields, or to the root of the structure. Like the Cornell Program Synthesizer, other commands consist of typing a period followed by the name of a nonterminal. This causes the editor to allow the user to enter the first field of this new nonterminal. The user can either enter another nonterminal designation or, if applicable, simply type a string that will become a terminal or leaf node. As well, *sds* provides target-independent commands such as .w (.r), which write (read) a subtree to (from) a file, .hide(show), to suppress(exhibit) detail of a subtree, .pick, which saves a pointer to the current node, and .put, which substitutes the current node with the previously picked node.

The target-specific editor is written using a formal syntax description similar to that used for the YACC compiler-compiler of Johnson [JOHN75]. The entire grammar for an *sds* binary tree editor is captured in one line[15]:

    tree = value tree tree : dotree(value,tree,tree2)

The phrase before the colon is the grammatical description of tree, the only production in the grammar of binary trees. The portion after the colon is SNOBOL4 code to perform an action (tree2 is the second argument named tree, tree*n* would be the SNOBOL argument for the *n*th tree token in a production list). In this example, the dotree subroutine contains SNOBOL code to display the value and the two subtrees in graphical form. Note that to change the representation of a binary tree node to one in which the value lay between the two tree pointers, one would simply have to change the production to transpose the words "value" and "tree":

    tree = tree value tree : dotree(value,tree,tree2)

Similarly, the dotree routine could be changed to store the binary tree in a disk-oriented form or to print it in an indented representation; the actions are independent of the creation routines of *sds*.

A document editor has also been written in *sds*. Of course, this implies the construction of a hierarchical grammar for a document, coupled with action rules for each production. A sample grammar for a small document system looks like:

    paper = title sect : center(title) nl nl generate(sect)
    sect = header pp sect : header nl nl put(pp) generate(sect)
    pp = text pp : break(text) nl generate(pp)

To the right of the colons lie production-specific SNOBOL code. We are concerned here only with the productions to the left of the colon.

To use this editor, the user would enter textual commands to create various levels of the subtree as follows. The prompt line gives the user an idea of location in the structure. The last item on the line is the current field (item on the right side of the production), while the preceding items are the types (items on the left side of the production) which brought the user to that field, i.e., the successive nodes of the tree branch. The root name paper, is implied at the beginning of each line.

First, the user types .paper, telling *sds* to begin a node of type paper, the root of the structure.

    prompt:
    user: .paper

The next prompt asks the user to type in a title and go to the next part of the production:

    prompt: title
    user: Interactive Editing Systems

sds is now ready to perform the sect production, but requires the user to issue the explicit command to create the section:

---

[15]Examples are adapted from [FRAS81].

prompt: `sect`
user: `.sect`

Having created the `.sect` record, the system prompts the user to fill in the header field:

prompt: `sect header`
user: `Introduction`

The user is now prompted to create a `.pp` record, and again must issue an explicit command:

prompt: `sect pp`
user: `.pp`

The user is prompted to enter text. In this mode, he is provided with a target-dependent text editor based on the Irons model:

prompt: `sect pp text`
user: `The interactive editor has become an essential...`

Upon terminating that paragraph, the user is prompted to create another, as the `pp` production is recursive:

prompt: `sect pp pp`
user: `.pp`

The user then types in the appropriate text:

prompt: `sect pp text`
user: `Though the editor has always been deemed...`

The command *up* goes up one level in the structure. This cause a production (`pp` = `text pp`) to be completed and an action to be performed; in this case, formatting of a paragraph:

prompt: `sect pp pp pp`
user: `up`

We go up one more level of the tree, formatting the first paragraph.

prompt: `sect pp pp`
user: `up`

While the user is entering text, *sds* is performing syntax-checking, flagging and prohibiting invalid structure at any point in the document.

Initial reaction to document creation by structure centers on the apparent "wordiness" necessary to get the job done, but Fraser contends that the explicit structure is almost identical to what one does implicitly with a compiler-based document language. In fact, the `.w` command would store the above paper as

```
.paper
Interactive Editing Systems
.sect
Introduction
.pp
The interactive editor has become an essential...
.pp
Though the editor has always been deemed...
```

A third application for *sds* is as a picture editor for simple line drawings. The structure editor, using the small, 6-line grammar described in [FRAS81], would create the multicolor letter "T" with the structure:

```
.branch
.color
blue
.line
0,20 20,20
.color
.red
.line
10,0 10,20
```

Other grammars used by *sds* include one for a subset of C [KERN78c].

4.7 Word Processors

WordStar

WordStar [MICR81] is one of the most popular word processing programs available for home computer systems. It runs on a variety of systems under the CP/M operating system, using the CP/M file system to maintain its files.

The conceptual model of text in WordStar is the quarter-plane of the Irons model. Control key combinations (special prefix characters are used as software shift keys to provide a large set of commands), function keys and cursor keys are used for command specification. WordStar combines the quarter plane model with a "virtual typewriter" model. The user is presented with a ruler line that simulates tab rack and margin ruler on conventional typewriters, and with commands to move virtual margin keys forward and backward on this ruler line. WordStar divides the file into logical pages that default to contain 55 lines (the number of lines on an 8-1/2-x-11 page, excluding margins). Most importantly, WordStar provides modest interactive editor/formatter capabilities for justified, monospaced text. As the user types in text, the lines are automatically justified. When text is changed, rejustification is not automatic, but is done on a per-paragraph or per-document basis by user command.

The screen is set up to provide extensive feedback to the user. The first line is a status line: it presents the filename of the document, the current page number, and the current line and column at which the cursor points; as soon as the cursor is moved, these latter values are changed. As well, the beginning of this line is used to echo the typed command. For instance, as in Figure 23, if the user types CTRL-Q on the keyboard, the textual representation ⁻Q is shown on the screen. The next few lines on the screen (above the ruler line) represent the current options. Here, since CTRL-Q was typed, the ⁻Q prefix options are displayed in the help area. The user then chooses one of the ⁻Q suffixes, which represent commands. A more sophisticated user can avoid this extensive prompting in two ways. First, if the entire command, say CTRL-QF is typed together quickly, it is executed without displaying the ⁻Q options. More explicitly, the user is given commands to change help levels. These help levels range from displays for the novice, containing complete options to those for the expert, containing no options at all. The full set of WordStar commands is shown in Figure 24. For errors, WordStar makes sure that the user has noticed the error by requiring an acknowledgment – by default the ESC key – to resume operation.

```
^Q          A:TEST.DOC    PAGE 1    LINE 3    COL 19
            ^Q PREFIX          (to cancel prefix, hit SPACE bar)

CURSOR: S=left Side screen  E=top screen    X=bottom          D=right enD line
        R=beginning file    C=end file      0-9, B, K, V, P = to marker

SCROLL:                     Z=continuous up        W=continuous down
DELETE TO END LINE:         DEL=left               Y=right
FIND, REPLACE:              F= find a string       A= find and substitute
REPEAT NEXT COMMAND:Q=repeat until key hit
L- - - -!- - - -!- - - -!- - - -!- - - -!- - - -!- - - -!- - - -!- - - -!- - - -!- - - -R
    this is text entered by the user.                                        <
    The quick brown fox jumped over the lazy dog.                            <
    abcdefghijklmnop ■
```

Figure 23. *WordStar screen [MICR81]*

As in the Irons model, editing is done on the displayed viewing buffer/editing buffer by driving the cursor around and typing. WordStar offers both insert mode and typeover mode.

A major flaw of WordStar is the lack of an undo facility: once a command is executed, it cannot be reverted. This reduces the freedom of experimentation that an author should have. The only recourse a user has is "undoing" an entire session with an abort command.

A problem with WordStar, and with most microcomputer editors, is lack of both main memory and disk space. WordStar, for instance, has its own paging routines to bring parts of documents in and out of memory. If the disks are of reasonable capacity, this offers no problem. However, for small systems with floppy disks and consequently small disk capacity, the amount of the disk needed for paging leaves little room for document storage. This causes, in some systems, the unfortunate situation in which a document that is being edited cannot be stored back on disk.

CPT 8000

CPT is a representative example of a commercial standalone word processing system. The Disktype 8000 has a page-size, monospace display, and two floppy disks to store files. CPT was the first word processing system to offer a 8-1/2-x-11 white screen with black characters, simulating a piece of paper in a typewriter [SEYP79]. In fact, the typewriter metaphor is consistently applied. A few lines up from the bottom of the page is the **typing line**, meant to simulate the paper bail on the platen of a typewriter. Input takes place on the typing line only.

No standard cursor keys exist on the CPT. Rather, the space bar moves the cursor forward on the typing line and the backspace key moves it backwards. There is no need for up and down cursor movement, since it is the document that travels up and down past the typing line. Keys are provided, therefore, to scroll the document up and down. Margins are set by moving right and left markers on the typing line. Five other keys specify character, word, line, paragraph and page elements for commands like delete, skip, move, and insert.

CPT provides three input modes. Manual mode simulates a typewriter; when the user reaches the right margin, a bell rings. Wraparound mode provides automatic carriage returns when the right margin is exceeded. Hyphenation mode performs automatic hyphenation when a word reaches a system-defined "hot zone," using an algorithm aided by an exceptions dictionary.

One interesting feedback mechanism of CPT is its error message facility. In the center of

^A	Cursor word left	^JS	Defines Status Line	
^B	Paragraph REFORM	^JV	Defines text moving	
^C	Scroll up screen	^K0-9	Set/Hide Place Markers	
^D	Cursor character right	^KB	Mark/Hide Block begin	
^E	Cursor up line	^KC	Block COPY	
^F	Cursor word right	^KD	Save file	
^G	Delete character right	^KE	RENAME file	
^H	Cursor character left	^KF	Directory ON/OFF	
^I	TAB advance	^KH	Hide/Display Block	
^J	Prefix HELP	^KJ	Delete file	
^K	Prefix Editing	^KK	Mark Block end	
^L	FIND/REPLACE AGAIN	^KL	Switch Logged drive	
^M	RETURN	^KO	COPY file	
^N	Insert carriage return	^KP	PRINT	
^O	Prefix Formatting	^KQ	Edit abandon	
^P	Enter control character	^KR	Read a file	← Deletes character left
^Q	Prefix cursor editing	^KS	Save file re-edit	ESC Error release
^R	Scroll down screen	^KV	Block move	RETURN Hard carriage return
^S	Cursor character left	^KW	Write Block to file	TAB tab
^T	Delete word right	^KX	Save file Exit	NO FILE MENU- (When no file is being created or edited)
^U	INTERRUPT commands	^KY	Block Delete	D Create or edit document file
^V	INSERT On/OFF	^OC	Center cursor line	E Rename file
^W	Scroll down line	^OD	Display DOT commands	F File Directory OFF/ON
^X	Cursor down line	^OE	Soft hyphen entry	H Set Help level
^Y	Delete line	^OF	Set margins,tabs as exist	L Change logged drive
^Z	Scroll up line	^OG	Paragraph tab	M Merge-Print
^JB	Defines REFORM	^OH	Hyphen Help ON/OFF	N Create, edit non-document file
^JD	Print directives	^OI	Set tab stop	O Copy file
^JF	Defines FLAG characters	^OJ	Justification ON/OFF	P PRINT, stop print, start print
^JH	Set HELP level	^OL	Set left margin	R Run program
^JI	Command Index	^ON	Clear tab stops	X Exit to system
^JM	Defines Tabs, Margins	^OP	Display page break ON/OFF	Y Delete file
^JP	Defines Place Markers	^OR	Set right margin	
^JR	Defines Ruler Line	^OS	Set line spacing	

^OT	Display Ruler	^QF	FIND
^OV	Variable tabs ON/OFF	^QK	Cursor Block end
^OW	Word Wrap Off/ON	^QP	Cursor previous position
^OX	Release margins	^QQ	REPEAT next command
^PM	Overprint next line	^QR	Cursor file beginning
^PO	Enter non-break space	^QS	Cursor screen left
^Q0-9	Cursor to Marker	^QV	Cursor source (Block, Find)
^QA	REPLACE	^QW	Downward scroll
^QB	Cursor Block beginning	^QX	Cursor screen bottom
^QC	Cursor file end	^QY	Delete to end of line
^QD	Cursor right end of line	^QZ	Upward Scroll
^QE	Cursor top screen	^Q←	Deletes to front of line

Figure 24. *WordStar commands*

the status line at the bottom of the screen is a 20-character area reserved for error messages. Rather than having terse error messages in this area, and as an alternative to removing some of the possibly offending text from the display to make room for a wordy error message, CPT rolls the lengthy error across this area like a captioned bulletin at the bottom of a television screen.

NBI System 3000

The NBI System 3000 is another popular commercial word processing system. It has a standalone processor, with file storage on floppy disk. Its conceptual model is very similar to that of WordStar described above. The interface uses a combination of option sheets and function keys; the display is a mapping of a screen-sized viewing buffer to a full-screen viewport. The user alters the documents by driving a cursor around the screen with cursor keys, overstriking characters or using appropriate function keys to effect the changes. Like WordStar, the NBI System 3000 supplies the user with option sheets to show available operations. It does not however, offer the help level commands of WordStar. In some cases, the user can operate without calling up an option sheet at all, and in other cases, as in WordStar, if the user is "faster" than the option sheet, it is not called up at all.

NBI presents an interesting alternative to the insert mode vs. overstrike mode "controversy." When the cursor is positioned over a character, typing will overwrite that character. When the cursor is positioned over a space, typing will invoke insert mode and all characters to the right of the cursor will be pushed to the right as necessary. NBI provides an extensive search and replace facility, allowing the user to perform case-insensitive searches and replacements on a case-by-case basis.

Along with these advantages are several inconsistencies. The commands set is not consient. The **line delete** command will delete the line in which the cursor is positioned, regardless of where the cursor lies in that line, while the **word delete** command will only delete a word if the cursor is positioned at the first character of that word. Although complete region selection and associated copying, moving, deletion, and storage are available, NBI provides no feedback as the areas are selected.

4.8 Integrated Environments

RIG, Apollo

The Rochester Intelligent Gateway (RIG) user interface [LANT79, LANT80] and the similar Apollo Aegis user interface [APOL82] are two examples of a relatively new trend in editing systems, one in which the editor is an integrated part of the interface presented to the user, rather than a user-invoked utility program.

Both the RIG and Apollo systems are based on the concept of a display or window manager as the primary interface to the system. These display managers gives the user the ability to create windows on the display surface, move these windows around, and change their size. On the Apollo these windows can overlap; in RIG the windows do not overlap but simply partition the display screen (see Figure 25).

As in Star, the windows are meant to simulate pieces of paper on a desk. More specifically, the window shows a rectangular portion of a two-dimensional **pad** (see Figure 25), an unbounded quarter-plane of text. Editing functions much like those in Irons-model editors are supplied to manipulate items in the pad.

So far, the systems sound much like a standard multi-window editor. In fact, one of the two types of windows, the **editing window**, fits that model exactly. The other type of window, the **process window**, is an editing window with an arbitrary user or system process attached to it. The process window has both a large **output pad** window on top and a smaller **input pad**

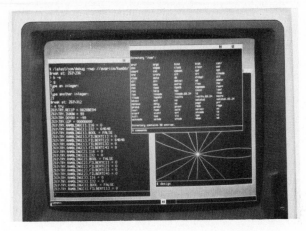

Figure 25. *RIG/Apollo Pads [APOL81]*

window directly underneath. For interactive processes, input is typed into the input pad and, much like a typewriter, when a carriage return is pressed, this text scrolls up over the "typing bar" into the output pad. In addition, output from the interactive process is written directly to the output pad. The result is a complete transcript, simulating output on a hardcopy terminal, of the interactive session. Multiple windows on the screen may be active at once; the user may be reading electronic mail in one process window, editing the file referenced in the mail in an editing window, and compiling that file in another process window. Returning to our editing concerns, we note that the output pad allows all editing functions (though often the system makes the pad's contents read-only so that they can be perused or selected but not altered). The user can now travel through the entire contents of an interactive session, and actually select previous input and output from the output pad and use it as input elsewhere in the system. For instance, the user might select a code fragment directly from the electronic mail window and insert it in the open editing window.

The major use made of this model is to tie to a process window the operating system command interpreter process. Now, the user types operating system commands into the input pad, and both this input and the output of the system programs invoked are stored in the output pad. Commands can be reexecuted simply by selecting their text in the output pad and inserting it in the input pad. Output from a program that is lying in an output pad can be selected and stored in a file. In fact, an entire output pad can be saved as a file if the user wants a transcript of an interactive session.

The ramifications of this concept are wide-ranging, much like the concepts imparted by the Star interface, but in the framework of a general-purpose computing system, rather than an office automation system. The editor does not create a preemptive environment [SWIN74], in which functions normally available to the user are suddenly cut off. Since the editor is now above the command interpreter (rather than being an applications program invoked by the command interpreter), the user can freely issue system commands interspersed with editing commands. No longer does the user have to leave the editor to do something as simple as reading electronic mail or listing the files in a directory; the user simply switches windows momentarily, executes the appropriate command, and returns to the previous window.

Smalltalk-80

Smalltalk-80, a research product of Xerox PARC's Software Concepts Group (originally the Learning Research Group), provides an even more integrated environment than described above. In fact, the paradigm of overlapping windows was developed as part of the Smalltalk-80 project [LRG76]. Composed of an object-oriented programming language and an integrated user interface, the Smalltalk-80* [GOLD82, GOLD83] system currently runs on several Xerox personal workstations (the Xerox 1100 Scientific Machine and the Dorado) with bitmapped raster displays and three-button mice (see Figure 26). The aim is to give the user an interface in which editing commands are always applicable and other capabilities that the user desires are at hand as well. Anything on the screen may be edited: document text, commands, program code, and so on. The user does not become trapped in modes (as in SOS above), but always has a full range of choices at any point in the editing session.

The conceptual model provided by the Smalltalk-80 user interface [GOLD82] is one of views, represented as labelled, rectangular, possibly overlapping pieces of paper on a desktop. A view is a particular way of displaying the information of a task or group of tasks for user inspection, alteration, storage, and retrieval of information. The views most used are standard system views, in which operations to alter size, location, label and level of detail are defined.

Menus are the other important entity in the Smalltalk-80 user interface. They exist in two varieties: fixed and pop-up. A fixed menu is a **subview** of a displayed view; the user moves a cursor over the menu items with a mouse and selects an item by pressing the leftmost mouse button. This action highlights the selection. Releasing the button invokes the selected command. A pop-up menu appears directly under the cursor when the user holds down one of the other mouse buttons. As the cursor is moved around the menu, the item underneath the cursor is suitably highlighted. Upon releasing the button, the item is selected and the menu disappears.

Since the screen space available to present a view may not be large enough to contain all the information that needs to be presented, Smalltalk-80 provides the **scroll bar**, a special type of menu that allows the user to select what portion of the view is to be made visible. It supports three general operations: **scroll up**, **scroll down**, and **jump**. The scroll bar is displayed as a vertical white rectangle that appears out to the left of a view's rectangle when that view is being used. This white rectangle represents the document continuum. Inside this rectangle is a smaller, gray rectangle. This represents the viewing buffer of the document, the amount of the document that is currently being viewed. For example, in Figure 27a, the gray bar indicates that about the last half is being viewed; in Figure 27b, the first half is being viewed; and in Figure 27c, the entire document is being viewed. To jump to a particular place in the document, the user puts the cursor in the gray rectangle, holds down the leftmost button, and drags the gray rectangle up and down by moving the mouse. Moving the rectangle simulates changing the placement of the viewing buffer on the document. Upon releasing the button, the view is changed to reflect this viewing buffer placement. To scroll down (up) the user places the cursor on the left (right) of the gray rectangle, and the cursor automatically changes to a down (up) arrow. Upon pressing the leftmost button for downward scrolling, the line of text closest to the

---

*Smalltalk-80 is a trademark of the Xerox Corporation

Figure 26. *Smalltalk-80 Screen and Mouse*

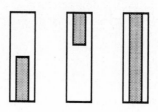

Figure 27. *Smalltalk-80 Scroll Bar*

line of text at the top of the view is moved to the cursor position. Upon pressing the leftmost button for upward scrolling, the line of text closest to the cursor is moved to the top of the view. Other menus include **confirmers**, which allow a user to select one of two displayed choices, and **prompters**, which allow the user to "fill-in-the-blank" in response to a question or message.

To edit text in a system-specified view, the user makes extensive use of the mouse and the supplied menus. Pressing and releasing ("clicking") the leftmost button on the mouse causes a caret to appear in the inter-character gap closest to the cursor. This essentially selects a zero-length string. If the user holds down the leftmost button, all the characters between the initial caret and the current position of the cursor are highlighted in reverse video. Releasing this button causes the highlighted text to become the active selection. Two clicks on the leftmost button while the cursor remains stationary select the word on which the cursor lies, unless the cursor is at the beginning or end of the document, in which case the entire document is selected, or unless the cursor lies just after (before) a left (right) parenthesis, square bracket, angle bracket, single quote, or double quote, in which case the text between the delimiter pair is selected.

Replacement fits naturally with the concept of selection. Inserting characters is simply a form of replacement. The user moves the cursor to the gap in which the string is to be inserted, does a single click to get the caret, and begins typing, which causes characters to be inserted at this spot: the user is essentially replacing the zero-length string with the string being typed (see Figure 28). If a larger area is selected, the typed-in text replaces the selection (the first typed character causes the deletion of the selected area.)

Copying and moving are done analogously. The proper selection is made and either the **copy** or the **cut** button is selected from the pop-up view menu controlled with the middle mouse button. Both commands store the selected text in a paste buffer; **copy** leaves the selected text

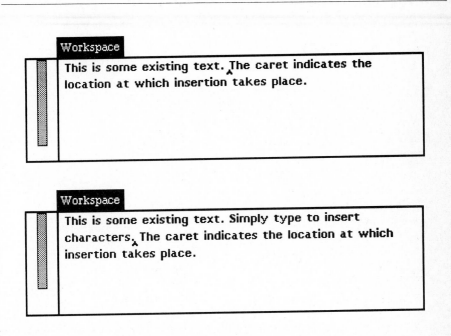

Figure 28. *Insertion in Smalltalk-80*

unscathed while cut deletes it. Now the user is free to perform any action; the **copy** and **cut** are finished. When desired, the user simply selects a destination point, selects the **paste** command in the menu, and the proper insertion is made. If the user has just selected and replaced text, **again**, another command in the pop-up menu, will hunt for the next occurrence of the pattern that was selected and replace it with the text used for the replacement. If the user selects text and then issues the **again** command, the system will simply search forward for the selected pattern, and if found, select it so the user may cut it or replace it (see Figure 29). An **undo** command allows the reversal of the previously issued command.

Most Smalltalk-80 commands are issued by either clicking a mouse button, or by the dual motion of first pressing a mouse button to select a menu item and then releasing the button to invoke the associated command. When a command is not available this way, the user simply finds some empty view space, types in the appropriate command, selects it, and then issues the **doIt** command. Later on, one may come back, edit that command in the normal way, and reissue it. Thus commands are edited as easily as text; indeed, commands are simply text. The **printIt** command is identical to **doIt**, with the exception that any output result is placed immediately after the command text to which **printIt** was applied and this result is automatically selected.

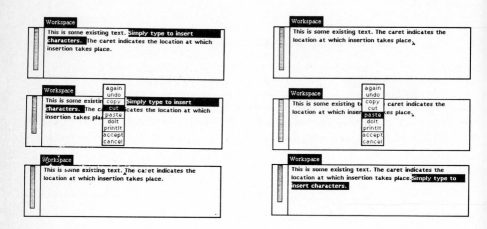

Figure 29. *Cut and Paste in Smalltalk-80*

In a, the user selects the text to be moved. In b, the user holds down the middle mouse button and the pop-up menu appears. The user moves the cursor over the   cut button, which is appropriately highlighted. In c, releasing the mouse button causes the selected text to be removed. In d, the user selects the re-insertion point with the left mouse button. In e, the user holds down the middle mouse button and the pop-up menu appears. The user moves the cursor over the e paste button, which is appropriately highlighted. In f, releasing the middle mouse button causes the previously cut text to be pasted in at the selection point.

The environment supports a wide range of tools for the development of Smalltalk-80 programs. While most are beyond the scope of this paper, we mention **browsers** as an interesting method for traversing hierarchies. Objects in the Smalltalk-80 language are built hierarchically. For instance, a **number** is a *class name* that is in the browser *class category* **numeric objects**. Similarly, the operation of addition is a *message selector* that is in the browser **numeric-number** *message category* **arithmetic**. To find information about these quickly, the user simply selects numeric objects in the class category subview in the browser, which brings up the appropriate classes in the class name subview. The user then selects Number in the class name view, which brings up the appropriate method categories in the message category subview. The user then selects arithmetic, which brings up all appropriate messages in the message selector subview. Choosing one of these message selectors, for example abs, causes the Smalltalk-80 procedure for that method to be brought up in the editing view below (see Figure 30a). The user is free to edit this procedure using the editing facilities described earlier. Pointing to an item in a subview further up the hierarchy replaces the subviews below, and allows the user to browse through new definitions. For instance, as in Figure 30b, selecting truncation and round off in the class category subview causes a new message category subview to be generated and the message selector subview to be changed. Subsequently, selecting truncated causes a new procedure to appear in the editing subview.

The browser is important not only for its convenient techniques for tree traversal, but for its notion of letting a user browse through an entire collection of information, examining and editing it at will. A browser-like interface would be attractive in other environments as well, such as that of examining a file system hierarchy or traversing a hierarchically-structured menu system. Indeed, the access to local and remote files is provided in the Smalltalk-80 system through appropriate browsers in which filename patterns are specified and filenames are selected for reading, retrieving, or editing.

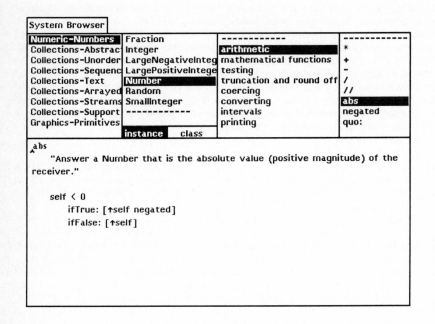

Figure 30. *Browser*

5. ISSUES

5.1 The State of Editor Design

While much is written about "the desirable human interface," most of it (unsupported) personal opinion, very little experimentation in determining the optimal editor interface has been done. Typically editor design is based not on concrete experimental results, but on market pressure to design systems that conform to today's worn technology (such as 24-x-80-character terminals, and half-duplex communication to timesharing systems). Rather than concentrating on desired functionality and ease of use, the editor designer is forced to devote large amounts of time to molding the user interface to the constraints of particular classes of limited input and output devices, producing a far-from-optimal interface.

In our editing model, the lexical phase of the command language processor, which composes tokens from lexemes, is followed by a syntactic phase, which parses sentences of these atomic tokens. In principle, we want each token's appearance and meaning to be unambiguous in all contexts, and its user image to be unique, easily remembered, and unobtrusive. For typed command languages, this is not the case: the user must correctly spell or abbreviate the needed tokens, usually from memory, and the system must be in the appropriate "command" mode so that command tokens are accepted as such, and not as literal text. In control-key interfaces, tokens are composed by overloading the alphanumeric keyboard with control or prefix keys to form cryptic combinations.

If tokens are atomic entities unto themselves, why do we need a lexical component to compose them at all? In fact, the token composition phase is one of the most treacherous parts of a user interface, and is, for all practical purposes, unnecessary with modern technologies. The pure function key interface, for example, assigns a token to a particular key; composition of tokens is not necessary. The flaw in this technique is that the number of function keys grows linearly with the number of tokens; a many-function editor would need a massive, untenable keyboard. One type of interface that begins to satisfy the criteria of atomic tokens without incurring the expense of linear growth of input devices is the menu interface, more explicitly, one that uses pop-up menus in temporary viewports and selection devices like the mouse (see Smalltalk-80 in Section 4). In general, menus supply composed tokens in a form the user easily recognizes. No memorization of tokens is needed, since the necessary images appear as needed; the user simply points to the appropriate image and selects it. The menu presents to the user only those tokens that are viable at any particular time, unlike the function keyboard, which is obliged to have all tokens at all times to avoid overloading. The menus are unobtrusive; when not in use they disappear and only pop up when called. Another interface satisfying this criteria is the Star interface. Star eliminates the problem of overloading commands by having a small set of general-purpose function keys such as open, move and find that provide the majority of tokens needed, a rich set of icons that serve as tokens as well, property sheets and option sheets that provide consistent access to tokens as well as a consistent method for composing new tokens in these sheets, and finally, window-specific menus containing selectable command tokens.

Design techniques pose another problem. Many editors in production today have been designed *by* programmers *for* programmers, and have been foisted upon the general public with little apparent regard for its needs. Many others appear to have been designed by non-programmers for non-programmers, and show little evidence of proper software engineering and language design principles, such as consistent user instruction sets and consistent syntax. Clearly few editors have been designed by rigorous examination of reasonable choices in interface and functionality, and even fewer are backed by a well-explained conceptual model. Rather, editing design has been ad hoc, with the editor often becoming a potpourri of contradictory techniques and functions, copying and inheriting poor design from previous systems ("we can always change it or write another one"). It is high time that editor designers, like programming language designers, commit their conceptual models and user interfaces to paper before implementation. This requires extensive search of the literature, analysis of alternatives, and experimental valida- tion of ideas, all traditional actions in science and engineering but disappointingly rare in this field.

5.2 The Modeless Environment

There has been much recent interest in so-called "modeless environments" [TESL81]. In fact, the term "modeless" is a bit of misnomer since no system can be truly without modes. What is intended is that modes be minimized, that designers move away from implementing special-purpose context-sensitive states and commands of the type that SOS has. The primary problem with modes is that they lock the user into a specialized and typically highly restricted functionality while in the mode, preempting the use of the normal set of functions and thereby severely limiting flexibility. With current techniques for command specification there is often a second problem, that of assigning different meanings to user actions as a function of the mode, as is the case in overloaded keyboards.

The goal of the modeless editor is to allow the user to have the flexibility to travel and to select operands without having to commit to a particular function and the particular options that it allows. In particular, the postfix form of command specification in which the operands precede the command is more conducive to minimizing modes than the prefix form. The latter is typically used to put the user in a temporary mode and then prompt for the operand(s): for example, **move** puts the user in a mode that requires the user to specify the source and then the destination. This style of guided dialogue, while useful for novices, is often frustrating and annoyingly time-consuming for experts. Furthermore, it enforces sequential specification of multiple operands, without providing the ability to edit them. Worst, of course, is that the user is locked into the dialogue, and cannot leave to browse, or to collect information with which to complete the command (see Tesler's painfully amusing example in TESL81).

With postfix syntax, the user spends most time browsing and selecting without committing to a particular function. When the function is specified, it is executed indivisibly and the user is back immediately in the familiar and universal operand selection "mode," free to browse, to create other window/viewport combinations and to select and revise selection of operands before specifying another operation. It would be possible to allow the user to escape from a temporary operation mode in prefix interaction, but a great deal more status-saving would be required.

In the case in which certain commands require more than a single operand followed by an operator, there are several alternatives in a postfix system: 1) split a compound operation into smaller primitive operations that fit the postfix constraint (as in two single-operand cut and **paste** commands to replace **move**); 2) allow multiple selection of operands, although this becomes difficult if order of specification is important; 3) allow the use of familiar editing functions for specifying parameters and for setting attributes by letting the user fill out a form and then execute a command based on this form; and 4) temporarily switch to infix specification. For an example of the last alternative, a **move** command that takes both a source and a destination would be specified in the normal way by selecting first the source and then **move**. Then, the system would enter temporary **move** mode, ask the user to select the destination, execute the **move** command and return to familiar operand selection mode.

The Star system uses the third alternative above, providing property sheet forms that do not preempt the user (as shown in Section 4). To issue the find command, for example, the user presses the find key, gets the property sheet, fills in the appropriate parameters, and then issues a command that actually does the search. Using the form metaphor, the user has the ability to select information from other parts of a screen as input to the form, and, of course, has the ability to edit the form as well. In fact, the form can be used to simulate a dialogue. As the user fills in particular information or toggles particular attributes, the system can provide further fields to be filled in. If the user goes back and edits one of the fields, all of the field values that depended upon one particular field value might be undone. (See the example of Star query-replace in Section 4.) Not only does the form metaphor simulate interactive dialogues, but it obviates the sequentiality and non-editability problems of conventional dialogues. Why then is filling in a form not considered "dangerous?" In fact, form filling is a mode of sorts, yet familiar functions can be used to edit it. Most importantly, the user can leave the context of the form, issue other commands, and return without loss of context.

5.3 Instant Editor/Formatters vs. Batch Formatters

The classical separation between form and content enforced by batch formatting is becoming increasingly less desirable. Space and layout constraints often force alteration of content to make text fit. Furthermore, text can be interpreted in a surprisingly different way when typeset than when it is printed as draft copy on a lineprinter. This, of course, is the reason it is typeset at all. That computer scientists, reporters, copy editors, and even professional printers have tolerated the system of marked-up alterations and specifications on typewritten copy or bad facsimiles of a final typeset galley is a result of economics and not an implicit confirmation of that system. The typesetting conventions that make it easier to understand text in printed form make it correspondingly easier to understand the online form. For all these purposes and especially for complex formatting tasks (tables, equations), interactive formatting is clearly highly desirable.

Yet, there is a strong camp advocating continued use of batch formatting systems, with possible softcopy review, to allow maximum flexibility and power, especially in terms of multiple interpretations of markup tags (which indicate, for example, different document styles and output devices). Allen et al. [ALLE81] advocate the use of softcopy output that is later more precisely formatted by a document compiler. They contend that the interactive user does not need a finely formatted document, but simply one that approximates the final printed result. The interactive system does not need to perform expert formatting; this is left to a batch document compiler. The underlying notion is that no matter how accurate interactive formatting systems can become, those (batch) methods that spend more time will produce higher-quality output.

Still, interactive editor/formatters seem to have compelling advantages over editors that have a separate, editable representation for formatting effects, and certainly over the separate interactive editing/batch compiling method. The ability to experiment with different formats is clearly invaluable to both author and transcriber, providing that there are no serious restrictions resulting from this facility. Having to "program" formatting effects is a mental burden and requires sophisticated, complicated code all too often; debugging a sequence of formatting codes is difficult unless a formatted copy of the same document exists for comparison.

On the other hand, the problem with some interactive editor/formatters, often called "what-you-see-is-what-you-get" editors is that, as Brian Kernighan has remarked, "what you see is all you've got." That is, it is just as uninformative and unhelpful to give a user a view of a beautifully formatted document with no clues as to how or why the formatting was effected as it is to give the user a file laden with complicated formatting codes without the rules for what these formatting codes will do. However, the stripping of formatting information is not necessary to interactively produce a finely formatted document. Referring back to our editor model in Part I, Section 1, however, we can interpret the finished document page as simply one of many useful **views**, but not the only one to which the user should be restricted. In fact, the property sheet of Star and the margin tags of ETUDE are simply specially tailored views of the document data structure. In particular, structure editing can be nicely done on representations that stress the structure and suppress formatting information – one can rearrange sections in an outline much more easily if only the section headings and the first line of each section are displayed, as in NLS. Also, as Jan Walker has pointed out [WALK81a], it is often important to know why a particular formatting effect is apparent; it is useful to be able to interrogate and alter the higher-level document object specification that caused the effect.

The principle of multiple views, one that has been sorely under-utilized in the hundreds of editors that have been created, shows that a completely reasonable solution to satisfy both camps is to provide whatever views each desires. The batch community might get a view that allows them to edit textual descriptions of formatting, equations and tables, while the interactive community might be given a view that allows interactive specification of tables, equations, as well as of the traditional simple (and local) formatting effects. Except for the additional implementation time, there is no reason to restrict the user to editing of a single interpretation/view; the multiple viewing principle needs to be adopted in systems of the future.

5.4 Structure/Syntax-Directed Editors vs. "Normal" Editors

With the increase in the number of structure editors, several designers have explained the rationale behind what seems at first to be a restrictive concept.

Advocates of structure editors claim that the specification of target data as well-connected, well-defined units enhance's the user's powers of creativity and composition. Engelbart, describing a key idea in NLS [ENGE68], writes:

> With the view that the symbols one works with are supposed to represent a mapping of one's associated concepts, and further that one's concepts exist in a "network" of relationships as opposed to the essentially linear form of actual printed records, it was decided that the concept-manipulation aids derivable from real-time computer support could be appreciably enhanced by structuring conventions that would make explicit (for both the user and the computer) the various types of network relationships among concepts . . . . We have found that in both offline and online computer aids, the conception, stipulation, and execution of significant manipulations are made much easier by the structuring conventions . . . . We have found it to be fairly universal that after an initial period of negative reaction in reading explicitly structured material, one comes to prefer it to material printed in the normal form.

Burkhart and Nievergelt [BURK80] concur with the view that while the structuring seems to be a restriction on the user (especially the novice), who may not want to be forced to keep track of the data hierarchically, the structuring would ultimately be performed anyway, "into chapters and paragraphs, procedures and modules, subpictures and patterns, as the semantics of the data may suggest."

Using his Cornell Program Synthesizer as an example, Teitelbaum claims the value of the syntax-directed editor is that a program being developed is always structurally sound, even if not complete. The use of structural templates eliminates mundane program development tasks. Indentation and prettyprinting are automatic, typographical errors are possible only in user-typed phrases, not in system-supplied templates, and such errors can be easily caught at runtime. The templates save keystrokes, as one typed command may generate a long template. Placeholders in the templates act as prompts, guiding the user along the proper path. The user never needs to get mired in low-level syntactic detail – the constructs are always conceptualized as abstract units, not as streams of tokens.

On the other side, Woods [WOOD81] claims that a good "standard" editor can do 95 percent of the program editing that a syntax-directed editor can, at much smaller development and computation costs. He claims that syntax-directed editing constrains the user interface, complicating operations that are normally easy in a standard editor. This is true of some operations in the available interfaces today, but is not an intrinsic restriction on future interfaces. He further claims that the syntax-directed approach promotes a multitude of editors. This is only partially true; editor generators such as the Cornell Synthesizer Generator, the GANDALF/ALOE project [NOTK79, FEIL80, MEDI81], and *sds* show that editors for very different targets can have the same basic editing operations. In fact, the regularity of the structure editor introduces the ability to produce formal descriptions to generate special-purpose editors. This parallels the trend to create parser-generators and compiler-generators from formal descriptions. Of course syntax-directed editors certainly have target-specific operations as well; but these operations then need not be supported by separate lexical and syntactical analyzers. Woods's claim that the representation and editing of a program as a parse-tree makes an editor harder to implement is certainly true, yet, again, the syntax-directed editor eliminates the need for a parser all together.

Notkin points out that syntax-directed editing may change the way programming is taught and described [NOTK79]. For instance, "nitty-gritty" details such as placement of statement delimiters like semicolons could be eliminated entirely, since the templates will carry whatever information is necessary to create a structurally correct program.

Morris and Schwartz [MORR81], among others, contend that syntax-directed editors are "profligate consumers of computer resources . . . . Parsing consumes processing power, the parse tree devours storage, and there is no solution but to supply plenty of each." With high-performance personal workstations possessing virtual memory, however, this is no longer a very important consideration.

We believe that given adequate machine resources and a well-engineered human interface (perhaps a two-dimensional syntax with interesting icons), there are many reasons to prefer a syntax-directed approach to editing. However, we know of no formal determination of tradeoffs between "normal" editors and structure/syntax-directed editors. We hope that controlled experiments in this area will result in the necessary data for an objective, informative evaluation of the utility of structure/syntax-directed editors.

6. CONCLUSION – PART II

6.1 Desiderata for Today's Editor

As in programming languages and most computer systems, the "desirability" of the syntax and semantics associated with an interactive editor is largely a matter of individual taste. Often, however, constraints imposed by old techniques and methodologies and acceptance of outmoded technologies (300-baud "glass teletypes," for example) force inferior modes of communication. Without being unduly constrained by the limitations of old-fashioned technology, we suggest our design criteria for an ideal interactive editor within the limits of today's modern technology. Thus, an ideal editor should have:

- A well-defined, consistent conceptual model, rather than a seemingly haphazard organization. The user must be familiar and comfortable with the "philosophy" behind the system.
- Documentation, both online in a help facility and offline in manuals, which explains the conceptual model as well as the details of the user interface and the functions of the system.
- A clear and concise user interface that is easy to learn and to use and that provides consistency across different targets such as text, pictures, and voice. Indeed, a good test of an efficient and pleasing interface is that authors will use the system to compose and revise manuscripts themselves. We believe that the author should not need to involve others (experts or "wizards" to advise, secretaries to make changes) in any phases of document creation or editing.
- An "infinite" undo/redo capability, enabling an author to experiment without concern of loss or damage to a document.
- Fast response time. No noticeable delay should exist for all but the most complex commands.
- Powerful facilities, with few restrictions and exceptions, to make possible everything that one can do to hardcopy with red pencil, ruler, scissors, and tape.
- Facilities that take advantage of computer capabilities to compensate for human limitations. Examples of existing facilities include global substitution of one pattern for another throughout a document, replication of a standard phrase or paragraph, and automatic renumbering of sections or references after (or while) a file is edited. Some of these facilities may duplicate human processes, others may be functions that are available only with the power of a computer.
- User access to shared information and files under controlled conditions (useful for a pool of researchers or documentors working in the same area, or for common access to dynamically updated management information).
- Ability to mix targets, such as text, graphics, programs, and forms, with ease.
- The ability to have multiple contexts on the same display surface, allowing the user to browse through and use a large assortment of familiar utilities and documents in an editing session. The editor should not force the user into a smaller, less powerful environment in which normally provided system functions are preempted. In fact, the editor should be part of a larger, integrated environment, allowing the user, in the middle of an editing session, to obtain information by looking through the file system, to use a desk calculator utility, or to retrieve an electronic mail message or a piece of data from a database system, with transparent return to the editing context.
- The ability to edit a close facsimile of the final composition, layout, and typography of the document without significant impact on computer response time.

6.2 Standardization

Several ANSI and ISO committees (ANSI X3J6 and X3V1, ISO/TC 97/SC 5/EGCLPT) are considering standardization of generic markup languages, text processing languages, text formatting, text editing, and text structures. We consider the agreement upon a standard editor as unrealistic at this time. What is needed first is a standard reference model for editing (for example, one based on the framework in Part I, Section 1). The acceptance of at least an interim reference model on which to base further research and development of editors will be helpful for a productive interchange of ideas in the editing field.

Another step towards standardization would be the definition of a set of operations, called a virtual editing protocol (VEP) [MAXE81, WILD82], that acts upon any medium, such as text, graphics, or voice. The VEP would not define *how* operations are performed on the medium, but simply what generic operations can be done on all media. The virtual editor for each medium accepts the medium-independent VEP and translates it to medium-dependent operations.

6.3 The Online Community

Just over ten years ago, in our first survey of the field [VAND71b], we concluded:

> Online composition and editing of programs, coupled with interactive debugging, has become an established, cost-effective use of computers. Similarly, minor text editing, such as the correction of typographical errors in memoranda, is cost-effective, since only teletypewriter consoles and minimal service from the CPU are required. In contrast, the imaginative use of computers for online composition and extensive manipulation of free-form text is still in the early stages of experimentation and user conversion. This is due partially to the high cost of CRT terminals that provide the human factors essential to general-purpose editing, partially to the high cost of system resources and implementation time for the sophisticated programs required, and partially to the long time required to wean users from traditional offline hardcopy processes. Hardware prices are coming down steadily, however, and as more users switch to online thinking, creating, and manipulating, the use of computers will become increasingly accepted (and judged cost-effective), hopefully to the same extent that numerical and data processing applications are already considered to be a legitimate use of the computer.

In the ensuing decade, this hope for the large-scale introduction of text processing was realized, as a result of rapidly decreasing hardware prices, the acceptance of word processing systems in business, the introduction of personal computers in hundreds of thousands of homes and offices, and the rapid growth of software for interactive editing. Regrettably, much text processing today is still done by transcription from hardcopy rather than by authors composing and editing online. This is due in part to generally poor interfaces (limited windows on alphanumeric screens and transcription-oriented software), and in part due to cultural resistance: typing, unfortunately, is not a universal skill and is still too often considered an inappropriate activity for executives and other high-level decision makers.

For the remainder of the decade and indeed the century we see an ever-increasing infiltration of editors. In one form or another they will become a fundamental tool of modern communication in all walks of life. They will be the key user interface to the workstations that will be used in the office, the classroom, the home, and any other place in which information is entered, edited and communicated. They will increasingly be used for do-it-yourself, high-quality document production with sophisticated typesetting effects, as well as for online browsing, studying, composing, and communicating.

As terminals and workstations become widely available and personal (i.e., become part of one's office or study furniture that, like a clock radio, are rarely, if ever, turned off) increasingly more of one's daily activities will be done via the computer, increasingly less via traditional paper and mechanical communication. There is, in fact, a kind of "critical mass" phenomenon, in which a knowledge worker switches from hardcopy to softcopy for most purposes, given fulltime availability of powerful local services and a high-performance information- and resource-sharing network. At that point, the Bush-Engelbart-Nelson visions of online communities will become commonplace, and editors will be the key interface to all manner of (softcopy) manuscript preparation and communication. We expect these editors to be suitable both for stream and structure editing, and for targets as diverse as text, pictures, and voice. The more intelligence the editor has of both the form and content of the manuscripts, the more powerful its capabilities will be.

Just as advances in technology in the past decade have provoked a marked change in editors, so will advances in intercomputer communication, speech synthesis and understanding, and character and handwriting recognition again change the way in which future editors are implemented. Imagine the following scenario:

Families, businesses, and individuals will receive a symbolic computer address much as one receives a telephone number. A user anywhere in the world with access to this address will be able to access the files at that network address as if they were on that user's own machine (subject to any confidentiality and security restrictions imposed). Interdocument links will easily be made by including this user address as the first search criterion in the link address. Multi-person collaborations will become economically and technically feasible, and will make distributed knowledge work an attractive alternative to physical travel. Tymshare's AUGMENT and Nelson's Xanadu* system are ongoing projects to bring these concepts and many other adventurous document organization ideas to the general public. NELS81 provides both an interesting history of the development of hypertext systems and a description of the Xanadu technical and organizational plans.

Each user will have a personal workstation with a high-resolution (several-hundred-points-per-linear-inch) bitmap display packaged in a flat, notebook-style package easily moved about a desk or carried in a briefcase [LRG76, KAY77, GRID82]. Interaction may be done in many ways. A wireless mouse or a touch-sensitive screen will allow for cursor movement. The cursor may be used not only for selection of entities from a menu, but also for drawing proofreader's symbols on a document or for entering text into the document. A symbol recognition program will understand the drawn symbols and perform the appropriate operation. If a symbol is inscrutable or ambiguous, the editor may notify the user using voice output. The user will have the choice of redrawing the symbol, or alternately, vocally inputting the commands (as well as, later, even natural-language text). While currently experimental and unportable, the use of eye-tracking schemes [BOLT81] may allow the editor to determine at what (large) area the user is looking, enabling it to correctly understand commands such as "delete *this* paragraph."

Before the turn of the century, the editing systems are likely to have taken the place of pen, paper, and typewriter – and not only for manuscript composition. For example, banks will have editors with preprinted "forms" that the user fills out using a keyboard or even natural handwriting. Documents will be interactive, compiled on demand especially for the requester. They will be further personalized with online annotation. Most importantly, schoolchildren will learn to both read and write with the editor and a nationwide library of online books.

In fact, much of the technology for the near-term editor of the 1980s is in place. Among the hardware are bitmapped personal workstations, pointing devices, precision laser printers, and digital phototypesetters; among the software are multi-window text and graphics editors, interactive formatters/typesetters, iconographic communications, and modeless environments. The key issue of the 1980s is the willingness of users and manufacturers to discard existing

---

* Xanadu is a registered trademark.

techniques for even better-researched, better-understood, and better-developed metaphors of user interaction.

In the broadest sense, most actions that people perform are editing operations of one form or another. In moving a car from here to there, making a shopping list, or playing chess, a person modifies or *edits* the state of some entity. In computing, most of the actions that people perform are editing operations as well. It is inevitable that the interactive editor will soon enter a new generation, a generation in which it forms the primary interface to the computer.

POSTSCRIPT

The majority of this document was edited using the *bb* editor running on a VAX 11/780 under Berkeley UNIX 4.1. Some parts of the document were occasionally edited using the Apollo editor, BBN's PEN editor, and Brown's CMS Editor. Besides these, the authors at one time or another have used ed, ex, vi, EMACS, SOS, the Cornell Program Synthesizer, FRESS, NLS, TECO, XEDIT, WordStar, Bravo, and Star.

Formatting was initially done using the TROFF package under UNIX. A revised version was translated to TEX by the use of keystroke macros in *bb* and through hand-translation for some parts. No interactive formatting was available; the authors had to rely on hardcopy printouts from a Varian electrostatic printer-plotter (approximately 5 pages/minute) to see the formatting that the TEX codes had produced. The text consists of approximately 100, single-spaced, 12-inch high pages. With around 50 drafts of the paper over more than two years, we have regrettably used just under one mile of paper to produce a final draft, excluding the reams of paper used in duplicating review copies.

Communication of machine-readable files and electronic mail was done through the *uucp* inter-UNIX telephone network and through the ARPANET.

ACKNOWLEDGMENTS

The authors would like to thank the numerous people who have contributed their time and thoughts to the production of this paper, especially Steve Derose, Doug Engelbart, Joan Haber, Phil Hutto, Barb Meier, Steve Reiss, Katy Roth, Dave Smith, Tim Teitelbaum, Jan Walker, and Nicole Yankelovich. We also thank the numerous researchers whose systems we have used as examples, and apologize for any misrepresentations that may appear. A special mention goes to Trina Avery, for her outstanding copy-editing and proofreading of multiple versions of the document, and to Steve Feiner, for his customary incisive comments and technical questions that resulted in more accurate explanations and descriptions. Rachel Rutherford's meticulous reading pointed out hundreds of places where we could clarify points for the reader; her delightful comments on the final draft were an important barometer of how well we were achieving our goals. Janet Incerpi answered our barrage of questions about and suffered our tirades over TEX. Mike Braca cheerfully produced photographs with virtually no notice. We gratefully acknowledge the reviewers, whose detailed critiques guided us towards a completely reorganized, clearer document. Finally, many thanks go to Adele Goldberg who provided us with patience and understanding beyond the call of duty, immediate turnaround despite our somewhat more sluggish speed, and most importantly, numerous critical and editorial comments that improved the paper.

CREDITS

Bravo, Smalltalk-80, and Star figures courtesy the Xerox Corporation. SOS figures © 1978, Digital Equipment Corporation. XEDIT figures © 1980, International Business Machines. WordStar figures © 1981, MicroPro, Inc. Etude figures courtesy MIT Laboratory for Computer Science.

7. REFERENCES

[Achu81] Achugbue, J.O.,"On the Line Breaking Problem in Text Formatting," in *Proc. ACM SIGPLAN/SIGOA Conference on Text Manipulation*, Portland, Oregon, June 1981, pp. 117–122.

[Albe79] Alberga, C.N., Brown, A.L., Leeman, G.B. Jr., Mikelsons, M., and Wegman, M.N.,"A Program Development Tool," Technical Report RC 7859, IBM Thomas J. Watson Research Center, Yorktown Heights, NY, September 1979.

[Alle81] Allen, T., Nix, R., and Perlis, A.,"PEN: A Hierarchical Document Editor," in *Proc. ACM SIGPLAN/SIGOA Conference on Text Manipulation*, Portland, Oregon, June 1981, pp. 74–81.

[Apol82] Apollo Computer Inc., *Apollo System User's Guide, Release 4.0*, Chelmsford, MA, April 1982.

[Arch81] Archer, J.,"The Design and Implementation of a Cooperative Program Development Environment," Ph.D. Thesis, Cornell University, Ithatca, NY, August 1981.

[Arno80] Arnold, C.R.C.,"Screen Updating and Cursor Movement Optimization: A Library Package," Technical Report, Department of Electrical Engineering and Computer Science, University of California, Berkeley, CA, September 1980.

[Bake80] Baker, R.,"Terminal Crunch," *The New York Times Magazine*, November 10, 1980.

[Bara81] Barach, D.R., Taenzer, D. H., and Wells, R.E.,"Design of the PEN Video Editor Display Module," in *Proc. ACM SIGPLAN/SIGOA Conference on Text Manipulation*, Portland, Oregon, June 1981, pp. 130–136.

[Baud78] Baudelaire, P.C.,"Draw," in *Alto User's Handbook*, Xerox Palo Alto Research Center, 3333 Coyote Hill Road, Palo Alto, CA, November 1978, pp. 97–128.

[Beac81] Beach, R.J., Beatty, J.C., Booth, K.S., and White, A.R.,"Documentation Graphics at the University of Waterloo," in *International Conference on Research Trends in Document Preparation Systems*, Lausanne, Switzerland, February 27-28, 1981, pp. 123–125.

[Bilo77] Bilofsky, W.,"The CRT Text Editor NED - Introduction and Reference Manual," R-2176-ARPA, Rand Corp., Santa Monica, CA, December 1977.

[BBN73] Bolt Beranek and Newman Inc., *TENEX Text Editor and Corrector Manual*, Cambridge, MA, October 1973.

[Bolt81] Bolt, R.A., "Gaze-Orchestrated Dynamic Windows," *Computer Graphics* 15, 3 (August 1981).

[Bork79] Bork, A., *Textual Taxonomy*, Educational Technology Center, Physics Department, University of California, Irvine, CA, October 4, 1979.

[Bork81] Borkin, S.A. and Prager, J.M.,"Some Issues in the Design of an Editor-Formatter for Structured Documents," Technical Report, IBM Cambridge Scientific Center, September 1981.

[Bowm81] Bowman, W., and Flegal, B.,"ToolBox: A Smalltalk Illustration System," *BYTE*, vol. 6, no. 8, August 1981, pp. 369–376.

[Brow81] Brown University Computer Center, *User's Guide to the Brown CMS Editor*, Brown University, Box 1885, Providence, RI, April 1981.

[Burk80]   Burkhart, H. and Nievergelt, J., "Structure-oriented Editors," Rep 38, Eidgenössische Technische Hochschule Zurich, Institute für Informatik, Zurich, Switzerland, May 1980.

[Burk81]   Burkhart, H. and Stelovsky, J., "Towards an Integration of Editors," in *International Conference on Research Trends in Document Preparation Systems*, Lausanne, Switzerland, February 27-28, 1981, pp. 9–11.

[Bush45]   Bush, V., "As We May Think," *The Atlantic Monthly*, vol. 176, no. 1, July 1945, pp. 101–108.

[Bush67]   Bush, V., "Memex Revisted," in *Science Is Not Enough*, Vannevar Bush, Ed., William Morrow and Co., 1967, pp. 75–101.

[Card76]   Card, S.K., Moran, P., and Newell, A., "The Manuscript Editing Task: A Routine Cognitive Skill," Report SSL-76-8, Xerox Palo Alto Research Center, 3333 Coyote Hill Road, Palo Alto, CA, December 1976.

[Card78a]   Card, S.K., "Studies in the Psychology of Computer Text Editing," Report SSL-78-1, Xerox Palo Alto Research Center, 3333 Coyote Hill Road, Palo Alto, CA, August, 1978.

[Card78b]   Card, S.K., English, W.K., and Burr, B.J., "Evaluation of Mouse, Rate-Controlled Isometric Joystick, Step Keys, and Text Keys for Text Selection on a CRT," *Ergonomics* **21** (1978), 601–613.

[Card79]   Card, S.K., Moran, P., and Newell, A., "The Keystroke-level Model for User Performance Time with Interactive Systems," Report SSL-79-1, Xerox Palo Alto Research Center, 3333 Coyote Hill Road, Palo Alto, CA, March 1979.

[Carm69]   Carmody, S., Gross, W., Nelson, T.H., Rice, D.E., and van Dam, A., "A Hypertext Editing System for the /360," in *Pertinent Concepts in Computer Graphics*, M. Faiman, J. Nievergelt, Ed., Illinois Press, March 1969, pp. 291–330.

[Cata79]   Catano, J., "Poetry and Computers: Experimenting with the Communal Text," *Computers and the Humanities* **13** (1979), 269–275.

[Cham81]   Chamberlin, D.D., King, J.C., Slutz, D.R., Todd, S.J.P., and Wade, B.W., "JANUS: An Interactive System for Document Composition," in *Proc. ACM SIGPLAN/SIGOA Conference on Text Manipulation*, Portland, Oregon, June 1981, pp. 82–91.

[Cher81]   Cherry, L., "Computer Aids for Writers," in *Proc. ACM SIGPLAN/SIGOA Conference on Text Manipulation*, Portland, Oregon, June 1981, pp. 61–67.

[Cole69]   Coleman, M., "Text Editing on a Graphic Display Device Using Hand-Drawn Proofreader's Symbols," in *Pertinent Concepts in Computer Graphics*, M. Faiman, J. Nievergelt, Ed., Illinois Press, March 1969, pp. 282–290.

[ComS67]   Com-Share, Inc., *QED Reference Manual*, Ann Arbor, MI, 1967.

[Coul76]   Coulouris, G.F., Durham, I., Hutchinson, J.R., Patel, M.H., Reeves, T., and Winderbank, D.G., "The Design and Implementation of an Interactive Document Editor," *Software - Practice and Experience* **6** (May 1976), 271–279.

[Cris65]   Crisman, P.A., ed., *The Compatible Time Sharing System: A Programmer's Guide*, 2ndedition, MIT Press, 1965.

[Deut67]   Deutsch, P. and Lampson, B., "An Online Editor," *Commun. ACM* **10**, 12 (December 1967), 793-799, 803.

[Digi78]   Digital Equipment Corporation, *VAX-11 Text Editing Reference Manual*, Maynard, MA, August 1978.

[Donz75]   Donzeau-Gouge, V., Huet, G., Kahn, G., Lang, B., and Levy, J.J.,"A Structure Oriented Program Editor: A first step towards computer assisted programming," Technical Report, IRIA-LABORIA, France, April 1975.

[Donz80]   Donzeau-Gouge, V., Huet, G., Kahn, G., and Lang, B.,"Programming Environments Based on Structured Editors: the MENTOR experience," Technical Report, INRIA, France, May 1980.

[Dzid78]   Dzida, W., Herda, S., and Itzfeldt, W.D., "User-Perceived Quality of Interactive Systems," *IEEE Trans. Software Engineering* **SE-4**, 4 (July 1978), 270–276.

[Elli80]   Ellis, C. and Nutt, G., "Office Information Systems and Computer Science," *Comput. Surveys* **12**, 1 (March 1980), 27–60.

[Embl78]   Embley, D.W., Lan, M.T., Leinbaugh, D.W., and Nagy, G., "A Procedure for Predicting Program Editor Performance from the User's Point of View," *International Journal of Man-Machine Studies* **10**, 6 (November 1978), 639–650.

[Embl81]   Embley, D.W. and Nagy, G., "Behavioral Aspects of Text Editors," *Comput. Surveys* **13**, 1 (March, 1981), 33–70.

[Enge63]   Engelbart, D.C.,"A Conceptual Framework for the Augmentation of Man's Intellect," in *Vistas in Information Handling*, P. Howerton, Ed., Spartan Books, Washington, DC, 1963, pp. 1–29.

[Enge68]   Engelbart, D.C. and English, W.K.,"A Research Center for Augmenting Human Intellect," in *Proc. FJCC*, vol. 33, no. 1, AFIPS Press, Montvale, NJ, Fall 1968, pp. 395–410.

[Enge73]   Engelbart, D.C., Watson, R., Norton, J.,"The Augmented Knowledge Workshop," in *Proc. NCC*, vol. 42, AFIPS Press, Montvale, NJ, June 4-8, 1973, pp. 9–21.

[Enge78]   Engelbart, D.C.,"Toward Integrated, Evolutionary Office Automation Systems," in *Proc. Joint Engineering Management Conference*, Denver, CO, October 16-18, 1978, pp. 63–68.

[Engl67]   English, W.K., Engelbart, D.C., and Berman, M.L., "Display-selection Techniques for Text Manipulation," *IEEE Trans. Hum. Factors. Electron.* **HFE-8**, 1 (March 1967), 5–15.

[Fajm73]   Fajman, R., "WYLBUR: An Interactive Text Editing and Remote Job Entry System," *Commun. ACM* **16**, 5 (May 1973), 314–322.

[Feil80]   Feiler, P.H. and Medina-Mora, R.,"An Incremental Programming Environment," Technical Report CMU-CS-80-126, Department of Computer Science, Carnegie-Mellon University, Pittsburgh, PA, April 1980.

[Fein81a]   Feiner, S., Nagy, S., and van Dam, A., "An Integrated System for Creating and Presenting Complex Computer-Based Documents.," *Computer Graphics* **15**, 3 (August 1981).

[Fein81b]   Feiner, S., Nagy, S., and van Dam, A., "Online Documents Combining Pictures and Text," *Proceedings of the International Conference on Research and Trends in Document Preparation Systems*, Lausanne, Switzerland (February 27-28, 1981).

[Fein82]   Feiner, S., Nagy, S., and van Dam, A., "An Experimental System for Creating and Presenting Interactive Graphical Documents," *Transactions on Graphics* 1, 1 (January 1982).

[Fins80]   Finseth, C.A., "A Theory and Practice of Text Editors," Technical Memo 165, MIT Laboratory for Computer Science, Cambridge, MA, June 1980.

[Fins82]   Finseth, C.A., "Managing Words: What Capabilities Should You Have with a Text Editor?," *BYTE*, vol. 7, no. 4, April, 1982, pp.242-282.

[Fole82]   Foley, J.D. and van Dam, A., *Fundamentals of Interactive Computer Graphics*, Addison-Wesley, Reading, MA, 1982.

[Fras79]   Fraser, C.W., "A Compact, Portable CRT-based Text Editor," *Software - Practice and Experience* 9, 2 (February 1979), 121-125.

[Fras80]   Fraser, C.W., "A Generalized Text Editor," *Commun. ACM* 23, 1 (March 1980), 27-60.

[Fras81]   Fraser, C.W., "Syntax-Directed Editing of General Data Structures," in *Proc. ACM SIGPLAN/SIGOA Conference on Text Manipulation*, Portland, Oregon, June 1981, pp. 17-21.

[Frei78]   Frei, H.P., Weller, D.L., and Williams, R., "A Graphics-Based Programming-Support System," *Computer Graphics* 12, 3 (August 1978), 43-49.

[Furu82]   Furuta, R., Scofield, J., Shaw, A., "Document Formatting Systems: Survey, Concepts, and Issues," *Comput. Surveys* 14, 3 (September 1982).

[Gold79]   Goldberg, A. and Robson, D., "A Metaphor for User Interface Design," in *Proc. Twelfth Hawaii International Conference on System Sciences*, vol. 6, no. 1, 1979, pp. 148-157.

[Gold80]   Goldberg, A. and Robson, D., "Sharing Problems: Personal Computers as Interpersonal Tools," Xerox Palo Alto Research Center, 3333 Coyote Hill Road, Palo Alto, CA. Keynote Address at the SIGSMALL/PC Symposium, Palo Alto, CA., September 1980.

[Gold82]   Goldberg, A., "The Smalltalk-80 System: A User Guide and Reference Manual," Xerox Palo Alto Research Center, 3333 Coyote Hill Road, Palo Alto, CA, March 1, 1982.

[Gold83]   Goldberg, A. and Robson, D., *Smalltalk-80: The Language and Its Implementation*, Addison-Wesley, Reading, MA, to appear 1983.

[Golc81]   Goldfarb, C.F., "A Generalized Approach to Document Markup," in *Proc. ACM SIGPLAN/SIGOA Conference on Text Manipulation*, Portland, Oregon, June 1981, pp. 68-73.

[Good81]   Good, M., "Etude and the Folklore of User Interface Design," in *Proc. ACM SIGPLAN/SIGOA Conference on Text Manipulation*, Portland, Oregon, June 1981, pp. 34-43.

[Good75]   Goodwin, N.C., "Cursor Positioning on an Electronic Display Using Lightpen, Lightgun or Keyboard for Three Basic Tasks," *Hum. Factors* 17, 3 (June 1975), 289-295.

[Gosl81]   Gosling, J., "A Redisplay Algorithm," in *Proc. ACM SIGPLAN/SIGOA Conference on Text Manipulation*, Portland, Oregon, June 1981, pp. 123-129.

[Gree80]   Greenberg, B.S.,"Multics EMACS: An Experiment in Computer Interaction," in *Fourth Annual Honeywell Softare Conference*, March 1980.

[GRID82]   GRiD Systems Corporation, *Compass Computer*, 2535 Garcia Avenue, Mountain View, CA, March 1982.

[GSPC79]   GSPC, "Status Report of the Graphic Standards Planning Committee," *Computer Graphics* **13**, 3 (August, 1979).

[Habe79]   Habermann, A.N., "An overview of the Gandalf Project," *Computer Science Research Review 1978-79*, Carnegie-Mellon University, Pittsburgh, PA (1979).

[Hamm81] Hammer, M., Ilson, R., Anderson, T., Gilbert, E.J., Good, M., Niamir, B., Rosenstein, L., and Schoichet, S.,"The Implementation of Etude, An Integrated and Interactive Document Production System," in *Proc. ACM SIGPLAN/SIGOA Conference on Text Manipulation*, Portland, Oregon, June 1981, pp. 137-146.

[Hans68]   Hansen, W.J.,"User Engineering Principles for Interactive Systems," in *Proc. FJCC*, vol. 39, AFIPS Press, Arlington, VA, Fall 1968, pp. 395-410.

[Hans71]   Hansen, W.J.,"Creation of Hierarchic Text with a Computer Display," Report ANL7818, Argonne National Laboratory, July, 1971.

[Haye81]   Hayes, P., Ball, E., and Reddy, R., "Breaking the Man-Machine Communication Barrier," *Computer* **14**, 3 (March 1981), 19-30.

[Haze80]   Hazel, P., "Development of the ZED Text Editor," *Software - Practice and Experience* **10**, 1 (January 1980), 57-76.

[Hero80]   Herot, C., Carling, R., Friedell, M., Kramlich, D., "A Prototype Spatial Data Management System," *Computer Graphics* **14**, 3 (July 1980).

[IBM67]   International Business Machines, *Magnetic Tape Selectric Typewriter*, New York, 1967.

[IBM69]   International Business Machines,"A Conversational, Context-Directed Editor," IBM Cambridge Scientific Center Report, Cambridge, MA, July 1969.

[IBM70]   International Business Machines, *System/360 Administrative Terminal System*, 1970.

[IBM80]   International Business Machines, *IBM Virtual Machine/System Product: System Product Editor User's Guide*, White Plains, NY, July 1980.

[Imag81]   Image Data Products, Ltd., *The Image Data Tablet*, 1-4 Portland Square, Bristol, England, 1981.

[Iron72]   Irons, E.T. and Djorup, F.M., "A CRT Editing System," *Commun. ACM* **15**, 1 (January 1972), 16-20.

[John75]   Johnson, S.,"YACC - Yet Another Compiler-Compiler," Bell Labs, Murray Hill, NJ, 1975.

[Jong82]   Jong, S.,"Designing a Text Editor? The User Comes First," *BYTE*, vol. 7, no. 4, April, 1982, pp. 284-300.

[Joy80a]   Joy, W. and Horton, M.,"Ex Reference Manual – Version 3.1," , Department of Electrical Engineering and Computer Science, University of California, Berkeley, CA, September 16, 1980.

[Joy80b]   Joy, W. and Horton, M.,"An Introduction to Display Editing with Vi," , Department of Electrical Engineering and Computer Science, University of California, Berkeley, CA, Setember 16, 1980.

[Joy81]   Joy, W. and Horton, M.,"TERMCAP," in *UNIX Programmers Manual, Seventh Edition, Berkeley Release 4.1*, June, 1981.

[Kay77]   Kay, A. and Goldberg, A., "Personal Dynamic Media," *Computer* **10**, 3 (March 1977), 31-43.

[Kell77]   Kelly, J.,"A Guide to NED: A New On-Line Computer Editor," R-2000-ARPA, Rand Corporation, Santa Monica, CA, July 1977.

[Kern75]   Kernighan, B.W. and Cherry, L.L., "A System for Typesetting Mathematics," *Commun. ACM* **18**, 3 (March 1975), 182–193.

[Kern78a]   Kernighan, B.W.,"A Tutorial Introduction to the UNIX editor," Bell Laboratories, Murray Hill, NJ, September 28,`1978.

[Kern78b]   Kernighan, B.W.,"Advanced Editing on UNIX," Bell Laboratories, Murray Hill, NJ, August 4, 1978.

[Kern78c]   Kernighan, B.W. and Ritchie, D.M., *The C Programming Language*, Prentice-Hall, Inc., Englewood Cliffs, NJ, 1978.

[Kern81]   Kernighan, B.W.,"PIC - A Language for Typesetting Graphics," in *Proc. ACM SIGPLAN/SIGOA Conference on Text Manipulation*, Portland, Oregon, June 1981, pp. 92–98.

[Kern82]   Kernighan, B.W. and Lesk, M.E., J. Nievergelt, G. Coray, J. Nicoud, A. Shaw, ed., *Document Preparation Systems*, North Holland, 1982.

[Knut79]   Knuth, D.E., *TEX and Metafont: New Directions in Typesetting*, Digital Press, Bedford, MA, December 1979.

[LRG76]   Learning Research Group,"Personal Dynamic Media," Technical Report SSL-76-1, Xerox Palo Alto Research Center, 3333 Coyote Hill Road, Palo Alto, CA, March 1976.

[Lamp78]   Lampson, B.W.,"Bravo Manual," in *Alto User's Handbook*, Xerox Palo Alto Research Center, 3333 Coyote Hill Road, Palo Alto, CA, November 1978, pp. 31–62.

[Lant79]   Lantz, K. and Rashid, R.,"Virtual Terminal Management in a Multiple Process Enviroment," in *Proc. 7th Symposium on Operating Systems Principles*, Pacific Grove, CA, December 10-12, 1979.

[Lant80]   Lantz, K.,"Uniform Interfaces for Distributed Systems," Computer Science Dept., University of Rochester, Rochester, NY, May 1980.

[Lede80]   Lederman, A.,"An Abstracted Bibliography on Programming Environments," Dept. of Electrical Engineering and Computer Science, MIT, Cambridge, MA, June 1980.

[Ledg80]   Ledgard, H., "The Natural Language of Interactive systems," *Commun. ACM* **23**, 10 (October 1980), 556–563.

[Lesk76]   Lesk, M.,"TBL - A Program to Format Tables," Technical Report 49, Bell Laboratories, Murray Hill, NJ, 1976.

[Lesk81]   Lesk, M.,"Another View," *Datamation*, vol. 27, no. 12, November, 1981, pp. 146.

[MacD80] MacDonald, N.H., Frase, L.T., and Keenan, S.A.,"Writer's Workbench: Computer Programs for Text Editing and Assessment," Bell Laboratories, Piscataway, NJ, 1980.

[MacL77] MacLeod, I.A., "Design and Implementation of a Display-oriented Text Editor," *Software - Practice and Experience* 7, 6 (November 1977), 771–778.

[Maxe81] Maxemchuck, N.F., and Wilder, H.A., "Virtual Editing: I. The Concept," *Proceedings of the International Conference on Research and Trends in Document Preparation Systems*, Lausanne, Switzerland (February 27-28, 1981).

[McCa67] McCarthy, J., Dow, B., Feldman, G., and Allen, J.,"THOR–A Display Based Timesharing System," in *Proc. SJCC*, vol. 30, AFIPS Press, Arlington, VA, Spring 1967, pp. 623–633.

[Medi81] Medina-Mora, R. and Notkin, D.S.,"ALOE Users' and Implementor's Guide," Technical Report, Department of Computer Science, Carnegie-Mellon University, Pittsburgh, PA, November, 1981.

[Meyr81] Meyrowitz, N. and Moser, M.,"BRUWIN: An Adaptable Design Strategy for Window Manager / Virtual Terminal Systems," in *Proc. 8th Symposium on Operating Systems Principles*, Pacific Grove, CA, December 1981.

[Micr81] MicroPro, *WordStar User's Guide*, MicroPro International Corp., 1299 Fourth Street, Suite 400, San Rafael, CA, 1981.

[Mike81] Mikelsons, M.,"Prettyprinting in an Interactive Programming Environment," in *Proc. ACM SIGPLAN/SIGOA Conference on Text Manipulation*, Portland, Oregon, June 1981, pp. 108–116.

[Mont82] Montgomery, E.B., "Bringing Manual Input Into the 20th Century: New Keyboard Concepts," *IEEE Computer* 15, 3 (March 1982), 11–18.

[Morr81] Morris, J.M. and Schwartz, M.D.,"The Design of a Language-Directed Editor for Block-Structured Languages," in *Proc. ACM SIGPLAN/SIGOA Conference on Text Manipulation*, Portland, Oregon, June 1981, pp. 28–33.

[Mukh80] Mukhopadhyay, A.,"A proposal for a hardware text processor," in *The Papers of the 5th Workshop on Computer Architecture for Non-Numeric Processing*, Pacific Grove, CA, March 11-14, 1980.

[Nass73] Nassi, I. and Shneiderman, B., "Flowchart Techniques for Structured Programming," *ACM SIGPLAN Notices* 8, 8 (August 1973).

[NBI81] NBI, Inc., *System 3000 Operator's Guide*, Boulder, CO, March 1981.

[Nels67] Nelson, T.H.,"Getting It Out of Our System," in *Information Retrieval: A Critical Review*, G. Schecter, Ed., Thompson Book Company, Washington, DC, 1967, pp. 191–210.

[Nels74] Nelson, T.H., *Computer Lib/Dream Machines*, Hugo's Book Service, Box 2622, Chicago, IL, 1974.

[Nels81] Nelson, T.H., *Literary Machines*, Box 128, Swarthmore, PA, 1981.

[Newm78] Newman, W.M.,"Markup," in *Alto User's Handbook*, Xerox Palo Alto Research Center, 3333 Coyote Hill Road, Palo Alto, CA, November 1978, pp. 85–96.

[Newm79] Newman, W., and Sproull, R., *Principles of Interactive Computer Graphics*, McGraw-Hill, New York, 1979.

[Norm81] Norman, D.A., "The Trouble with UNIX," *Datamation*, vol. 27, no. 12, November, 1981, pp. 139–150.

[Notk79] Notkin, D.S. and Habermann, A.N., "Software Development Environment Issues as Related to Ada," Carnegie-Mellon University, Pittsburgh, PA, 1979.

[Ossa76] Ossanna, J., "NROFF/TROFF User's Manual," Technical Report 54, Bell Laboratories, Murray Hill, NJ, 1976.

[Pete80] Peterson, J.L., "Computer Programs for Detecting and Correcting Spelling Errors," *Commun. ACM* **23**, 12 (December 1980).

[Prus79] Prusky, J.N., *FRESS Resource Manual*, Department of Computer Science, Brown University, Box 1910, Providence, RI, 1979.

[Reid80a] Reid, B.K., "A High-Level Approach to Computer Document Formatting," in *Proc. 7th Annual ACM Symposium on Programming Languages*, January 1980, pp. 24–30.

[Reid80b] Reid, B.K., "Scribe: A Document Specification Language and its Compiler," Ph.D. Thesis, Department of Computer Science, Carnegie-Mellon University, Pittsburgh, PA, 1980.

[Reid80c] Reid, B.K. and Walker, J.H., *Scribe User's Manual*, Third edition, Unilogic, Ltd, 605 Devonshire St., Pittsburgh, PA, 1980.

[Reid81] Reid, B.K. and Hanson, D., "An Annotated Bibliography of Background Material on Text Manipulation," in *Proc. ACM SIGPLAN/SIGOA Conference on Text Manipulation*, Portland, Oregon, June 1981, pp. 157–160.

[Reis81] Reiss, S.P., Lustig, M., and Medvene, L., *BB User's Guide*, Department of Computer Science, Brown University, Providence, RI, 1981.

[Rice71] Rice, D.E. and van Dam, A., "An Introduction to Information Structures and Paging Considerations for On-line Text Editing Systems," in *Advances in Information Systems Science*, J. Tou, Ed., Plenum Press, New York, NY, 1971, pp. 93–159.

[Robt79] Roberts, T., "Evaluation of Computer Text Editors," Report SSL-79-9, Xerox Palo Alto Research Center, 3333 Coyote Hill Road, Palo Alto, CA, November 1979.

[Robg79] Robertson, G., McCracken, D., and Newell, A., "The ZOG Approach to Man-Machine Communication," Technical Report CMU-CS-79-148, Department of Computer Science, Carnegie-Mellon University, Pittsburgh, PA, Ocbober 1979.

[Sand78] Sandewall, E., "Programming in an Interactive Environment: the LISP experience," *Comput. Surveys* **10**, 1 (March 1978), 35–71.

[SeyJ81] Seybold, J., "Xerox 'Star'," *The Seybold Report* **10**, 16 (April 27, 1981).

[SeyP78] Seybold, P.B., "Tymshare's Augment: Heralding a New Era," *The Seybold Report on Word Processing* **1**, 9 (October 1978), 1–16.

[SeyP79] Seybold, P.B., "The CPT 8000 and 6000 Word Processing Systems," *The Seybold Report on Word Processing* **2**, 1 (February 1979), 1–16.

[Smit82] Smith, D.C., Irby, C., Kimball, R., Verplank, B., and Harslem, E., "Designing the Star User Interface," *BYTE*, vol. 7, no. 4, April, 1982, pp.242-282.

[Snee78] Sneeringer, J., "User-interface Design for Text Editing: A Case Study," *Software - Practice and Experience* **8** (1978), 544–557.

[Stal80]   Stallman, R.M., "EMACS Manual for TWENEX Users," AI Memo 556, MIT Artificial Intelligence Laboratory, Cambridge, MA, August 17 1980.

[Stal81]   Stallman, R.M., "EMACS: The Extensible, Customizable Self-Documenting Display Editor," in *Proc. ACM SIGPLAN/SIGOA Conference on Text Manipulation*, Portland, Oregon, June 1981, pp. 147–156.

[Stro81]   Stromfors, O. and Jonesjo, L., "The Implementation and Experiences of a Structure-Oriented Text Editor," in *Proc. ACM SIGPLAN/SIGOA Conference on Text Manipulation*, Portland, Oregon, June 1981, pp. 22–27.

[Sufr81]   Sufrin, B., "Formal Specification of a Display Editor," Technical Monograph PRG-21, Programming Research Group, Oxford University Computing Laboratory, June 1981.

[Suth63]   Sutherland, I.E., "THOR–A Display Based Timesharing System," in *Proc. SJCC*, vol. 23, Spartan Books, Baltimore, MD, Spring 1963, pp. 329.

[Swin74]   Swinehart, D., "Copilot: A MUltiple Process Approach to Interactive Programming Systems," Ph.D. Thesis, Stanford Artificial Intelligence Laboratory Memo AIM-230, Stanford University, Palo Alto, CA, July 1974.

[Symb81]   Symbolics, Inc., *Symbolics Software*, 21150 Califa Street, Woodland Hills, CA, 1981.

[Teit81a] Teitelbaum, T., and Reps, T., "The Cornell Program Synthesizer: A Syntax-directed Programming Environment," *Commun. ACM* **24**, 9 (September 1981).

[Teit81b] Teitelbaum, T., Reps, T., and Horwitz, S., "The Why and Wherefore of the Cornell Program Synthesizer," in *Proc. ACM SIGPLAN/SIGOA Conference on Text Manipulation*, Portland, Oregon, June 1981, pp. 8–16.

[Teiw77]   Teitelman, W., "A Display Oriented Programmer's Assistant," Report CSL-77-3, Xerox Palo Alto Research Center, 3333 Coyote Hill Road, Palo Alto, CA, March 1977.

[Tesl79]   Tesler, L., "Home Text Editing: A Tutorial," Xerox Palo Alto Research Center, 3333 Coyote Hill Road, Palo Alto, CA, 1979.

[Tesl81]   Tesler, L., "The Smalltalk Environment," *BYTE*, vol. 6, no. 8, August 1981, pp. 90–147.

[Thim78]   Thimbleby, H., "Character Oriented Text Editing," Computer Systems Laboratory, Queen Mary College, London University, London, England, November 1978.

[Tilb76]   Tilbrook, D., "A Newspaper Page Layout System," M.Sc. Thesis, Department of Computer Science, University of Toronto, 1976.

[Toll65]   Tolliver, B., "TVEDIT," Stanford Time-Sharing Memo No. 32, Dept. of Computer Science, Stanford University, Palo Alto, CA, 1965.

[Turb81]   Turba, T.N., "Checking for Spelling and Typographical Errors in Computer-Based Text," in *Proc. ACM SIGPLAN/SIGOA Conference on Text Manipulation*, Portland, Oregon, June 1981, pp. 51–60.

[vanD71a] van Dam, A., *FRESS (File Retrieval and Editing SyStem)*, Text Systems, Barrington, RI, July 1971.

[vanD71b] van Dam, A. and Rice, D.E., "On-line Text Editing: A Survey," *Comput. Surveys* **3**, 3 (September 1971), 93–114.

[vanW81] van Wyk, C.J.,"A Graphics Typesetting Language," in *Proc. ACM SIGPLAN/-SIGOA Conference on Text Manipulation*, Portland, Oregon, June 1981, pp. 99–107.

[VIP69]   VIP Systems, *VIPcom User's Guide*, Washington, DC, 1968.

[Walk81a] Walker, J.H.,"Personal communication," , July 1981.

[Walk81b] Walker, J.H.,"The Document Editor: A Supporting Environment for Preparing Technical Documents," in *Proc. ACM SIGPLAN/SIGOA Conference on Text Manipulation*, Portland, Oregon, June 1981, pp. 44–49.

[Whit81] White, A.R.,"Pic – A C-based illustration language," , Dept. of Computer Science, University of Waterloo, Waterloo, Ontario, Canada, 1981.

[Wild82] Wilder, H.A., and Maxemchuck, N.F., "Virtual Editing: II. The Interface," *Proceedings of SIGOA Conference on Office Automation Systems*, Philadelphia, PA (June 1982).

[Wood81] Woods, S.R.,"Z - The 95 Percent Program Editor," in *Proc. ACM SIGPLAN/SIGOA Conference on Text Manipulation*, Portland, Oregon, June 1981, pp. 1–7.

[Xero82] Xerox Corporation, *8010 STAR Information System Reference Guide*, 1341 West Mockingbird Lane, Dallas, TX, 1982.

DOCUMENT PREPARATION SYSTEMS
J. Nievergelt, G. Coray, J.D. Nicoud, A.C. Shaw (eds.)
North-Holland Publishing Company, 1982

Document Formatting Systems: Survey, Concepts, and Issues*

Richard Furuta, Jeffrey Scofield, and Alan Shaw

Department of Computer Science
University of Washington
Seattle, Washington 98195

Abstract

Formatting systems are concerned with the physical layout of a document for hard and soft copy media. This paper characterizes the formatting problem and its relation to other aspects of document processing, describes and evaluates several representative and seminal systems, and discusses some issues and problems relevant to future systems. The emphasis is on topics related to the specification of document formats; these include the underlying document and processing models, functions performed by a formatter, the formatting language and user interface, variety of document objects, the integration of formatters with other document processing tasks, and implementation questions.

Categories and Subject Descriptors: H.4.1 **[Information Systems Applications]**: Office Automation—*word processing;* I.7.0 **[Text Processing]**: General; I.7.1 **[Text Processing]**: Text Editing; I.7.2 **[Text Processing]**: Document Preparation; K.2 **[Computing Milieux]**: History of Computing—*software*

General Terms: Algorithms, design, human factors, languages

Additional Key Words and Phrases: Formatters, document preparation, editors, text manipulation, word processing

---

*This work was supported in part by the National Science Foundation under grants numbered MCS-7826285 and MCS-8004111.

1. Introduction

Document preparation involves two principal tasks: defining the content and structure of a document, and generating the document from specifications of its appearance. The first part is typically called editing while the second, the subject of this paper, is known as formatting. More precisely, formatting is concerned with the layout of document objects on hardcopy media, usually paper, and various softcopy devices, such as video displays.

While text processing, especially editing, has long been a major application of computers, it is only recently that particular attention has been given to formatting systems. The reasons are a combination of technology and economics. Because of increasing costs of manually-produced documents, decreasing costs of computers and storage, and the availability of high-quality computer-controlled printers, typesetters, and display devices, it has become both feasible and worthwhile to use computer formatting systems for a wide variety of technical, business, and literary documents, such as letters, memos, invoices, brochures, reports, papers, and books. Many experimental and commercial systems have been developed for offices, laboratories, publishers, and, in fact, virtually any enterprise that uses written documents.

Our aims in this paper are to characterize the formatting problem and its relation to other aspects of document processing, to describe and evaluate several representative and seminal systems, and to discuss some issues and problems relevant to future systems. The emphasis is on topics related to the specification of document formats; these include the underlying document and processing models, functions performed by a formatter, the formatting language and user interface, variety of document objects, the integration of formatters with other document processing tasks, and implementation questions. A number of important related areas are not covered in any detail; for example, there is little discussion of font design, the characteristics of typical output devices, commercial typesetting programs, or particular applications such as newspaper production.

2. The Formatting Problem

2.1. Object Model of Documents

In order to discuss formatters and their functions and to distinguish formatting from other aspects of document preparation, it is convenient to use an object model of documents [Shaw 80], somewhat analogous to that in programming languages. The model introduces a uniform terminology which is useful when comparing and evaluating various systems and ideas, and it allows a more precise definition of terms such as editing, formatting, and viewing.

A *document* is an object composed of a hierarchy of more primitive objects. Each object is an *instance* of a *class* that defines the possible constituents and representations of the instances. Some typical document classes are business letters, papers for a particular journal or conference, theses, and programs in a given language; common lower-level classes include such document components as sections, paragraphs, headings, footnotes, tables, equations, matrices, figures, polygons, and character fonts.

Objects are further classified as either *abstract* or *concrete*. To each abstract object, there corresponds one or more concrete object(s). An abstract object is denoted by an identifier and the class to which the object belongs. One example could be the identifier "the" in the class *word*, indicating the abstract word object "the." Another abstract object may be the identifier "plus" in the class *operator*, denoting the operator for addition. We will sometimes use the term *logical* object as an informal synonym for abstract object.

Concrete objects are defined over one or more two-dimensional *page spaces* and represent the possible formatted images of abstract objects. For example, a particular paragraph of a document, an abstract paragraph object, may be represented concretely in many different ways depending on font, hyphenation conventions, line length, and other concrete variables.

Example: The extended abstract for this paper [Shaw, Furuta, and Scofield 80] has the logical objects (partially) defined and structured as follows:

⟨ExtendedAbstract⟩ = (⟨Header⟩, ⟨Body⟩, ⟨References⟩)
⟨Header⟩ = (⟨Title⟩, ⟨Authors⟩ ⟨Affiliation⟩)
⟨Body⟩ = ⟨Introduction⟩ ⟨Section 1⟩ ⟨Section 2⟩ ⟨Section 3⟩
⟨References⟩ = ...

.

.

.

⟨Title⟩ = "Document Formatting Systems: Survey, Concepts, and Issues"

⟨ExtendedAbstract⟩ is an instance of the class of extended abstracts specified for a particular conference; similarly, ⟨Section 2⟩ is an instance of the class of sections. The notation *(A, B, ..., F)* denotes the unordered *set* of objects *A, B, ..., F*; and *A B ... F* means the object *sequence A* followed by *B* followed by ... followed by *F*. Thus the ⟨Header⟩ consists of the object sequence ⟨Authors⟩ ⟨Affiliation⟩ and the object ⟨Title⟩. The two-dimensional representations of these abstract objects define the concrete objects of the document. In this case, one set of concrete objects appears in a technical report containing the extended abstract while another appears in a conference proceedings.

Document processing consists of executing various operations to define, manipulate, and view abstract and concrete objects. For this purpose, we distinguish between *ordered* and *unordered* objects. Many textual objects, such as paragraphs and words, are normally ordered, implying that we can speak of the first one, the last one, the next one, the preceding one, and so on. On the other hand, there are many objects that are more naturally treated as unordered for particular applications; these may include the elements of a figure or table, parts of mathematical equations, and pieces of unrelated text. In the ordered case, document processing involves working in order through a *sequence* of objects. By contrast, processing a set of unordered objects allows arbitrary selection of objects and even interleaving of the operations.

2.2. Editing, Formatting, and Viewing

Within the object model framework, we can consider the major operations of document processing as mappings from objects to objects. *Editing* operations are defined as mappings from either abstract to abstract objects or concrete to concrete objects. Conventional text editing operations map logical text objects to logical text objects; for example, a text insertion or deletion may be a mapping from strings to strings or from paragraphs to paragraphs. Also, editing operations on an already formatted document produce concrete objects from concrete objects. An example of this type of editing is interactively inserting or deleting text from an already formatted paragraph, thereby mapping concrete paragraphs to concrete paragraphs; interactive layout operations such as moving formatted text, tables, or figures around a document are also in this category.

Mappings from abstract objects to concrete objects are defined as *formatting* operations. Standard examples are transforming a logical character to its representation in a particular font, producing a two-dimensional word with possible hyphenation from a logical word, mapping a paragraph into a sequence of lines, and breaking an abstract document into pages. In the non-textual domain are mappings such as those that transform an abstract directed graph to a line drawing (for example, producing flow charts), operations for producing two-dimensional mathematical objects from a possibly one-dimensional (string) specification of an expression, and functions for constructing or laying out a table from a list of its entries.

An important part of an abstract to concrete object mapping is the page space domain of the concrete object. The constraints on page spaces are often the cause of complex interactions among formatting operations. For example, a paragraph-to-lines mapping may cause hyphenation in a word; and a paragraph-to-lines mapping may be modified because a section-to-pages operation leaves a first or last line of a paragraph on a page by itself (known as a *widow*). Different page spaces are possible, depending on the viewing medium and on the application. These include a sequence of identical rectangular areas or boxes, which correspond to conventional hardcopy pages; a rectangular box bounded, say, in the horizontal direction but unbounded vertically—typically viewed by vertical scrolling; and boxes that are unbounded in two or more directions, for example, full, half, or quarter planes that could be viewed by displaying small rectangular areas (*windows*) of the region.

It is useful to distinguish between formatting a document and displaying some part of the resulting concrete object. This leads to a definition of *viewing* mappings that produce hardcopy and softcopy images from concrete objects. An example is a concrete formatted object, defined in some normalized coordinate system, that may be viewed on a display screen and on paper by two different viewing mappings. A viewing mapping might also be the result of either windowing or scrolling some concrete object. The separation of formatting and viewing also permits a device-independent treatment of formatting. In the simplest case, our viewing mappings take the role of output device drivers.

To summarize, we have divided document processing operations into three types—editing, formatting, and viewing—depending on the domain and range objects:

1. Editing: Abstract Objects → Abstract Objects,
                Concrete Objects → Concrete Objects.

2. Formatting: Abstract Objects → Concrete Objects.

3. Viewing: Concrete Objects → Output Devices.

Many other kinds of operations, such as numbering figures, equations, or pages, correcting spelling, and indexing terms, deal directly with the objects resulting from either editing or formatting. Spelling correction and figure or equation numbering can be performed with abstract objects and, consequently, may be done before formatting; on the other hand, page numbering and automatic indexing require the concrete objects produced from formatting. One other important class of operations is *filing*. Like most computer systems, document-processing systems require facilities for storing and accessing files of abstract and concrete objects. While we acknowledge their importance, we will, for the most part, ignore filing issues. We also do not discuss those applications that involve mappings from concrete to abstract objects, such as on-line character or sketch recognition.

2.3. Formatting Functions

Our study of a variety of abstract and corresponding concrete objects used in text, tables, mathematical equations, and figures has led to the following set of general formatting functions. At a more detailed level than our mapping definition, these functions describe what formatters do.

1. Selection of Primitive Concrete Objects

The usual selection task is the retrieval of particular characters within a specified *font*, where a font is a set of concrete character objects having the same size and style. Also included are variably-sized symbols such as summation (Σ) for an arbitrary expression, special symbols such as a company logo, and atomic figure elements, for example, points, lines, curve segments, and filled-in-areas.

2. Horizontal and Vertical Placement of Objects

Examples of horizontal placement are operations to indent, tab, flush, and center. Vertical placement occurs when skipping lines, starting a new paragraph or section, and placing equations, figures, and tables on a page. Some objects, such as subscripts, require explicit placement in both vertical and horizontal directions.

3. Horizontal and Vertical Alignment

By object alignment, we mean the horizontal or vertical placement of an object relative to some other object(s). Operations such as aligning " = " signs in equations, centering a table entry, lining up decimal points, or "pretty-printing" a structured program fall into this category. Alignment can be viewed as a simple form of constraint satisfaction.

4. Break-up of Abstract Objects into "Paged" Concrete Objects

This function includes break-up of objects into lines and pages, with page header and footnote handling, and is the central task of most text formatters.

5. Scaling

Objects may be expanded or reduced in size to fit into an allocated space, to be compatible with other elements of the document, or to improve their appearance.

These five general functions are often used in a cooperative and ordered manner. For example, alignment involves placement which requires selection of primitive objects, and the first three functions are performed before page break-up. It would be desirable to define these functions more precisely, for example, for systems design purposes, but much research remains to be done before this can be accomplished. Some ideas on how this could be approached have been given by Guttag and Horning [Guttag and Horning 80] where algebraic axioms and predicate transformers are employed to specify the design of a display interface. For our purposes, the object model, formatting definition, and list of formatting functions provide a useful framework for surveying past systems and discussing formatting issues and concepts.

3. Representative and Seminal Systems

In this section, we discuss the history and evolution of document formatting by investigating some important original and representative systems.

It is useful to define some further terminology, shown in Figure 1, to describe the actions involved in document processing. We call the mental image of the document the *intended document*. This is mapped, by an editing step which we call *specifying*, into a physical form consisting of intermixed specifications and text called the *document description*. The document description identifies the abstract objects of the document. The formatting and viewing mappings, as defined in Section 2.2, produce the *formatter output* and the *visible concrete document*, respectively. The visible concrete document is produced on a particular hardcopy or softcopy display medium. Some formatters provide both a high-level specification language and also a lower-level language for defining the meanings of new specifications. This lower-level language is the *definition language*.

Although editing and formatting systems have been physically separated and developed individually for some time, formatting and viewing systems have typically been tied firmly together. In particular, in many systems the document description contains low-level information that requires a specific output device to be used to view the visible concrete object. There are two ways to separate formatting and viewing. The weaker of the two is provided by a *device-independent description* in which the same document description can be used (without change) to prepare formatter output for viewing on different devices. This is done either by rerunning the formatter after changing some parameters or by running different versions of the formatter. A stronger separation can be found in a few systems that also produce *device-independent formatter output*. Here, the same formatter output can be viewed to produce a visible concrete document on any of a number of different devices.

In selecting the systems to be discussed, we tried to pick those original early systems that were the first to present important ideas and which affected the designs of later systems; those systems that underwent a clear, clean, controlled, evolutionary development over the years; and those systems which to us represent present and future trends. When other factors were about the same, we preferred those systems with understandable, thorough descriptions in the open literature and those we have actually used. For purposes of presentation, these systems have been divided into two groups: the *pure formatters* and the *integrated editor/formatters*.

Pure formatters accept a document description, previously prepared by a separate editing system. The formatter output may then be viewed, producing the visible concrete document. (Others sometimes call the pure formatters "document compilers" or "batch-mode formatters.") Although many of the earliest formatters had an associated text editor, they are included in this

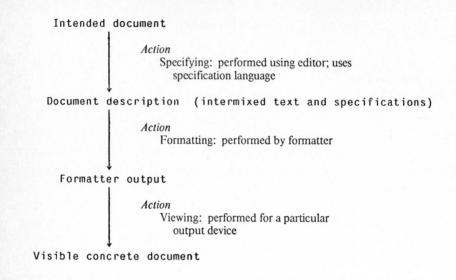

Figure 1: Steps in document processing.

class because the objects operated on by the editor and the formatter were logically disjoint. The editors in these early systems were provided out of necessity since general-purpose text editors were not common. This contrasts with the integrated nature of the editing and the formatting functions in the second group, the integrated editor/formatters.

Integrated editor/formatters allow one to view the visible concrete document while creating and modifying the document description, without leaving the editor/formatter. In other words, editing, formatting, and viewing are combined into one unified system. In the most general form, the user directly manipulates an exact representation of the visible concrete document. A form more closely resembling the pure formatters allows occasional viewing of the visible concrete document, and that only on request. (Integrated editor/formatters are also known as "document interpreters" or as "interactive formatters.")

We describe the pure formatters in the next three sections, followed by a discussion of the integrated editor/formatters in Section 3.4. We found a few systems which, while not meeting the criteria for inclusion in the preceding categories, address unique problems or present ambitious solutions. A brief discussion of four of these systems appears in Section 3.5. Finally, a number of research laboratories are attempting to provide systems which combine the best features of the pure formatters with the best features of the integrated editor/formatters. Three of these projects are mentioned in Section 3.6.

CALL FOR PAPERS

The aim of this conference is to survey the state of the art of computer aids for document preparation.

Papers are solicited on

- Picture editing

- Text processing

- Algorithms and software for document preparation and other related topics

Detailed abstracts should not exceed five pages; they *must* be sent before October 31, 1980 to the Program Chairman. Selected authors will be notified by November 30.

Duration of one presentation will be of either 25 or 45 minutes.

Figure 2: A sample document.

Document descriptions specifying this document will be presented in later figures.

3.1. The First Generation Formatters

The first widely known pure formatters appeared in the 1960's. The available devices were quite limited: the output device was, at best, a simple typewriter-like printer and the input was, at worst, from punched cards. The formatting functions provided were at a quite low, machine-language-like, level of action. Most objects were related to the lines and pages of the document (the *format* of the document). Only a few objects associated with the document's logical *content* were supported: words and sometimes sentences and paragraphs. The formatting languages were fixed and non-extensible. The appearance of the formatting commands seemed quite ad hoc. For example, it is not always clear which commands took parameters or how many parameters were expected. However, defaults were provided for most unspecified parameters. Additionally, it was not possible to structure the document, for example, by applying scoping rules to definitions and collecting related sequences of commands into single units.

The document descriptions for these early systems consist of formatting commands and layout specifications intermixed with the text (i.e., the data). This form continues to be reflected in recent pure formatters. Two different styles emerge for distinguishing commands from text. The first is to differentiate distinct command lines and data lines by a particular character in column one of the command lines; the period, as popularized by the RUNOFF system, seems especially pervasive. The second style, used in the FORMAT system, is to precede the command by a reserved *escape* character. The end of the command is marked either by some delimiting character or, if the commands are of a uniform length, after the appropriate number of characters have been encountered. The early formatters also introduced the use of reserved characters to signal actions of a limited scope; for example, "¢" in FORMAT caused the subsequent character to be capitalized.

3.1.1. RUNOFF

RUNOFF, an early, influential formatter, appeared in 1964 on the Compatible Time Sharing System (CTSS) at MIT [Saltzer 65]. With its separate companion editor, TYPSET, RUNOFF accepted a document description prepared on an upper/lower-case typewriter-like device with limited capabilities; it produced formatter output for viewing on the same device. This early version of RUNOFF had only eighteen primitive, low-level operations, all oriented to formatting the visible concrete document page. This orientation is especially apparent from a list of the available objects and the manipulations which could be performed: individual lines (center, break, undent, literal), collections of lines (set line length, initiate and terminate filling and justification, indent blocks of lines), arrangement of lines in vertical space (single space, double space, leave blank vertical space), pages (headers, paper length, begin new page, print page numbers), and files (append—that is, switch to the specified file for the rest of the input). All operations dealt with the physical format of the document; none dealt with the logical content of the document.

The appearance of the input language is illustrated by the document description shown in Figure 3; the visible concrete document to be produced is in Figure 2. Input lines are in one of two modes, command or text. It is not possible to change the meaning of special characters. In particular, commands cannot be signalled by any character other than the period. It is also not possible to modify the actions of particular commands (e.g., to turn off automatic breaking of lines). A command parameter, when present, is an integer or string literal; no more general expressions are provided.

Despite its inflexibility, cumbersome nature, limited functionality, and commands oriented to the output page, the early RUNOFF is an important system historically. It brought text formatting to the attention of many people. Elements of its design, particularly the two-mode form of input with separate text and command lines, have been adopted by many subsequent systems. RUNOFF has continued to develop over the years, increasing both in functionality and also in the range of objects provided.

```
.center
CALL FOR PAPERS
.space 2
The aim of this conference is to survey the state of the art of
computer aids for document preparation.
.nojust
.space 1
Papers are solicited on
.space 1
.indent 10
.undent 2
- Picture editing
.space 1
.undent 2
- Text processing
.space 1
.undent 2
- Algorithms and software for document preparation and other
related topics.
.indent 0
.space 1
.adjust
Detailed abstracts should not exceed five pages; they must be
sent before October 31, 1980 to the Program Chairman.  Selected
authors will be notified by November 30.
.space 1
Duration of one presentation will be of either 25 or 45 minutes.
```

Figure 3: Document description for RUNOFF to produce
the document of Figure 2.

    Command lines begin with a period ("."). The other lines are text lines. Since there was no significant blank character in RUNOFF (unpaddable space character), ".nojust" is invoked before the itemized listing to prevent extra spaces from being inserted into the lines. Filling of lines continues. ".adjust" restores justification. ".indent" resets the left margin, ".undent" decreases the ".indent" for the one line following. The underlined word in the next to last paragraph would have to be produced by the editor (TYPSET) before running RUNOFF since RUNOFF did not have facilities for underlining.

3.1.2. FORMAT

    FORMAT was developed for use on the IBM S/360 computer. The first published descriptions appeared in the late 1960's [Berns 68, Berns 69, Ehrman and Berns 71]. As with RUNOFF, a text editor was provided. Although physically in the same program as FORMAT, the editing functions were, again, logically distinct. FORMAT ran in a batch-processing environment. The document description was given entirely in upper case on punched cards; characters not explicitly capitalized were automatically converted into lower case. The visible concrete document was viewed on a line printer with upper- and lower-case letters.

Again, as with RUNOFF, many commands manipulate concrete page-oriented physical objects: groups of lines (filling, justification, defining length) and pages (breakup, numbering, defining height, multiple columnation, specifying headers and footers). Others, however, address more logical, content-oriented, objects: words (producing alphabetical listing of words used), phrases (underlining, centering, capitalizing, horizontal spacing between sentences), and paragraphs (indenting, placing blank lines between paragraphs, eliminating widows). Unlike the treatment of characters in RUNOFF, FORMAT's operations may apply to individual characters (specifying case, overprinting). Horizontal spacing commands (tabbing) as well as vertical spacing commands are also provided.

Figure 4 presents the document of Figure 2 specified for processing by FORMAT. Three types of commands are present. The *character-level commands* are reserved characters that appear in the text but have special meanings. *Phrase-level commands* are single letters that may be grouped together. A group of phrase-level commands is preceded by the escape character ")" and terminated by a blank. Some phrase-level commands specify a particular action (e.g., terminating the current line), and others act as toggles, (i.e., the first use starts an action, the next terminates it). The third type of command, the *paragraph-level commands*, do not cause immediate formatting actions but establish values for the general attributes of the document, for example, the left margin position, the page length, or the meaning associated with special characters.

No macro facility is provided and it is not possible to modify the actions of particular commands. It is possible to redefine the reserved characters that invoke various character-level commands. Arguments, when present, are literals. No expressions or variables are allowed.

The treatment of the document description as one long string of characters makes direct correction of the description extraordinarily difficult. For example, ending a word in column 80 of a card requires leaving column 1 of the next card blank. Therefore, one must use the associated editor to effect any changes. Further, the document description is difficult to read as it reflects so little of the structure of the document. Some rudimentary features are provided to help handle some of the more routine writing tasks, in particular, the paragraph-level command "DICTIONARY" which produces an alphabetized list of the words used in the document. In this paper, features of this kind are collectively known as *writer's workbench* features. (The term "writer's workbench," was inspired by E. Ivie's "Programmer's Workbench" [Ivie 77, Reid 80a, Cherry 81].)

```
)V
INDENTATION OF COLUMNS ON LEFT AND RIGHT IS (0,0),(5,0)
PARAGRAPH INDENT IS 0 PRINT POSITIONS
SEPARATION LINES BETWEEN PARAGRAPHS ARE 1
TABS ARE SET AT RELATIVE COLUMN POSITIONS 5
NONTRIVIAL BLANK IS REPRESENTED BY SPECIAL CHARACTER 44 (#)
GO
)M¢ CALL FOR PAPERS )M¢LLP ¢THE AIM OF THIS CONFERENCE IS TO SURVEY THE STATE OF
 THE ART OF COMPUTER AIDS FOR DOCUMENT PREPARATION. )P ¢PAPERS ARE SOLICITED ON
)LLH2W1 ##- )T ¢PICTURE EDITING )HLLH2W1 ##- )T ¢TEXT PROCESSING )HLLH2W2 ##- )T
 ¢ALGORITHMS AND SOFTWARE FOR DOCUMENT PREPARATION AND OTHER RELATED TOPICS. )HP
 ¢DETAILED ABSTRACTS SHOULD NOT EXCEED FIVE PAGES; THEY )U MUST )U BE SENT BEFOR
E ¢OCTOBER 31, 1980 TO THE ¢PROGRAM ¢CHAIRMAN. ¢SELECTED AUTHORS WILL BE NOTIFIE
D BY ¢NOVEMBER 30. )P ¢DURATION OF ONE PRESENTATION WILL BE OF EITHER 25 OR 45 M
INUTES.
```

Figure 4: Document description for FORMAT to produce
the document of Figure 2.

The lines following the ")V" until the line containing "GO" are paragraph-level commands, defining global attributes which hold until they are reset. Each symbol within the text following the escape symbol ")" and preceding the next blank is a phrase-level command which has a more limited scope of action. Some, such as ")P", the begin paragraph command, and ")L", the terminate current line command, have an immediate effect. Others, such as ")M", center phrase, and ")¢", capitalize phrase, serve as toggles. The first appearance turns the action on, the next turns the action back off. Character-level commands, represented by special symbols ("¢", capitalize next character, and "#", significant blank, in this document) affect the next character only. Notice that ¢ is both a phrase-level and a character-level command. Input is expected to come from cards. Characters are converted to lower case unless a "capitalize" command is in effect. The end of a line has no special significance within the input.

Clearly this is an early system, inflexible and low-level in nature by today's standards; for example to produce ten blank lines, one must enter ")LLLLLLLLLLLL". The style of input has been designed to use the entire punched card and not for readability or ease of entry.

But again, it incorporates design features which show up quite regularly in later systems. Most visible is the embedding of commands within the text and the use of an escape character to signal the switch from the text to the command mode. The use of reserved characters or strings to initiate certain, fairly short-lived, actions is common in later systems. Also significant is the provision of commands which manipulate logical objects (FORMAT's *paragraph* command), and commands which provide writer's workbench features. Both of these ideas are developed substantially by later pure formatters.

3.2. The First Structured Formatters

The late 1960's and early 1970's found the development of a new generation of formatters (the *first structured formatters*) based on lessons learned from using the early, first generation ones. Superficially, the document description still looked the same; both of the systems we discuss in this section are certainly RUNOFF descendants. However, the functions performed increased both in number and in sophistication. Ideas were incorporated from other areas of computer science. Macros provided a way to collect commonly used sequences of commands, to define new commands, and to reflect the logical structure of the document in the input. Conditional control statements, general arithmetic expressions, string and integer variables, and block structuring were borrowed from programming languages, providing structure in the input representation of the document. Writer's workbench features were added to make the formatters easier to use for the writer of a document: sections were automatically numbered, tables of contents and indices were created during formatting of the document, footnotes were properly numbered and placed, and so forth. Kaiman [Kaiman 68] proposed an early system which anticipated many of these developments.

It is in these first structured formatters that we see the idea that document formatting is more than just taking a sequence of words and forming them into lines which are then moved around on a printed page. Instead, the document consists of logical objects (sentences, paragraphs, sections) and the purpose of the formatter is to allow the manipulation of these objects.

Low-level primitives were still found intermixed with this higher-level view of documents. While higher-level commands could be created from the lower levels by using the macro definition facility, the lower-level primitives remained visible to the user. The inability to hide lower-level primitives is still present in current formatters.

Another significant difference between the first generation formatters and the first structured formatters was the increasing sophistication of the document processing environment and of the available output devices. Providing a means for creating text input was no longer considered a problem which needed to be solved by the formatter. Instead, a general purpose text editor was assumed to exist to take over this function. However, the formatting package still included the facilities for handling the different output devices. Thus although editing had been separated from formatting, viewing and formatting were still contained in the same system package.

It is interesting to compare the first structured formatters with the commercial systems produced for the VideoComp phototypesetter, originating with PAGE-1 [Pierson 72] in the middle 1960's. These commercial systems were derived from M. Barnett's earlier work at MIT [Barnett 65]. Like the first structured formatters, PAGE-1 borrowed many ideas from programming languages. Further, both PAGE-1 and the first structured formatters provided more sophisticated features for mapping objects into page spaces. However, applying similar ideas in different environments produced substantially different systems. PAGE-1 was intended for use in commercial typesetting and emphasized the definition of the concrete objects needed to control the typesetter, rather than the abstract objects useful in document specification.

3.2.1. PUB

PUB was developed at the Stanford Artificial Intelligence Laboratory, beginning in 1971, for use on the PDP-10 computer [Tesler 72]. Its designers called it a "document compiler," illustrating the parallel between translating a document description into formatter output and compiling programming language statements into an executable form. Initially, the output could be viewed only on a standard video or hardcopy terminal or on a line printer. Many other viewing devices were subsequently added.

PUB's commands manipulate the same kinds of low-level objects as did FORMAT: lines, pages, words, phrases, sentences, and paragraphs. Several higher-level objects are also provided: columns (multiple columns of text on a page), footnotes, and sections and subsections. Sections and subsections are automatically numbered and contain a heading that can also be used to generate a table of contents. Individual characters or groups of characters can be overprinted to form new characters. The "REQUIRE" statement can be used to cause part of the input to be taken from another file.

PUB's designers made an attempt to classify the constituent parts of some of the objects. Paragraphs are defined to consist of three parts: the "crown," the "vest," and the "hem." The crown is the first line of the paragraph, and the vest is the remainder. The hem is the last line of the vest.

A page in PUB is made up of *areas*. Areas are of two types: those which continue across subsequent pages (type *text*) and those which exist on only one page, truncating their contents when they fill up (type *title*). An area must be given a name and may be positioned arbitrarily on the page. However, at least one of the areas on each page must be named "text." By default, a page contains three areas: two of type *title*, named "heading" and "footing," and one of type *text* named "text." The last line of a text area is used only to eliminate widows, otherwise it is left blank.

The formatting language is similar to RUNOFF in appearance; Figure 5 provides an example specification. Some symbols and sequences of symbols have special meaning within text lines, but most actions can be redefined to be associated with a different control character.

A macro facility is provided which allows grouping of commands, control characters, and text. Macros can have arguments and may be declared to be recursive.

A number of Algol-like features are provided in PUB, most adopted from the SAIL

```
.TURN ON "↓", "_", "#"
.SINGLE SPACE
.INDENT 0
.PREFACE 1
.ONCE CENTER
CALL FOR PAPERS

The aim of this conference is to survey the state of the art of
computer aids for document preparation.

Papers are solicited on
.SKIP 1
.BEGIN INDENT 3, 5, 5 ; PREFACE 1 ;

-#Picture editing

-#Text processing

-#Algorithms and software for document preparation and other
related topics
.END
.SKIP 1

Detailed abstracts should not exceed five pages; they
↓_must_↓ be sent before October 31, 1980 to the Program
Chairman.  Selected authors will be notified by November 30.

Duration of one presentation will be of either 25 or 45 minutes.
```

Figure 5: Document description for PUB to produce
the document of Figure 2.

PUB uses Stanford's extended version of the ASCII character set. Command lines start with a period ("."). Text lines do not. The period marks a command line, not the beginning of a command. Therefore, multiple commands can be placed on a single line, separated by semicolons if necessary to prevent ambiguity, or a single command could span several command lines. Commands could also be included in the text if surrounded by "{" and "}". Each paragraph starts with a blank line which causes a paragraph break (technically, the paragraph break also ends the preceding paragraph). "ONCE" is a special scoping command which applied to any command means the scope of the command is the following paragraph. Thus in this example, "ONCE CENTER" means that the next input line should be centered. This is a specialized scoping rule. More generally, definitions made following a "BEGIN" are in effect until the matching "END". The "#" represents a significant blank, the "↓_" begins underlining, the "_↓" ends it.

programming language [VanLehn 73]. Most notable is that of block structuring. Portions of the manuscript may be grouped into *blocks*, bracketed by "BEGIN" and "END" statements. Document parameters set by declarations within a block revert to their original values at the termination of the block. Similarly, macros and variables defined within a block hold only for the duration of the block. Another kind of grouping, the *clump*, also is provided. Clumps are bracketed by "START" and "END" statements. The main difference between a block and a clump is that declarations made in a clump continue to hold after the clump is exited. Thus, clumps are used in defining compound statements which can change the global environment.

Variables may be defined and used in other commands. Constants may be string, decimal, or octal. A number of predefined variables provide information about the document being produced. For example, CHAR denotes the number of characters printed so far on the current line; LMARG denotes the current left margin, the value of which can be changed through assignment; and DATE denotes the present date. A complete set of arithmetic and logical operations are available to allow expressions to be formed from variables and constants. Special purpose operators, such as the unary "↑", which capitalizes its string operand, are also defined. An if...then...else statement allows conditional compilation of parts of the manuscript.

Certain identifiers can be declared to be *counters*. The value associated with a counter can be incremented and printed in any of a number of ordinal number systems. Use of counters makes it possible to refer to section numbers and page numbers symbolically within the text. PUB replaces the symbolic name with the actual section number or page number.

A special form of macro, called a *response*, is triggered by specified character sequences in the text, by changes to particular counters, or by the filling up of an indicated area. The response can be used to print page headings, define character sequences to mark the beginning of paragraphs, and to provide many other useful functions.

A document can be divided into arbitrarily named *portions* which are then processed sequentially. Portions are used to collect the information needed to generate, for example, a table of contents or a set of end notes. The "SEND" command is used to send text and commands to a portion. When processing reaches a portion, the portion issues the "RECEIVE" command to retrieve the collected information which is then processed. Since the "RECEIVE" command will optionally sort the collected information using provided sort keys, portions may also be used to implement indexes. A special portion called "FOOT" is defined by the system. Footnote text is sent to FOOT for placement at the bottom of the page.

The PUB language is perhaps as much a programming language as it is a document formatting language. Certainly the document formatting features are the ones most commonly used. The programming language constructs allow implementation of many additional features. However, the implementation of extensions through macros in PUB, as well as in later systems, means that extensions to the formatting language add to the available set of commands instead of replacing lower-level commands with higher-level commands. Consequently, lower-level commands may interact with higher-level commands in unexpected ways.

One significant contribution by PUB is the incorporation of block structuring. The document specification can more directly represent the relationships between abstract objects through the use of sequential and nested blocks. Additionally, the inclusion of programming language constructs adds to the ability to extend the formatting language. The extensive group of writer's workbench tools which have been developed using PUB's powerful set of constructs is another significant contribution.

3.2.2. NROFF

NROFF is the UNIX operating system's formatter, intended to produce documents on various typewriter-like terminals [Ossanna 74]. This formatter was developed at Bell Laboratories in the early to mid-1970's on the PDP-11, and was derived from the earlier ROFF [Thompson and Ritchie 75] which itself was derived from RUNOFF.

In this section, we will discuss only "bare NROFF." The many macro packages, preprocessors, and postprocessors that have been developed for use with NROFF and the closely related TROFF (for phototypesetters) will be discussed in the next section.

The objects supported by NROFF commands are basically the same as those supported by PUB: lines, pages, words, phrases, sentences, and paragraphs. Overprinting of characters can be used to form new characters.

Programming language-like features have been provided but are not as general as those in PUB. For example, NROFF provides *environments* which are similar to PUB's blocks in that they allow the collection of certain document parameters. It is possible to switch to a new environment in a push-down fashion and later to restore the previous environment. However, it is only possible to define three environments (numbered 0 through 2) and environments can only be pushed down to a maximum depth of ten. Additionally, only certain attributes of the documents are actually local to the environment; many attributes are global and not affected by environment switching. Environments are also not nested: undefined local attributes are given a default value, not the value of the previously entered environment. Therefore, the concept of environment switching is quite different from PUB's block structuring and less powerful as well. The same idea is applied to input files. Input can be obtained from multiple files which can be pushed down upon each other to a maximum depth of five.

NROFF's substitutes for variables are called "number registers" and "strings." The values in number registers and strings can be displayed in the text, modified, used in expressions (if numeric), or invoked as commands (if strings). Predefined numeric registers provide system information which can be included in the text (e.g., the current page number and the current date).

Macros can be defined and can be recursive. Up to nine parameters can be provided on macro invocation. Conditional control statements allow selective inclusion of input text lines. Built-in condition names allow testing for such cases as even or odd page number.

It is as interesting to notice what has not been explicitly provided in NROFF as it is to notice what has been provided. Not defined are facilities for handling page headings, page footings, multiple columns on a page, or footnotes. Instead, there are more general mechanisms called *traps* and *diversions*, which, when combined with macros, can be used to implement these facilities. Traps cause the invocation of a macro at a given spot on the output page and therefore can be used to generate page headings and page footings. Diversions cause formatted text to be diverted into a macro definition which can be invoked later as a command, causing the processed contents to be treated as input at that point. Essentially, diversion provides a mechanism for defining macros containing formatted text as the body of the macro. Diversion combined with traps can be used to implement footnotes. Adding in page positioning commands allows implementations of multiple columns on a page.

The formatting language itself consists of separate commands and text. Two groups of commands are provided. The first appears on separate lines and is distinguished from text by either a "." or a "'" at the beginning of the line. If a "'" is used, a command which would normally terminate a text line will not perform the termination. This form resembles RUNOFF quite closely in appearance; details may be seen in the example in Figure 6. The second group of commands are flagged within a text line with the escape character "\". This group provides the same kinds of functions as do the special characters used in PUB and FORMAT. User-defined commands of the first form are written as macros, possibly with parameters. User-defined macros or strings can redefine NROFF commands, previously defined macros, or previously defined strings by reusing the name. User defined commands of the second form are stored as strings and cannot have parameters.

Bare NROFF is an extremely low-level and difficult language to use. Parts of the language seem unintended for human use. In fact, this is probably the case; many parts are used primarily by the formatter's preprocessors.

There is no denying the immense popularity of the UNIX document-processing system. As will become clear in the next section, this popularity is largely due to the system's ability to evolve, providing facilities to meet changing needs and becoming more powerful and convenient to use. NROFF and TROFF are the basis for this ability to adapt. Their flexibility allows the implementation of many much more usable document-processing programs.

```
.ll 70
.ce 1
CALL FOR PAPERS
.sp 1
The aim of this conference is to survey the state of the art of
computer aids for document preparation.
.sp 1
Papers are solicited on
.sp 1
.in +5
.ti -2
-\ Picture editing
.sp 1
.ti -2
-\ Text processing
.sp 1
.ti -2
-\ Algorithms and software for document preparation and other
related topics.
.in
.sp 1
Detailed abstracts should not exceed five pages; they
.ul 1
must
be sent before October 31, 1980 to the Program Chairman.
Selected authors will be notified by November 30.
.sp 1
Duration of one presentation will be of either 25 or 45
minutes.
```

Figure 6: Document description for NROFF to produce
the document of Figure 2.

    Command lines begin with ".", the remaining lines are text lines. The escape character "\" is used to give the following character special meaning. "\ ", used here, is an unpaddable space character (significant blank). ".in +5" increases the current left margin by 5 characters, ".in" restores it to its previous value.

    With the exception of the "\ " sequence, this simple example could also be processed successfully by ROFF, NROFF's predecessor. Other mechanisms existed in ROFF to provide unpaddable spaces.

3.3. Structured Formatters With Many Objects

In this section, we discuss three of the most interesting and influential pure formatting systems in current use: Scribe, TEX, and that provided by the modern UNIX system. We call these systems "structured formatters with many objects" in recognition of the increased sophistication and flexibility of the systems, particularly with respect to definition of new logical objects within the document.

Each of these systems has generated much interest and discussion. Efforts are being made to prepare computer-system-independent versions of each: two separate companies have formed to market different variants of Scribe; the American Mathematical Society is preparing a portable Pascal implementation of TEX; and the entire UNIX operating system, not just the formatters, has been converted to run on several different computers.

The functionality of these systems has increased substantially from that of the earlier pure formatters. TEX and the UNIX formatting system can include complicated mathematical equations in their documents. Table specification in UNIX is particularly easy. Objects can be integrated, especially in the UNIX system, which allows inclusion of mathematical expressions in tables and, in a recent addition, inclusion in text of line drawings which can, in turn, contain text. Each of these systems can produce output for a variety of devices; Scribe provides device-independent description, TEX produces device-independent formatter output.

The philosophies behind the user interfaces of these systems differ greatly. The separation between TEX and Scribe is greatest, with the UNIX formatting system falling in between the two. The TEX user is viewed as being an author who wants to position objects exactingly on the printed page, producing a document with the finest possible appearance. Consequently, its emphasis is on the power and flexibility of the formatting language. It may be expected that TEX will become easier to use as new macro packages and preprocessors are developed. The Scribe user is viewed as an author who is more interested in easily specifying the abstract objects within his document, leaving the details of the appearance of objects to an expert who establishes definitions mapping the author's objects to the printed page. The emphasis is on simplicity in the input language and provision of writer's workbench tools.

Each system includes some interesting organizational and implementation details. TEX presents formatting as an optimization problem. Here, the purpose of line filling is not to fit text as densely as possible into an area, but to reduce undesirable effects such as excessive hyphenation and widows. Scribe makes an attempt to separate the content of the document from the formatting actions by using a mostly declarative language. Scribe also allows easy definitions of new environments through partial modification of existing environments. All definitions and global declarations must precede any text. Changes to the standard environments are therefore easy to detect during later modification of the document. The UNIX system is organized as a set of small programs which may be connected together in a variety of configurations. Its "building block" approach contrasts with that of TEX and of Scribe which are both implemented as large, monolithic programs.

3.3.1. The UNIX document-formatting tools

The UNIX formatting system is a part of the larger collection of document-processing tools available within the UNIX operating system [Kernighan, Lesk, and Ossanna 78]. Figure 7 summarizes the available tools. The formatting package, which has developed and grown substantially over the years, consists of the sibling formatters NROFF and TROFF, and of a number of macro packages, preprocessors, and postprocessors. The system is one of the first with non-trivial capabilities for formatting text, tables, mathematical equations, and, recently, line drawings. Indeed, TEX is the only other modern pure formatter with comparable formatting capabilities.

Before discussing the components of the UNIX formatting system, some general observations may be in order about the UNIX programming environment [Ritchie 78]. The overall aim of this environment is to provide a powerful set of tools with a simple, and often extraordinarily terse, command language syntax. The expected user seems to be an experienced professional, a person with frequent contact with the computer system. The easy interconnection of processes through the mechanism of *pipes*, which connect the output from one process to the input of another process, encourages development of systems that consist of a set of separate programs, each performing a single function. The intention is to provide a set of *software tools* [Kernighan and Plauger 76]: programs that are continually improved by much trial, error, discussion, and redesign. When new requirements develop, the tendency is to produce a new program derived from the already existing one rather than to increase the functionality and complexity of the original. Creation of new software is preferred to modification of old since modification threatens to introduce weaknesses into previously stable parts of the system. This philosophy is reflected strongly in the organization of the formatting system as a set of distinct preprocessors and postprocessors to the central RUNOFF-like formatters. We also find different programs with similar or identical input languages producing output reflecting slightly differing requirements (e.g., EQN and NEQN for processing mathematical equations that produce input for TROFF and NROFF, respectively). We note in passing that this philosophy also seems to encourage development of an unusually wide variety of document analysis-programs, such as programs for gathering statistics on word frequencies [McMahon, Cherry, and Morris 78].

We shall now discuss several of the document-formatting tools available on the UNIX system. The most commonly used method for extension of a pure formatting language has been through

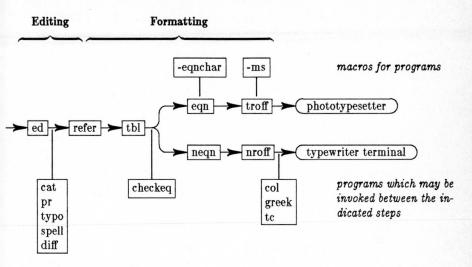

- *ed*: line-oriented text editor
    - *cat*: list file without pagination
    - *pr*: list file and paginate for printing
    - *typo*: detect spelling errors using statistical analysis
    - *spell*: detect and attempt to correct spelling errors with dictionary
    - *diff*: compare files, generate troff commands to place marginal bars when differences found
- *refer*: generate bibliographic citations. Refer has its own separate subsystem for maintaining the bibliography data base file.
- *tbl*: table formatter
- *eqn* and *neqn*: mathematical equation formatters
    - *checkeq*: make sure that equation is syntactically correct before passing it on to eqn or neqn
    - *eqnchar*: macro package specifying special characters normally unknown in troff
- *troff* and *nroff*: RUNOFF-like formatters
    - *ms*: macros for partial separation of content from format
    - *col*: convert nroff output to print on devices without reverse scrolling
    - *greek*: convert nroff output to print Greek characters on Teletype 37
    - *tc*: convert troff output to print on Tektronix 4024 DVST terminal

Figure 7: Some of the document-processing tools available on UNIX, Version seven.

macro definitions. We describe one UNIX macro package, the -ms macros, which makes a low-level attempt to provide an input language separating format from content. We also discuss four TROFF preprocessors: EQN, which formats mathematical expressions; TBL, a table formatter; REFER, which looks up bibliographic references and generates TROFF commands to produce a properly formatted citation within the text; and PIC, which allows string descriptions of line drawings.

3.3.1.1. TROFF/NROFF

In Section 3.2.2, we discussed the functions available in NROFF, the UNIX formatter producing output for typewriter-like devices. Now we wish to discuss TROFF [Ossanna 76], which prepares output for phototypesetters.

The input languages accepted by TROFF and NROFF are nearly identical. Thus, all of the discussion about NROFF also applies to TROFF. TROFF must support additional functions since a phototypesetter has more capabilities than does even the most sophisticated typewriter-like printer. However, NROFF typically ignores those TROFF commands which it cannot carry out (for example, changing character sizes) and thus maintains input language compatibility. There are a few commands which are present only in TROFF or only in NROFF but, since it is possible to determine which formatter is being used while the formatting is going on and conditionally to include or exclude input lines, it is always possible to set up an input file which will be acceptable to both formatters. However, it will, at times, take quite a bit of work to set up this file. Thus, a weak form of device-independent description is provided by these formatters.

TROFF and NROFF have been modified over the years to support special functions needed by the various preprocessors. The documents which TROFF produces can be typographically very complex. Text, mathematical equations, tables, and line drawings can all be specified and combined. TROFF and NROFF may be considered to be useful primarily for implementation of higher-level document-specification languages. Using TROFF directly to set complex documents is more complicated than almost anyone would wish. Macro packages and preprocessors are essential for effective use [Kernighan 76].

3.3.1.2. The -ms macro package

Let us now look at one of the available NROFF/TROFF macro packages, the -ms macros [Lesk 76b]. Objects supported here are simple but certainly higher-level than those provided by the bare formatters. They include indented and unindented paragraphs, footnotes, section headings, indented outlines, and blocks of text which are to be kept together within a column of text. Commands are provided for changing fonts, for increasing or decreasing type point size, and for specifying the number of columns on the page.

We include one example document description, specified using the -ms macros, as Figure 8 (we will later show descriptions of this same document in Scribe, Figure 16, and in GML, Figure 20). One interesting object used in the example is a document heading. It consists of document title, authors' names and affiliations, and document abstract. The positioning of this object with respect to neighboring objects varies with the type of document being produced. In fact, fields of this object can appear in more than one place in the final printed document. If "released paper format" (.RP) had been specified at the beginning of the -ms input file, a separate cover page containing the document header object and the current date would have been generated. The title and author information would have been repeated on the first page of the text. Thus abstract objects can be represented multiply in the concrete form of the paper and some abstract objects can be unordered with respect to their neighbors.

As the example illustrates, NROFF/TROFF commands are needed to augment the -ms macros with even simple text. Setting more complicated text requires that the values in registers used by macros be altered by commands in the text. The values within these registers can be device-dependent, for example, the width of a column or the spacing between lines of text. Some separation of format from content has been achieved, but the separation is not complete.

With UNIX macros, the entire underlying implementation language remains visible during formatting. Indeed, use of the underlying language may be necessary to achieve certain effects. The syntax of the newly defined commands is fixed by the semantics imposed by the formatter on macro invocations. Further, since macro commands are implemented by grouping commands from the base formatting language, the commands which can be implemented are limited by the functionality of the formatter itself. Another approach, which may be used to provide additional commands, is to create a "filter" program, one through which the input passes before reaching the base formatter. While still limited by the functionality of the base formatter, this approach allows definition of a syntax appropriate for the problem being solved, and allows hiding of parts of the base formatting language. This is the approach used with great success by the various NROFF/TROFF preprocessors.

3.3.1.3. EQN

EQN, a TROFF preprocessor (and the related NEQN, an NROFF preprocessor) provide a high-level declarative language for specifying mathematical equations within TROFF-prepared documents [Kernighan and Cherry 75].

Objects specified using the language are viewed as being enclosed in rectangular boxes. The language specifies the relationships between boxes. Thus, larger boxes are built from smaller

```
.TL
Extended Abstract
.br
Document Formatting Systems:   Survey, Concepts, and Issues*
.AU
Alan Shaw, Richard Furuta, and Jeffrey Scofield
.AI
Department of Computer Science
University of Washington
Seattle, WA   98195, U.S.A.
.AB
Formatting, the final part of the document preparation process, is
concerned with the physical layout of a document for hard and soft
copy media....  Our aims are to characterize the formatting problem
and its relation to other aspects of document processing, to
evaluate several representative and seminal systems, and to
describe some issues and problems relevant to future systems.
.AE
.FS
*This research was supported in part by the National Science
Foundation under grant number MCS-782685.
.FE
.NH
The Formatting Problem
.PP
In order to discuss formatters and their functions and to
distinguish formatting from other aspects of document
preparation, it is convenient to use an
.I
object
.R
model of documents [Shaw 80], somewhat analogous to that in
programming languages.
.PP
A document is an object...
.NH
Representative and Seminal Systems
.NH 2
Pure Formatters
.PP
Some typical first generation formatters...
```

Figure 8: A document description using the -ms macros.

(Continued on the following page)

This figure shows input to either NROFF or TROFF using the -ms macros. The document specified is the first part of the extended abstract for this paper [Shaw, Furuta, and Scofield 80]. The case of commands is significant. Upper-case commands are defined by the -ms macros. Lower-case commands are NROFF/TROFF commands. The title of the document is placed between the ".TL" and the ".AU" commands. The NROFF/TROFF command ".br" (break) was necessary to separate the text "Extended Abstract" from the rest of the title. Authors' names, between ".AU" and ".AI", and authors' address, between ".AI" and ".AB" follow. The text between ".AB" and ".AE" is the paper's abstract. The title, authors' names, authors' address, and abstract will be placed on the first page of the text, formatted properly based on conventions established within the macro package. For example, the title will be centered and underlined when the formatter is NROFF, centered and written in a larger point size in boldface when the formatter is TROFF. The footnote, located between ".FS" and ".FE" could not be placed in the header since the header information is treated specially. ".NH" defines a section heading which will be numbered ("1." and "2." in this example), ".NH 2" a subsection heading, also numbered ("2.1." here), and so on. ".PP" defines the beginning of a paragraph. Text following ".I" is set in italics. ".R" restores the normal (roman) font.

Figure 8, concluded.

---

boxes. An equation specification in EQN is quite aural in form. Figure 10 presents an EQN specification of the equation shown in Figure 9. As this example shows, the EQN specification is close to what would be recited by a person reading the equation from left to right.

The equation specification is delimited by the ".EQ" and ".EN" commands. Equations can also be specified within a text line if surrounded by defined delimiter characters. Reserved words are used within the specification to indicate relative positioning of the object-containing boxes, to specify symbols not present on the keyboard, and to identify parts of the equation requiring different typographic settings. Spacing of the equation description is not significant except where necessary to delimit a reserved word. Reserved words can be defined or redefined by the user through a limited macro definition facility.

EQN equations are easily included in tables and in text. It is possible to use TROFF strings within an equation specification, but not TROFF commands. However, this is not really a limitation since the EQN language can be used to specify almost any desired equation.

The language is defined by a context-free grammar and implemented using a compiler-compiler. Some of the benefits of this approach are discussed in Section 4.3.

$$\frac{1}{2\pi} \int_{-\infty}^{\sqrt{y}} \left(\sum_{k=1}^{n} \sin^2 x_k(t) \right) \left(f(t) + g(t) \right) dt$$

Figure 9: A sample mathematical equation [Knuth 79c, page 91].

Figure 10 shows specification of this equation in EQN. Figure 18 shows this equation specified in TEX.

3.3.1.4. TBL

TBL, the UNIX system's table preprocessor, defines a simple, non-extensible, declarative language which allows specification of fairly complex tables [Lesk 76a]. The TBL language specifies rectangular tables with entries which may be numeric or textual (either short phrases or formatted blocks of text, possibly including mathematical equations). Any entry within the table may be enclosed with a box or separated from adjacent objects with either horizontal or vertical rules (these rules may be either double or single). In fact, the table itself may be enclosed with a box. Adjacent table entries (again, either horizontally or vertically) may be merged to form a single, larger, entry. Certain low-level font and type-size changes may be specified within this language.

The model of tables used in this system is an object which consists of a sequence of rows which are divided into columns. Row templates are used to describe the positioning of entries within the columns (or, as mentioned, within a sequence of the adjacent boxes defined by the row and column divisions). The templates used now differ from those in the original version of TBL, which used column templates.

Figure 12 specifies the table of Figure 11. Table definitions in the TBL language consist of a line of global options, a sequence of line templates (also called the table format), and a sequence of lines defining the rows of the table. Blocks of text to be formatted over several lines can be included within the table as in:

```
Column 1 information⊕T{
A multi-line block of text to be formatted by TROFF and
placed in the table as the second column
T}⊕Column 3 information
```

Columns are separated by the tab character, represented by "⊕". Table entries can include NROFF/TROFF commands. EQN equation specifications may also be included. Either EQN

```
.EQ
1 over {2 pi} int from {- inf} to {sqrt y}
left ( sum from k=1 to n sin sup 2 x sub k (t) right )
left ( f(t) + g(t) right ) dt
.EN
```

Figure 10: The equation of Figure 9 specified in EQN.

Text enclosed in brackets, "{" and "}", is *grouped* and syntactically treated as if it were a single unit. "sub" means subscript, "sup" means superscript, "left (" and "right)" bracket a group which is surrounded by parentheses large enough to enclose the group's contents. Notice that EQN will automatically set function names, for example "sin," in a roman font instead of in the italic font used for the other textual material in the finished equation.

---

or TBL can be run first without altering the results although efficiency considerations dictate that TBL be run before EQN. This flexibility is possible since TBL acts by generating NROFF/ TROFF commands and macros; the actual calculation of the values needed for formatting the table is delayed until NROFF/TROFF is invoked. Most NROFF/TROFF commands work properly within the TBL definition, but some formatting commands that alter environmental attributes used by TBL will have unforeseen effects. With this exception, text and mathematical equations have been integrated with tables.

3.3.1.5. REFER

The function of the NROFF/TROFF preprocessor REFER [Lesk 78] is to retrieve a particular citation from a centrally maintained bibliography database given an imprecise form of the citation. When the citation is found, strings are generated which NROFF/TROFF macros (for example, -ms) use to print the complete reference and to insert the appropriate citation into the text. By default, citations are numeric. The -ms macros place the references in footnotes; the citation itself is the superscripted number that refers to the footnote. The appearance of the citation can be changed by redefining the macros. Also, some REFER options allow other citation and reference formats to be specified. REFER options can indicate that references are to be collected, not alphabetized, and then listed at the end of the text. Citations can be numeric, can consist of the senior author's last name and the date, or can consist of the first n initials of the last name. Authors' names can be printed in the references with last name first or first name last.

The input document contains imprecise citations consisting of a sequence of key words and authors' names. A citation for the report defining REFER could look like this:

AT&T Common Stock		
Year	Price	Dividend
1971	41-54	$2.60
2	41-54	2.70
3	46-55	2.87
4	40-53	3.24
5	45-52	3.40
6	51-59	.95*

* (first quarter only)

Figure 11: A sample table [Lesk 76a, page 7].

Figure 12 shows specification of this table in TBL. Figure 19 shows this table specified in TEX.

```
.[
Lesk inverted indices UNIX 1978
.]
```

REFER would find the complete citation in its database and generate the appropriate strings to allow the NROFF/TROFF macros to place a complete reference and proper citation into the text. A separate language is used within the database to specify entries, as shown in Figure 13.

REFER is particularly interesting for two reasons. First, it serves a purpose quite different from the other NROFF/TROFF preprocessors. The other preprocessors all provide languages for describing new objects simply. REFER provides what we have called a "writer's workbench" tool. Second, the implementation is of interest. The central bibliography available at Bell Laboratories contains over 4000 entries. Searching this large central database for references would be prohibitively expensive without an efficient means. Inverted indices provide this efficiency. Briefly, an inverted file [Knuth 75], which contains the inverted indices, is like a book index: the values of the attributes within the records are the lookup keys and keys point to the records in which they are contained. The Bell Laboratories implementation uses a precomputed hash table for quick retrieval of the lookup keys.

```
.TS
allbox;
c s s
c c c
n n n.
AT&T Common Stock
Year⊕Price⊕Dividend
1971⊕41-54⊕$2.60
2⊕41-54⊕2.70
3⊕46-55⊕2.87
4⊕40-53⊕3.24
5⊕45-52⊕3.40
6⊕51-59⊕.95*
.TE
* (first quarter only)
```

Figure 12: Document description for TBL to produce the table
of Figure 11 [Lesk 76a, page 7].

The table begins with the ".TS" command and ends with the ".TE" command. Note that the final line is outside the body of the table itself. Global options, specified by keywords, are declared once, at the beginning of the table definition, between the ".TS" command, which marks the beginning of the table, and the terminating ";". The global option "allbox," used here, causes each entry in the table, and the table itself, to be enclosed within a box. Other global options can, for example, cause the table either to be centered within the available horizontal space or cause the table to expand in width to fill the available space.

Row templates, which follow the global options and are terminated with a ".", consist of codes which represent characteristics of column entries within the row. A single line of codes is given for each row in the table, one code per column. When there are more rows in the table than templates, the last template given holds for the remaining rows. Templates used here specify that an entry is to be centered within a field ("c"), that the previous entry in the row should span into the current field ("s"), and that numbers are to be aligned at their decimal points ("n"). Left justification, right justification, vertical spanning, and centering of blocks of left adjusted text can also be specified. Templates can also indicate that horizontal and vertical lines be drawn between entries, alter the font used, and so on. New templates can be defined in the middle of a table, changing the table's format.

The remainder of this table definition is data to be entered into the table using the formats defined by the templates. Extra columns in the text are ignored. Rows are entered one at a time with columns separated by the tab character, represented as "⊕" in this figure. Vertical and horizontal rulings between individual entries and rows, and vertical spanning may also be specified at this time, if desired.

```
%T Document Formatting Systems:   Survey, Concepts, and Issues
[Extended Abstract]
%A A. C. Shaw
%A R. Furuta
%A J. Scofield
%R Technical Report 80-10-02
%D October 1980
%I Department of Computer Science, University of Washington
%C Seattle, WA
```

Figure 13: A REFER database entry.

Each field of the entry is flagged by a two-symbol code: the character "%", followed by a letter indicating what the field is (for example, "A" for author, "T" for title). See the references for a full listing of this entry [Shaw, Furuta, and Scofield 80].

3.3.1.6. PIC

A recent addition to the UNIX document-processing system is the picture specification language PIC [Kernighan 81a, Kernighan 82]. This one-dimensional string language, implemented as a TROFF preprocessor, provides a way to specify line drawings, possibly with enclosed text, equations, or other TROFF specified material, within typeset documents. Thus PIC adds an important class of figure objects to those expressible within the UNIX system and partially integrates the other mathematical and text objects with these figure objects.

PIC's primitive objects are the box, line, arrow, circle, ellipse, arc, and B-spline. Heavy reliance on associating symbolic names with objects, on describing positions relative to other objects, and on default values for object size, orientation, and other attributes, allows a simple, flexible, and high-level description of figures. It is, however, possible to specify the concrete attributes of the object in an exact, low-level manner. Objects may be scaled, translated, or placed with respect to an identified point in a figure. Invisible objects can be used to help in specifying figures. A macro facility is provided, allowing creation of a hierarchy of figure objects. Additionally, objects can be collected together into a *block* (syntactically represented by delimiting a sequence of specifications with "[" and "]" brackets). The block may then be manipulated as a single object. Figure 14 presents an example.

The approach taken to picture specification is similar to, but at a higher level than that used in the Lawrence Livermore system, discussed in Section 3.5.2. IDEAL, another TROFF preprocessor for figure descriptions using quite a different approach, is discussed in Section 3.5.3.

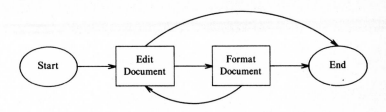

```
.PS
ellipse "Start"; arrow
B1:box "Edit" "Document"; arrow
B2:box "Format" "Document"; arrow
E2:ellipse "End"
arc -> cw from top of B1 to top of E2
arc -> cw from bottom of B2 to bottom of B1
.PE
```

Figure 14: An example using the PIC language.

Specifications in PIC consist of the name of a primitive object, ellipse, box and arc in this example, followed by optional specification of object attributes. Text contained in quotes is displayed, centered inside the object. Specifications are either written one per line or separated by semicolons. By default, the figure is assumed to grow from left to right. Names followed by a colon label the following object, allowing symbolic references to the location of the object. The position of the objects could also have been specified without labels by using ordinal values. For example, the first arc could have been described as:

```
arc -> cw from top of 1st box to top of last ellipse
```

The two arcs specified here are drawn in a clockwise fashion (cw) and contain an arrowhead (->).

3.3.1.7. Discussion of the UNIX system

By any standards, the UNIX formatting system is a successful one. An informal evaluation conducted for *Physical Review Letters* compared UNIX composition to the typewriter composition method already in use at the journal for articles with a moderate amount of mathematical and tabular text [Lesk and Kernighan 77]. UNIX reduced the keyboard time needed to prepare the articles, averaging 2.4 times as fast as typewriter composition. Further, total estimated composition costs per page decreased by one-third with UNIX.

As previously indicated, a large part of the success of this system is its unique ability to change incrementally to meet more sophisticated demands. Paradoxically, the system's highly modular design has also discouraged integration between different types of objects and between the languages used to describe these objects. Section 4.7.2 continues this point.

3.3.2. Scribe

We find a different approach to document processing in Scribe, developed in the late 1970's by B. Reid at Carnegie-Mellon University [Reid 80a, Reid and Walker 80, Reid 80b, Reid 81]. In the pure formatters already discussed, the user of the system retains most of the responsibility for the appearance of the final printed document. In Scribe, this responsibility is given to the formatter. The emphasis in the document description language is on the logical content of the document, not on its physical format. Formatting details are determined by the system, varying for individual types of documents and for different output devices. Other systems permit their users to specify the logical structure of the document, most generally through use of commands defined using the system's macro facility, but the user can also specify the concrete form of the document directly through the low-level positioning commands which remain available for use. The Scribe user is required to specify the logical structure of the document. For the most part, lower-level positioning commands have not been provided.

One result of this philosophy is that the object types which the Scribe system can handle are limited to those which can currently be described completely by their content, without resorting to use of concrete object positioning commands. In essence, this means that Scribe currently is restricted to fairly simple textual objects. There are no facilities, for example, for line drawings, complex tables, and complicated mathematical expressions. TEX and the UNIX document formatting system attempt to allow any object to be specified, although perhaps with great difficulty. Unlike these, Scribe contents itself with the easy specification of objects sufficient to provide many, but certainly not all, of the commonly needed document types.

Another result of this strong separation of content from format is that document descriptions stated using Scribe are highly portable. Not only can the same document description be used at different computer sites, but the same document description can be used to produce visible concrete documents for viewing on different devices; the necessary details are supplied by the Scribe system.

Environments and Commands

Declaring a Scribe document to be of a particular type (for example, article, letter, thesis) specifies the attributes of the global environment for the document. An environment encloses document text, which itself may include a sequence of nested environments (for example, italic phrase, or section heading). Another way of describing an environment is as a partial definition of the concrete attributes for the logical object it contains (for example, left margin, or typeface). Unspecified attributes are generally inherited from the surrounding environment. Formatting, then, involves applying the environment attributes to the text contained within the environment. The definitions of the attributes of the environments provided for each individual document type are contained in the central *Scribe database.* The person responsible for maintaining the Scribe database at a particular site may add new document types to the database or remove old ones. Similarly, environment definitions in existing document types can be added, deleted, or modified. Importantly, this means that the particular environments which are available within a particular document depend on the type of the document; different document types may provide different environments.

Text within an environment may be simply a string of characters, a paragraph containing a sequence of sentences or a sequence of paragraphs. Text objects are available within all environments since these objects are defined internally by the Scribe compiler, not in the database.

A number of low-level features for creation of new objects are available, such as overprinting of characters and a macro facility. However, these features are not meant for the general user and are not described in the basic language tutorial [Reid and Walker 80].

We present two examples of Scribe input. Figure 15 presents the same document already presented for the other pure formatters. Figure 16 is included to give an idea of how Scribe would be used to specify a more generally needed document type.

Keywords, preceded by the reserved escape symbol "@" and followed, optionally, by a delimited argument, name either environments or commands. Environments have been discussed above. Commands differ from environments in three major ways. First, they are generally associated with a point in the document rather than with a region of the document. They may also associate information with that point in the document. For example, the command "@Label(*LabelName*)" marks a particular location in the document, saving the section number and output page number for retrieval in other parts of the document. Second, the actions associated with commands are "hard-wired" into the Scribe system. The actions cannot be modified as can the list of attributes associated with environments. And third, many of the commands are procedural in nature. The environment mechanism is declarative.

A particularly useful feature of the Scribe system is its facility for defining and modifying environment definitions. These changes may be either global or local in scope. Global changes can only be specified at the beginning of the document specification, before any document text is encountered. The @Define command is used to define a new environment globally. For example, the command:

```
@Define(Unfilled,Justification=no)
```

```
@Style(indent=0,spacing=1,spread=1)
@Heading(CALL FOR PAPERS)

The aim of this conference is to survey the state of the art of
computer aids for document preparation.

Papers are solicited on
@Begin(Itemize)
Picture editing

Text processing

Algorithms and software for document preparation and other related
topics
@End(Itemize)

Detailed abstracts should not exceed five pages; they @i(must) be
sent before October 31, 1980 to the Program Chairman.  Selected
authors will be notified by November 30.

Duration of one presentation will be of either 25 or 45 minutes.
```

Figure 15: Document description for Scribe to produce
the document of Figure 2.

Environment and command keywords are preceded by the escape character "@" which cannot be changed, and are optionally followed by delimited arguments or delimited text. The delimiters can be just about any matched pair of brackets. The position of keywords on the input line is not significant. Paragraphs are flagged with a blank line. The @Style command modifies global attributes of the document. If a @Style command is included, it must appear at the beginning of the input file before any text is encountered. Here, the "indent" argument specifies how much a paragraph should be indented, "spacing = 1" means the document should be single spaced, "spread" indicates how many blank lines should be left between paragraphs. The "@i" environment contains a text string to be italicized. An equivalent way to specify any environment with delimited string argument is to use @Begin and @End command brackets. Thus the italicized string "@i(must)" could equivalently have been specified as "@Begin(i)must@End(i)".

---

defines a new environment, named "Unfilled," in which text is not justified. More usefully, @Define can be used to create new environments defined by *analogy* to existing environments: "The environment I want to specify is exactly the same as this existing environment except for these changes...." For example, the "Quotation" environment, used for displaying large quotations, narrows both its margins. The command:

```
@Define(QuoteButFullRight=Quotation,RightMargin=+0)
```

```
@Make(article)
@Center(Extended Abstract)
@Heading(Document Formatting Systems:  Survey, Concepts, and Issues@foot<This
research was supported in part by
the National Science Foundation under grant number MCS-7826285.>)
@Center(Alan Shaw, Richard Furuta, and Jeffrey Scofield)
@Center(Department of Computer Science
University of Washington
Seattle, Washington  98195, U.S.A.)

@PrefaceSection(Abstract)

Formatting, the final part of the document preparation process, is
concerned with the physical layout of a document for hard and soft
copy media....  Our aims are to characterize the formatting problem
and its relation to other aspects of document processing, to evaluate
several representative and seminal systems, and to describe some
issues and problems relevant to future systems.

@Section(The Formatting Problem)

In order to discuss formatters and their functions and to distinguish
formatting from other aspects of document preparation, it is
convenient to use an @i(object) model of documents@Cite(ShawModel),
somewhat analogous to that in programming languages.

A document is an object composed of a hierarchy of more primitive
objects....

@Section(Representative and Seminal Systems)

@SubSection(Pure Formatters)

Some typical first generation formatters...
```

Figure 16: A sectioned document specified in Scribe.

This figure presents the same document segment as that specified in Figure 8. Documents of type "article" may be divided into numbered sections to three levels. (The first two, Section and SubSection are shown here.) This example document consists of a title, authors' names and address, an abstract, and portions of the first few sections of the document. "@Cite(ShawModel)" refers to an entry in the bibliographic database for this document. In the printed document, a citation to the reference will be placed in the text at this point. Scribe will automatically generate a list of references and a table of contents for this document.

---

provides a new environment, named "QuoteButFullRight," with the same attributes as "Quotation" except for the right margin, which is not narrowed. Similarly, existing environments can be globally altered through the @Modify command which allows new values to be specified for attributes of an existing environment:

```
@Modify(Itemize,RightMargin=0)
```

would change the RightMargin attribute associated with the "itemize" environment in every place in which the environment was used within the document.

Local changes to an environment are made using the @Begin command. For example:

```
@Begin(quotation,RightMargin=0)
```

changes the RightMargin attribute for this use of "Quotation" only. Unfortunately, local environment changes can introduce subtle output device dependencies into the document description since many environmental attributes are defined in extremely device dependent ways. We return to this subject again in Section 4.2.3.

Writer's Workbench Features

A major factor in the popularity of the Scribe system is its large number of writer's workbench tools. Many of these tools were also found in PUB and a few in the UNIX system. Scribe has a mechanism for collecting text during the processing of a document and then treating this derived text as input to the formatter at the end of the run. This mechanism is used, for example, to generate a table of contents or an index. Objects such as sections of a document, footnotes, or elements in an itemized list can be numbered automatically. A cross-reference facility allows symbolic reference to page numbers or section numbers of objects within the document. Scribe provides page-layout aids which assist in placing footnotes and which will move a figure forward until enough blank space is found on a page to insert it. Similar aids are also available in most of the other pure formatters discussed. Additionally, individual document types may include useful options. For example, selecting the "Draft" option can cause diagnostic information related to the document description to be included within the visible concrete document.

A bibliography management facility is available. No central bibliography database is provided; each user maintains a personal bibliography containing specifications for a set of references. The form of entries in this database quite closely resembles that used in REFER (see Section 3.3.1.5 and Figure 13). In Scribe, the user defines a unique identifier for each entry in the bibliography. Citations within a document use this identifier to select the desired reference. The Scribe system fills in the text of the actual citation in an appropriate format for the document type. At the end of the document, a list of references is generated, also in an appropriate format for the document type. Citations and references can be generated in a number of different formats, such as those of the *Communications of the ACM* and *Information Processing Letters*. Unlike REFER, Scribe completely regenerates its internal bibliographic lookup tables each time they are needed.

Finally, Scribe includes some basic facilities for managing large documents. Large documents can be broken up into a number of different computer files and ordered into a tree structure.

Global definitions made in the root apply to all nodes. Any subtree can be formatted separately without requiring that the entire document be processed. Auxiliary files are updated so page numbers, figure numbers, and cross references, for example, in other parts of the document will be correct the next time they are processed. This feature not only aids the individual author who is working on a large document, but also aids groups of authors who are each working on separate sections of a document. We discuss these facilities further in Section 4.5.2.

3.3.3. TEX

TEX was developed by D. Knuth of Stanford University in the late 1970's to provide high-quality typesetting of books containing much mathematical material [Knuth 79a]. The system concentrates on the arrangement of objects in the visible concrete document. New and interesting algorithms have been developed for breaking paragraphs into lines, for collecting lines into pages, and for hyphenation—for the tasks, in other words, which are normally performed automatically by a formatter. The specification language allows the description of extremely complex textual, tabular, and mathematical concrete objects.

The specification language appears to emphasize the expression of this wide range of objects rather than ease of use. Some ideas have been borrowed from other systems; most notably, the math-mode language resembles EQN. However, the specification languages are more unified in TEX than in the UNIX system. In particular, features of TEX's math mode language, such as ellipses, are used in non-mathematical specifications more often than are features of EQN. On the other hand, the assessment by one of the implementors of the UNIX document processing system is that TROFF is more powerful than TEX [Kernighan 81b] since TEX does not provide page layout mechanisms as general as TROFF's traps which can associate a macro invocation with a position on the output page. Another difference is that TEX does not include primitives for specifying line drawings as do the newer versions of TROFF [Kernighan 81c].

The Boxes and Glue Model

Concrete objects are modelled as two-dimensional *boxes* connected to each other by *glue*. Boxes define the size of the object they contain and provide a reference point which is used to align the box with other boxes, either horizontally or vertically. Aligning two boxes produces an enclosing box. Typical box contents are characters, words, lines, paragraphs, and pages. Glue provides space between boxes. Glue has a natural size and may be stretched or compressed according to given constraints. Line justification may be thought of as pulling the objects on the ends of the line apart, or pushing them together, until the desired width has been reached. Since the glue put between sentences has more stretchability than the normal glue placed between words, line justification will cause more space to be added between sentences than between words. Similarly, a phrase can be centered within a line by placing glue of infinite stretchability at both ends of the phrase.

The Formatting Language

The formatting language uses control sequences preceded by a special escape character, usually "\". Other characters also have special meaning, but all special characters can be redefined, including the escape character. Specifications are *grouped* if surrounded by set brackets, "{" and "}". Definitions made within a group persist only until the end of the group, unless they are defined to be global. Thus one common use of groups is to specify a change with limited scope, say, a switch to an italic font. Because a group is treated as a unit, groups are also often used as arguments to commands. Both of these uses may be seen in the text example presented in Figure 17.

A separate math mode is provided for specification of mathematical equations. Inline mathematical-equation specifications are delimited by the character "$". Displayed mathematical specifications are delimited by "$$". Figure 18 shows a specification for the displayed equation previously presented in Figure 9.

TEX's math-mode language is similar to EQN's. The primary difference between the languages is that TEX uses no reserved words; escape sequences are used instead. Special symbols are used, however, to specify some operations such as superscripting, invoked by "↑", and subscripting, invoked by "↓". Overall, TEX math mode and EQN seem quite close in their abilities to specify complicated equations. However, using TEX math mode requires more knowledge of typographic conventions than does EQN. In the example, the TEX math-mode user must remember to type "\sin" since typographic convention indicates that function names are to be set in a different type face from variable names.

A macro facility is included which allows definition of new commands. TEX macro definitions are somewhat unusual when compared to those of other formatting systems in that they offer a limited facility for defining new command syntaxes, similar to that provided in PUB by the response macros. As with the other systems, the body of the TEX macro definition includes a sequence of formatting language specifications that defines the macro's action. However, a definition also includes a parameter pattern with embedded argument placeholders. When the macro is invoked, tokens in the invocation string are matched against tokens in the parameter pattern. Tokens corresponding to the embedded argument placeholders are substituted into the definition's body, which is then evaluated.

This macro facility is a powerful tool for simplifying and extending the specification language. Indeed, much of the "basic" language is implemented within a macro package, as may be noted

```
\input basic % defines the standard macros, formatting parameters
\parskip 10pt
\parindent 0pt % no indentation
\def\yskip{\vskip3pt}
\def\textindent#1{\noindent
    \hbox to 19pt{\hskip0pt plus1000pt minus 1000pt#1 }\!}
\def\hang{\hangindent19pt}
\hsize 4in
\ctrline{\bf CALL FOR PAPERS}
\vskip 24pt
The aim of this conference is to survey the state of the art of
computer aids for document preparation.

Papers are solicited on
{\parskip 0pt
\par\yskip\textindent{$\bullet$}\hang Picture editing
\par\yskip\textindent{$\bullet$}\hang Text processing
\par\yskip\textindent{$\bullet$}\hang Algorithms and software for
document preparation and other related topics}

Detailed abstracts should not exceed five pages; they {\sl must} be
sent before October 31, 1980 to the Program Chairman.  Selected
authors will be notified by November 30.

Duration of one presentation will be of either 25 or 45 minutes.

\vfill % fill out rest of page with space
\end
```

Figure 17: Document description in TₑX specifying the document of Figure 2.

Text following a percent sign, "%", is commentary and is ignored by TₑX. The first seven lines of the specification establish macros and formatting parameters. "\parskip" defines the space which is to be left between paragraphs and "\parindent" the indentation at the beginning of each paragraph. The definitions of "\yskip", "\textindent", and "\hang" are adapted from Appendix E of the TₑX reference manual [Knuth 79c, page 165]. "\yskip" will leave a small amount of vertical space. "\textindent" and "\hang" will be used in specifying lists of items flagged with a bullet in the left margin. "\hsize" establishes the document's line width.

The text of the document begins with line nine. Notice the difference in line nine in syntax between a group used as an argument to a command or macro, in this case as argument to "\ctrline" which centers the argument on the line, and a group used to limit the scope of a formatting parameter, here "\bf" which switches to a bold face font. "\vskip" specifies vertical blank space. "\noindent" inhibits indentation of the first line of the following paragraph. A blank line terminates the preceeding paragraph, contributing its lines to the current page; the "\par" command could have been used instead. Notice that the measurements expressed in these specifications are stated in points (a point is 0.013837 inch) and therefore are highly oriented to the visible concrete document.

```
$$ {1 \over 2\pi} \int\limitswitch↓{-\infty}↑{\sqrt y}
\bigglp \sum↓{k=1}↑n \sin↑2 x↓k(t) \biggrp
\biglp f(t)+g(t)\bigrp\,dt $$
```

Figure 18: The equation of Figure 9 specified
in TEX [Knuth 79c, page 149].

This specification is extremely similar in form to that in EQN. See Figure 10 and the text for discussion. "\limitswitch" causes the limits to be placed above and below the integral sign. By default (in this example, the default would have been used if the specification had been "...\int↓{-\infty}..."), limits are placed to the right of the integral sign. "\bigglp" and "\biggrp" are particular parenthesis characters somewhat larger than "\biglp" and "\bigrp" which themselves are slightly larger than the standard left and right parenthesis. Spaces have been added to improve readability but only those separating control sequences from subsequent letters are actually required.

---

in the example of Figure 17. The American Mathematical Society has sponsored creation of another macro package, called AMS-TEX, designed to make specification of mathematical papers in TEX easier [Spivak 80].

Tables are handled as text. Two commands of particular use in defining tables are "\halign" and "\valign". The group following a "\halign" contains, first, a (horizontal, hence the "h") row template, and then a sequence of row entries to be specified using the template. See Figure 19 for an example table specification. The "\valign" command performs much the same function except that a (vertical) column template is given and specifications are by column, not by row.

Again, the division of a TEX table specification into two parts, template and entries, is similar to the UNIX specification. Use of the formatting language to specify table templates rather than using special characters, as in TBL, means that TEX's language is more general. However, TEX's table specifications are quite a bit more complex than are TBL table specifications, and the TBL language is easier to use. Once again, macro packages will undoubtedly be developed to make TEX table specification much simpler.

Line and Page Break-up

Among the most important contributions of TEX are its concrete-document model and the algorithms used in the system's implementation. The TEX reference manual [Knuth 79c] includes a description of the hyphenation routine, a list of the modes TEX gets into while processing a document, and a brief discussion of the methods used for breaking paragraphs into lines and for making lists of lines into pages. This last topic has been described in more detail in

```
$$\vbox{\tabskip 0pt
\def\|{\vrule height 9.25pt depth 3pt}
\def\.{\hskip-10pt plus 10000000000pt}
\hrule
\hbox to 150pt{\|\.AT&T Common Stock\.\|}
\hrule
\halign to 150pt{#\tabskip 0pt plus 100pt
⊗\hfill#⊗#⊗\ctr{#}⊗#⊗\hfill#⊗#\tabskip 0pt\cr
\|⊗\.Year\.\hfill⊗\|⊗\.Price\.⊗\|⊗\.Dividend\.\hfill⊗\|\cr
\noalign{\hrule}
\|⊗1971⊗\|⊗41--54⊗\|⊗$\$$2.60⊗\|\cr\noalign{\hrule}
\|⊗2⊗\|⊗41--54⊗\|⊗2.70⊗\|\cr\noalign{\hrule}
\|⊗3⊗\|⊗46--55⊗\|⊗2.87⊗\|\cr\noalign{\hrule}
\|⊗4⊗\|⊗40--53⊗\|⊗3.24⊗\|\cr\noalign{\hrule}
\|⊗5⊗\|⊗45--52⊗\|⊗3.40⊗\|\cr\noalign{\hrule}
\|⊗6⊗\|⊗51--59⊗\|⊗.95\spose*⊗\|\cr\noalign{\hrule}}
\vskip 3pt
\hbox{* (first quarter only)}}}$$
```

Figure 19: Document description for TEX to produce the table
of Figure 11 [Knuth 79c, page 108].

The designer of this table has decided that the table is to be 150 points wide (slightly under 2.1 inches). The table specification may be divided into four major parts. The first three lines provide some overall definitions of parameters and macros available within the specification. The next three lines specify the major heading of the table. The next eleven lines specify the body of the table. The final two lines specify the text which is to appear beneath the table as a footnote to the rightmost number in the last row of the table.

The group making up the table body contains two parts. The first defines a template which will be used in placing the seven column entries which make up each row (the bars adjacent to the three columns, specified as "\|", are considered to be separate column entries). Specifications for column entries are separated by the alignment tab, "⊗". The template ends with the first "\cr". Row specifications follow, each ended with "\cr". Row entries are separated by the "⊗". In essence, entries are substituted into the template, externally replacing the corresponding "#". The "\noalign{\hrule}" which follows each row entry specifies the horizontal bar separating the rows in the visible concrete document.

a later paper [Knuth and Plass 81]. In essence, TEX tries to determine the "best" way to break each paragraph into lines, using a dynamic programming algorithm, where "best" means the way with the least hyphenation and with the glue settings that result in the least amount of "badness." The badness of a glue setting is high if the glue had to be stretched or compressed to a point close to its limits. The badness associated with a particular point can be affected manually by specifying a "penalty" for a break occurring at the point. If the penalty is negative, then the break is favored; if positive, then the break is discouraged. A similar algorithm is used in placing lists of lines onto pages. Here, TEX tries to avoid ending a page with a hyphenated line and tries to avoid isolated lines on the top or the bottom of a page.

3.4. Integrated Editor/Formatters

In this section we discuss those systems which combine the features of an interactive text editor with those of a document formatter, a group which we call the integrated editor/ formatters. We do not discuss those systems which are primarily editors with a few formatting functions included. EMACS [Stallman 80, Stallman 81] is one of the more complicated systems of this kind.

These systems are divisible into two broad categories. In the first, represented here by QUIDS, the objects used in formatting have been integrated with those used in editing, but the editing and formatting functions have not been integrated. Only occasional viewing of the visible concrete document is permitted. In the second, both objects and functions have been integrated. Editing changes are shown directly on a representation of the visible concrete document. We describe four systems exhibiting this kind of integration: Bravo, Star, and Smalltalk, all developed by Xerox, and the Wang Word Processor. The use of multiple viewing windows and high-quality graphics devices by the Xerox systems is also of interest.

Two general observations may be made comparing the integrated editor/formatters to the pure formatters. The first is that the integrated editor/formatters tend to be more configuration-dependent than do the pure formatters. The range of devices used by the different systems is quite wide, ranging from standard CRT terminals to bit mapped displays with associated graphical input devices. Unlike the recent pure formatters, each system's design seems to be heavily influenced by the environment in which it operates. The second observation is that the sophistication of the objects used in these systems is less than that of those used in the pure formatters, especially when compared to those in the group we called the "pure formatters with many objects." None of the integrated editor/formatters provides objects at the abstract level used in Scribe or allows the careful control over the appearance of the visible concrete document provided by TEX. However, integrated editor/formatters are being developed which use these kinds of abstract and concrete objects. They will be discussed in Section 3.6.

3.4.1. QUIDS

One of the first published descriptions of a system which combined editing functions with formatting functions in a unified manner was that of QUIDS (QUick Interactive Documentation System), designed and implemented in the mid-1970's at the University of London [Coulouris, et al. 76]. QUIDS' editing functions are oriented to document text rather than to computer program text. Consequently, the basic editing unit is the paragraph, not the line. Additionally, the system allows incremental viewing of the visible concrete document on request during preparation of the document description. The system integrates functions to edit, format, view, file, and print documents. However, the complexity of the object types permitted is quite limited. The system can only be used for very simple textual objects; no mathematics, line drawings, or other more complex objects can be represented or manipulated.

The model of the document employed within QUIDS is a sequence of abstract objects: paragraphs, tables, section and subsection headings, and associated titles. Most of these objects are logically ordered into a tree and assigned numbers based on the path from the root of the tree: section headings are numbered 0, 1, 2, 3, ...; subsection headings 1.0, 1.1, ...; and paragraphs 1.0.1, 1.0.2, and so on. These numbers are used within the system to identify the particular objects. Other objects represent non-sequential text, for example, page headings and footnotes. Low-level formatting parameters, such as those establishing the width of the margins, are also specified by commands and stored within the internal form of the document.

The system uses a standard CRT terminal as the interactive device. The QUIDS language consists of commands divided into three groups. Initially, the user is in ">" mode (">" is the prompt displayed in this mode). The user types commands to edit an existing document (positioning within the document), file or print the document, or select one of the other modes. In "*" mode, commands can be entered to specify parameters for global options controlling the formatting of the document; for example, whether or not a title is printed at the top of each output page. In the " ' " mode, the user enters a command to select one of the abstract object types (e.g., paragraph or section heading) and then enters the document text associated with the object. " ' " mode commands also specify the low-level formatting parameters mentioned above.

As might be noted from this discussion, commands are not selected from menus displayed on the screen. The user must remember what commands are possible and in which mode they may be used. Additionally, it is clear that a more sophisticated hardware configuration with a pointing device could be used to advantage. Significantly, the user does not manipulate a direct representation of the final document, but instead alters a logical representation of the document. Views of the final document are only presented when requested.

This simple, limited system has combined the editing and formatting functions and integrated the objects manipulated by each of these functions. However, a distinct separation of commands relating to each of these functions has also been retained; in particular, the "'" mode provides formatting commands and the ">" mode provides editing commands. Unfortunately, the formatting commands provided in this system are low-level in nature and oriented to the visible concrete document. The editing commands, however, operate at a higher level, representing the document as a structured set of ordered abstract objects. This separation contrasts strikingly to the approach taken in the Xerox systems, discussed below, in which editing and formatting have been more completely integrated.

3.4.2. Alto, Bravo, and Star

The Xerox Alto is a personal computer/workstation developed in 1973 [Thacker, et al. 79]. It includes an 8.5-inch by 11-inch bitmapped display with a resolution of about 70 pixels per inch, a typewriter keyboard, and a positioning device called the mouse. Over the years, a number of important and influential document preparation systems have been developed which take advantage of the special input/output capabilities of this workstation.

One of the most influential of these systems is the integrated text editor/formatter Bravo [Lampson 78]. This editor/formatter cleanly combines editing, formatting, viewing, filing, and production of hardcopy text documents. An option allows direct editing of an exact representation of the visible concrete document; the results of editing on the appearance of the visible concrete document are reflected immediately in the display. Multiple display windows are used to allow simultaneous manipulation of different documents or of different parts of the same document.

A limited number of object types are provided: characters, words, lines, paragraphs, and documents. Editing operations act either on individual objects or on a sequence of objects of one of these types. Objects are selected by positioning a cursor which is controlled by the mouse. Associated with character and paragraph objects are concrete attributes called *looks*. Looks are formatting properties that define the appearance of the object. Thus, character looks describe the character's font, its size, and its baseline (to allow superscripting and subscripting). Paragraph looks describe the shape of the text in the paragraph, e.g., the margins, the space between lines, if the paragraph is justified or centered, and the default character looks for characters within the paragraph. Looks are not always visible; only their side effects, the visible concrete objects, are normally seen. Looks can be modified; modification of an object's looks alters the appearance or positioning of the object on the display.

An interesting idea, which is used in many commercial systems but has been implemented quite generally in Bravo, is the partial specification of document types using *forms* (templates). Forms are document skeletons with appropriate looks, headings, and other components already in place, and with textual indicators describing those fields that must be provided by the user.

Forms are particularly useful for standard document types, such as business letters, inter-office memos, and technical reports, where much of the formatting information and some of the components (e.g., headers) are pre-defined. Creating a document of a particular type simply involves replacing the fields in the template with the actual document text; the retained looks in the form assure the proper formatting.

Bravo only provides for manipulation of simple text. Mathematical expressions, figures, and footnotes are not included, but there is provision for paging, page headers and footers, and up to two columns. There is little structuring of the objects in the text: looks are associated only with particular objects and are not related to each other. Thus making uniform changes to a document is difficult. In particular, changing the appearance of concrete objects associated with a particular abstract object type involves individual modification of each instance of the abstract object type. It is not generally possible, for instance, to change the font of all section headings in a document with one command; one must do each change individually.

Documents can contain more than just simple text, however, since a number of drawing packages are available that allow creation of figures to be merged into Bravo documents. Markup [Newman 78] adds both freehand drawings and figures constructed with straight lines. It can also be used to add text to drawings produced by other packages. Draw [Baudelaire 78] is used for drawings which require precise placement of curves, as well as lines and text, within a figure.

Alto, Bravo, Markup, Draw, and other research systems developed in Xerox laboratories provided the experimental basis for a number of commercial products. The most recent and interesting of these is the office workstation called Star, announced in 1981 [Seybold 81, Smith, et al. 82]. This product is an integrated office system that provides document preparation, filing, electronic mail, and data processing functions, all within a uniform command syntax and interpretation. Star's machine has many improvements over the Alto, such as a larger high-resolution bitmapped display.

Document preparation in Star involves the direct manipulation of the visible concrete document, but with a wider range of objects than Bravo. Document objects include mathematics and line graphics with shading. Star also features multiple overlapped display windows, object *properties* which are a generalization of Bravo's looks, and pictorial symbols or *icons* for representing all system objects on the display screen. Examples of system objects represented by icons are documents, file folders, file drawers, in- and out-baskets, disks, printer devices, and object directories. A command typically involves the selection of an object (actually of the icon representing the object) with a mouse and the invocation of an operation by further object selections or keyboard entry.

3.4.3. Smalltalk

Smalltalk [Goldberg and Kay 76, Ingalls 78, Shoch 79, Byte 81] is neither a formatter nor an editor, but an interactive programming language and system based on object classes and instances, and on message passing. Developed and used in an experimental research setting originally on the Xerox Alto computer (described in the previous section), it has demonstrated the usefulness of class/instance language facilities in a number of editing, formatting, and related applications, and has been a productive testbed for interactive techniques on a bitmapped display screen. This work has influenced several modern systems, such as Star and the systems presented in Section 3.6.

Editors for creating and modifying a wide variety of different objects, including text, freehand drawings, and character fonts, have been constructed. Formatting and viewing are integrated with editing: the resulting user interfaces deal with concrete objects and the screen layouts are closely associated with the object class and instance definitions. The same language, Smalltalk, is used both for programming objects and for invoking them; i.e., the interactive user language and the extender language are the same. A particularly useful systems feature is the subclass/superclass mechanism through which class attributes may be inherited. This permits a new class, a subclass, to be defined by modifying and extending a previously-defined class, the superclass.

The user interface contains an interesting window package that permits the definition and use of any number of screen windows simultaneously; the "active" window may overlap inactive ones in screen space, analogous to a sloppy stack of sheets of paper. This feature appears particularly applicable to the document preparation environment. Several parts of the same document or several documents can be viewed simultaneously and processed, by displaying them in their own windows. These and other Smalltalk features strongly influenced the design of Star's user interface.

One particularly interesting system written in Smalltalk is ThingLab [Borning 79, Borning 81], which can be used to manipulate simulated objects whose interactions are governed by constraints. For example, a rectangle containing text may be constrained so that the text completely fills the rectangle. If the user changes the width of the rectangle, the height is automatically adjusted and the text rejustified so that the text still completely fills the rectangle; similarly, a change in the amount of text will cause a corresponding change in the size of the rectangle. The constraints may be very general; each constraint description includes a number of methods that may be used to satisfy it. The system is also able to satisfy some circular constraints. Although ThingLab is not a document-processing system, its constraint techniques could be useful in future systems for expressing and solving some formatting problems.

3.4.4. The Wang Word Processor

The Wang Word Processor is one of many commercial formatting systems that became available in the late 1970's. It is a self-contained, multi-user system with a dedicated processor and peripherals. Its design stresses ease of use, achieved through an integrated editor/formatter with a simple set of commands. Editing operations are applied directly to a representation of the concrete document that is continuously displayed on a CRT device. Text and commands are entered by single keys on a keyboard or by selection from a menu, and hardcopy output is produced for a typewriter terminal or a phototypesetter.

Most commands are entered by single keystrokes, and reside in the document as special characters. For example, indentation is accomplished by a special indentation key that inserts an "indent" command character into the document. Other, more global formatting commands are applied to an entire section of the document, usually interactively under the control of the user. For example, the system handles pagination and hyphenation by displaying each division point and requesting the user to make a decision about the division to be made. In all cases, the effects of the commands are immediately visible in the concrete representation.

The Wang system deals with a small set of the most useful abstract objects: words, phrases, paragraphs, and page headings. It allows operations on these objects such as hyphenation of words, centering or underlining of phrases, and filling or justification of paragraphs. A number of lower-level commands are also available to allow the construction of other objects. For example, characters may be placed as superscripts or subscripts, and special commands may be used to control horizontal and vertical spacing. As usual, the system places all these objects into lines and pages.

In addition to operations that introduce local formatting actions, there is a set of concrete attributes associated with each page (expressed in a template language) that determine its global characteristics, such as line and page length, tab settings, and inter-line spacing.

The set of commands may be extended through a general macro facility called a *glossary* that allows sequences of keystrokes to be named and called when desired. This facility includes limited recursion and conditional statements, and hence is quite powerful. Glossary entries are created just as is any document, using the full power of the system. However, there is no way to alter the behaviors of the built-in commands nor any notion of variables or expessions.

Although this system offers only modest formatting capabilities, it appears responsive and easy to use. The integration of formatting and editing may help somewhat to make up for the lack of more sophisticated features. For example, although the system cannot automatically determine how to hyphenate words, it can produce hyphenations fairly painlessly by performing them interactively.

On the other hand, the commands and objects of the system are all at a rather low level. The lack of a higher-level structure makes it difficult to restructure the document automatically after it has been changed. For example, the addition of a few new phrases may require that the entire hyphenation process be repeated for long sections of the document. In Section 3.6 we describe systems that attempt to retain the flexibility of integrated editing and formatting, while also making document restructuring easier by maintaining information about the high-level structure of the document.

3.5. Other Systems

In this section, we present four interesting, unrelated systems. KATIB/HATTAT, a pure formatter, formats and typesets documents in Arabic script, perhaps the most difficult alphabet to typeset. The TRIX/RED formatter is contained within an extensive document-processing system which allows composition of quite elaborate documents containing intermixed color graphics (figures), text, and mathematical equations. IDEAL, a TROFF preprocessor, is a language for textually describing two-dimensional figure objects using a system of simultaneous equations to define the relationships between significant points in the figure object. And GML, implemented as a macro package for a RUNOFF-like pure formatter, includes a high-level declarative document specification language and many writer's workbench tools.

3.5.1. KATIB and HATTAT

The programs KATIB and HATTAT, written in the mid 1970's by P. MacKay of the Department of Classics at the University of Washington, formatted and typeset documents using the Arabic and the Roman alphabets [MacKay 77]. Arabic script writing is extraordinarily complicated. The shape and size of each letter is highly context sensitive, depending not only on the surrounding letters but also on the entire word in which the letter appears. Thus, while there are only 29 separate letters in Arabic (and no differing upper and lower cases), a high-quality typesetting job requires that more than 900 separate symbols be used. As MacKay wrote in 1977 [MacKay 77]: "The normal policy of every Orientalist journal in North America, even if it will still consent to print Chinese, cuneiform, or hieroglyphic, is to refuse all Arabic script text. Arabic is not merely 'penalty copy,' it is prohibited copy."

MacKay's system consists of two separate programs. KATIB (which means "writer" or "scribe" in Arabic) performs the page formatting functions. HATTAT ("calligrapher" in Arabic) specifies the penstrokes to be used in forming the characters which KATIB has placed on the page. Importantly, it is HATTAT which determines the actual shape of the individual characters. KATIB only estimates the size of the characters by using the average value of the possible forms. Clearly, formatting and viewing have been separated in this system. KATIB also handles details of intermixing Arabic text (written from right to left) with Roman text (written from left to right). Input is entered in the Roman alphabet, from left to right; it is not necessary to type English or Latin text backwards. Arabic letters are represented phonetically. Output from HATTAT is then processed by a phototypesetter.

The formatting language is surprisingly general, but unfortunately assembly-language-like in appearance. The language is based on one designed by David Packard [Packard 73] for a system which handled intermixed English, Latin, and Greek text. Numeric variables may be defined, assigned values, used (along with constants) in expressions, and tested in conditional statements. Synonyms (i.e., macros), each with a two character name, may be defined and invoked within the text by preceding the name with a reserved escape character.

3.5.2. TRIX/RED

The document preparation system at Lawrence Livermore Laboratories [Beatty, Chin, and Moll 79], developed in the middle through late 1970's, produces visible concrete documents, in color, containing text, mathematical equations, and graphics for display on high-resolution output devices. The system, consisting of a group of separate programs, can be logically divided into four parts: TRIX, which contains a distinct text editor (TRIX/AC) and text formatter (TRIX/RED); PCOMP, which compiles picture descriptions written in the string language PICTURE, producing low-level graphics primitives; TV80LIB, a set of routines allowing applications programs to generate figures for inclusion in the document; and REDPP, which merges the various outputs of the preceding parts into a single output stream, directed to a specific output device. Thus, two different languages are defined, one for text, the other for pictures.

The document description processed by TRIX/RED is RUNOFF-like in appearance with separate text and command lines. In some cases, the argument for a command may be several lines long. A special delimiter line is used to mark the end of a multi-line argument. Mathematical equations can be defined either in the picture language (by drawing them) or with TRIX/RED. When TRIX/RED is used, components of the equation are first defined, then combined into larger parts, and finally displayed. For example, a fraction could be produced by first defining the numerator and the denominator; then defining the fraction to be the numerator placed over the denominator, separated with a line; and then finally directing that the composite object be displayed. This is a crude form of nested boxes. Unfortunately, the language for specifying equations is quite cumbersome. A limited form of nesting of environments is available for low-level typographic directives (e.g., selecting fonts, or point sizes). A macro facility, permitting text and numeric arguments, is available to allow extension of the language.

The PICTURE language, processed by PCOMP, is a context-free language with reserved words. The language, while not very powerful, is able to describe a useful range of figures. Primitive objects are lines, circles, and other geometric forms. Their position is specified within a coordinate space. Other attributes, such as radius of a circle, can also be specified. Simple text-formatting operations are available within the language so text objects can be included within a picture. All objects can be colored, filled in, rotated about an axis, and scaled. No control structures (e.g., iteration, conditionals, or macros) are available. PICTURE language statements can either be embedded in the file processed by TRIX/RED or maintained separately. However, since TRIX/RED and PCOMP are separate programs, integration of the output from the two is awkward: the user of the system must specify to TRIX/RED how much space the picture will take and cannot use TRIX/RED commands within PICTURE language input.

Figures and drawings can also be generated by applications programs through calls to routines in TV80LIB. While PCOMP is not interactive, some of these applications programs are, so interactive picture editing is possible.

The final part of the package, REDPP, merges the output from TRIX/RED, PCOMP, and TV80LIB routines, producing an output file for display on a particular device. Formatting and viewing have been separated in this system. TRIX/RED performs the page formatting, producing a representation which is device independent. REDPP performs the viewing function.

Again, as with UNIX, the organization of this system into separate programs has both advantages and disadvantages. We discuss these further in Section 4.7.2. Still, this is an ambitious system, certainly one of the few to treat characters as picture objects which may be colored, rotated and scaled.

3.5.3. IDEAL

C. Van Wyk has developed an interesting one-dimensional (string) language for specifying line drawings in a document [VanWyk 80, VanWyk 81]. In this language, an object class is defined in two parts, a declarative section and an instruction section. The declarations specify the relations, or constraints, that must hold among the points of the object. These relations lead to a system of simultaneous equations that the points must satisfy. The instruction section of the object definition gives instructions for connecting points and for drawing other objects by invoking or calling them. When an object is invoked, additional relations, equations, and instructions may be inserted in the call. These "parameters" further specify the equations and must result in a unique solution for the point variables. At this stage, the instruction part may be executed with the solution points, drawing, for example, points, lines, text, circles, and rectangles.

The language has been implemented in C as a TROFF preprocessor called IDEAL. While it requires perhaps too much mathematical sophistication for general use, the language may be practical with an interactive or less mathematical user interface. It is significant chiefly because of its methods for declaring and solving constraint equations.

3.5.4. GML

The Generalized Markup Language (GML) was developed by C. F. Goldfarb of IBM over a period of years in the early to middle 1970's. GML first became available for general use in 1978 and is now part of IBM's Document Composition Facility [IBM 80a, IBM 80b, Goldfarb 81a, Goldfarb 81b].

GML is a pure formatter, implemented using macros written for the SCRIPT formatter. SCRIPT is a RUNOFF-like pure formatter first developed in the late 1960's [Madnick and Moulton 68, IBM 80c]. GML provides high-level declarative specifications, called *tags*, which are associated with points in the document text. Figure 20 contains more information about the specification language. Notice that the commands of the underlying implementation language (SCRIPT) remain available for use.

GML also incorporates many desirable writer's workbench features. Included are automatic numbering of list elements, chapters, and footnotes; symbolic referencing to page numbers or other numbers associated with parts of the document; and facilities for collecting and formatting information to be included in a table of contents and in an index.

3.6. Some Current Developments

We wish to present three experimental systems still under development and not yet completely specified to conclude our discussion of representative and seminal systems. All combine the idea of high-level declarative object specification, taken from some of the recent pure formatters, with the idea of continuous viewing of the visible concrete document, as in some of the integrated editor/formatters.

3.6.1. JANUS

JANUS [Chamberlin, et al. 81, Chamberlin, et al. 82] is an integrated editor/formatter under development at the IBM Research Laboratory in San Jose. JANUS uses a work station with keyboard, joystick, and two screens. One screen is used to show the specification of a document in a declarative specification language; the other shows the corresponding page of the visible concrete document as it would appear if printed. The two screens can be thought of as being

```
:frontm.
:titlep.
.se tl = 'Document Formatting Systems:   Survey, Concepts, and Issues'
.se ea = 'Extended Abstract'
:title.&tl. [&ea.]:fnref refid=funds.
:fn id=funds.
This research was supported in part by the National Science Foundation
under grant number MCS-7826285.
:efn.
:author.Alan Shaw
:author.Richard Furuta
:author.Jeffrey Scofield
:address.
:aline.Department of Computer Science
:aline.University of Washington
:aline.Seattle, Washington   98195, U.S.A.
:eaddress.
:etitlep.
:abstract.
:p.Formatting, the final part of the document preparation process, is
concerned with the physical layout of a document for hard and soft
copy media....   Our aims are to characterize the formatting problem
and its relation to other aspects of document processing, to evaluate
several representative and seminal systems, and to describe some
issues and problems relevant to future systems.
:body.
:h2.The Formatting Problem
:p.In order to discuss formatters and their functions and to distinguish
formatting from other aspects of document preparation, it is
convenient to use an :hp1.object:ehp1. model of documents [Shaw 80],
somewhat analogous to that in programming languages.
:p.A document is an object composed of a hierarchy of more primitive
objects....
:h2.Representative and Seminal Systems
:h3.Pure Formatters
:p.Some typical first generation formatters...
```

Figure 20: GML specification to produce the sectioned document of Figure 16.

The figure presents the same document segment as that given in Figures 8 and 16. This GML specification uses the "starter set" tags. Other sets would provide different tags. Tags begin with a colon and end with a period. They consist of a tag name followed by an optional list of attribute-value pairs. Attributes either provide additional information (e.g., a short form of the title) or provide formatting parameters. A text argument follows the period. Pairs of tags which are defined as delimiting a multi-line argument are flagged with ":" and ":e" respectively.

(Continued on the following page)

This document description consists of two major parts: the front matter, beginning with the ":frontm." tag, and the body, beginning with the ":body." tag. The body and the front matter are formatted differently. The front matter contains a title page which is delimited by ":titlep." and ":etitlep." tags. The SCRIPT ".se" command, used in the third and fourth lines of the description, associate the document text to the right of the " = " with the symbol name to the left. "&tl." retrieves the string associated with the symbol "tl". Note that the period in "&tl." is part of the specification and not part of the text. Symbols are used in this example since the argument to the ":title." tag must fit onto a single line. The ":fnref refid = funds." tag retrieves the number of the identified footnote, here the one tagged with ":fn id = funds." which contains an id attribute corresponding to that used in the footnote reference. The actual implementation of the "starter set" tags prohibits inclusion of footnotes within the front matter, although the implementation could be changed to permit them. ":p." tags a paragraph. ":h2." and ":h3.", used in the body, specify text for section and subsection headings.

Figure 20, concluded.

---

two separate fixed-size windows on different representations of the document. Editing is performed on the document description rather than on the representation of the final document. Published material does not indicate how Janus will aid the correlation of information on the two screens. Correlation may be awkward unless the system's user interface is carefully designed.

The description language is closely related to GML, associating high-level, declarative tags with particular locations in the document. The current prototype implementation uses Pascal language procedures to define new tags.

A JANUS document is specified as a collection of *galleys*. One galley might contain document text and another might contain footnote text. Points in different galleys are marked as corresponding to each other. This allows a footnote, for example, to be correlated with its reference in the body of the text. The correlation is used in placing material from different galleys on the same physical page. The actual placement of galley material onto physical pages is done using information contained in *page templates*. There may be a number of page templates associated with any particular document, for example, a title page template, a body page template, and a template for the appendices. Each template indicates where the material from each of the galleys contributing to the page may be placed, and specifies certain "fixtures" such as page headings.

JANUS also allows the user to point to a particular object on the page (say, a figure) and drag it to a new location. The rest of the page is reformatted accordingly. This feature permits local overriding of placement decisions made by the formatter and is implemented by creating a special page template to represent the manually altered page. Consequently, a manually repositioned item on a page will remain in its new location, even if surrounding material is reformatted. Further discussion of issues raised by this feature is in Section 4.5.1.

3.6.2. Etude

Etude [Good 81, Hammer, et al. 81a, Hammer, et al. 81b, Ilson 80], an integrated editor/ formatter being implemented at MIT, uses a bitmapped terminal. A Scribe-like model of document structure is combined with an internal model based on the boxes and glue of TEX. A document page consists of a collection of page spaces. Objects placed in these page spaces are obtained from one or more *subdocuments*, a concept closely resembling JANUS' galleys. As in Scribe, Etude document type definitions are collected into a database. The editing language uses English-like commands. Special keys are associated with the more commonly used commands. A help facility is provided and a menu of commands is produced on request.

The document is displayed using four windows. One window displays paginated text in final form. Associated with this window is another window containing format information. This information window is placed at the margin of the text window. The displayed format information corresponds to the adjacent line in the text window. The third window serves as an interaction window, displaying prompts and echoing typed input. The fourth window shows the system's status.

3.6.3. Yale's PEN

PEN [Allen, Nix, and Perlis 81], under development at Yale University, presents another possible organization for an integrated editor/formatter. It differs from JANUS and Etude in its scope and goals. Rather than building a complete prototype of a future system, PEN presents a smaller experimental testbed. Like Etude, PEN includes a Scribe-like hierarchical model to describe the abstract structure of a document and a TEX-like boxes and glue model to describe the relationships between concrete objects. Unlike JANUS and Etude, PEN's document model does not incorporate pagination, thus allowing for a simpler formulation.

One of the interesting aspects about a PEN document is its tree representation. For textual material, the internal nodes of this tree represent a hierarchy of objects within the document, for example, chapter, section, and paragraph. Internal nodes are instances of a template for the object they represent. Further, each node's type includes a specification of the type and number of those nodes which can be its children, thus placing constraints on the legal relationships among objects in the tree. Leaves of the tree contain primitive objects. In the case of text, these primitive objects are expressed using the boxes and glue model. A Smalltalk-like model of object invocation is used. Editing and formatting operations on a node are carried out by asking the node to perform the operation. It is the node's responsibility to perform the operation in an appropriate fashion; the action associated with a particular operation varies depending on the node to which the operation is applied.

One portion of the formatting problem which has been investigated in more detail is the specification of mathematical formulae. PEN includes a specification language called PEN-MATH. Since PEN-MATH is based on APL, it allows concise specification of mathematical structures such as arrays and sequences. PEN views the objects described by a PEN-MATH specification as being entirely contained within a leaf of the tree (these objects are not directly incorporated into PEN's object hierarchy). However, PEN-MATH extends PEN's object-oriented structure. In particular, parameters (called *looks*) may be passed to an operator, altering the way in which the operator displays itself and its operands. Thus the specification for *a* multiplied by *b*, "a✕b", may be displayed as "a✕b", "a•b", or "ab" depending on the parameters passed to the operator.

4. Issues and Concepts

The previous sections have identified a number of issues and concepts that suggest ideas for further research and that should also be of use in the design and evaluation of formatting systems.

4.1. Document and Processing Models

A formatter is easier to understand and to design if it is based on a consistent model of documents and of the operations used in processing them. Current systems offer some interesting and useful models, but much development remains to be done.

4.1.1. Document models

Because the notion of classes and instances is a powerful means of characterizing sets of related objects, a document model like the class/instance model described in Section 2.1 seems to be a natural choice. A further advantage is that this is an integrated model of abstract and concrete documents. Existing models have tended to be either concrete or abstract, but not both.

Abstract Models

The underlying form of the model presented in Section 2.1 is tree-structured, as may be seen in the example class <ExtendedAbstract>. However, the notion of ordered and unordered subtrees allows a flexibility of expression not present in strictly tree-structured models such as those of the XS-1 system [Burkhart and Nievergelt 80].

One limitation of any tree-structured model is that it cannot directly represent all the necessary relations among the objects in documents, since some violate the nesting restrictions of trees. Such relations are rather common, since parts of a document very often refer to other parts by name, by section number, or by page number.

A model of abstract documents that does not have this limitation is a generalized graph structure, such as the one used in the Hypertext Editing System (HES) [Carmody, et al. 69, vanDam and Rice 71], in the NLS system [Engelbart and English 68, Engelbart, Watson, and Norton 73, vanDam and Rice 71], and in PIE [Goldstein and Bobrow 80, Goldstein and Bobrow 81]. By assigning particular structural meanings to the links in the graph, this model can be used to represent any relations among the objects of a document. For example, the relation between a footnote reference in the main text and the footnote to which it refers may be modelled in this way. This model could also be used to represent desired spatial relations among concrete objects.

Since trees are more comprehensible than general graphs, and since many documents are primarily tree-structured, it may be more desirable to use a tree-structured model and to include general relations among objects as subsidiary information. For example, Scribe allows references between objects, although they are not directly included in Scribe's essentially tree-structured model.

It should be noted that neither HES, XS-1, nor PIE is chiefly a formatting system. In fact, no formatting system today offers a sufficiently explicit model for abstract documents. Scribe's notion of "document types" and PEN's tree structure come closest to this goal.

Concrete models

A model for concrete documents must deal with two-dimensional components of the page. In general, the details of particular concrete primitives, such as characters, are hidden by considering them to reside inside simpler figures, such as rectangles or parallelograms. The model developed for EQN, with nested and juxtaposed rectangular boxes, has proven simple and very natural. The more refined model used in TEX, which places glue between the boxes, is the most complete model for concrete documents that has been implemented and tested.

Current experimental systems, such as Etude, JANUS, and PEN, may help to determine whether TEX's model can be made even more useful by being integrated into a higher-level model for concrete documents. Etude and JANUS attempt to provide a high-level concrete document that consists of a set of related *galleys* to be placed into definable concrete page spaces. All three systems attempt to integrate this concrete model with a model for abstract documents.

4.1.2. Processing models

Models for the processing of documents are rather diverse. The traditional processing method that was used in all early formatters accumulates characters into lines and pages, and takes appropriate action when these spaces threaten to overflow; these actions are taken immediately, without looking ahead into the document. This model has proven far too limited to offer flexible control over the appearance of the final document, largely because of this lack of look-ahead.

The syntax-driven model of the formatting process is based on the parsing of a context-free language. This model has been used for two slightly different purposes. In the first case, the syntax is that of an already existing language (in general, a programming language). This approach has been used to reformat programs into a more legible form, and has the characteristic that the input and output are syntactically identical strings. In the second case, the syntax is that of a language used to describe the objects of the document, and the resulting concrete output is very different from its input description. This approach is used in EQN and in the math mode of TEX. Although syntax-driven techniques are very powerful when applied to languages with easily described grammars, they cannot readily be applied to textual objects such as paragraphs, or other objects with less regular structure.

The processing model used in TEX for paragraph layout, described in Section 3.3.3, is the most satisfactory to date. However, since the use of penalty values to control the concrete appearance of objects is not based on a direct statement of the desired appearance of the document, the choice of penalty values appears to be a task requiring a fair amount of experience. A more direct way of specifying the desired appearance would be even more useful.

The use of constraints to specify desired properties of objects, as is done in IDEAL and in ThingLab, leads to a processing model in which the system attempts to satisfy all constraints simultaneously. The equation-solving technique used in IDEAL is quite powerful, although rather stringent restrictions must be placed on the types of equations allowed. Further, this technique is clearly limited to problem domains that are essentially numeric. The more flexible technique used in ThingLab includes equation solving as a particular case, but is much more general and may be used with constraints that are not numeric.

The development of document and processing models must be undertaken together, since they interact very strongly. For example, an attractive document model may be rejected if it cannot lead to good models for the processing of the document.

4.2. Formatting Functions

4.2.1. Kinds of objects

Formatters must have facilities for dealing with many kinds of objects. Current systems provide a variety of textual objects, a few systems offer mathematical and tabular objects, and fewer yet offer pictorial objects.

There are many other useful specialized object types that need to be formatted, such as musical notation, chemical diagrams, chess positions, and crossword puzzle diagrams. In each case, it should be possible to take advantage of the structure of the objects to simplify their specification. One challenge for future general-purpose formatters will be to provide such new and useful object types, to allow users to create their own object types, and to define a uniform framework in which objects of all types may be used.

4.2.2. Composition of objects

Documents consist of simple objects combined into more complex ones. For the most part, this structuring is conveniently done at the abstract level. That is, the user should describe the abstract object composition of the document, and the formatter should transform this structured abstract object into a structured concrete one.

There are two levels of definition that may be used in the construction of abstract documents. The first is the creation of new classes and subclasses. A user may want to define an entirely new document class such as "business letter," or may want to create a subclass by further specifying an existing class. An example of a subclass of the "business letter" class would be a "form letter" class with a fixed body. Instances of "form letter" would need to supply only a recipient, as the body would be supplied by the subclass. This notion of classes and subclasses is similar to that of Smalltalk.

The creation of new classes and subclasses is not allowed in all systems, and in systems where even a partial facility is provided (Scribe, TEX, TROFF), it is often so difficult that it is not intended for the casual user. In addition, few systems provide a mechanism for encapsulating the details of new classes. In many cases, the behavior of classes is controlled by global variables that may be inadvertently changed, either directly or through the use of conflicting low-level commands. Since the creation of new classes and subclasses is often the easiest and most natural way for a user to specify a desired document (or, even more so, a series of similar documents), ways of simplifying this task should be developed. This topic is discussed further in Section 4.3.3.

The second level of definition used in the construction of abstract documents is the definition of instances of an already defined class, for example, the definition of a particular paragraph and its body. All formatters allow this sort of definition, although it is not always thought of in the terms used here.

Structural information about classes of objects can be used by formatters to govern the composition of abstract objects and to simplify the user's task. Class information can be used, for example, to insure that objects are correctly formed, or, in interactive systems, to suggest prompts for parts of the structure to be entered next. Classes can also supply default values for attributes of their instances. This can substantially simplify the creation of new objects, allowing the user to concentrate on only the aspects of objects that distinguish them from the default for the class.

Some limited structural checking is performed by Scribe, which defines different kinds of object substructures depending on the type (i.e., the class) of the document being constructed. The PEN system has formalized this notion and performs even stronger checking. No other modern system offers functions of this sort. In TROFF, for example, abstract objects are most often bracketed by pairs of opening and closing commands, but TROFF does not check that such opening and closing brackets are properly nested, or that the enclosed material is of the correct type.

4.2.3. Abstract-to-concrete mappings

All present formatting systems severely limit the ways in which abstract-to-concrete mappings are performed for structured abstract objects. For example, most systems simply change a sequence of abstract objects into a corresponding sequence of concrete objects, and provide no control over the orderings of the objects and of their parts. This requires the user to specify completely the ordering of objects (such as bibliographic references), when it may be more desirable to allow the formatter to choose the ordering. Recent systems have offered more control, but this is usually limited to a few special cases such as figures that may be reordered with respect to the surrounding text.

TROFF and TEX allow users to define new abstract objects, while TBL and EQN support a large number of built-in abstract objects. However, because none of these systems have a general way for users to express concrete attributes of objects, much of the desired control over their concrete representations must be built into their implementations from the beginning.

Scribe has more flexible mechanisms whereby the concrete attributes of its abstract objects, or "environments," may be modified at any time, and this modification may be local (to only a single instance of an object), or global (applying to all objects of the class). A limitation of this system is that it relies on the existence of a fixed universe of concrete attributes; there is no mechanism provided for extending the set of attributes.

4.2.4. Relations among concrete objects

Formatters should provide a means for expressing relations among concrete objects. For example, it should be possible to align designated parts of the concrete representation of nearby objects, to constrain the allowed distances between them (imposing either a minimum or a maximum distance, or both), or to specify objects whose size depends on the placement of nearby objects.

Only one system, TEX, permits constraints on distances between all types of objects, accomplished by means of glue specifications. Since there is usually glue between all pairs of adjacent objects, a very fine degree of control over the distances between them is possible. However, this scheme does not work for specifying distances between objects that are not directly adjacent, for specifying alignments of objects, or for making sizes of objects depend on other objects.

One result of the lack of a means to express relations between objects is that all recent formatters contain a number of rather low-level functions to allow concrete specifications. These facilities are similar to the strictly concrete control that was offered by earlier formatters such as FORMAT and RUNOFF. For example, EQN and TEX have many types of "space" characters that must be used to move parts of equations around when the provided structuring methods are not adequate. For the same reason, Scribe has low-level features for tabulation and a number of other positioning commands.

Controlling the concrete representations by low-level spacing commands is rather unsatisfactory for two reasons. In the first place, it causes the user to be concerned with very low-level details when in fact often only high-level notions of alignment are involved. In the second place, use of these low-level spacing commands makes it very hard to change the document: a small change in one place will often require that all of the spaces be recalibrated. If the alignment constraints could be stated directly, this recalibration would not be necessary.

Another result is that common kinds of control over relations must often be built into formatters as special cases. For example, EQN and TEX provide special-purpose "alignment" operators; these allow designated parts of adjacent equations to be aligned, but cannot be used to solve general two-dimensional alignment problems. As another example, both TEX and Scribe offer special predefined operations for dealing with footnotes, which require control over the maximum distance between concrete objects to guarantee that the footnote will be on the same page as its reference.

In each case, these concrete functions violate the goal that the user be freed from low-level details. In many ways, this is similar to the dilemma faced in the design of higher-level languages, where the attempt to eliminate low-level details restricts the programmer's control.

Two methods of solving this dilemma are found in recent systems designed for the formatting of graphics; these systems offer much greater flexibility in expressing relations among objects. The first of these, the PIC language, provides predefined names for the key parts of objects and ways of specifying how the named parts of objects are to be spatially related. To some extent, it also allows the size of an object to depend on its relation to other objects.

The means for specifying these relations is very simple: objects are described in a sequence, and a point on each new object is placed either at an absolute location or in a described relationship to a point on an existing object. This simplicity also limits the complexity of relations that may be represented. No cyclic relations may be represented, and, with the exception of arc definitions, it is not possible to represent a relation between one object and several others. This structure may thus be somewhat cumbersome for very complex relations.

The IDEAL system allows even more flexible relations among graphical objects. In this system, relations among objects are represented by equations involving points on the objects, expressed as complex numbers. The system solves these equations to determine the actual points to be used. In this way, any desired relations among the points of the objects may be expressed, providing that the resulting equations admit a solution. However, a possible weakness is that equations are not always a natural means for representing desired relations.

Both of these systems have the drawback that relations among objects must be completely specified, although the use of defaults helps to reduce the problem. However, neither system provides a way of expressing general constraints on the concrete appearance of objects and allowing the system to choose the appearance that best satisfies these constraints. For example, the user cannot specify a range of allowable values instead of a single value. Experiments with methods for specifying and satisfying more general constraints, such as those of ThingLab, may provide insight into more flexible ways of expressing relations.

If formatters had better facilities for composing objects and more control over their concrete forms and relations, the number of primitive predefined objects could be decreased. For example, it would not be necessary to include a special kind of object, such as a figure, that may be reordered with respect to surrounding text, or a special command for aligning equal signs in adjacent equations. Formatters could provide only characters and line segments as primitives, and all of the normal objects could be built from them.

4.2.5. Page spaces

Many characteristics of documents are best described as properties of the page spaces into which the document objects are placed, rather than as properties of the objects themselves. For example, pages are most often built from nested and juxtaposed spaces for page headers, footnotes, figures, and so forth. However, few formatters permit much control over the page spaces occupied by concrete objects; most do not allow these spaces to be either nested or juxtaposed, and require them to have a bounded rectangular shape. The lack of a general means for specifying such structures means that they must be treated awkwardly, as properties of document objects or as special cases.

Further, even more complex shapes are often required. For example, a page may be shaped like a rectangle with a smaller rectangle removed; the surrounding rectangle may contain text while the removed rectangle can be used for a figure. Even three-dimensional spaces could be considered—for example, layouts for transparent overlays could be designed in this manner. As the layout of pages becomes more and more complex, the task may become too complicated to be handled conveniently by a pure formatter. An integrated system may be needed, so that the user may see immediately the results of changes. The lack of sufficient control over page layout has meant that general-purpose formatters are not used for document types, such as magazines and newspapers, for which this control is essential.

Two of the experimental systems described above, JANUS and Etude, have proposed more flexible methods for specifying the nesting of page spaces; further research should attempt to provide even more control. If this research is successful, general-purpose formatters could be used for a number of layout problems for which more specialized programs have traditionally been used.

From the preceding discussion of objects, composition, abstract-to-concrete mappings, relations, and page spaces, it is clear that even current formatters are very limited in the formatting functions that they offer. Some of the limitations are historical, and are caused by former restrictions on output devices. Some are due to the lack of efficient algorithms for implementing the desired functions. Others, such as inadequate control over relations among concrete objects or the inability to format objects into complex page spaces, arise because it has proven difficult to design a language for expressing the desired functions.

4.3. Formatting Language

The usefulness of a formatting system is very dependent upon the formatting language used to specify documents. The document specification language must be able to express the structure and content of many different kinds of objects. Some means of controlling the abstract-to-concrete mapping of the objects is also required. Finally, the language may also allow the user to create new classes of objects.

Few systems give an explicit description of their formatting language. With the exception of EQN, no formatting language has even included its grammar in its published description, as do most modern programming languages. It is therefore often very difficult to determine whether an undesired feature of the concrete document is the result of an error in the formatting system or is due to a misunderstanding of the syntax or semantics of the formatting language. In addition, the absence of a precise semantic description often makes it impossible to determine the effects of combinations of operations provided by the language.

Future formatting systems should provide more precise descriptions of the syntax and semantics of their formatting language. There is a great deal of benefit to be derived from the explicit use of a rich context-free language like that of EQN; such a language insures great flexibility and internal consistency. Many other benefits of this approach are discussed in the original paper on EQN [Kernighan and Cherry 75].

Since formatting systems are used by a wider variety of people than conventional programming systems, it is important that the language be easy to use and to understand. It is also important, however, that the language be capable of describing any desired document. Much of the difficulty of designing a formatting language is caused by the conflict between these two goals.

4.3.1. Declarative languages

One approach that has been used to make formatting languages easier to understand is to make them declarative rather than procedural. Since documents are essentially passive in nature, and themselves perform no processing, this is a natural approach. It also allows the formatting process to be understood without a knowledge of programming concepts. With a declarative language, the document is viewed as a series of declarations that elaborate its structure and content. The abstract-to-concrete mapping is controlled by associating "properties" with the objects.

The power of a declarative language can be increased by using templates for describing parameterized structures, that is, structures of which part is constant and part is supplied later as an argument. Templates are a very natural means of specification, since the template language can be designed so that the template graphically resembles the class of structures that it encodes. Templates represent a natural method for extending declarative languages; in a well-designed language, named templates can be used in the same manner as structures that are built into the language.

Among the pure formatters, the declarative approach is taken most notably by Scribe, where concrete properties associated with text are defined by environments. Default properties supplied by Scribe's database may be supplemented or overridden in each case by the user. Scribe uses templates in some special cases, such as the representation of formats for dates and for numerical quantities, but does not really allow the language to be extended by means of templates.

Some integrated editor/formatters also offer what is essentially a declarative language. For example, both Bravo and Star define the appearance of objects by associating low-level properties with them. As described in Section 3.4.2, Bravo is conventionally used with a set of template files (forms) that simplify the process of creating new documents. A very similar facility is offered by PEN, where the templates are called "default instances" of objects.

The power and naturalness of templates is also demonstrated in both TEX and UNIX. Although their languages are chiefly procedural, both systems use a template language to specify table formats.

4.3.2. Procedural languages

Many systems treat the formatting process as a series of operations to be applied to objects, much in the style of a traditional programming language. This has the advantage that the formatting language can be made extremely powerful. The inclusion in the language of only a small number of programming constructs can help to insure that a user will be able to perform any function that is desired, since the formatting language can then presumably be used to calculate any computable function at all. This approach does have the corresponding disadvantage that a user unfamiliar with programming concepts will be unable to understand the more advanced features of the system.

In a purely functional system, the abstract-to-concrete mapping would be controlled only by the operations that were performed on the objects. In most systems, however, there is also a set of global variables that control this mapping. In addition, there is usually some way for particular values of the global variables to be associated with particular objects by entering a nested scope for the duration of the processing of the objects. Upon leaving the scope, the old values of the global variables are restored. This is the method used by PUB, TROFF, and TEX.

A procedural formatting language also allows the language itself to be extended easily through the definition of macros or procedures. If properly designed, the language can permit the extended operations to be used exactly as the built-in operations. In PUB, TROFF, and TEX, the user can define macros including recursion and conditional tests. PUB has an especially large number of programming constructs, including procedures and iteration in its later versions. These insure that a user will be able to produce almost any desired document.

Formatters could benefit from even more ideas from conventional programming languages. Much could be gained by allowing variables and expressions of many types, including both traditional types such as integers and strings, and also abstract and concrete objects. In addition, such formatters should offer the kinds of debugging facilities that are provided by programming language systems. This is necessary because the increased power of procedural languages makes it harder to diagnose their failures.

As shown by TEX and UNIX, it is possible for a system to be a mixture of both declarative and procedural languages. One scheme, proposed for the JANUS system, provides a declarative language to describe particular documents, and a procedural language to define classes of documents by implementing the constructs of this declarative language. Many other organizations are possible. Again, there are similarities to the design of higher-level programming languages, which most often consist of a mixture of declarations and executable statements.

4.3.3. Class definitions

There are a variety of mechanisms for defining new classes. In a declarative language this may be done either, as in PEN, by using a template to represent a class of objects by means of a single, partially-specified object, or, as in Scribe, by the simpler process of associating an environment name with a set of concrete properties.

In a procedural language, this may be done either by explicitly declaring classes as in Simula [Birtwistle, et al. 79] or Smalltalk, or, as in most current formatting systems, by the simpler method of associating a procedure or macro with the new class. This procedure or macro is used to produce instances of the new class by calling or invoking it with appropriate arguments, most often a stream of text. The more explicit class/instance method has greater promise, however, since it permits more control over objects. For example, this method could be used to insure that objects of a class were correctly structured.

Some systems, such as Scribe and JANUS, have separated the language used to describe classes from that used to describe instances of the classes. In both cases, this is done so that the general user need not be concerned with class definition. However, it also has the drawback that it may tend to draw too sharp a distinction between a class of objects and a single object. Usually there is a spectrum of objects in use, from a very generic class of "documents" at the top, through a number of more and more highly specified objects with fairly constant formats (such as "technical reports" or "newsletters"), down to particular instances of documents (such as "Technical Report #37") at the most specific level. As described in Section 4.2.2, it is often as natural for a user to want to create a new subclass (a more specified form of an existing class) as it is to want to create a particular instance of a document. There is a danger, then, that too great a distinction between the languages used to describe classes and instances would make it difficult to create natural and economical descriptions of such a hierarchy of objects.

4.4. Integration of Objects

Systems that deal with a large number of different kinds of objects have often failed to provide a uniform framework for handling them. For example, the UNIX system offers separate languages and programs for its different classes of objects. It is worth investigating the advantages of a single language and set of commands for all these classes.

The UNIX system also places some limitations on the ways objects may be nested. For example, it is not possible to include one table as an entry in another, or to include graphical objects within a mathematical one. This is caused partly by the fact that the formatting processors communicate by one-directional pipes and are designed so that objects of one kind are all processed at once by a single program. This means that, for example, the results of formatting a table containing mathematics cannot easily be used as input to the formatting process for another mathematical object.

As another example, TEX integrates the formatting of textual, tabular, and mathematical objects into a single language. However, the integration is not complete because there are separate "modes" for handling text and mathematics. TEX thus fails to provide a single set of commands that is applicable to all objects.

Future research should attempt to find a single set of primitive operations (or properties, for declarative systems) that may be used in the creation and manipulation (or description) of objects of all types. This would insure that objects may be nested in arbitrary combinations, and would reduce the amount of detail present in a formatting system based on these primitive operations. The Star system uses an especially small set of universal commands, and Smalltalk and its applications use a single mechanism for applying operations to all objects. These systems are thus rich sources of ideas for integrating objects.

4.5. Integration of Document Processing Functions

In addition to integrating different types of objects into a single framework, systems should also attempt to integrate the many different functions performed in the preparation of a document. Systems in which these functions are not integrated require the use of a large number of unrelated environments. For example, one environment may be an editor, another may be the command interpreter of an operating or filing system, and a third may be the formatting system itself. Different commands and operations are used in each environment, and even the styles of interaction may be different for the different environments. There is usually a fairly large amount of mental effort and time required to move from one environment to another.

4.5.1. Integration of editing and formatting

The greatest gains in this area come from the integration of editing and formatting, as in the systems described in Section 3.4. In a system where these functions are not integrated, the document preparation process is a cyclic activity of refining the document description, generating the resulting document, and finding flaws in the concrete appearance of the document. This process is repeated until the concrete appearance is satisfactory. An integrated editor/formatter reduces the effort of this task by making the generation of the concrete document a part of a single document creation procedure. In simple systems, the current concrete appearance of the document may be viewed on request.

This process may be carried even further, so that the formatting and viewing functions are carried out continuously, and the user may be considered to be applying operations directly to the finished document. This immediacy allows the document to be manipulated partly through the physically intuitive notions of moving objects around on a two-dimensional surface. It also reduces the amount of detail that a user must remember, since it is no longer necessary to be able to "predict" the system's actions when it is given a set of commands. Instead, the system's actions become immediately apparent.

The drawback of existing integrated editor/formatters is that the high-level structure of the document is not represented. Since the user manipulates only the concrete document, its abstract structure is obscured. This makes it difficult not only to manipulate logical entities as a unit, but also to generate several versions of the same document according to different formatting conventions.

Two experimental systems, JANUS and Etude, attempt to provide concrete and abstract information simultaneously. In these systems, the user may edit both the abstract structure of the document and its concrete format. Although similar in this respect, the two systems differ in their emphasis. In Etude, the user is expected to deal chiefly with the concrete form of the document, except when direct manipulation of its abstract structure is desired. In JANUS, on the other hand, the user is expected to be concerned chiefly with the abstract form of the document, perhaps checking its concrete appearance from time to time. Editing of the concrete document is intended only as a means of overriding the actions of the formatter. Although this is an attractive means of controlling the abstract-to-concrete mapping, it is of limited use unless the changes are also made a permanent part of the abstract document. Otherwise, there will be serious problems in maintaining consistency between the two versions of the document.

Integrated systems make it possible for programming to be done in an entirely new way. Rather than describing the desired actions symbolically, the user may actually carry out the actions, which are remembered by the system. The system may then be asked to repeat the actions at a later time. This technique is powerful, yet simple enough to be used by people with no knowledge of programming. It has been used in a number of experimental programming systems [Smith 75, Curry 78], and work is going on to include it in the Star system [Halbert 81].

New methods for creating classes of objects can also be used in an integrated system. ThingLab, for example, implements an attractive technique that allows a user to define a class by constructing a particular instance of the class. This idea may be applied to document systems as well. For example, a class of form letters could be constructed by creating a single prototypical form letter. Instances of this class would specify different recipients but would otherwise be identical to the prototype.

Future systems could benefit from even further integration. For example, the creation of primitive graphical objects, special characters, and new character fonts may be made an integral part of the document preparation process.

4.5.2. Integration of other functions

In order to be most useful, document preparation systems must offer more than just editing and formatting functions. Even the earliest formatting systems attempted to provide a number of more general document preparation functions, such as the "dictionary" command of FORMAT. More of these writer's workbench facilities should be available, including detection and correction of spelling errors; generation of outlines, tables of contents, indices, and concordances; and citation of bibliographic references. A number of general resources, such as dictionaries, thesauruses, and manuals of writing style, would also be useful.

When a document becomes very large, changes are most often made only to part of the document; the other parts are unchanged, or are changed only slightly. In this case it is much more efficient if the changed parts can be reformatted separately, without reformatting the entire document. The reformatting is complicated somewhat by the fact that parts of the document often refer by name, section number, or page number to other parts. This means that a change to one section may require changes (perhaps small ones) to the sections that refer to them.

Scribe solves these problems by allowing a document to be broken into a number of modules that may be formatted either separately or as a unit, and handles the references between these modules automatically. However, the user must state explicitly where the divisions into modules are to be made, and these divisions need not be related to the logical structure of the document.

The class/instance model outlined in Section 2.1 defines a document as being structured from a number of nested simpler objects such as paragraphs, sections, and so on. A document preparation system based on this model could use the high-level structure of the document, together with a knowledge of the references from one object to another, to determine automatically parts of the document to be formatted separately, and could allow many kinds of changes to be propagated through the entire document automatically.

There are also advantages in keeping historical versions of a single document and in maintaining families of related documents that have some parts in common. A system that understood these notions would allow the integration of a facility for comparing documents in order to determine their differences. This comparison could be used to determine the portions of a document that have changed since its previous version, or to capture the differences between the members of a family of documents. The PIE system has suggested a way of achieving these goals. PIE also allows the creation of alternate versions that may be maintained consistently in parallel. However, its ideas have not yet been tried in a formatting system.

Even more elaborate tools may be envisioned. For example, a system could help to maintain documents in a partial state of composition by maintaining an outline of parts not yet written, and could allow this outline to be easily fleshed out later. Improved facilities for allowing multiple authors to work on a document without conflict could be added. This might include, for example, a means of making comments on sections and a means of "locking" sections for exclusive access while they are being worked on. Recent programs in the UNIX system analyze aspects of the style and readability of documents [Cherry 81]; some potential also exists for the application of artificial intelligence and other techniques to the deeper analysis of document style and content.

4.6. User Interface

Every formatting system provides the user with a means of accessing the operations for creating, viewing, and modifying documents. The quality of the interface presented to the user may be judged in part by the following criteria:

- The amount of detail that the user must memorize in order to use the system.

- The amount of mental and physical effort that is required to perform common functions.

- The average number of errors made by the user, especially including errors from which recovery is difficult.

- The amount of time that the user is required to wait for the system to perform its functions, such as the time required for an integrated editor/formatter to update the contents of a screen, or the time required for a pure formatter to create a concrete document for viewing.

The overall design of a formatting system contributes a great deal to the quality of the interface. Ideally, a system should be based on a small number of powerful operations, so that it is simple enough to be easily understood (and hence memorized) by its intended users. Similarly, a system designed around a small number of organizing principles (such as a single context-free language) may be made very consistent. This allows the behavior of the system to be predicted easily and reduces the amount of memorization required. Finally, as stated in Section 4.5.1, a highly integrated editor/formatter may also reduce the amount of memorization required, since the user no longer must predict the behavior of such a system.

Another desirable feature of a system is the ability to provide access to a freely chosen subsystem oriented to a certain class of user or to a restricted class of problems. This has been referred to as *filtering* [Goldberg and Robson 79]. For example, a beginning user may learn only a very small set of commands, and this set may be increased as the user becomes more and more familiar with the system. At each stage, the user is able to access only commands that are well understood, thus reducing the possibility of error.

In recent years, a growing number of empirical studies of interactive systems have been performed, giving quantitative insight into the importance of the various aspects of user interfaces. Both the hardware and the software features of interfaces have been investigated [ACMC 81, Card, English, and Burr 78, Card, Moran, and Newell 80, Shneiderman 80]. Increasingly, research of this type is being used to assist the intuition of the user interface designer.

4.6.1. Software improvements

Many software techniques have been developed to improve aspects of the interface, but most of these improvements require compromises in other areas. For example, using long identifiers as command names tends to reduce the amount of detail that the user must remember, since the command names may be made descriptive of their action. However, it tends to increase the amount of physical effort required for the user to enter a command, since it takes more keystrokes to enter a long name than a short one. Similarly, long command names make it easier to mistype a command, an error from which it is easy to recover. However, they also make it physically harder to type one command when another is intended, an error from which recovery may be more difficult.

As another example, prompting for portions of commands and data reduces the amount of detail that the user must memorize, but it increases the amount of data that must be emitted by the system, thus increasing the amount of time required for the system to perform its functions. The use of menus reduces the amount of detail that must be memorized, the number of errors in entering commands, and the amount of physical effort required to enter commands, but it also has the drawback that it increases the amount of time required for a system to perform display functions and that it requires the user to read more material between commands.

Multiple windows have been used to decrease the mental effort involved in switching from one context to another, since they allow a number of contexts to be maintained simultaneously. For example, they may contain menus, prompting information, or views of several different parts of a document. However, their use increases the amount of time required for display functions, and introduces the mental task of correlating the information found in different windows.

As the above examples illustrate, it is impossible to achieve simultaneously all of the desirable properties of an interface for all classes of users. However, one can do much better by taking into account the characteristics of the intended user. For example, a system may be intended for an expert user who may be expected to memorize all of the details of a system. In this case, the design of the interface would probably emphasize a reduction of the physical effort required of the user. In other cases, the design of the interface may attempt to minimize the amount of detail to be memorized. In the most general case, a single system may offer a number of different user interfaces. This may be accomplished by implementing entirely separate interfaces; however, a more general and more consistent system will result from the use of filtering to provide access to well-defined subsystems.

4.6.2. Hardware improvements

The user interface may also be improved through the use of hardware techniques, such as high-resolution displays and graphical input devices, dedicated computers, large storage facilities, and high-bandwidth connections. For example, the time required for the system to perform display functions may be reduced by increasing the bandwidth between the processor and the display device. Higher bandwidth than that available under a large timesharing system may be achieved on a single-user computer with a dedicated display. If the bandwidth is sufficiently high, many of the software techniques described above become practical, because there is little time spent waiting for the system.

Graphical input devices such as the mouse, light pen, and joystick substantially reduce the physical effort required to select and position objects. For example, they are used successfully for the selection of items from a menu. Bitmapped displays and their extensions can allow the manipulation of many different types of objects, such as colored objects and halftone images.

4.7. Implementation

The utility of a practical document processing system also depends significantly on its implementation. For example, an appealing model or formatting language may need to be rejected if it is impossible to build efficiently. Aside from choosing low-level data structures and algorithms, an implementation may also attempt to decompose the formatting problem into small independent pieces and to provide device independence. Another aspect of an implementation is the ease with which it fits into a larger system of which it is part. Each of these is now discussed in turn.

4.7.1. Data structures and algorithms

The published material of the earliest systems placed little emphasis on their data structures and algorithms, although they may often be deduced from the other information about the systems. For example, the document model used by HES is based rather directly on a data structure for representing segments of text linked into a graph structure, with pointers in the text that refer to locations in other text segments. Recently, a certain number of new algorithms and data structures have appeared. A notable example is the dynamic programming algorithm for paragraph layout in TEX, which is probably the first clearly described and non-trivial algorithm to be employed for this task.

The *sticky pointer* data structure [Fischer and Ladner 79] provides a mechanism that can be used to associate pointers with textual data. In this scheme, the pointers are kept entirely separate from the data and point to a tree structure that in turn points to a linked list containing the text. The advantage of this structure is that it allows the data to change freely without requiring constant updating of the pointers. Sticky pointers have already been used in the implementation of a text editor [Robertson 81a, Robertson 81b]. They may also be useful for an integrated editor/formatter, where the structure and properties of objects in the document could be represented separately from the objects themselves. Modifications to the document contents could be handled very quickly while keeping the structure up to date.

The familiar concept of an inverted file used in REFER also appears applicable to a number of other document-processing tasks that require a search of a set of textual objects that do not change frequently. For example, it could be used to locate a particular quotation in a large work.

In addition to these relatively low-level techniques, some interesting methods have been used for the implementation of formatting systems as a whole. For example, EQN, PIC, and IDEAL are constructed by means of a context-free language parser, generated using a compiler-compiler. In general, these and other preprocessors have proven very useful in systems that are broken down into separate programs.

4.7.2. Decomposition of the formatting problem

An implementation may be based on a single large program, as are TEX and Scribe, or factored into a number of smaller programs, as is done in the UNIX system. A factored system may be broken into small programs that process different types of objects, as under UNIX, or it may be broken into programs that handle different parts of the formatting problem. For example, some systems use one program to format a document into a series of lines, and use a different program to place these lines onto pages.

One advantage of a factored approach is that each of the programs may be very simple and fairly easy to understand. Further, it is possible to set up a configuration of programs that is tailored to the complexity of the document to be formatted. This allows the overall system resource requirements for a particular document to be reduced. The disadvantage of this organization is that it may tend to multiply the number of languages used in the system (as is true under UNIX), and also will multiply the number of programs to be maintained. There is also likely to be a certain amount of duplication of code among the separate programs, such as the code required to parse the formatting language.

The advantage of a single program is that it seems to make it easier to offer a single integrated system for handling all types of objects. As observed in Section 4.4, the use in UNIX of many small programs communicating by one-directional pipes tends to limit the possible nesting of different kinds of objects. Further, with a single program it is easier to provide a single language for describing documents. On the other hand, a single large program must be much more complicated, and also cannot be tailored to the document.

One of the fundamental difficulties of the formatting problem is that the processing of objects depends not only on the objects themselves, but on the larger objects of which they are part. For example, the concrete appearance of a sentence is not known until the paragraph of which it is part is mapped into a set of lines; there is not enough information to format the sentence when taken by itself. However, the concrete appearance of an object (a paragraph in this example) clearly depends upon the objects from which it is composed. Therefore, neither a strictly top-down nor a strictly bottom-up algorithm can be used.

Besides complicating the formatting process itself, this fact has implications about the ways in which formatting systems may be broken down into small programs. That is, unless a certain amount of control over the concrete appearance is relinquished, it is not possible in general to break down the formatting problem into a number of completely independent programs that handle different objects. In the example above, it would not be possible to format the paragraph without formatting its component sentences or to format the sentences without formatting the paragraph of which they are part.

As another example, TEX exercises much more control than earlier formatters over the concrete appearance of paragraphs because it tries many different ways of placing words into lines. This interdependence could be carried even further. A system could try many different ways of placing words into both lines and paragraphs in order to choose the one that gives the pages the best appearance. For example, words could be formatted more tightly to eliminate a widow on the following page. In systems that separate the formatting of paragraphs into lines from the layout of lines onto pages, this would not be possible.

On the other hand, the resulting simplification makes it worth looking for cases in which the formatting problem can be decomposed. An example appears in the Arabic language system KATIB/HATTAT, where the placing of characters into lines is separated from the determination of the concrete forms of the individual characters, by using average values for the widths of characters. This method of decomposition may perhaps be extended to other cases where the different concrete forms of a given class of abstract objects do not show too much variation in size.

It should also be noted that decomposition can provide device-independence. The viewing of a concrete document may be separated from the rest of the formatting process, allowing the same concrete document to be produced on a number of different devices without requiring that it be reformatted each time. This may be accomplished through a device-independent formatter output that is translated by the viewing process into low-level commands for controlling a particular device.

A decomposition of the formatting problem is achieved in the UNIX system by having the programs for separate objects perform a high-level "pre-formatting" function; almost all of the actual solutions to formatting problems are handled in the final pass through the low-level formatter TROFF. This approach, while very appealing, increases the amount of processing time required to produce a document from its description.

4.7.3. Interface to host environment

Many formatting systems today are designed as application programs under existing operating systems. One of the difficulties of this embedding occurs if it is desired to ensure that the formatting system could also function (without much change) under a different operating system. Independence of particular operating system features tends to increase the portability of the formatting system and of the abstract documents themselves. These can be very important goals, especially if a standardized means for exchange of documents is to be developed. At the same time, however, dependence upon a particular operating system often increases the usability and efficiency of a formatting system.

For example, Scribe is designed to execute in the environment of a generic operating system that makes only modest demands upon the specific operating system in which it is embedded, and does not try to provide a sophisticated interface to any system functions [Reid 80b, Appendix B]. The central requirements are the ability to access files with names formed from short character strings, and the ability to perform simple operations on these files, such as reading, writing, deleting, and determining date of creation.

Because Scribe's interface to the operating system is so simple, it is impossible for Scribe to provide a complete or integrated interface to its documents. It is necessary, for example, for the user to communicate with the command interpreter of the operating system to ask for a list of current files containing documents. Adding this function to Scribe would make the file interface more difficult to move to another system.

Scribe and the UNIX formatters have proven easy to move to new operating systems because they use only features, such as programs and text files, that are present in nearly all current systems. However, a formatting system that used interprocess communication more complex than that offered by files or pipes would be more difficult to make portable, because there is not as much agreement about how these facilities should be provided. Similarly, formatters that rely on specialized hardware not present in all operating systems could not easily be moved to systems not supporting this hardware.

5. Concluding Remarks

We have defined the nature of the formatting problem, surveyed some significant systems, and presented a number of concepts and outstanding issues and problems. Despite the impressive achievements in this fast-moving field, it is evident from our analysis in the preceding pages that much remains to be done before realizing the potential inherent in computer, display, and printing technology—a hardware technology that makes it feasible, in principle, to specify, manipulate, and view the appearance of documents with an unprecedented degree of control, precision, flexibility, speed, and economy.

As they are developed further, formatting systems will remain a major part of such applications as publishing and word processing, but they will also become a major utility available in most general purpose computer systems. Even more generally, a complete package of integrated editors, formatters, and other tools for computer-aided writing and reading of documents will be an important component of the computer system of the future.

Acknowledgments

We are grateful to the following people for reading and offering helpful comments on various parts of the paper: A. Borning, D. Chamberlin, G. Coulouris, S. Johnston, B. Kernighan, J. King, D. Knuth, B. Lampson, M. Lesk, P. MacKay, H. Moll, B. Reid, J. Saltzer, L. Tesler, C. Van Wyk, and J. Zahorjan.   We wish to acknowledge the assistance in obtaining certain references provided by G. Kimura, J. Saltzer, P. Samson, and L. Tesler.   D. Knuth, G. Kimura, B. Kernighan, and B. Rice helped us obtain material used in the figures.   Thanks are also due to B. Reid for his assistance in producing typeset versions of this paper.   A. Goldberg and the referees made many constructive suggestions.   This paper was specified in Scribe and printed on the Xerox Dover laser printer at Stanford University.   Figures 7 and 9 were produced using TEX and Figures 11 and 14 with the UNIX document production tools.

This work was supported in part by the National Science Foundation under grants numbered MCS-7826285 and MCS-8004111.   An extended abstract [Shaw, Furuta, and Scofield 80] of this paper was presented at the International Conference on Research and Trends in Document Preparation Systems, held in Lausanne, Switzerland, in February 1981.

6. References

[ACMC 81]   ACM Computing Surveys.   *ACM Computing Surveys* 13(1), March 1981. Special Issue: The Psychology of Human-Computer Interaction.

[Allen, Nix, and Perlis 81]
                 Todd Allen, Robert Nix, and Alan Perlis.   PEN: A hierarchical document editor.   *Proceedings of the ACM SIGPLAN SIGOA Symposium on Text Manipulation, SIGPLAN Notices* 16(6):74-81, June 1981.   The proceedings of the conference containing this paper are also available as *SIGOA Newsletter* 2(1&2), Spring/Summer 1981.

[Barnett 65]   Michael P. Barnett. *Computer Typesetting: Experiments and Prospects.* The MIT Press, 1965.

[Baudelaire 78] Patrick C. Baudelaire. Draw Manual. In B. W. Lampson and E. A. Taft (editors), *Alto User's Handbook.* Computer Science Laboratory, Xerox Palo Alto Research Center, 1978.

[Beatty, Chin, and Moll 79]
                 John C. Beatty, Janet S. Chin, and Henry F. Moll. An interactive documentation system. *SIGGRAPH '79 Proceedings, Computer Graphics* 13(2):71-82, August 1979.

[Berns 68]   Gerald M. Berns. The FORMAT program. *IEEE Transactions on Engineering Writing and Speech* EWS-11(2):85-91, August 1968.

[Berns 69]   Gerald M. Berns. Description of FORMAT, a text-processing program. *Communications of the ACM* 12(3):141-146, March 1969.

[Birtwistle, et al. 79]
                 Graham M. Birtwistle, Ole-Johan Dahl, Bjorn Myhrhaug, and Kristen Nygaard. *Simula Begin,* Second edition. Van Nostrand Reinhold, 1979.

[Borning 79]   Alan Borning. *ThingLab—A constraint oriented simulation laboratory.* Ph.D. thesis, Stanford University, Stanford, Calif., 1979. Available as technical report SSL-79-3 from Xerox Palo Alto Research Center, Palo Alto, Calif., and as Technical Report No. STAN-CS-79-746, Stanford Computer Science Department, Stanford University, Stanford, Calif.

[Borning 81]   Alan Borning. The programming language aspect of ThingLab, a constraint-oriented simulation laboratory. *ACM Transactions on Programming Languages and Systems* 3(4):353-387, October 1981.

[Burkhart and Nievergelt 80]
                 H. Burkhart and J. Nievergelt. Structure-oriented editors. Berichte des Instituts fuer Informatik 38, Eidgenoessische Technische Hochschule Zuerich, May 1980.

[Byte 81]   Byte Magazine. *Byte* 6(8), August 1981. Special issue on Smalltalk.

[Card, English, and Burr 78]
                 Stuart K. Card, William K. English, and Betty J. Burr. Evaluation of mouse, rate-controlled isometric joystick, step keys, and text keys for text selection on a CRT. *Ergonomics* 21(8):601-613, 1978.

[Card, Moran, and Newell 80]
        Stuart K. Card, Thomas P. Moran, and Alan Newell. The keystroke-level
        model for user performance time with interactive systems. *Communications of*
        the ACM 23(7):396-410, July 1980.

[Carmody, et al. 69]
        Steven Carmody, Walter Gross, Theodor E. Nelson, David Rice, and Andries
        van Dam. A hypertext editing system for the /360. Technical Report, Center
        for Computer and Information Sciences, Brown University, March 1969. Also
        contained in M. Faiman and J. Nievergelt, editors. *Pertinent Concepts in*
        Computer Graphics. University of Illinois, Urbana, Ill., March 1969, pp. 291-
        330.

[Chamberlin, et al. 81]
        Donald C. Chamberlin, James C. King, Donald R. Slutz, Stephen J. P. Todd,
        and Bradford W. Wade. JANUS: An interactive system for document
        composition. *Proceedings of the ACM SIGPLAN SIGOA Symposium on Text*
        Manipulation, SIGPLAN Notices 16(6):82-91, June 1981. The proceedings of
        the conference containing this paper are also available as *SIGOA Newsletter*
        2(1&2), Spring/Summer 1981. This report was also issued as IBM Computer
        Science Research Report Number RJ3006 (37371), IBM Research Laboratory,
        San Jose, Calif., December 1980.

[Chamberlin, et al. 82]
        Donald C. Chamberlin, James C. King, Donald R. Slutz, Stephen J. P. Todd,
        and Bradford W. Wade. JANUS: An interactive document formatter based
        on declarative tags. IBM Computer Science Research Report RJ3366 (40402),
        IBM Research Laboratory, January 1982.

[Cherry 81]   Lorinda Cherry. Computer Aids for Writers. *Proceedings of the ACM*
        SIGPLAN SIGOA Symposium on Text Manipulation, SIGPLAN
        Notices 16(6):61-67, June 1981. The proceedings of the conference containing
        this paper are also available as *SIGOA Newsletter* 2(1&2), Spring/Summer
        1981.

[Coulouris, et al. 76]
        G. F. Coulouris, I. Durham, J. R. Hutchinson, M. H. Patel, T. Reeves, and
        D. G. Winderbank. The design and implementation of an interactive
        document editor. *Software—Practice and Experience* 6(2):271-279, April-June
        1976.

[Curry 78]   Gael Alan Curry. *Programming by Abstract Demonstration.* Ph.D. thesis,
        University of Washington, Seattle, Wa., March 1978. Also issued as Technical
        Report 78-03-02, Department of Computer Science, University of Washington.

[Ehrman and Berns 71]
John R. Ehrman and Gerald M. Berns. FORMAT, A Text Processing Program. SLAC Report 135, Stanford Linear Accelerator Center, July 1971.

[Engelbart and English 68]
Douglas C. Engelbart and William K. English. A research center for augmenting human intellect. *Proceedings, Fall Joint Computer Conference* 33:395-410, 1968.

[Engelbart, Watson, and Norton 73]
Douglas C. Engelbart, Richard W. Watson, and James C. Norton. The augmented knowledge workshop. ARC Journal Accession Number 14724, Stanford Research Center, March 1973. Paper presented at the National Computer Conference, June 1973.

[Fischer and Ladner 79]
Michael J. Fischer and Richard E. Ladner. Data Structures for Efficient Implementation of Sticky Pointers in Text Editors. Technical Report 79-06-08, Department of Computer Science, University of Washington, June 1979.

[Goldberg and Kay 76]
Adele Goldberg and Alan Kay (editors). Smalltalk-72 Instruction Manual. Report No. SSL-76-6, Xerox Palo Alto Research Center, March 1976.

[Goldberg and Robson 79]
Adele Goldberg and Dave Robson. A Metaphor for User Interface Design. *Proceedings of the Twelfth Hawaii International Conference on System Sciences* 1:148-157, 1979.

[Goldfarb 81a]
C. F. Goldfarb. Use of an integrated text processing system in commercial textbook production. *Abstracts of the Presented Papers, International Conference on Research and Trends in Document Preparation Systems,* Lausanne, Switzerland:121-122, February 1981.

[Goldfarb 81b]
C. F. Goldfarb. A generalized approach to document markup. *Proceedings of the ACM SIGPLAN SIGOA Symposium on Text Manipulation, SIGPLAN Notices* 16(6):68-73, June 1981. The proceedings of the conference containing this paper are also available as *SIGOA Newsletter* 2(1&2), Spring/Summer 1981.

[Goldstein and Bobrow 80]
Ira P. Goldstein and Daniel G. Bobrow. A layered approach to software design. Report No. CSL-80-5, Xerox Palo Alto Research Center, December 1980.

[Goldstein and Bobrow 81]
Ira Goldstein and Daniel Bobrow. An experimental description-based programming environment: Four reports. Report No. CSL-81-3, Xerox Palo Alto Research Center, March 1981.

[Good 81]   Michael Good. An ease of use evaluation of an integrated editor and formatter. Technical Report MIT/LCS/TR-266, Massachusetts Institute of Technology Laboratory for Computer Science, November 1981. This is a revised version of Good's M.S. thesis, August 1981.

[Guttag and Horning 80]
John Guttag and James J. Horning. Formal specification as a design tool. *Conference Record of the Seventh Annual ACM Symposium on Principles of Programming Languages*:251-261, January 1980. Also issued as Report No. CSL-80-1, Xerox Palo Alto Research Center, Palo Alto, Calif., (January 1980).

[Halbert 81]   Daniel C. Halbert. An example of Programming by Example. Master's thesis, University of California, Berkeley, Calif., June 1981.

[Hammer, et al. 81a]
Michael Hammer, Richard Ilson, Timothy Anderson, Edward J. Gilbert, Michael Good, Bahram Niamir, Larry Rosenstein, and Sandor Schoichet. Etude: An integrated document processing system. Office Automation Group Memo OAM-028, Massachusetts Institute of Technology Laboratory for Computer Science, February 1981. Presented at the 1981 Office Automation Conference, March 23-25, 1981.

[Hammer, et al. 81b]
Michael Hammer, Richard Ilson, Timothy Anderson, Edward J. Gilbert, Michael Good, Bahram Niamir, Larry Rosenstein, and Sandor Schoichet. The implementation of Etude, an integrated and interactive document production system. *Proceedings of the ACM SIGPLAN SIGOA Symposium on Text Manipulation, SIGPLAN Notices* 16(6):137-141, June 1981. The proceedings of the conference containing this paper are also available as *SIGOA Newsletter* 2(1&2), Spring/Summer 1981. This report was previously issued as Office Automation Group Memo OAM-026, Massachusetts Institute of Technology Laboratory for Computer Science, Cambridge, Mass. (December 1980).

[IBM 80a]   *Document Composition Facility—Introduction to the Generalized Markup Language: Using the starter set,* IBM Corporation, 1980. Order number SH20-9186-0.

[IBM 80b]   *Document Composition Facility Generalized Markup Language: Starter set reference,* IBM Corporation, 1980. Order number SH20-9187-0.

[IBM 80c]   *Document Composition Facility: User's Guide,* IBM Corporation, 1980. Order number SH20-9161-1.

[Ilson 80]   Richard Ilson. An integrated approach to formatted document production. Technical Report MIT/LCS/TR-253, Massachusetts Institute of Technology Laboratory for Computer Science, August 1980. This is Ilson's M.S. thesis.

[Ingalls 78]   Daniel H. Ingalls. The Smalltalk-76 programming system design and implementation. *Conference Record of the Fifth Annual ACM Symposium on Principles of Programming Languages*, January 1978.

[Ivie 77]   Evan L. Ivie. The Programmer's Workbench—A machine for software Development. *Communications of the ACM* 20(10):746-753, October 1977.

[Kaiman 68]   Arthur Kaiman. Computer-aided publications editor. *IEEE Transactions on Engineering Writing and Speech* EWS-11(2):65-75, August 1968.

[Kernighan 76]   Brian W. Kernighan. A TROFF tutorial. Internal Memorandum, Bell Laboratories, August 1976. In *Documents for Use With the Phototypesetter*, Version seven.

[Kernighan 81a] Brian W. Kernighan. PIC—A crude graphics language for typesetting. Computer Science Technical Report 85, Bell Laboratories, January 1981.

[Kernighan 81b] B. W. Kernighan. Review of 'TEX and METAFONT: New directions in typesetting'. *Computing Reviews* 22:299-301, July 1981. Review number 38,151.

[Kernighan 81c] Brian W. Kernighan. A typesetter-independent TROFF. Computer Science Technical Report 97, Bell Laboratories, 1981.

[Kernighan 82]   Brian W. Kernighan. PIC—A language for typesetting graphics. *Software—Practice and Experience* 12(1):1-21, January 1982. A preliminary version of this paper appeared in the *Proceedings of the ACM SIGPLAN SIGOA Symposium on Text Manipulation, SIGPLAN Notices* 16(6), June 1981, and *SIGOA Newsletter* 2(1&2), Spring/Summer 1981.

[Kernighan and Cherry 75]
                 Brian W. Kernighan and Lorinda L. Cherry. A system for typesetting mathematics. *Communications of the ACM* 18(3):151-157, March 1975. Also available as Computer Science Technical Report No. 17, Bell Laboratories, Murray Hill, N.J. (Revised, April 1977).

[Kernighan and Plauger 76]
                 Brian W. Kernighan and P. L. Plauger. *Software Tools.* Addison Wesley, 1976.

[Kernighan, Lesk, and Ossanna 78]
　　　　　B. W. Kernighan, M. E. Lesk, and J. F. Ossanna, Jr. UNIX Time-Sharing System: Document Preparation. *The Bell System Technical Journal* 57(6):2115-2135, July-August 1978.

[Knuth 75]　　Donald E. Knuth. *The Art of Computer Programming: Volume 3, Sorting and Searching.* Addison-Wesley, 1975, pages 552-557, section 6.5.

[Knuth 79a]　　Donald E. Knuth. TₑX *and Metafont: New Directions in Typesetting.* Digital Press and the American Mathematical Society, 1979.

[Knuth 79b]　　Donald E. Knuth. Mathematical typography. In TₑX *and Metafont: New Directions in Typesetting,* part 1. Digital Press and the American Mathematical Society, 1979. Reprinted from the *Bulletin* (New Series) *of the American Mathematical Society* 1(2):337-372, March 1979. Josiah Willard Gibbs lectures, presented January 4, 1978.

[Knuth 79c]　　Donald E. Knuth. TₑX, a system for technical text. In TₑX *and Metafont: New Directions in Typesetting,* part 2. Digital Press and the American Mathematical Society, 1979. Based on Stanford Artificial Intelligence Laboratory Memo AIM-317.3/Computer Science Department No. STAN-CS-78-675, Stanford University, Stanford, Calif. (September 1979).

[Knuth and Plass 81]
　　　　　Donald E. Knuth and Michael F. Plass. Breaking paragraphs into lines. *Software—Practice and Experience* 11(11):1119-1184, November 1981. Also issued as Technical Report No. STAN-CS-80-828, Stanford Department of Computer Science, Stanford, Calif. (November 1980).

[Lampson 78]　　Butler W. Lampson. Bravo manual. In B. W. Lampson and E. A. Taft (editors), *Alto User's Handbook.* Computer Science Laboratory, Xerox Palo Alto Research Center, 1978.

[Lesk 76a]　　M. E. Lesk. Tbl—A program to format tables. Computer Science Technical Report 49, Bell Laboratories, September 1976.

[Lesk 76b]　　M. E. Lesk. Typing documents on the UNIX system: Using the -ms macros with TROFF and NROFF. Internal Memorandum, Bell Laboratories, October 1976. In *Documents for Use With the Phototypesetter,* Version Seven.

[Lesk 78]　　M. E. Lesk. Some applications of inverted indexes on the UNIX System. Computing Science Technical Report 69, Bell Laboratories, June 1978.

[Lesk and Kernighan 77]
M. E. Lesk and B. W. Kernighan. Computer typesetting of technical journals on UNIX. *Proceedings, National Computer Conference* 46:879-888, 1977. Also available as Computer Science Technical Report No. 44, Bell Laboratories, Murray Hill, N.J. (June 1976).

[MacKay 77]   Pierre A. MacKay.   Setting Arabic with a computer.   *Scholarly Publishing* 8(2):142-150, January 1977.

[Madnick and Moulton 68]
Stuart E. Madnick and Allen Moulton. SCRIPT: An on-line manuscript processing system. *IEEE Transactions on Engineering Writing and Speech* EWS-11(2):92-100, August 1968.

[McMahon, Cherry, and Morris 78]
L. E. McMahon, L. L. Cherry, and R. Morris. UNIX Time-Sharing System: Statistical Text Processing. *The Bell System Technical Journal* 57(6):2137-2154, July-August 1978.

[Newman 78]   William M. Newman. Markup User's Manual. In B. W. Lampson and E. A. Taft (editors), *Alto User's Handbook*. Computer Science Laboratory, Xerox Palo Alto Research Center, 1978.

[Ossanna 74]   Joseph F. Ossanna. NROFF Users' Manual—Second Edition. Internal Document, Bell Laboratories, September 1974.

[Ossanna 76]   Joseph F. Ossanna. NROFF/TROFF User's Manual. Computer Science Technical Report 54, Bell Laboratories, October 1976.

[Packard 73]   David W. Packard. Can scholars publish their own books? *Scholarly Publishing* 5(1):65-74, October 1973.

[Pierson 72]   John Pierson. *Computer Composition using PAGE-1.* Wiley-Interscience, 1972.

[Reid 80a]   Brian K. Reid. A high-level approach to computer document formatting. *Conference Record of the Seventh Annual ACM Symposium on Principles of Programming Languages,* January 1980.

[Reid 80b]   Brian K. Reid. *Scribe: A Document Specification Language and its Compiler.* Ph.D. thesis, Carnegie-Mellon University, Computer Science Department, Pittsburgh, Pa., October 1980. Also issued as Technical Report CMU-CS-81-100.

[Reid 81]   B. K. Reid. The Scribe document specification language and its compiler. *Abstracts of the Presented Papers, International Conference on Research and Trends in Document Preparation Systems,* Lausanne, Switzerland:59-62, February 1981.

[Reid and Walker 80]
                 Brian K. Reid and Janet H. Walker. *SCRIBE Introductory User's Manual,* Third Edition, Preliminary Draft. UniLogic, Ltd., Pittsburgh, 1980. Previous editions were issued by Carnegie-Mellon University, Computer Science Department, Pittsburgh, Pa.

[Ritchie 78]   D. M. Ritchie. UNIX Time Sharing System: A retrospective. *The Bell System Technical Journal* 57(6):1947-1969, July-August 1978.

[Robertson 81a] Ken Robertson. ESP, A Direct Access Editor: ESP user's guide. Technical Note 134, Computer Science Laboratory, University of Washington, April 1981.

[Robertson 81b] Kenneth Ray Robertson. ESP: A direct access editor. Master's thesis, University of Washington, Seattle, Wa., 1981.

[Saltzer 65]   J. Saltzer. Manuscript typing and editing: TYPSET, RUNOFF. In Crisman, P. A., editor, *The Compatible Time-Sharing System: A programmer's guide,* Second Edition, section AH.9.01. The MIT Press, 1965.

[Seybold 81]   Jonathan Seybold. Xerox's 'Star'. *The Seybold Report* 10(16), April 27, 1981.

[Shaw 80]   Alan C. Shaw. A model for document preparation systems. Technical Report 80-04-02, Department of Computer Science, University of Washington, April 1980.

[Shaw, Furuta, and Scofield 80]
                 Alan Shaw, Richard Furuta, and Jeffrey Scofield. Document Formatting Systems: Survey, Concepts, and Issues [Extended Abstract]. Technical Report 80-10-02, Department of Computer Science, University of Washington, October 1980. Also available in the *Abstracts of the Presented Papers, International Conference on Research and Trends in Document Preparation Systems,* Lausanne, Switzerland, 47-52, February 1981.

[Shneiderman 80]
                 Ben Shneiderman. *Software Psychology.* Winthrop, Cambridge, Mass., 1980.

[Shoch 79]   John F. Shoch. An overview of the programming language Smalltalk-72. *SIGPLAN Notices* 14(9):64-73, September 1979.

[Smith 75]   David Canfield Smith. *PYGMALION: A creative programming environment.* Ph.D. thesis, Stanford University, Stanford, Calif., June 1975. Also issued as Stanford Artificial Intelligence Laboratory Memo AIM-260 and as Computer Science Department Report No. STAN-CS-75-499.

[Smith, et al. 82]   David Canfield Smith, Charles Irby, Ralph Kimball, and Bill Verplank. Designing the Star User Interface. *Byte* 7(4):242-282, April 1982.

[Spivak 80]   Michael Spivak. *The Joy of* TEX: *A gourmet guide to typesetting technical text by computer,* Version -1. American Mathematical Society, 1980.

[Stallman 80]   Richard M. Stallman. EMACS manual for TWENEX users. AI Memo Number 555, Massachusetts Institute of Technology Artificial Intelligence Laboratory, September 1980.

[Stallman 81]   Richard M. Stallman. EMACS, The extensible, customizable self-documenting display editor. *Proceedings of the ACM SIGPLAN SIGOA Symposium on Text Manipulation, SIGPLAN Notices* 16(6):147-156, June 1981. The proceedings of the conference containing this paper are also available as *SIGOA Newsletter* 2(1&2), Spring/Summer 1981. This report is a revised version of AI Memo Number 519, Massachusetts Institute of Technology Artificial Intelligence Laboratory, Cambridge, Mass. (June 1979).

[Tesler 72]   Larry Tesler. PUB: The document compiler. Operating Note 70, Stanford Artificial Intelligence Project, September 1972.

[Thacker, et al. 79]
        C. P. Thacker, E. M. McCreight, B. W. Lampson, R. F. Sproull, and D. R. Boggs. Alto: A personal computer. Technical Report CSL-79-11, Xerox Palo Alto Research Center, August 1979. Also contained in Siewiorek, Bell, and Newell, *Computer Structures: Readings and Examples*, second edition.

[Thompson and Ritchie 75]
        K. Thompson and D. M. Ritchie. *UNIX Programmer's Manual,* Sixth edition. Bell Telephone Laboratories, Inc., 1975, entry ROFF(1).

[vanDam and Rice 71]
        Andries van Dam and David E. Rice. On-line text editing: A survey. *ACM Computing Surveys* 3(3):93-114, September 1971.

[VanLehn 73]   Kurt A. VanLehn. SAIL User Manual. Report Number STAN-CS-73-373, Stanford Department of Computer Science, July 1973. Also issued as Stanford Artificial Intelligence Laboratory Memo AIM-204.

[VanWyk 80]   Christopher John Van Wyk. *A Language for Typesetting Graphics.* Ph.D. thesis, Stanford University, Stanford, Calif., June 1980.

[VanWyk 81]   Christopher J. Van Wyk. A graphics typesetting language. *Proceedings of the ACM SIGPLAN SIGOA Symposium on Text Manipulation, SIGPLAN Notices* 16(6):99-107, June 1981. The proceedings of the conference containing this paper are also available as *SIGOA Newsletter* 2(1&2), Spring/Summer 1981.

DOCUMENT PREPARATION SYSTEMS
J. Nievergelt, G. Coray, J.D. Nicoud, A.C. Shaw (eds.)
© North-Holland Publishing Company, 1982

Choosing Better Line Breaks*

MICHAEL F. PLASS

Xerox Palo Alto Research Centers
3333 Coyote Hill Road
Palo Alto, California 94304, U.S.A.

DONALD E. KNUTH

Computer Science Department
Stanford University
Stanford, California 94305, U.S.A.

This article discusses a new approach to the problem of dividing the text of a paragraph into lines of approximately equal length. Instead of simply making decisions one line at a time, the method considers the paragraph as a whole, so that the final appearance of a given line might be influenced by the text on succeeding lines. A system based on three simple primitive concepts called 'boxes', 'glue', and 'kerfs' provides the ability to deal satisfactorily with a wide variety of typesetting problems in a unified framework, using a single algorithm that determines optimum breakpoints. This algorithm avoids backtracking by a judicious use of the techniques of dynamic programming. Extensive computational experience confirms that the approach is both efficient and effective in producing high-quality output.

INTRODUCTION

The software of a document preparation system may be divided into several parts, depending upon the function performed: user interface (getting the input from the user, perhaps interactively), system interface (conversion between the internal and external representations of the documents and font descriptions), control (getting the different parts of the system to work together in a coherent way), and translation (a non-trivial conversion from one representation to another). Underlying all of these kinds of software are basic algorithmic building blocks. The most fundamental of these pervade the software at all levels; examples are various kinds of table lookup algorithms, and algorithms for manipulation of linked data structures. Others are applicable only to some particular aspect of the system as a whole. Hyphenation algorithms would fall into this latter class; although hyphenation could, in principal, be treated as a table lookup problem, it is usually advantageous to summarize the hyphenation rules in some more compact form, and then to use a table of exceptions. Another example would be algorithms for parsing, i.e., for converting from a flat, string-oriented input representation to a structured internal representation; the lessons learned from compiler construction can be helpful in this area. There are special purpose algorithms for converting from one description of a font (say a polygonal outline) to another (say a bit matrix). The chief purpose of this report is to describe a particular special-purpose algorithm, for the problem of breaking paragraphs into lines.

Before we plunge into the details of the line-breaking problem, we should consider how it fits into the system as a whole. One of the most important aspects of a document preparation system is the *model* it presents to the user. A model will ideally have the following properties:

- *Simplicity* — a simple model can be concisely explained and easily understood in terms of just a few primitive concepts. A user who understands the underlying model and has a particular task in mind will be able to figure out how to do it without searching a lengthy manual to discover the right 'feature' to use.

---
* This research was supported in part by the National Science Foundation under grants IST-7921977 and MCS-7723738; by Office of Naval Research grant N00014-76-C-0330; by the IBM Corporation; by Addison–Wesley Publishing Company; and by the Xerox Corporation. 'TEX' and 'Tau Epsilon Chi' are registered trademarks of the American Mathematical Society. This report contains substantial excerpts from an earlier paper appearing in Software—Practice and Experience[11], © John Wiley & Sons, Ltd., used by permission.

- *Generality* — a general model allows the user create any document that can be produced with the available hardware.
- *Naturalness* — a natural model conforms well with the user's notion of how the document is put together.

For example, one possible model of a document is simply a list of items, where each item specifies a font, a character, and a position on the page. This model is certainly simple and quite general, but for the user trying to prepare a document consisting mostly of text, it is not at all natural. It is, however, quite an appropriate model for the output device to present to the typesetting software, since the final internal representation of the document will generally be easy to convert to this form (easy for a computer, that is).

Another possible model would be the 'typewriter model', in which the user just gives a string of characters, perhaps including characters to start a new line or a new page. This model is much more natural for most applications, and also very simple, but it is lacking in generality. It can serve, however, as the starting point for a more general model, at the cost of some of its simplicity and naturalness.

A case can be made that the model that is finally presented to the user should sometimes sacrifice some simplicity and/or generality to make the user interface more natural, or to achieve some other goal. Perhaps a goal is to separate the task of the author from that of the document designer; then the model presented to the author should not be fully general, or else the intentions of the document designer could be circumvented. Or it might be hard for a novice user to figure out how to apply a simple model to obtain some common desired result; in such a case a long list of different features might be preferable. But if the user's model can be expressed completely in terms of a simpler, more general internal model, many advantages can be obtained. In the first example, the document designer can express the document design in terms of the internal model, and so obtain the necessary generality. In the second example, if the features used by the novice are implemented by building on top of a simple, general model, they will be just as useful as if they had been implemented on a case-by-case basis. The advanced user, on the other hand, will not be limited to this set of features, but will have access to the power and flexibility obtained through the combination of primitive functions.

The remainder of this article will concentrate on one particular model for the contents of a document, and one particular algorithm for operating on this model. The algorithm, as mentioned above, is aimed at solving the problem of breaking a paragraph into lines, and in this article we will develop only those aspects of the model that are relevant to this problem.

The line-breaking problem is informally called the problem of 'justification', since it is the 'J' of 'H & J' (hyphenation and justification) in today's commercial composition and word-processing systems. However, this tends to be a misnomer, because printers have traditionally used justification to mean the process of taking an individual line of type and adjusting its spacing to produce a desired length. Even when text is being typeset with ragged right margins (therefore 'unjustified'), it needs to be broken into lines of approximately the same size. The job of adjusting spaces so that left and right margins are uniformly straight is comparatively laborious when one must work with metal type, so the task of typesetting a paragraph using last century's technology was conceptually a task of justification; nowadays, however, it is no trick at all for computers to adjust the spacing as desired, so the line-breaking task predominates the work. This shift in relative difficulty probably accounts for the shift in the meaning of 'justification'; we shall use the term 'line breaking' in this chapter to emphasize the fact that the central problem of concern here is to find breakpoints.

The traditional way to break lines is analogous to what we ordinarily do when using a typewriter: A bell rings (at least conceptually) when we approach the right margin, and at that time we decide how best to finish off that line, without looking ahead to see where the next line or lines might end. Once the typewriter carriage has been returned to the left margin, we begin afresh without needing to remember anything about the previous text except where the previous line starts. Thus we don't have to keep track of many things at once; such a system is ideally suited to human operation, and it also leads to simple computer programs.

Book printing is different from typing primarily in that the spaces are of variable width. Traditional practice has been to assign a minimum and maximum width to interword spaces, together with a normal width representing the ideal situation. The standard algorithm for line breaking (see, for example, Barnett[1], page 55) then proceeds as follows: Keep appending words to the current line, assuming normal spacing, until reaching a word that does not fit. Break after this word, if it is possible to do so without compressing the spaces to less than the minimum; otherwise break before this word, assuming it is possible to do so without expanding the spaces to more than the given maximum. Otherwise hyphenate the offending word, putting as much of it on the current line as will fit; if no suitable hyphenation points can be found, this may result in a line whose spaces exceed the given maximum.

There is no need to confine computers to such a simple procedure, since the data for an entire paragraph is generally available in the computer's memory. Experience has shown that significant improvements are possible if the computer takes advantage of its opportunity to 'look ahead' at what is coming later in the paragraph, before making a final decision about where any of the lines will be broken. This not only tends to avoid cases where the traditional algorithm has to resort to wide spaces, it also reduces the number of hyphenations. In other words, line breaking decisions provide another example of the desirability of 'late binding' in computer software.

One of the principal reasons for using computers in typesetting is to save money, but at the same time we don't want the output to look cheaper. A properly programmed computer should, in fact, be able to solve the line-breaking problem better than a skilled typesetter could do in a reasonable amount of time (unless we give this person the liberty to change the wording in order to obtain a better fit). For example, Duncan[2] studied the interword spacing of 958 lines that were manually typeset by a "most respectable publishers' printer" that he chose not to identify by name, and he found that nearly 5% of the lines were quite loosely set; the spaces on those lines exceeded 10 units (i.e., $\frac{10}{18}$ of an em), and two of the lines even had spaces exceeding 13 units. We shall see later that a good line-breaking algorithm can do better than this.

Besides the avoidance of hyphens and wide spaces, we can improve the traditional line-breaking method by keeping the spaces nearly equal to the normal size, so that they rarely approach the minimum or maximum limits. We can also try to avoid rapid changes in the spacing of adjacent lines; we can make special efforts not to hyphenate two lines in a row, and not to hyphenate the second-last line of a paragraph; and so on. Given any mathematical way to rate the quality of a particular choice of breakpoints, we can ask the computer to find breakpoints that optimize this function.

But how is the computer to solve such a problem efficiently? When a given paragraph has n optional breakpoints, there are 2^n ways to break it into lines, and even the fastest conceivable computers could not run through all such possibilities in a reasonable amount of time. In fact, the problem sounds suspiciously like the infamous bin-packing problem, which is well known to be NP-complete[3]. Fortunately, however, each line is to consist of contiguous information from the paragraph, so the line-breaking problem is amenable to the techniques of discrete dynamic programming[4,5]; this means there is a reasonably efficient way to attack it. We shall see that the optimum breakpoints can be found in practice with only about twice as much computation as needed by the traditional algorithm; the new method is sometimes even faster than the old, when we consider the time saved by not needing to hyphenate so often. Furthermore the new algorithm is capable of doing other things that are useful in laying out pages, such as setting a paragraph one line longer or one line shorter than normal.

Formulating the Problem

For our purposes, a *paragraph* is a sequence $x_1, x_2, ..., x_m$ of m items, where each individual item x_i specifies a *box*, *glue*, or a *kerf*.

- A box refers to something that is to be typeset: either a character from some font of type, or a black rectangle such as a horizontal or vertical rule, or something built up from several characters such as an accented letter or a mathematical formula. The contents of a box may be extremely complicated, or extremely simple; the line-breaking algorithm does not peek inside a box to see what it contains, so we may consider the boxes to be sealed and locked. As far as we are concerned, the only relevant thing about a box is its *width*. The width of a box may be zero, and in fact it may even be negative, athough negative widths must be used with care and understanding. We use the notation 'box(w)' to denote a box of width w.

- Glue refers to blank space that can vary its width in specified ways; it is an elastic mortar used between boxes in a typeset line. A glue specification x includes just three numbers of relevance to line breaking: $width(x)$ is the 'ideal' or 'normal' width; $stretch(x)$ is the 'stretchability'; $shrink(x)$ is the 'shrinkability'.

  For example, the amount of space between two words in a line often contains the glue specification $width(x) = \frac{1}{3}$ em, $stretch(x) = \frac{1}{6}$ em, $shrink(x) = \frac{1}{9}$ em, where one em is the set size of the type being used (approximately the width of an uppercase 'M' in classical type styles). The actual amount of space occupied by this glue can be adjusted when the line containing it is justified to some desired width; if the normal width is too small the adjustment is proportional to $stretch(x)$, and if the normal width is too large the adjustment is proportional to $shrink(x)$. A glue item with width w, stretch y and shrink z will be denoted by 'glue(w, y, z)'. Notice that, for the purposes of actually choosing the line breaks, a box can be considered to be equivalent to a glue item with zero stretch and shrink; we will maintain the distinction, however, because there is a big difference between boxes and glue in othe parts of the document system (otherwise it would just produce blank sheets of paper).

- A kerf describes a place in the paragraph where a break is possible, and specifies what is supposed to go into the lines just before and after the break (if the paragraph is broken at this place), or what is used in place of the break (if no break happens here). Specifically, the kerf specification x contains three lists of boxes and glue: $prebreak(x)$ contains the boxes and glue to be appended onto the end of the line just before the break; $postbreak(x)$ contains the boxes and glue to be appended onto the beginning of the line immediately following the break; $join(x)$ contains the boxes and glue to be inserted into the line in case no break is chosen at this kerf. For the purposes of line breaking, the exact composition of these lists is not important, but merely the sums of the widths, stretches, and shrinks; we will continue to think of them as lists, however, to keep the model closer to reality. In addition to the three lists, the kerf specification may include a number $penalty(x)$ that quantifies how undesirable a break at x would be, and a boolean flag $hyph(x)$ that tells whether or not a break at this kerf is to be counted as a hyphenation. The hyphenation flag is useful in avoiding breaks that would cause consecutive lines to end with hyphens.

Any fixed unit of measure can be used for the dimensions *width*, *stretch*, and *shrink*; TEX uses printers' points, which are slightly less than $\frac{1}{72}$ inch. In this paper we shall specify all dimensions in term of *machine units* equal to $\frac{1}{18}$ em, assuming a particular size of type, since the widths turn out to be integer multiples of this unit in many cases; the numbers in our examples will be as simple as possible when expressed in terms of machine units.

In order to better internalize the abstract concepts embodied in the definitions of boxes, glue, and kerfs, let us think of how they can be applied to the typesetting of straight text material, such as a newspaper article or a short story. A typesetting system will put such a paragraph into the abstract form we want in the following way:

(1) If the paragraph is to be indented, the first item will be an empty box whose width is the amount of indentation; alternatively, it could be a glue item with the requisite width and with zero stretch and shrink.

(2) Each word of the paragraph becomes a sequence of boxes for the characters of the word, including punctuation marks that belong with that word.

(3) Each interword space becomes a kerf with *prebreak* and *postbreak* empty, *penalty* zero, *hyph* false, and *join* containing a glue item corresponding to the recommended spacing conventions of the fonts of type in use. The glue might be different in different contexts; for example, TEX will make the glue specifications following punctuation marks slightly different from the normal interword glue.

(4) At each place within the words where a hyphenation is permissible, there is a kerf with *postbreak* and *join* empty, *penalty* nonzero, *hyph* true, and *prebreak* containing a box with a hyphen inside.

(5) Explicit hyphens and dashes in the text will be followed by kerfs with all three lists empty, *hyph* true, and with the penalty as appropriate.

(6) At the very end of the paragraph, a kerf z is appended, with *prebreak*(z) containing zero-width glue with zero shrink and infinite (or very large) stretch, *postbreak* empty, *penalty* zero, *hyph* true (to try to avoid a hyphenation in the next-to-last line), and *join* containing an infinite width item, so as to force a break at this kerf.

This translation of the paragraph will cause it to be justified, with both margins straight. If we wanted it to be set with a ragged right margin, then in (3) we would use a fixed width glue in *join* and a zero-width glue with some arbitrary non-zero amount of stretch in *prebreak*. It would also be necessary to include this same glue after the hyphen in the *prebreak* of (4) and in the *prebreak* of (5). We will see later that the box-glue-kerf model can also be used to solve many of the more esoteric typesetting problems that come up in practice.

It should be noted that the translation into boxes, glue, and kerfs would normally be done entirely by the typesetting program, given the text of the paragraph and some description of the style desired. The strength of the model is that the same line breaking algorithm can be used to meet the requirements of many different styles, so that the advantages of a good line breaking algorithm can be made to apply uniformly to them all.

DESIRABILITY CRITERIA

According to this definition of line breaking, there are 2^n ways to break a paragraph into lines, if the paragraph has n legal breakpoints that aren't forced. For example, let's consider the paragraph of Figure 1, which is taken from Grimm's Fairy Tales[6]. There are 129 kerfs in this paragraph, not counting the forced break at the end, and so it can be broken into lines in 2^{129} ways, a number that exceeds 10^{38}. But of course most of these choices are absurd, and we need to specify some criteria to separate acceptable choices from the ridiculous ones. For this purpose we need to know (a) the desired lengths of lines, and (b) the lengths of lines corresponding to each choice of breakpoints, including the amount of stretchability and shrinkability that is present. Then we can compare the desired lengths to the lengths actually obtained.

We shall assume that a list of desired lengths $l_1, l_2, l_3, \ldots$ is given; normally these are all the same, but in general we might want lines of different lengths, as when fitting text around an illustration. Let the actual length of the jth line be denoted by L_j; this is calculated in the obvious way by adding together the widths in the list formed by concatenating the *postbreak* of the kerf at the beginning of the line, the boxes, glue, and *joins* of the kerfs included in the line, and the *prebreak* of the kerf at the end of the line. In a similar fashion we find the total stretchability Y_i and the total shrinkability Z_i. Now we can compare the actual length L_j to

Figure 1. An example paragraph that has been typeset by the 'first-fit' method. Small triangles show permissible places to divide words with hyphens; the adjustment ratio for spaces appears at the right of each line.

In olden times when wishing still helped one, there ₊₁₁
lived a king whose daughters were all beautiful; and ₊₁₂
the youngest was so beautiful that the sun itself, which ₊₀₀₁
has seen so much, was astonished whenever it shone in ₊₀₀₀
her face. Close by the king's castle lay a great dark ₊₀₇₆
forest, and under an old lime-tree in the forest was a ₊₁₄₄
well, and when the day was very warm, the king's child ₊₀₀₀
went out into the forest and sat down by the side of the ₊₀₀₀
cool fountain; and when she was bored she took a ₊₀₀₁
golden ball, and threw it up on high and caught it; and ₊₇₀₀
this ball was her favorite plaything.   ₊₀₀₁

Figure 1. An example paragraph that has been typeset by the 'first-fit' method. Small triangles show permissible places to divide words with hyphens; the adjustment ratio for spaces appears at the right of each line.

the desired length l_j by seeing if there is enough stretchability or shrinkability to change L_j into l_j; we define the *adjustment ratio* r_j of the jth line as follows:

If $L_j = l_j$ (a perfect fit), let $r_j = 0$.

If $L_j < l_j$ (a short line), let $r_j = (l_j - L_j)/Y_j$, assuming that $Y_j > 0$; the value of r_j is undefined if $Y_j \leq 0$ in this case.

If $L_j > l_j$ (a long line), let $r_j = (l_j - L_j)/Z_j$, assuming that $Z_j > 0$; the value of r_j is undefined if $Z_j \leq 0$ in this case.

Thus, for example, $r_j = \frac{1}{3}$ if the total stretchability of line l is three times what would be needed to expand the glue so that the total line length would change from L_j to l_j.

According to this definition of adjustment ratios, the jth line can be justified by letting the width of all glue items x_i within that line be

$$width(x_i) + r_j \, stretch(x_i), \quad \text{if } r_j \geq 0;$$
$$width(x_i) + r_j \, shrink(x_i), \quad \text{if } r_j < 0.$$

For if we add up the total width of that line after such adjustments are made, we get either $L_j + r_j Y_j = l_j$ or $L_j + r_j Z_j = l_j$, depending on the sign of r_j. This distributes the necessary stretching or shrinking by amounts proportional to the individual glue components $stretch(x_i)$ or $shrink(x_i)$, as desired.

For example, the small numbers at the right of the individual lines in Figure 1 show the values of r_j in those lines. A negative ratio like $-.881$ in the third line means that the spaces in that line are narrower than their ideal size; a fairly large positive ratio like $.965$ indicates a very 'loose' fit.

Although there are 2^{129} ways to break the paragraph of Figure 1 into lines, it turns out that only 49 of these actually will result in breaks whose adjustment ratios do not exceed 1 in absolute value; this means that the spaces between words after justification will lie between $width(x_i) - shrink(x_i)$ and $width(x_i) + stretch(x_i)$. Furthermore, only 30 of these 49 ways to make 'nice' breaks will do so without introducing hyphens. One of these ways appears in Figure 1; another way, slightly better, is obtained by moving 'the' from the eighth line down to the ninth.

Our main goal is to find a way to avoid choosing any breakpoints that lead to lines in which the words are spaced very far apart, or in which they are very close together, because such lines are distracting and harder to read. We might therefore say that the line-breaking problem is to find breaks such that the adjustment ratio in each line never exceeds one in absolute value, with the minimum number of hyphenations subject to this condition. Such an approach was taken by Duncan et al.[7] in the early 1960s, and they obtained fairly good results. However, this condition depends only on the values of $width(x_i) - shrink(x_i)$ and $width(x_i) + stretch(x_i)$, not on $width(x_i)$ itself, so it does not use all the degrees of freedom

Figure 2. The paragraph
of Figure 1 when the
'best-fit' method has been
used to find successive
breakpoints.

In olden times when wishing still helped one, there ·₁₂₁
lived a king whose daughters were all beautiful; and ·₁₁₂
the youngest was so beautiful that the sun itself, which ·₁₄₁
has seen so much, was astonished whenever it shone ·₁₄₄
in her face. Close by the king's castle lay a great dark ·₁₄₁
forest, and under an old lime-tree in the forest was a ·₁₄₄
well, and when the day was very warm, the king's child ·₁₄₁
went out into the forest and sat down by the side of ·₁₁
the cool fountain; and when she was bored she took a ·₁₄₁
golden ball, and threw it up on high and caught it; ·₄₀₂
and this ball was her favorite plaything. ·₀₀₁

present in our data. Furthermore, such stringent conditions may not be possible to achieve; for example, if each line of our example were to be 418 units wide, instead of the present width of 421 units, there would be no way to set the text of Figure 1 without having at least one very tight line or loose line, i.e., a line with the magnitude of the adjustment ratio greater than one.

We can do a better job of line breaking if we deal with a continuously varying criterion of quality instead of the yes/no tests on the magnitude of the adjustment ratios. Let us therefore give a quantitative rating of the *badness* of the jth line by finding a formula that is nearly zero when $|r_j|$ is small but grows rapidly when $|r_j|$ takes values exceeding 1. Experience with TeX has shown that good results are obtained if we define the badness of line j as follows:

$$\beta_j = \begin{cases} \infty, & \text{if } r_j \text{ is undefined or } r_j < -1; \\ 100|r_j|^3, & \text{otherwise.} \end{cases}$$

Thus, for example, the individual lines of Figure 1 have badness ratings that are approximately equal to 0, 7, 68, 18, 5, 0, 69, 72, 90, 49, 0, respectively. Note that a line is considered to be 'infinitely bad' if $r_j < -1$; this means that glue will never be shrunk by more than its *shrink* value. However, values of $r_j > 1$ are only finitely bad, so they will be permitted if there is no better alternative.

A slight improvement over the method used to produce Figure 1 leads to Figure 2. Once again each line has been broken without looking ahead to the end of the paragraph and without going back to consider previous choices, but this time each break was chosen so as to minimize the 'badness plus penalty' of that line. In other words, when choosing between alternative ways to end the jth line, given the ending of the previous line, we obtain Figure 2 if we take the minimum possible value of $\beta_j + \pi_j$; here β_j is the badness as defined above, and π_j is the amount of penalty associated with the kerf at the end of the line. In our example, the penalty is 50 at a hyphenation and zero everywhere else. Figure 2 improves on Figure 1 by moving words down from lines 4, 8, and 10.

The method that produces Figure 1 might be called the 'first-fit' algorithm, and the corresponding method for Figure 2 might be called the 'best-fit' algorithm. We have seen that best-fit is superior to first-fit in this particular case, but other paragraphs can be contrived in which first-fit finds a better solution; so a single example is not sufficient to decide which method is preferable. In order to make an unbiased comparison of the methods, we need to get some statistics on their 'typical' behavior. Therefore 300 experiments were performed, with line widths ranging from 350 to 649 in unit steps; although the text for each experiment was the same, the varying line widths made the problems quite different, since line-breaking algorithms are quite sensitive to slight changes in the measurements. The 'tightest' and 'loosest' lines in each resulting paragraph were recorded, as well as the number of hyphens introduced, and the

*Figure 3. This is the 'best
possible' way to break the
lines in the paragraph
of Figures 1 and 2, in
the sense of fewest total
'demerits' as defined in
the text.*

In olden times when wishing still helped one, there ₋₀₂₁
lived a king whose daughters were all beautiful; and ₋₀₁₂
the youngest was so beautiful that the sun itself, which ₋₀₉₁
has seen so much, was astonished whenever it shone ₋₀₄₄
in her face. Close by the king's castle lay a great dark ₋₀₈₄
forest, and under an old lime-tree in the forest was ₋₇₀₃
a well, and when the day was very warm, the king's ₋₀₈₁
child went out into the forest and sat down by the side ₋₀₄₄
of the cool fountain; and when she was bored she took ₋₀₉₁
a golden ball, and threw it up on high and caught it; ₋₀₀₄
and this ball was her favorite plaything.   ₀₀₀₁

comparisons came out as follows:

	min j	max j	hyphens
first-fit < best-fit	69%	35%	12%
first-fit = best-fit	26%	50%	77%
first-fit > best-fit	5%	15%	11%

Thus in 69% of the cases, the minimum adjustment ratio in the lines typeset by first-fit was less than the corresponding value obtained by best-fit; the maximum adjustment ratio in the first-fit lines was less than the maximum for best-fit about 35% of the time, etc. We can summarize this data by saying that the first-fit method usually typesets at least one line that is tighter than the tightest line set by best-fit, and it also usually produces a line that is as loose or looser than the the loosest line of best-fit. The number of hyphens is about the same for both methods, although a more detailed study of the experimental data shows that the superiority of best-fit is especially pronounced in the cases where the lines are rather narrow.

We can actually do better than both of these methods by finding an 'optimum' way to choose the breakpoints. For example, Figure 3 shows how to improve on both Figures 1 and 2 by making line 6 a bit looser, therefore avoiding a rather tight 7th line and a fairly loose 10th line. This pattern of breakpoints was found by an algorithm that will be discussed in more detail below. It is globally optimum in the sense of having fewest total 'demerits' over all choices of breakpoints, where the demerits assessed for the jth line are computed by the formula

$$\delta_j = \begin{cases} (1 + \beta_j + \pi_j)^2 + \alpha_j, & \text{if } \pi_j \geq 0; \\ (1 + \beta_j)^2 - \pi_j^2 + \alpha_j, & \text{if } -\infty < \pi_j < 0; \\ (1 + \beta_j)^2 + \alpha_j, & \text{if } \pi_j = -\infty. \end{cases}$$

Here β_j and π_j are the badness rating and the penalty, as before; and α_j is zero unless both line j and the previous line ended on kerfs marked as hyphenations, in which case α_j is the additional penalty assessed for consecutive hyphenated lines (e.g., 3000). We shall say that we have found the best choice of breakpoints if we have minimized the sum of δ_j over all lines j.

The above formula for δ_j is quite arbitrary, like our formula for β_j, but it works well in practice because it has the following desirable properties: (a) Minimizing the sum of squares of badnesses not only tends to minimize the badness per line, it also provides secondary optimization; for example, when one particularly bad line is inevitable, the other line breaks will also be optimized. (b) The demerit function δ_j increases as π_j increases. (c) Adding 1 to β_j instead of using the badness β_j itself will minimize the total number of lines in cases where there are several ways to break with approximately zero total badness.

For example, the total demerits charged for the paragraphs in Figures 1, 2, and 3 are 26304 for first-fit, 10491 for best-fit, and 7063 for optimum-fit. In the first-fit and best-fit methods, each line is likely to come out about as badly as any other; the optimum-fit method, by contrast, tends to have its bad cases near the beginning, since there is less flexibility in the opening lines.

Further Applications

Before we look at how an optimizing algorithm can work, let us consider in more detail how we can use the primitives of boxes, glue, and kerfs to solve a wide variety of typesetting problems. Some of these are straightforward extensions to the simple applications of the last section, while others seem at first to be quite unrelated to the ordinary task of line breaking.

Combining paragraphs

If the desired line widths are not all the same, we might want to typeset two paragraphs with the second one starting in the list of line lengths where the first one leaves off. This can be done simply by treating the two paragraphs as one, i.e., appending the second to the first, assuming that each paragraph begins with an indentation and ends with the forced paragraph-end break.

Patching

Suppose that a paragraph starts on page 100 of some book and continues on to the next page, and suppose we want to make a change to the first part of that paragraph. We want to make sure that the last line of the new page 100 will end at the right-hand margin just before the word that appears at the beginning of page 101, so that page 101 doesn't have to be redone. It is easy to specify this condition in terms of our conventions, simply by forcing a line break (using a kerf with *prebreak* and *postbreak* empty, and *join* containing an impossibly large item) at the desired place, and discarding the subsequent text. The ability of the optimum-fit algorithm to 'look ahead' means that it will find a suitable way to patch page 100 whenever it is possible to do so.

We can also force the altered part of the paragraph to have a certain number of lines, k, by using the following trick: Set the desired length l_{k+1} of the $(k+1)$st line equal to some number θ that is different from the length of any other line. Then an empty box of width θ that occurs between two forced-break items will have to be placed on line $k+1$.

Avoiding 'psychologically bad' breaks

Since computers don't know how to think, at least not yet, it is reasonable to wonder if there aren't some line breaks that a computer would choose but a human operator might not, if they somehow don't seem right. This problem does not arise very often when straight text is being set, as in newspapers or novels, but it is quite common in technical material. For example, it is psychologically bad to break before 'x' or 'y' in the sentence

A function of x is a rule that assigns a value y to every value of x.

A computer will have no qualms about breaking anywhere unless it is told not to; but a human operator might well avoid bad breaks, perhaps even unconsciously.

Psychologically bad breaks are not easy to define; we just know they are bad. When the eye journeys from the end of one line to the beginning of another, in the presence of a bad break, the second word often seems like an anticlimax, or isolated from its context. Imagine turning the page between the words 'Chapter' and '8' in some sentence; you might well think that the compositor of the book you are reading should not have broken the text at such an illogical place.

During the first year of experience with TEX, the authors began to notice occasional breaks that didn't feel quite right, although the problem wasn't felt to be severe enough to warrant corrective action. Finally, however, it became difficult to justify our claim that TEX has the world's best line-breaking algorithm, when it would occasionally make breaks that were semantically annoying; for example, the preliminary TEX manual[9] has quite a few of these, and the first drafts of that manual were even worse.

As time went on, the authors grew more and more sensitive to psychologically bad breaks, not only in the copy produced by TEX but also in other published literature, and it became desirable to test the hypothesis that computers were really to blame. Therefore a systematic investigation was made of the first 1000 line breaks in the *ACM Journal* of 1960 (which was composed manually by a Monotype operator), compared to the first 1000 line breaks in the *ACM Journal* of 1980 (which was typeset by one of the best commercially available systems for mathematics, developed by Penta Systems International). The final lines of paragraphs, and the lines preceding displays, were not considered to be line breaks, since they are forced; only the texts of articles were considered, not the bibliographies. A reader who wishes to try the same experiment should find that the 1000th break in 1960 occurred on page 67, while in 1980 it occurred on page 64. The results of this admittedly subjective procedure were a total of

> 13 bad breaks in 1960,
> 55 bad breaks in 1980.

In other words, there was more than a four-fold increase, from about 1% to a quite noticeable 5.5%! Of course, this test is not absolutely conclusive, because the style of articles in the *ACM Journal* has not remained constant, but it strongly suggests that computer typesetting causes semantic degradation when it chooses breaks solely on the basis of visual criteria.

Once this problem was identified, a systematic effort was made to purge all such breaks from the second edition of Knuth's book *Seminumerical Algorithms*[8], which was the first large book to be typeset with TEX. It is quite easy to get the line-breaking algorithm to avoid certain breaks by simply including a penalty of, say, 999 in the wordspace kerf; then the bad break is chosen only in an emergency, when there is no other good way to set the paragraph. It is possible to make the typist's job reasonably easy by reserving a special symbol (e.g., ⊗) to be used instead of a normal space between words whenever breaking is undesirable. Although this problem has rarely been discussed in the literature, the authors subsequently discovered that some typographers have a word for it: they call such spaces 'auxiliary'. Thus there is a growing awareness of the problem.

It may be useful to list the main kinds of contexts in which auxiliary spaces were used in *Seminumerical Algorithms*, since that book ranges over a wide variety of technical subjects. The following rules should prove to be helpful to compositors who are keyboarding technical manuscripts into a computer.

1. Use auxiliary spaces in cross-references:

> Theorem⊗A   Algorithm⊗B   Chapter⊗3   Table⊗4   Programs E and⊗F

Note that no ⊗ appears after 'Programs' in the last example, since it would be quite all right to have 'E and F' at the beginning of a line.

2. Use auxiliary spaces between a person's forenames and between multiple surnames:

> Dr.⊗I.⊗J. Matrix   Luis⊗I. Trabb⊗Pardo   Peter Van⊗Emde⊗Boas

A recent trend to avoid spaces altogether between initials may be largely a reaction against typical computer line-breaking algorithms! Note that it seems better to hyphenate a name than to break it between words; e.g., 'Don-' and 'ald E. Knuth' is more tolerable than 'Donald' and 'E. Knuth'. In a sense, rule 1 is a special case of rule 2, since we may regard 'Theorem A' as a name; another example is 'register⊗X'.

3. Use auxiliary spaces for symbols in apposition with nouns:

> base⊗b   dimension⊗d   function⊗$f(x)$ string⊗s of length⊗l

However, compare the last example with 'string⊗s of length l⊗or more'.

4. Use auxiliary spaces for symbols in series:

$$1,\!\otimes\!2, \text{ or} \otimes\!3 \qquad a,\!\otimes\!b, \text{ and}\otimes\!c \qquad 1,\!\otimes\!2, \ldots,\!\otimes\!n$$

5. Use auxiliary spaces for symbols as tightly-bound objects of prepositions:

$$\text{of}\otimes\!x \qquad \text{from } 0 \text{ to}\otimes\!1 \qquad \text{increase } z \text{ by}\otimes\!1 \qquad \text{in common with}\otimes\!m$$

This does not apply with compound objects: For example, 'of $u\otimes$and$\otimes v$'.

6. Use auxiliary spaces to avoid breaking up mathematical phrases that are rendered in words:

$$\text{equals}\otimes\!n \quad \text{less than}\otimes\!\epsilon \quad \text{mod}\otimes\!2 \quad \text{modulo}\otimes\!p^\epsilon \quad (\text{given}\otimes\!X)$$

Also type 'If $t\otimes$is ...', 'when $x\otimes$grows'. Compare 'is$\otimes$15,' with 'is 15$\otimes$times the height'; and compare 'for all large$\otimes n$' with 'for all $n\otimes$greater than$\otimes n_0$'.

7. Use auxiliary spaces when enumerating cases:

$$(\text{b})\otimes\text{Show that } f(x) \text{ is } (1)\otimes\text{continuous}; (2)\otimes\text{bounded}.$$

It would be nice to boil these seven rules down into one or two, and it would be even nicer if the rules could be automated so that keyboarding could be done without them; but subtle semantic considerations seem to be involved in many of these instances. Most examples of psychologically bad breaks seem to occur when a single symbol or a short group of symbols appears just before or after the break; one could do reasonably well with an automatic scheme if it would associate large penalties with a break just before a short non-word, and medium penalties with a break just after a short non-word. Here 'short non-word' means a sequence of symbols that is not very long, yet long enough to include instances like 'exercise$\otimes$15(b)', 'length$\otimes 2^{35}$', 'order$\otimes n/2$' followed by punctuation marks; one should not simply consider patterns that have only one or two symbols. On the other hand it is not so offensive to break before or after fairly long sequences of symbols; e.g., 'exercise 4.3.2–15' needs no auxiliary space.

Many books on composition recommend against breaking just before the final word of a paragraph, especially if that word is short; this can, of course, be done by using an auxiliary space just before that last word, and the computer could insert this automatically. Some books also give recommendations analogous to rule 2 above, saying that compositors should try not to break lines in the middle of a person's name. But there is apparently only one book that addresses the other issues of psychologically bad breaks, namely a nineteenth-century French manual by A. Frey[10], where the following examples of undesirable breaks are mentioned (vol. 1, p. 110):

$$\text{Henri}\otimes\text{IV} \qquad \text{M.}\otimes\text{Colin} \qquad 1^{\text{er}}\otimes\text{sept.} \qquad \text{art.}\otimes\!25 \qquad 20\otimes\text{fr.}$$

It seems to be time to resurrect such old traditions of fine printing.

Recent experience of the authors indicates that it is not a substantial additional burden to insert auxiliary spaces when entering a manuscript into a computer. The careful use of such spaces may in fact lead to greater job satisfaction on the part of the keyboard operator, since the quality of the output can be noticeably improved with comparatively little work. It is comforting at times to know that the machine needs your help.

Author lines

Most of the review notices published in *Mathematical Reviews* are signed with the reviewer's name and address, and this information is typeset flush right, i.e., at the right-hand margin. If there is sufficient space to put such a name and address at the right of the final line of the paragraph, the publishers can save space, and at the same time the results look better because there are no strange gaps on the page (see Figure 4). During recent years the composition software used by the American Mathematical Society was unable to do this operation, but the amount of money saved on paper made it economical for them to pay someone to move the reviewer-names up by hand whenever possible, applying scissors and (real) glue to the computer output.

The author-line problem can be solved by using a kerf between the paragraph and the author's name that has the following specifications:

$$
\begin{array}{ll}
prebreak: & \text{glue}\,(0, 10000, 0) \\
postbreak: & \text{glue}\,(0, 10000, 0) \\
join: & \text{glue}\,(w, 10000, 0) \\
penalty: & p
\end{array}
$$

where w is the minimum amount of white space desired between the last word of the the the paragraph and the author's name, if the latter does not occur on its own line, and p is a positive penalty to encourage the algorithm to save the extra line if possible, even it it has to shrink some spaces to do it.

> This is a case where the name and address fit in nicely
> with the review.   *A. Reviewer* (Ann Arbor, Mich.)

> But sometimes an extra line must be added.
>   *N. Bourbaki* (Paris)

Figure 4. The author-line problem.

Ragged margins

In the previous section we discussed how to produce ragged right margins. Occasionally it is also desirable to be able to typeset ragged left margins; this can be done in essentially the same way as ragged right margins, except that the stretchy glue is moved from the *prebreak* specification to *postbreak*. Also, the paragraph should be started with a glue item with the same stretchability as in the *postbreak*, and the stretchy glue should be taken out of the forced break at the end of the paragraph. Notice that this will set the last line of the paragraph to be roughly the same size as the rest; this is probably what is wanted for ragged-left text.

If the stretchy glue is included in both *prebreak* and *postbreak*, a 'ragged centered' setting is obtained, which might be useful on a title page or poster.

These constructions for ragged margins essentially minimize the largest gap between the margins and the text on any line; and subject to that minimum they essentially minimize the largest gap on the remaining lines; and so forth. The reason is that our definitions of 'badness' and 'demerits' imply in this case that the sum of demerits for any choice of breakpoints is approximately proportional to the sixth powers of the individual gaps.

Hyphenation of ligatures

Early versions of TₑX could not allow discretionary hyphens in ligatures because the model for line breaking was originally formulated with a less general concept than kerfs. Later, each of the authors independently invented a variety of kerf, primarily to allow just these hyphenations.

For example, if the ligature 'ff' occurs in a word such that it is legal to hyphenate between the two letters, it would be represented by a kerf with *prebreak* containing 'f-', *postbreak* containing 'f', *join* containing 'ff', *hyph* true, and *penalty* as appropriate for a hyphenation.

Further applications

The reader who is interested in seeing even more complicated applications of the line breaking algorithm, applied to the typesetting of computer programs and to entries in a sophisticated index, is referred to the earlier paper on line breaking by the present authors[11]. That paper predates the notion of kerfs, but it is not difficult to reformulate those solutions in terms of generalized kerfs.

DESCRIPTION OF THE ALGORITHM

The general ideas underlying the optimum-fit algorithm for line breaking can probably be understood best by considering an example. Figure 5 repeats the text of the earlier figures, set at a different width. It includes little vertical marks to indicate 'feasible breakpoints' found by the algorithm. A *feasible breakpoint* is a place where the text of the paragraph from the beginning to this point can be broken into lines whose badness does not exceed a given tolerance; in the case of Figure 5, this tolerance was taken to be 100. Thus, for example, there is a tiny mark after 'fountain;' since there is a way to set the paragraph up to this point with 'fountain;' at the end of the 7th line and with none of lines 1 to 7 having an adjustment ratio exceeding unity.

The algorithm proceeds by locating all of the feasible breakpoints and remembering the best way to get to each one, in the sense of fewest total demerits. This is done by keeping a list of 'active' breakpoints, representing all of the feasible breakpoints that might be a candidate for future breaks. Whenever a potential breakpoint b is encountered, the algorithm tests to see if there is any active breakpoint a such that the line from a to b has an acceptable badness. If so, b is a feasible breakpoint and it is appended to the active list. The algorithm also remembers the identity of the breakpoint a that minimizes the total demerits, when the total is computed from the beginning of the paragraph to b through a. When an active breakpoint a is encountered for which the line from a to b has an adjustment ratio less than -1 (i.e., when the line can't be shrunk to fit the desired length), breakpoint a is removed from the active list. Since the size of the active list is essentially bounded by the maximum number of words per line, the running time of the algorithm is bounded by this quantity (which usually is small) times the number of potential breakpoints.

For example, when the algorithm begins to work on the paragraph in Figure 5, there is only one active breakpoint, representing the beginning of the first line. It is infeasible to have a line starting there and ending at 'In', or 'olden', ..., or 'lived', since the glue between words does not accumulate enough stretchability in such short segments of the text; but after the next word 'a' is encountered, a feasible breakpoint is found. Now there are two active breakpoints, the original one and the new one. After the next word 'king', there are three active breakpoints; but after the next word 'whose', the algorithm sees that it is impossible to squeeze all of the text from the beginning up to 'whose' on one line, so the initial breakpoint becomes inactive and only two active ones remain.

Skipping ahead, let us consider what happens when the algorithm considers the potential break after 'fountain;'. At this stage there are eight active breakpoints, following the respective text boxes for 'child', 'went', 'out', 'side', 'of', 'the', 'cool', and 'foun-'. The line starting after 'child' and ending with 'fountain;' would be too long to fit, so 'child' becomes inactive. Feasible lines are found from 'went' or 'out' to 'fountain;' and the demerits of those lines are 276 and 182, respectively; however, the line from 'went' actually turns out to be preferable, since there are substantially fewer total demerits from the beginning of the paragraph to 'went' than to

Figure 5. A somewhat
wider setting of the
same sample paragraph,
by the optimum-fit
method. Tiny vertical
marks show 'feasible
breakpoints' where it is
possible to break in such
a way that no spaces need
to stretch more than their
given stretchability.

In olden times when wishing still helped one, there lived a king whose daughters were all beautiful; and the youngest was so beautiful that the sun itself, which has seen so much, was astonished whenever it shone in her face. Close by the king's castle lay a great dark forest, and under an old lime-tree in the forest was a well, and when the day was very warm, the king's child went out into the forest and sat down by the side of the cool fountain; and when she was bored she took a golden ball, and threw it up on high and caught it; and this ball was her favorite plaything.

'out'. Thus, 'fountain;' becomes a new active breakpoint. The algorithm stores a pointer back from 'fountain;' to 'went', meaning that the best way to get to a break after 'fountain;' is to start with the best way to get to a break after 'went'.

The computation of this algorithm can be represented pictorially by means of the network in Figure 6, which shows all of the feasible breakpoints together with the number of demerits charged for each feasible line between them. The object of the algorithm is to compute the *shortest path* from the top of Figure 6 to the bottom, using the demerit numbers as the 'distances' corresponding to individual parts of the path. In this sense, the job of optimal line breaking is essentially a special case of the problem of finding shortest paths in an acyclic network; the line-breaking algorithm is slightly more complex only because it must construct the network at the same time as it is finding the shortest path.

Notice that the best-fit algorithm can be described very easily in terms of a network like Figure 6: it is the algorithm that simply chooses the shortest continuation at every step. And the first-fit algorithm can be characterized as the method of always taking the leftmost branch having a negative adjustment ratio (unless it leads to a hyphen, in which case the rightmost non-hyphenated branch is chosen whenever there is a feasible one). From these considerations we can readily understand why the optimum-fit algorithm tends to do a much better job.

Sometimes there is no way to continue from one feasible breakpoint to any other. This situation doesn't occur in Figure 6, but it would be present below the word 'so' if we had not permitted hyphenation of 'astonished'. In such cases the first-fit and best-fit algorithms must resort to infeasible lines, while the optimum-fit algorithm can usually find another way through the maze.

On the other hand, some paragraphs are inherently difficult, and there is no way to break them into feasible lines. In such cases the algorithm we have described will find that its active list dwindles until eventually there is no activity left; what should be done in such a case? It would be possible to start over with a more tolerant attitude toward infeasibility (a higher threshold value for the badness). Alternatively, TEX takes the attitude that the user wants to make some manual adjustment when there is no way to meet the specified criteria, so the active list is forcibly prevented from becoming empty by simply declaring a breakpoint to be feasible if it would otherwise leave the active list empty. This results in an overset line and an error message that encourages the user to take corrective action.

Figure 7 shows what happens when the algorithm allows quite loose lines to be feasible; in this case a line is considered to be infeasible only if its adjustment ratio exceeds 10 (so that there would be more than two ems of space between words). Such a setting of the tolerances would be used by people who don't want to make manual adjustments to paragraphs that cannot be set well. The tiny marks that indicate feasible breakpoints have varying lengths in this illustration, with longer marks indicating places that can be reached via better paths; the tiny dots are for breakpoints that are just barely feasible. Notice that all of the potential breakpoints in Figure 7 are marked, except for a few in the first two lines; so there are considerably more feasible

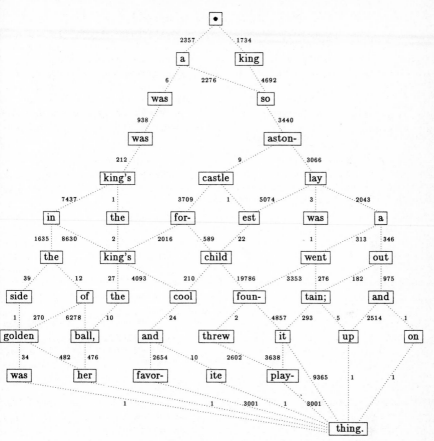

Figure 6. This network shows the feasible breakpoints and the number of demerits charged when going from one breakpoint to another. The 'shortest path' from the top to the bottom corresponds to the best way to typeset the paragraph, if we regard the demerits as distances.

breakpoints here than there were in Figure 5, and the network corresponding to Figure 7 will be much larger. There are 836,272,858 feasible ways to set the paragraph when such wide spaces are tolerated, compared to only 81 ways in Figure 5. However, the number of active nodes will not be significantly bigger in this case than it was in Figure 5, because it is limited by the length of a line, so the algorithm will not run too much more slowly even though its tolerance has been raised and the number of possible settings has increased enormously. For example, after 'fountain;' there are now 17 active breakpoints instead of the 8 present before, so the processing takes only about twice as long although huge numbers of additional possibilities are being taken into account.

When the threshold allows wide spacing, the algorithm is almost certain to find a feasible solution, and it will report no errors to the user even though some rather loose lines may have been necessary. The user who wants such error messages should set the tolerance lower; this not only gives warnings when corrective action is needed, it also improves the algorithm's efficiency.

Figure 7. *When the tolerance is raised to 10 times the stretchability, more breakpoints become feasible, and there are many more possibilities to explore.*

In olden times when wishing still helped one, there lived a king whose daughters were all beautiful; and the youngest was so beautiful that the sun itself, which has seen so much, was astonished whenever it shone in her face. Close by the king's castle lay a great dark forest, and under an old lime-tree in the forest was a well, and when the day was very warm, the king's child went out into the forest and sat down by the side of the cool fountain; and when she was bored she took a golden ball, and threw it up on high and caught it; and this ball was her favorite plaything.

One of the important things to note about Figure 7 is that breakpoints can become feasible in completely different ways, leading up to different numbers of lines before the breakpoint. For example, the word 'seen' is feasible both at the end of line 3:

'In olden ... lived/ a ... young-/ est ... seen'

and at the end of line 4:

'In olden ... helped/ one, ... were/ all ... beau-/ tiful ... seen',

although 'seen' was not a feasible break at all in Figure 5. The breaks that put 'seen' at the end of line 3 have substantially fewer demerits than those putting it on line 4 (approximately 1.68×10^6 versus 1.28×10^{10}), so the algorithm will remember only the former possibility. This is an application of the dynamic-programming 'principle of optimality', which is responsible for the efficiency of our algorithm[4]: the optimum breakpoints of a paragraph are always optimum for the subparagraphs they create. But the interesting thing is that this economy of storage would not be possible if the future lines were not all of the same length, since differing line lengths might well mean that it would be much better to put 'seen' on line 4 after all; for example, we have mentioned a trick for forcing the algorithm to produce a given number of lines. In the presence of varying line lengths, therefore, the algorithm would need to have two separate list entries for an active breakpoint after the word 'seen'. The computer cannot simply remember the one with fewest total demerits, because the optimality principle of dynamic programming would not be valid in such a case.

Figure 8 is an example of line breaking when the individual lengths are all different. In such cases, the need to attach line numbers to breakpoints might mean that the number of active breakpoints substantially exceeds the maximum number of words per line, if the feasibility tolerance is set high; so it is desirable to set the tolerance low. On the other hand, if the tolerance is set too low, there may be no way to break the paragraph into lines having a desired shape. Fortunately, there is usually a happy medium in which the algorithm has enough flexibility to find a good solution without needing too much time and space. The data in Figure 9 shows, for example, that the algorithm did not have to do very much work to find an optimal solution for Galileo's remarks on circles, when the adjustment ratio on each feasible line was required to be 2 or less; yet there was sufficient flexibility to make feasible solutions possible.

COMPUTATIONAL EXPERIENCE

The TEX typesetting system uses an algorithm similar to the one described in the previous section. Since TEX must deal with other aspects of typesetting, such as leaders, lines with attached footnotes or cross references or page-break marks, and with spacing both inside and immediately outside of math formulas, the implementation of the line breaking algorithm

The area of a
circle is a mean propor-
tional between any two regular
and similar polygons of which one
circumscribes it and the other is isoperimetric with it. In addition, the area
of the circle is less than that of any circumscribed polygon and greater than that
of any isoperimetric polygon. And further,
of these circumscribed polygons, the one
that has the greater number of sides has
a smaller area than the one that has
a lesser number; but, on the other
hand, the isoperimetric polygon
that has the greater num-
ber of sides is the
larger.

— Galileo Galilei (1638)

I
turn, in the
following treatises, to
various uses of those triangles
whose generator is unity. But I leave out
many more than I include; it is extraordinary how
fertile in properties this triangle is. Everyone can try his hand.

— Blaise Pascal (1654)

Figure 8. Examples of line breaking with lines of different sizes.

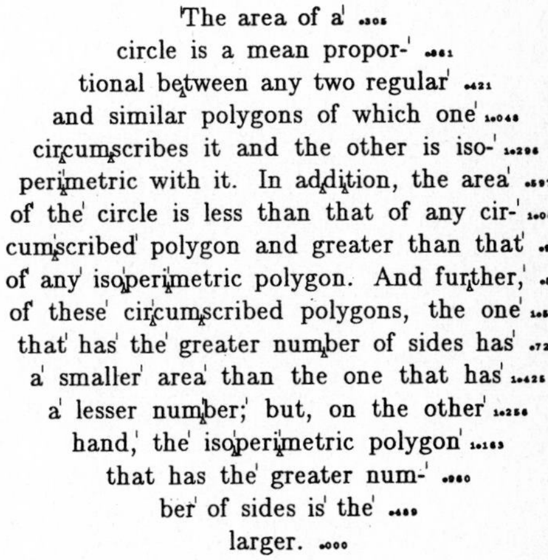

Figure 9. Details of the feasible breakpoints in the first example of Figure 8, showing how the optimum solution was found.

'The area of a' ₌₀₀
circle is a mean propor-' ₌₀₁
tional between any two regular' ₌₂₁
and similar polygons of which one' ₁₀₄₄
circumscribes it and the other is iso-' ₁₂₉₄
perimetric with it. In addition, the area' ₌₀₇
of the circle is less than that of any cir-' ₁₀₀₇
cumscribed polygon and greater than that' ₌₇₃
of any isoperimetric polygon. And further,' ₌₀₃
of these circumscribed polygons, the one' ₁₀₀₁
that has the greater number of sides has' ₌₇₂₆
a smaller area than the one that has' ₁₀₄₂₁
a lesser number; but, on the other' ₁₀₂₆₆
hand, the isoperimetric polygon' ₁₀₁₀₃
that has the greater num-' ₌₀₀
ber of sides is the' ₌₀₁
larger. ₌₀₀₀

is quite complex. (A complete description of TEX's algorithm will appear elsewhere[12].) Experience has shown that the general algorithm is quite efficient in practice, in spite of all the things it must cope with.

So many parameters are present, it is impossible for anyone actually to experiment with a large fraction of the possibilities. A user can vary the interword spacing and the penalties for inserted hyphens, explicit hyphens, and adjacent flagged lines. In addition, TEX's algorithm has some more refinements we have not covered here, each with its own parameters: An extra penalty can be charged whenever a very tight line is next to a loose one, or a very loose line is next to a normal one. TEX's approach for hyphenation is to first try setting the paragraph without any hyphenations, and then only if a certain tolerance is exceeded are the discretionary hyphens inserted. In the presence of so many parameters, one could perform computational experiments for years and not have a completely definitive idea about the behavior of this algorithm. Even with fixed parameters there is a significant variation with respect to the kind of material being typeset; for example, highly mathematical copy presents special problems. An interesting comparative study of line breaking was made by Duncan et al.[7], who considered sample texts from Gibbon's *Decline and Fall* versus excerpts from a story entitled *Salar the Salmon*; as expected, Gibbon's vocabulary forced substantially more hyphenated lines.

On the other hand, we have seen that the optimizing algorithm leads to better line breaks even in children's stories like Grimm's fairy tales, where the words are short and simple. It would be nice to have a quantitative feeling for how much extra computation is necessary to get this improvement in quality. Roughly speaking, the computation time is proportional to the number of words of the paragraph, times the average number of words per line, since the main loop of the computation runs through the currently active nodes, and since the average number of words per line is a reasonable estimate of the number of active nodes in all but the first few lines of a paragraph (see Figures 5 and 7). On the other hand, there are comparatively few active nodes on the first lines of a paragraph, so the performance is actually faster than this rough estimate would indicate.

Detailed statistics were kept when TEX's first large production, *Seminumerical Algorithms*[8], was typeset using the above procedure. This 700-page book has a total of 5526 'paragraphs' in its text and answer pages, if we regard displayed formulas as separators between independent paragraphs. The 5526 paragraphs were broken into a total of 21,057 lines, of which 550 (about 2.6 per cent) ended with hyphens. The lines were usually 29 picas wide, which means 626.4 machine units in 10-point type and about 677.19 machine units in 9-point type, roughly twelve or thirteen words per line. The threshold values were normally both set to 200, so that the spaces between words ranged from a minimum of 4 units to a maximum of $6 + 3\sqrt[3]{2} \approx 9.78$ units. The penalty for breaking after a hyphen was 50, and 3000 demerits were charged for consecutive hyphens and for adjacent lines with large adjustment ratio changes. The second (hyphenation) pass was needed on only 279 of the paragraphs, i.e., about 5% of the time; a feasible solution without hyphenation was found in the remaining 5247 cases. The second pass would only try to hyphenate uncapitalized words of five or more letters, containing no accents, ligatures, or hyphens, and it turned out that exactly 6700 words were submitted to the hyphenation procedure. Thus the number of attempted hyphenations per paragraph was approximately 1.2, only slightly more than needed by conventional nonoptimizing algorithms, and this was not a significant factor in the running time.

The main contribution to the running time came, of course, from the main loop of the algorithm, which was executed 274,102 times (about 50 times per paragraph, including both passes lumped together when the second pass was needed). The total number of break nodes created was 64,003 (about 12 per paragraph), including multiplicities for the comparatively rare cases that different fitness classifications or line numbers needed to be distinguished for the same breakpoint. Thus, about 23% of the legal breakpoints turned out to be feasible ones, given these comparatively low values of the tolerances. The inner loop of the computation

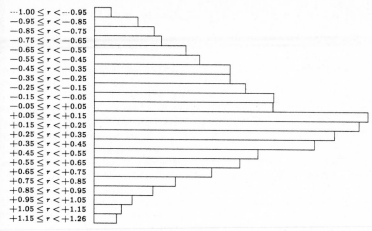

Figure 10. The adjustment ratios for interword spaces in a 700-page book.

was performed 880,677 times; this is the total number of active nodes examined when each legal breakpoint was processed, summed over all legal breakpoints. Note that this amounts to about 160 active node examinations per paragraph, and 3.2 per breakpoint, so the inner loop definitely dominates the running time. If we assume that words are about five letters long, so that a legal break occurs for every six characters of input text including the spaces between words, the algorithm costs about half of an inner-loop step per character of input, plus the time to pass over that character in the outermost loop.

And how about the output? Figure 10 shows the actual distribution of adjustment ratios r in the 15,531 typeset lines of *Seminumerical Algorithms*, not counting the 5526 lines at the ends of paragraphs, for which $r \approx 0$. There was also one line with $r \approx 1.8$ and one with $r \approx 2.2$ (i.e., a disgraceful spacing of 12.6 units); perhaps some reader will be able to spot one or both of these anomalies some day. The average value of r over all 21,057 lines was 0.08, and the standard deviation was only 0.403; about 67% of the lines had word spaces varying between 5 and 7 units. Furthermore the author believes that virtually none of the 15,531 line breaks are 'psychologically bad' in the sense mentioned above.

Anyone who has experience with typical English text knows that these statistics are not only excellent, they are in fact too good to be true; no line-breaking algorithm can achieve such stellar behavior without occasional assists from the author, who notices that a slight change in wording will permit nicer breaks. Indeed, this is another source of improved quality when an author is given composition tools like TₑX to work with, because a professional compositor does not dare mess around with the given wording when setting a paragraph, while an author is happy to make changes that look better, especially when such changes are negligible by comparison with changes that are found to be necessary for other reasons when a draft is being proofread. An author knows that there are many ways to say what he or she wants to say, so it is no trick at all to make an occasional change of wording.

Theodore L. De Vinne, one of America's foremost typographers at the turn of the century, wrote[13] that 'when the author objects to [a hyphenation] he should be asked to add or cancel or substitute a word or words that will prevent the breakage ... Authors who insist on even spacing always, with sightly divisions always, do not clearly understand the rigidity of types.' Another interesting comment was made by G. B. Shaw[14]: 'In his own works, whenever [William Morris]

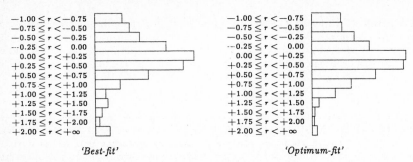

'Best-fit'   'Optimum-fit'

Figure 11. The distribution of interword spaces found by the best line-at-a-time method, compared to the distribution found by the best paragraph-at-a-time method, when difficult mathematical copy is typeset without human intervention.

found a line that justified awkwardly, he altered the wording solely for the sake of making it look well in print. When a proof has been sent to me with two or three lines so widely spaced as to make a grey band across the page, I have often rewritten the passage so as to fill up the lines better; but I am sorry to say that my object has generally been so little understood that the compositor has spoilt all the rest of the paragraph instead of mending his former bad work.'

The bias caused by Knuth's tuning his manuscript to a particular line width makes the statistics in Figure 10 inapplicable to the printer's situation where a given text must be typeset as it is. So another experiment was conducted in which the material of Section 3.5 of *Seminumerical Algorithms* was set with lines 25 picas wide instead of 29 picas. This sample text, which deals with the question 'What is a random sequence?', was chosen because it most closely resembles typical mathematics papers containing theorems, proofs, lemmas, etc. The optimum-fit algorithm now had to work harder than it did when the material was set to 29 picas, primarily because the second pass was needed about thrice as often (49 times out of 273 paragraphs, instead of 16 times); furthermore the second pass was much more tolerant of wide spaces in order to guarantee that every paragraph could be typeset without manual intervention. There were about 6 examinations of active nodes per legal breakpoint encountered, instead of about 3, so the net effect of this change in parameters was to nearly double the running time for line breaking. The reason for such a discrepancy was primarily the combination of difficult mathematical copy and a narrower column measure, rather than the 'author tuning', because when the same text was set 35 picas wide the second pass was needed only 8 times.

It is interesting to observe the quality of the spacing obtained in this 25-pica experiment, since it indicates how well the optimum-fit method can do without any human intervention. Figure 11 shows what was obtained, together with the corresponding statistics for the best-fit method when it was applied to the same data. About 800 line breaks were involved in each case, not counting the final lines of paragraphs. The main difference was that optimum-fit tended to put more lines into the range $.5 \leq r \leq 1$, while best-fit produced considerably more lines that were extremely spaced out. The standard deviation of spacing was 0.53 (optimum-fit) versus 0.65 (best-fit); 24 of the lines typeset by best-fit had spaces exceeding 12 units, while only 7 such bad lines were produced by the optimum-fit method. An examination of these seven problematical cases showed that three of them were due to long unbreakable formulas embedded in the text, three were due to the rule that TEX does not try to hyphenate capitalized words, and the other one was due to TEX's inability to hyphenate the word 'reasonable'. Cursory inspection of the output indicated that the main difference between best-fit and optimum-fit, in the eyes of a casual reader, would be that the best-fit method not only resorted to occasional wide spacing, it also tended to end substantially more lines with hyphens: 119 by comparison with 80. An author who cares about spacing, and who therefore will edit a manuscript until it can be typeset satisfactorily, would have to do a significant amount of extra work in order to get the best-fit method to produce decent results with such difficult copy, but the output of the optimum-fit method could be made suitable with only a few author's alterations.

PROBLEMS AND REFINEMENTS

Books on typography frequently discuss a problem that may be the most serious consequence of loose typesetting, the occasional gaps of white space that are called 'houndsteeth' or 'lizards' or 'rivers.' Such ugly patterns, which run up through a sequence of lines and distract the reader's eye, cannot be eliminated by a simple efficient technique like dynamic programming. Fortunately, however, the problem almost never arises when the optimum-fit algorithm is used, because the computer is generally able to find a way to set the lines with suitably tight spacing. Rivers begin to be prevalent only when the tolerance threshold has been set high for some reason, for example when an unusually narrow column is being justified. Another case that sometimes leads to rivers arises when the text of a paragraph falls into a strictly mechanical pattern, as when a newspaper lists all of the guests at a large dinner party. Extensive experience with TEX has shown, however, that manual removal of rivers is almost never necessary after the optimum-fit algorithm has been used.

The box-glue-kerf model applies in the vertical dimension as well as in the horizontal, so TEX is able to make fairly intelligent decisions about where to start each new page. The tricks we have discussed for such things as ragged-right setting correspond to analogous vertical tricks for such things as 'ragged-bottom' setting. However, the current implementation of TEX keeps each page in memory until it has been output, so TEX cannot store an entire document and find strictly optimum page breaks using the algorithm we have presented for line breaks. The 'best-fit' method is therefore used to output one page at a time.

Experiments have been made with a two-pass version of TEX that does find globally optimum page breaks. This experimental system also helps with the positioning of illustrations as near as possible to where they are cited, and it addresses the difficult layout problems posed by extensive footnotes in certain scholarly works. Many of these issues can be resolved by extending the dynamic programming technique and the model of this paper, but some closely related problems can be shown to be NP-complete[15].

REFERENCES

[1] Michael P. Barnett, *Computer Typesetting: Experiments and Prospects*, M.I.T. Press, Cambridge, Mass., 1965.

[2] C. J. Duncan, "Look! No hands!,' *The Penrose Annual* 57, 121–168 (1964).

[3] Michael R. Garey and David S. Johnson, *Computers and Intractability*, W. H. Freeman, San Francisco, 1979.

[4] Richard Bellman, *Dynamic Programming*, Princeton Univ. Press, Princeton, N.J., 1957.

[5] M. Held and R. M. Karp, 'The construction of discrete dynamic programming algorithms,' *IBM Systems J.* 4, 136–147 (1965).

[6] Jakob Ludwig Karl Grimm and Wilhelm Karl Grimm; 'Der Froschkönig (The Frog King),' in *Kinder- und Hausmärchen*, first published in Berlin, 1812. For the history of this story see Heinz Rölleke, *Die Altese Märchensammlung der Brüder Grimm*, Fondation Martin Bodmer, Cologny-Genève, 1975, pp. 144–153.

[7] C. J. Duncan, J. Eve, L. Molyneux, E. S. Page, and Margaret G. Robson, 'Computer typesetting: an evaluation of the problems,' *Printing Technology* 7, 133–151 (1963).

[8] Donald E. Knuth, *Seminumerical Algorithms*, Vol. 2 of *The Art of Computer Programming*, second edition, Addison–Wesley, Reading, Massachusetts, 1981.

[9] Donald E. Knuth, *TEX and METAFONT: New Directions in Typesetting*, American Mathematical Society and Digital Press, Bedford, Massachusetts, 1979.

[10] A. Frey, *Manuel Nouveau de Typographie*, Paris (1835), 2 vols.

[11] Donald E. Knuth and Michael F. Plass, 'Breaking paragraphs into lines,' *Software—Practice and Experience,* 11, 1119–1184 (1981).

[12] Donald E. Knuth, *Tau Epsilon Chi: A System for Technical Text*, book in preparation.

[13] Theodore Low De Vinne, *Correct Composition*, Vol. 2 of *The Practice of Typography*, Century, New York, 1901. The cited material appears on pages 138 and 206.

[14] George Bernard Shaw, 'On Modern Typography,' *The Dolphin* 4, 80–81 (1940).

[15] Michael F. Plass, 'Optimal pagination techniques for automatic typesetting systems,' Ph.D. thesis, Stanford University, June 1981.

Document Preparation Systems
and Commercial Typesetting

John W. Seybold

Seybold Publications, Inc., Box 644, Media, PA 19063

Abstract. *The setting for the development of methods of photocomposition is described, along with the various "generations" of such equipment. The history of the use of computer programs for the production of typeset output is traced. Hardware/software systems for inputting, editing and formatting text materials are considered, along with the implications of such systems with respect to their editorial and production environments. Similarities and differences between "commercial" applications and "document preparation systems" are also considered.*

1. Introduction

Computer applications for document processing, on the one hand, and for commercial typesetting, on the other, have, on the whole, represented two different and unrelated approaches to text processing. They have evolved from different needs and each has followed its own course. Yet it may well be that, in the new era of microcomputer technology, their paths are converging. Nevertheless, despite their disparate antecedents there is a certain commonality of approach, and there are obviously ways to bridge the gaps between the two disciplines. Moreover, each has something to learn from the other.

For example, in the commercial typesetting area some of the batch input and editing techniques will be found to be quite comparable to those which have evolved to deal with problems of documentation. In the field of document processing, interactive editing capabilities which have long been applied in the publishing industry—especially in newspapers—are now more common.

In the matter of pagination, problems and solutions will also be found to be quite similar in nature.

The bridge between the two disciplines has developed not only out of the similarity of tasks which each is required to perform, but also because those who are users of document preparation systems sometimes wish, and often need, to present their final output in the form of typeset pages, finding it necessary to develop programs to "drive" typesetters or to convert their files into a form in which they can be processed through commercial typesetting hardware and software systems.

2. The Evolution of Commercial Systems

In this article the term "commercial typesetting" will take on a broader meaning than is customarily attached to it. In the publishing industry, "commercial" typesetting is one of three major categories of activity in which typesetting (or "composition") take place. One is the newsaper industry. A second is the "in-plant" market. The third is "commercial" or trade typesetting. In the first two classifications, typesetting is an internal byproduct of writing, editing and publishing. In the third case it is a service business with respect to which writing, editing and publishing activities have traditionally been carried forward very much at arm's length.

However, in the context of this analysis we shall use the term "commercial typeset-ting" to describe the activities involved in typesetting and otherwise preparing for publi-cation a product of a certain kind, whether these activities are undertaken for profit, in a "trade" sense, or are carried forward "in-house" to service the needs of writers and editors engaged either by publishers or by others for whom "publishing" is a secondary require-ment in the support of a product or activity, as is the case with documentation.

Thus, in the sense which is relevant for this paper, "commercial typesetting" has more to do with the appearance of the product (its aesthetic properties) and the processing steps necessary to achieve this result, than with the question of whether or not the activity is performed by traditional (or even "new era") tradespeople.

Typesetting as it once was. For the purposes of this examination it seems hardly necessary to trace the beginnings of typesetting from the fourteenth-century origins of "movable type," attributed especially to Johan Gutenberg. That the western world experienced a cultural revolution as a result of the impact of the typesetting and printing technology set into motion at that time can hardly be doubted, although it may be as useful to assert that the technology came into being because the ferment of the times demanded it. But for the frame of reference pertinent to this particular study we need go no further back than the first half of the twentieth century. What has happened since then—in the areas of printing and reprographics generally, of computer hardware and software, and of imaging (or "typesetting") technology—is what we are now concerned with.

Although some "hand composition" (à la Gutenberg) still takes place, the vast bulk of the typesetting activity which occurred in the first half of the twentieth century was performed by one of two methods: linotype (or "slugcasting") and Monotype. Both of these processes were invented toward the end of the nineteenth century. Ottmar Mergenthaler developed the first practical "circulating matrix" machine, whereby a keyboard operator caused brass molds or matrices to be transported to an "assembler", with "spacebands" separating individual words. The keyboard operator made "end-of-line" decisions so that the width of the assembled characters would be less than the intended "measure" or line length by an amount that could be compensated for by virtue of the expansion of wedge-shaped spacebands, pressed upward by a lever until the line of characters occupies the desired space and can be cast as a "slug." This slug, created from molten metal, was then positioned with many others into a frame which represented a page or a "form" of (for example) two, four or eight pages, and locked up to be mounted on a letterpress printing press. For longer runs impressions could be taken from the pages of raised type and electrotype or stereotype printing plates were cast.

The alternative typesetting process, developed by Tolbert Lanston, was "Mono-type." Here an operator at a keyboard perforated a wide paper ribbon. Each character that he called for was identified by a combination of holes in this ribbon, and the width of the character, determined by its location on the casting matrix to be mounted in the machine, was "known" to the keyboard by a particular mechanical layout for the font in question and signalled to the operator by the mechanical movement of a revolving counter. Thus the operator could make the appropriate end-of-line decision and at the end of each line he would key in the value which the counter informed him represented the amount by which the line was "short" of its required length. The tape was then read by a Monotype casting machine, starting at the end of the job so that for each line the necessary justification statistics would be known by the machine in order that it could position certain wedges in such fashion that interword spaces cast would be of the required width to cause the line to justify.

With Monotype, each character or space was cast from hot lead separately, and deposited in a tray so that the output could be carefully removed and positioned for lock-up in the same manner as if the characters had been cast as slugs.

The Monotype approach generally yielded more attractive results because, despite the need to design characters to a common system of measurement (18 units to the printer's em), the type face designer could assign to individual characters whatever width values he chose. The matrix which held these character molds permitted a "font" to consist (most commonly) of 225 positions. Each character of the text type face ("roman") could be different in width from that of the "italic," and "small caps" could also be used. With linotype, on the other hand, it was common for italic characters to occupy the same brass matrix as the roman font (and hence assume their widths), with the operator setting a "rail" to indicate which of the two images should be included in the slug. This requirement compromised the design of the italic characters and represented only one of the respects in which the appearance of type cast from linotype was considered inferior to that created by the Monotype method.

Despite the aesthetic superiority of Monotype, linotype was the more economical process, and it prevailed for newspaper setting. Gradually, especially in the United States, linotype became the predominant device for the setting of even so-called "quality" book work, as more attention was directed by vendors of linotype machines to the design of improved book faces.

Note that these two techniques were particularly congenial for printing by letterpress. They both resulted in a raised mirror image of type characters, capable of transferring ink from roller to paper, and capable of withstanding sufficient pressure to avoid wear during a good many thousands of printing impressions.

Both techniques avoided the need to "distribute" types after printing since, unlike hand composition, they could be thrown into the melting pot in order to salvage for reuse the lead and other metals from which they were cast. Therefore new work was always composed from new or recycled metal.

Aside from "hot type" and some handsetting with "foundry" types, what else was available for composition? Only the photographing of characters drawn by pen, or the carving or etching of characters into wood or metal blocks—excepting, of course, the possibility of printing by means of mimeograph or hectograph ("ditto"). Here the typewriter could be used (ornamented by handwork on stencil or "master"). The quality of either mimeograph or ditto left much to be desired and only a relatively small run—perhaps several hundred copies—could be obtained from a stencil or paper ditto master. It was also not possible to produce "signatures" from forms or four, eight, sixteen, 32 or 64 pages since these "office duplicators" generally could handle nothing much larger than 8½ × 11 or A-4-sized pages. The collation and binding of the product was therefore also inferior.

But beginning in the late 1930s, and especially after World War II, the lithographic printing process became more and more popular, with improved presses and greater attention to quality control. This process, in its "offset lithography" form, gradually improved to the point where it was virtually indistinguishable by the layman from letterpress, and where relatively long press runs (of several hundred thousand) were possible.

The offset process, as it is generally known in the U.S. ("litho" overseas), does not require the use of raised type. (For that matter, neither does gravure). Hot metal type-setting thus became somewhat of a liability since it was necessary to produce "repro proofs" and photograph these in order to obtain the negatives or positives from which litho plates are made. Whether a liability or not, setting in metal was no longer a necessity, and the lithographic process was certainly more appropriate for the inexpensive reproduc-tion of illustrations, avoiding costly and time-consuming photoengraving processes.

Strike-on techniques. The time was ripe, therefore, for an alternative typesetting tech-nology, photographic in nature. Some "strike-on" typesetting also was introduced, with modifications in the typewriter to permit the use of more attractive proportional type characters, although to "justify" such composition was exceedingly difficult until the IBM "Composer," based upon the magnetic-tape selectric typewriter, came into being in the 1960s. The development of improved electrographic office copiers in the 1950s and 1960s also stimulated the use of "strike-on" techniques for short runs of small documents, as a much more desireable substitute for "ditto" and mimeographic reproduction, and in the meantime the use of paper printing plates for small offset ("multigraphic" or "duplica-tor") presses permitted the use of strike-on for internal memoranda and documentation where aesthetic considerations were not compelling and the economics of the cheaper process overcame the lack of economy in the use of paper as well as the inability to achieve "information compression" when the type images were monospaced rather than proportional.

In the latter connection, it is readily evident that "true printers' type"—or characters so designed—make for documents that are more readable, more understandable because of the available of a larger character repertoire of symbols and faces, and more compact or "compressed" in terms of numbers of words per page.

The phototypesetter. Efforts to design a photographic typesetter began to bear fruit as early as the late 1940s and in the 1950s several such machines were introduced. The first two were based upon the principles of linotype and Monotype, respectively, and were known as "first-generation" devices. Shortly thereafter, "second-generation" phototype-setters were offered and gained some acceptance. These did not imitate the (inappro-priate) technology of the hot metal machines but were designed from new beginnings. Soon a wide range of choices came into being, at various price levels, offering trade-offs in cost, quality of output, speed, and flexibility. Then in the late 1960s and early 1970s, "third generation" high-speed cathode ray tube typesetting machines ("CRT typeset-ters") entered the marketplace, first at prices in hundreds of thousands of dollars, and even before 1980 at prices from \$50,000 to \$120,000.

"Fourth generation" machines, using a laser to perform the task of character genera-tion and photographic exposure, also put in their appearance in the late 1970's and early 1980's.

For the most part, phototypesetters expose images onto photographic paper or film. The development of these photo-sensitive materials requires the use of a processor and dryer and this fact may have inhibited acceptance of the technology in the office environ-ment. "Dry" photo processes, using a "dry silver" emulsion, have so far not been widely accepted, but more recently electrographic typesetting devices have been introduced.

Here the office copier "engine," or something comparable forms characters by means of electrostatic or magnetic charges on a silenium (or similar) drum or belt, and transfers "toner" (wet or dry) onto paper. Such an engine can be used in order to create "camera ready" copy, which would be photographed for platemaking in the same manner as if it had been exposed onto light-sensitive materials, or—with some sacrifice in quality—it could be employed for multi-copy (reprographic) purposes.

By the early 1980's, hot metal machines no longer represented the prevailing method of setting type. Although still viable or even necessary in a few applications, and still persisting in out-of-the-way locations, the common method of setting type today is photographic, even if letterpress printing is still employed. (New letterpress platemaking techniques have been invented which permit the creation of raised images from light-sensitive materials.) In fact, the prediction today is that for some applications, before many years have passed, type images will be formed directly upon the surfaces of printing plates so that even "phototypesetters" will not be needed. And it is predicted, as well, that many printed products will be created on demand by reprographic engines driven by digital impulses, in such fashion that each book, leaflet or brochure will or could be produced serially, in its entirety, before another copy is even "typeset."

3. Functions of the Typesetting Device

The earliest phototypesetters were electro-mechanical devices. With the passage of time more components have become electronic in nature, and fewer are mechanical. Hence prices of such offerings have been reduced dramatically despite the inflationary spiral all around us. Reliability has been significantly improved as well.

Three aspects of typesetting machines deserve particular attention. One is character selection. From a grid, matrix, disk or drum of photographic masters, characters must be selected one at a time for exposure. Over the years the mechanical masking out of unwanted characters has given way to exposure by selective "flashing" of rotating master images, and now, with third or fourth-generation machines, by painting characters or entire lines of type through the technique of generating strokes or raster dots on a CRT tube or directly upon paper.

Sizing of images was accomplished by the interposition of scaling lenses. Now sizing is frequently accomplished by changing stroking or matrix patterns through electronics.

Character positioning (escapement or laydown) was initially performed by moving the film plane across the exposure area or by stepping the image-carrying light beam with mirror or prism. These techniques still exist, but increasingly the entire page area, up to the full width of a broadsheet newspaper, is exposed by deflecting a cathode ray electron beam or laser light source, with appropriate electronic or optical corrections to deal with problems of image distortion.

The relation to text formatting. Since electronics were now used so extensively to control the character-generating features of the typesetter it was only natural to consider the application of electronics to deal with the formatting of the text to be typeset, and even perhaps to use the same electronic system to perform both functions. But this did not happen in the first instance, and it is unlikely that in the long run a sharing of such electronic tasks will be considered advisable.

4. Driving the New Typesetters

The first phototypesetting machines were not driven by computers. Computers had not yet been removed from the scientific and military environments where they were first applied. Instead, these devices were activated and controlled by complex electrical switching relays. For the first generation machines input was created in precisely the same manner as was the case for hot metal. Thus the Intertype Fotosetter was a "direct input device" which looked exactly like a linecaster keyboard. The Monophoto keyboard was precisely the same as for Monotype. The first applications of computer technology were, moreover, applied to the automation of hot metal linecasting, rather than to the driving of phototypesetters. In order to pick up this strand of the narrative it is necessary to explain that a technique was developed in the early 1930s to activate hot metal linecasters from perforated paper tape. These were "teletypesetting" keyboards—a typewriter-like device with a paper tape punch attached, and a tray which contained a comb-like arrangement of metal plates from which character width information could be derived. A six-level "TTS" paper tape, containing text, line-ending decisions, and relevant codes, such as "return and elevate" to signal the end of a line, and "upper rail" to activate the alternate (bold or italic) matrix positions, was prepared by the operator and subsequently "read" by a mechanical reader attached to the linecasting machine, whose "fingers" sensed the presence or absence of holes in the tape and sent this information electrically to solenoids which actually depressed the keys and bars of the linecaster keyboard, just as if they were activated manually.

This method was not widely used, however, until after World War II. As was the case with direct input, the operator had to make his own end-of-line decisions, and he was assisted in this process by observing the juxtaposition of two pointers, one of which kept track of cumulating character width values and the other the interword space expansion potential. Linotype fonts were redesigned to a "unit" system so that width values could indeed be counted. Initially the counting process was purely mechanical, but later it became electronic.

The introduction of computers. In the early 1960s the possibility arose that TTS or other similar keyboards could be used to produce paper tape in an "idiot" mode. In other words, the operator would only have to key in the relevant text and some of the command codes (such as to effect a change to bold face), but was not obliged to make end-of-line decisions. The paper tape so perforated could then be inserted into a reader connected to a computer and a new tape would be reperforated which would include end-of-line signals. It was no longer necessary for the keyboards to retain information as to character widths. These could be stored in the computer. The task was, after all, purely one of computation: to determine when enough units had been accumulated, considering the number of interword spaces, so that the line fell within justification range. Then the "return and elevate" codes, inserted at the line endings by the computer program, would cause the linotype machine to justify the line.

This is the process known as "justification." However, to take care of those situations in which justification cannot be achieved between words, it was also necessary for the computer program to be able to determine whether or not the "straddle words" that made the line either too long or too short, could be broken (hyphenated) within justification range. In some of the earlier approaches an operator was called upon to make only these decisions. The reperforator unit would "beep" and call his attention to the word which prevented line justification by its inclusion or exclusion.

Since programmable computers were now available, algorithms were developed which (with some modest degree of accuracy) provided the necessary hyphenation points.

It may be seen that this great breakthrough contributed only one simple improvement to the typesetting process. The keyboarder or input operator, freed from the need to think about how lines were, in most instances, to be terminated, could key at a faster rate. Just as the TTS keyboard itself contributed to the volume of input since the depression of keys was no longer immediately tied to the casting of lines, so now the operator's fingers could serve merely to transfer letters from manuscript to paper tape.

Turning now, to the phototypesetting process, it was not long before direct input on keyboards attached to the typesetter was replaced by paper tape input. Initially this consisted of input perforated by teletypesetter-like devices, but naturally such keyboards had to contain "counting logic," whether stored electronically or mechanically. It was not long before it became evident that the same computer technology which could make end-of-line decisions for hot metal linecasters could do the same thing for phototypesetting devices, even though these were more complex—offering a much greater typographic versatility in terms of fonts and sizes which could be provided on line.

The correction process. One important limitation of photographic typesetting has always been that it is, in essence, a "blind" process. Once the input was fed into the computer program so that line endings and hyphenations could be determined, and the computer output (in the form of paper magnetic tape) was fed into the typesetter, the photographic film or paper removed and developed, then and only then could you see what you had created and it was clearly less than perfect. Keyboarding errors, or "literals" can never be avoided. Where strings of commands are also included such errors are even more likely. And there are also errors introduced by the composition process itself, such as faulty hyphenation. One of the advantages of conventional hot metal composition was that you could remove the very letters or line slugs that contained mistakes and replace them with others. Making such manual corrections is more difficult with photographic output since it can only be accomplished by "paste-up," and this is often impossible where errors require the resetting of entire paragraphs which will, when corrected, break or fit differently. Various approaches have been taken to alleviate these problems.

5. The Beginning of Typesetting "Systems"

It now became necessary to address more systematically the ways in which computers could be used to accept and format input intended for photographic typesetting devices. One method was for the operator to produce "hard copy" at the time of initial input, and for this hard copy to be proofread, and then to "merge" in the newly-perforated corrections before the paper tape was fed into the computer. *Paper tape merging devices* were thus constructed which could search for character strings, meanwhile punching out a *clean tape* up to the point where the correction was to be made.

A second method was to read the text into the computer, store it on magnetic tape or disk, obtain a printout while doing so, and then "update the file" by some method of addressing the locations where the corrections were needed. The correction messages for this "batch" program were themselves perforated on paper tape and a computer correction or update program would search for the points where changes were required and substitute new information for old.

Such correction programs often involved addressing the stored text according to printout line numbers, or spaces within the line, although the input of line numbers, accompanied with matching strokes of characters, plus their corrections, were also sometimes used. If necessary, words such as "delete" or "substitute"—or mnemonics therefore—were employed, and occasionally the programs were clever enough to encompass commands to move paragraphs or other blocks of text from one location in the file to another.

Often such changes were made before the text was formatted for typesetting purposes, on the theory that no purpose would be served by going to the expense of running a computer composition or format program on faulty input, and incurring the additional expense of setting such text in type. On the other hand, even if pre-composition checking and correction did occur, not all errors could be detected, especially those errors pertaining to formatting problems—faulty command codes or codes which produced undesireable results which could not be foreseen. Almost invariably, then, it was necessary to correct and reprocess text which had already been through the "composition pass," whether it had gone on to the typesetter or had been represented again by means of some kind of printout.

Perplexing problems caused by inadequate solutions usually arose. Some composition programs did not produce output which was itself reprocessible. It was necessary to go back to the input file, where lines broke differently, if you could indeed locate the point at which changes were desired in such a file. Then you would have to go through the entire process all over again. In other cases two files were created: one which could be used to drive a typesetter and another which could be reprocessed but which otherwise resembled the output file. Or one file was sometimes output which could either be used to send to the typesetter (where certain kinds of information would be ignored) or back into the computer for correction (where commands required for the typesetting process would be disregarded).

Because computer files intended for typesetting were often very long it was usually necessary to reprocess them in their entirety. This was occasioned by the serial nature of such data. If one plunged into the middle of such a file to institute a change one might not know or be able to restore all relevant conditions. For example, a command might be inserted into the middle of a paragraph for the purpose of italicizing a word, but one might not think to go back out of italics into the pre-existing type face (if one knew what it was!) with the result that the remainder of the document would be set in italics, or even worse, 36 point bold display.

One thing that clearly emerged from this experimentation (and we must remember that by this time we were no longer in the laboratories but attempting to produce commercially-viable products to a deadline) was that better correction procedures were clearly necessary and that they should if possible be interactive in nature, so that when changes were entered not only could one verify that they had been keyed correctly but also that one could determine immediately or reasonably soon thereafter what the effect of such changes would in fact be. In other words, there was a pressing need for a correction or update program which was *interactive* not only in the sense of implementing the changes, but in the broader sense of permitting the user to interact with the composition program itself.

The need for an on-line editorial system. At the same time that the commercial typesetting industry was struggling with the problem of how to transform words from a manuscript to paginated and typeset text pages, the newspaper industry was seeking to develop better solutions for handling wire service copy. Stories written by correspondents for these services (Associated Press and United Press International, for example) were being transmitted all over the country and indeed all over the world. While hard copy printouts were once considered sufficient, permitting local editors to pick up whatever they desired, modifying it by pen or pencil, and passing it on to the composing room for input into "the system," it was also possible to receive the same text in machine-readable form to be fed directly into a typesetter, or into a computer for composition formatting. However, most newspapers do not wish to print such stories intact, and the manner in which the stories were transmitted more or less assumed that some editing would take place, since corrections and "add-ons" were transmitted as separate takes. Hence the need for a way to review the stories on a video screen, to correct or modify them to suit local interests and editorial tastes, and then to transmit them through the system for typesetting. In the early 1970s such a terminal (the Harris 1500) was developed which accepted wire service input from paper tape and which enabled the editor to punch out an updated tape after he had made his changes.

Interestingly, that terminal was adopted by the commercial typesetting industry for the incorporation of changes in previously keyboarded local material even before it gained widespread acceptance in the area for which it had been intended.

Nevertheless, newspaper editorial systems were quick to develop. Initially they functioned in an environment in which reporters' stories were captured by OCR (optical character recognition) and then edited on video screens. Later, as union prohibitions were overcome and the economics of video terminal input were demonstrated, OCR gave way to direct VDT reporter input, and similar input of classified ads by the "telly ad takers."

The implications of an on-line editorial system. What made the transition occur so quickly, and in such a far-reaching manner, especially in the United States, was not just the advantage of avoiding the rekeyboarding of editorial (and classified) input. It was the *editorial control* which the system provided. A crude way of describing this was to use the term "the automation of the office boy." The all-electronic newsroom was to be a "paperless" environment, where all copy flow took place "through the system." While paper has not been entirely eliminated there is no question but that today the overwhelming proportion of editorial material appears in print without ever having been reproduced as hard copy. The process is quicker, easier, relatively trouble-free, and provides the managing editors with virtually total control of all of those processes which previously involved a confused and tortuous relationship between writer, editor, proofreader and composing room.

Directories and cross directories. One of the features of newspaper editorial systems which makes them so powerful has been the development of file management programs especially conceived for these applications. Elaborate structures of various types have been created to facilitate the effective use of video terminals by people who are not only not familiar with computers but who would be hostile toward the use of any procedures which were not virtually transparent and trouble free and which did not provide instantaneous response. For example, the editor who "logs on" to his terminal may or may not have to provide a password, but once he is recognized (whether or not the terminal he is sitting at is "his") a certain level of security permitting him to access certain files and certain levels of files is immediately provided. He will be provided with his own "queue" or "queues" which may not be accessible to anyone else. Certain routing procedures are probably implied so that when he hits the "send" key the story he is working on will be automatically routed to his supervising editor, and when he hits the "next" key the next story destined for him will be brought onto the screen, according to a predefined sequence such as "LIFO," (last in, first out), or "FIFO", (first in, first out), or some arrangement which brings the "urgents" in ahead of any of the others. Not only will messages queued for his "in basket" be available for him when he logs on, but he may be reached with a message signal, or message line, at any time, with some messages made available even if he does not store his open story, and others waiting until he chooses to dispose of or store whatever it is that he is working on.

The reporter or editor can jump from one hierarchical sequence to another. If the "tree structure" approach is implemented he may be permitted to move up or down this structure, perhaps being confined to his "desk" (e.g., sports), or with read-only privileges to certain other desks (e.g., "national"), or for other queues or baskets for his edition of the paper, or other papers (such as the morning rather than the evening edition). He can call up directories, and specify whether he wants them "long" or "short" or of a certain length, in terms of the amount of the story beginning which will be displayed along with the tag lines. The directory will also have certain attributes so that, by means of cross directories he may be able to ask for a long or short directory of all sports stories which have been written or edited by a certain person, destined for a certain page of the newspaper, and already sent to the typesetting machine.

It is possible for there to be "edit trace" features which will reveal what changes have been made or suggested (either in terms of deletions or insertions) by the last person who opened that story, and it is also possible, in arranging procedures for copy flow, for every version or certain versions of the story to be spun off for archival purposes onto magnetic tape.

Demands upon the system. The implications to system architecture of these and other features are quite profound. First of all, in a newspaper environment, catastrophe strikes if a system goes down. Virtually all components must be redundant, including all files. In the second place, response times must be virtually instantaneous. One would expect to wait less than five seconds before a requested story from any place in the system could be accessed by a particular terminal. One would not want to wait more than ten or fifteen seconds at most for a

Left: Atex terminals at Newsday on Long Island have been used by writers and editors since 1975.

Right: A terminal from System Integrators displays a short directory—in this instance a listing of wire service stories, including slug name, ID number, source, date and time entered, and length. Stories can be called merely by positioning the cursor on the appropriate line.

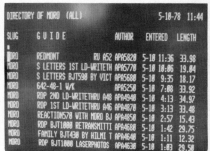

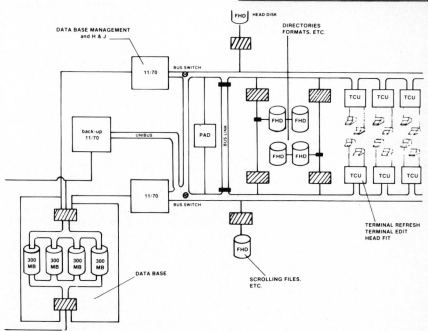

The Logicon TPS/6000 system, as it was installed at the Washington Star, illustrates a typical minicomputer configuration for newspaper editorial and classified use. Each TCU or terminal control unit supports editing and composition functions on a number of terminals, while the data base managers maintain all files in a form instantly accessible to users anywhere on the system. Note the back-up features and the four 300-MB disks.

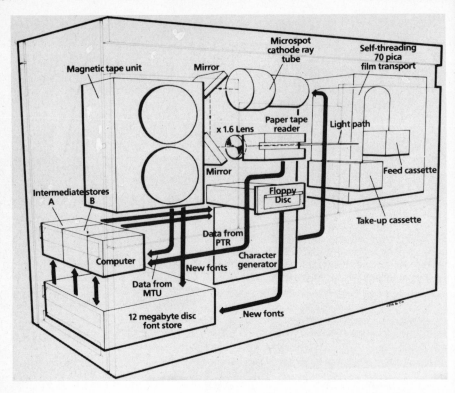

The diagram is labeled with the following components:

Magnetic tape unit, Mirror, Microspot cathode ray tube, Self-threading 70 pica film transport, x 1.6 Lens, Paper tape reader, Light path, Mirror, Feed cassette, Intermediate stores A B, Floppy Disc, Take-up cassette, Computer, Data from PTR, New fonts, Character generator, New fonts, Data from MTU, 12 megabyte disc font store, New fonts

Above: The Mergenthaler Linotron 404 CRT typesetter design is similar to that of most of the third-generation photocomposition devices. The only mechanical element in the machine is the film transport mechanism which moves the photographic material across the CRT tube.

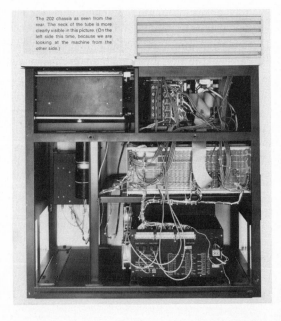

Right: The Linotron 202 is a very popular, low-cost third-generation cathode ray tube typesetter, widely used throughout the world, offering a wide variety of type faces on line, with setting speeds in the range of 600 lines per minute. This article has been composed on such a machine.

Above: Xenotron is a supplier of display ad composition work stations such as the Xenotron Video Composer shown here. Commands can be issued either from keyboard or tablet, and the stylus can also be used to indicate shapes and positions of text blocks. The screen display simulates the size and position of type to be generated by the final output device.

Right: Another similar display ad workstation is the AM 4800, which represents a current version of the original Harris 2200. Here the operator is holding typeset output of an ad designed on the 4800.

special directory, constructed by the use of cross directory functions, to come to the screen, and one would want to be able to get any story listed in that directory merely by placing the cursor on the listing and hitting a "fetch" key. And perhaps even more demanding upon the system is the response time expected for "h&j". For those editors charged with copy fitting responsibilities: if the editor makes changes and asks that the story be sent for composition formatting and brought back for his review, he would expect that not more than ten or fifteen seconds would elapse before he could bein to work on that story in its "hyphenated and justified" format. This means that the composition programs must be multi-threaded and/or re-entrant and possibly also that the system will route the story to whatever processor has the capacity at the moment. In addition, there are "copy fit" routines which provide even faster responses for copy depth estimates, and "head fit" routines which permit only the headlines to be counted for fitting, with an immediate report as to the extent to which the proposed wording is over or under the allotted width.

For classified ad takers, it is possible to send the ad to the system for copy fitting and to calculate the charge according to number of lines and other features while the placer is waiting on the phone. A credit check will also probably be run against the ad placer's phone number, and yet the ad taker will be expected to accept and to input, error-free, perhaps as many as 20 or 30 such ads per hour—or even more—during peak periods.

It is interesting to observe that the systems developed for the newspaper industry do not, generally speaking, consist of large main frame computers. Networks of minicomputers are generally used, and the operating systems have been especially designed to avoid irrelevant overhead demands.

To provide sufficient response time at the terminal level the architecture of the system tends to be of one of two varieties: the use of dual-ported memory plugged into a (Digital Equipment) PDP-11 unibus, or the use of intelligent terminals with a considerable amount of RAM with high-speed (e.g., 19,200 baud or better) data transfer from the host.

6. Software For Composition

Newspaper systems of the kind just described have been evolving for nearly twenty years, and especially since the mid 1970s when on-line video terminals began to be introduced in the United States for input and editing by journalists and for the taking of classified ads. The sophisticated features which such systems now offer presently go quite a distance beyond the capabilities available in the so-called "word processing" environment, and contain many features not necessary for "document processing" applications.

But not all typesetting systems in use today contain the same features as those required by newspapers, and while there is a great deal of commonality—even to the extent that some vendors can supply virtually the same hardware and software to newspaper and non-newspaper users—the requirements outside of the newspaper industry tend to place more emphasis upon batch processing, on the one hand, and highly-interactive processing on the other. It would seem probable that the batch processing approaches have more in common with those which we generally think of for purposes of "document processing."

A brief description of the evolution of systems for computerized composition may be helpful to provide some background for understanding where things stand at this particular juncture in the continuing evolution of text processing.

As we have already indicated, the first software for composition consisted of a single pass which read paper tape (which had been input in a "non-counting" mode without line-ending decisions) and formatted it for hot metal linecasting machines with TTS paper tape readers. This means that the program counted character widths and interword spaces in order to determine where to break the line in order to bring it within justification range, and also hyphenated "straddle" words where this was necessary in order to achieve justification.

In point of fact the program did not really "justify" lines but merely brought them within justification range; it was the linecasting machine's task to utilize its space band expansion capability to achieve the actual setting of justified text, presuming that all lines had indeed been broken within justification range.

Even the very early programs coped with the changing of fonts; a second font (bold or italic) was "duplexed" on the same linecaster matrices. Paper tape input contained "up the rail" and "downrail" command codes which would cause the typesetting device to activate a lever in order to position matrices in the alternative setting mode. In some cases character arrangements differed between the two fonts and translate tables were utilized to take this condition into account.

Since manual adjustments had to be made by the operator in order to permit the casting of each available point size, or to alter "body lead" (which determined the distance between lines) the initial programs were not concerned with the need to consider the effect of point size changes on the justification task during the processing of a given "take."

The next step was to develop the capability of "allocating" different outputs to machines with different set-ups, so that an input tape or a series of such tapes, could be analyzed by the processing program and computed according to the requirements of individual jobs and then routed to output devices already equipped with the desired magazines of type already mounted and the jaws set to the required measure. Thus the "torn tape" method evolved in newspaper applications, whereby the perforator operator ("keyboarder") would walk to the nearest of several paper tape readers, mount his tape to be accepted for input by the central processing unit on a polling basis, and a machine operator adjacent to a bank of linotype machines would tear from a cascading accumulation of computer-processed tape the most recent take, wind it onto a reel and mount it on the linecaster for which it was designated, reading the symbols on the tape leader for the necessary information to accomplish this.

When second-generation phototypesetters were introduced the torn-tape method of allocation was no longer necessary since now one machine offered the ability to set a variety of faces and sizes, even intermixing them within a given line. A program to drive such a typesetter thus became more complex since:

a.) the program had to cope with size changes

b.) it was necessary to take into account the different set width values of each font

c.) the arrangement of available characters or symbols might well differ from one font to another.

Moreover, some of these typesetting devices were driven as "slaves"—indeed, programmers preferred this condition—rather than in a manner in which the output device used its own internal logic to justify lines which the program merely brought within justification range.

If the computer program were permitted to accomplish precise justification it could then take more variables into account in the making of end-of-line decisions, or even in the implementation of decisions already made. Unlike their hot metal predecessors, photo-typesetting machines could usually handle spacing in fine increments, and could either add or take away hardly-discernible side bearing allowances between the escapement values of individual characters, in addition to "putting out" the customary variable interword spaces.

Other composition tasks. For photocomposition and even for hot metal setting, the task of composition involved more than the mere making of end-of-line decisions, including hyphenation. For example, individual lines, such as headings, could be set centered, or flush left or right, or "leadering" might be required. Ragged setting—left, right or center—might also be specified, or material might be justified but indented left, right or center, or with various combinations, such as indents within indents.

Some indents must "hang"—that is, the first line is not indented but the balance of the lines in the paragraph will be—or the value of the indent must be determined by the width of a combination of characters and spaces unknown to the input operator (a "variable" indent). The indent might be continued for a predetermined number of lines, or until some other command removes the condition.

All of these requirements seem trivial when one considers the task of inputting and composing tabular material, coping with a number of rows and columns of text, with some entries to be centered, or decimally-aligned within columns, and others to be justified, or even to be "run over" to succeeding rows within the same column. "Straddle heads" might be required to be centered optically over more than one column.

Correcting errors. Since photocomposing devices offer more opportunities for typographic flexibility, and to in order to achieve the varieties of setting which they made possible, it was clearly necessary to include more command codes within the text stream, and consequently the possibility of error multiplied accordingly. Mistakes are more readily made in typing illogical sequences of characters than in the typing of familiar words. But even for the preparation of relatively simple text the task of making corrections was considerably more complex than with the preparation of input for setting in hot metal.

With hot metal setting you had merely to remove and replace the offending characters or line slugs. With photocomposition output you had to cut and paste (or strip film) and to accomplish this so that the patched areas would not be discernible as such. Attention therefore focussed upon ways in which the final typeset output could be made perfect before it was set in type, and failing this, for the efficient incorporation of changes in the text prior to reprocessing.

The first correction program was introduced by Rocappi, a computer composition service bureau founded by this writer in the year 1963. This program was part of a "multiple-pass" system whose phases also accomplished galley composition and "pagination" (page make-up). Input (via paper tape) was read into the computer and stored on magnetic tape while a line-numbered printout was obtained. This printout could be proofread for typographic errors or for coding errors. A paper tape containing correction messages could then be prepared. These messages addressed the original text by line numbers and by interword spaces within the line. Programs of a similar nature were developed by others, some of which located the errors within a given line by matching the string of characters which were in error:

20 teh, the

Words could be added or deleted in much the same manner. It was more difficult to transfer blocks of text.

The updated magnetic tape was then formatted (in Rocappi's Phase II) into justified lines, during the "h&j" (hyphenation and justification) pass. Again a printout was produced so that errors could be located and these would be more readily apparent since typesetting commands had now been acted upon and to some extent their consequences could be revealed on the printout. Words to be set in italic might be underlined (so that it was easier to detect the omission of the command to return again from italic to roman). Other font changes could be identified by overprints of assigned font numbers or some similar convention. The lines of text themselves, while not appearing to be justified on the printout, could nevertheless be inspected in order to review their line endings and the hyphenation solutions which the program had effected.

Subsequent passes in the Rocappi system provided for pagination of the line-justified output, and driver programs for a variety of phototypesetters. Ultimately many pre- and post-processors were added in order to cope with data base needs, such as the sorting and sequencing of "entries" of records, and the "explosion" of such records, as would be the case with parts and price lists, or catalogs and bibliographic materials.

Composition systems. By the mid 1960s the user had his choice of a number of programs or composition systems, most notably for the RCA 301, the IBM 1620, and the Digital Equipment PDP-8, as well as for the Honeywell 200. The 301 and the PDP-8 were particularly well suited for this more sophisticated application, involving printouts and correction procedures, since magnetic tape decks for these machines were relatively inexpensive and neither rigid nor floppy disks were then available or, if available, affordable within the context of a viable commercial operation.

Nevertheless there were significant differences in program conception and design. One important difference had to do with the manner in which the "h&j'd" output could be corrected. Some programs wrote out the composed output file directly in the language of the internal photocomposition device, with the consequence that this output was not reprocessible through the composition pass again. If changes were required (as determined by the reading of the h&j'd printout or of final, typeset galleys) it would be necessary to update the original input file, or a subsequent file which antedated the h&j'd version. As we have already suggested, this led to complications since it was difficult to locate the position in the input file which corresponded to the offending portion of the output. Three solutions emerged. One permitted the updating of the h&j'd version since the latter was maintained as a separate file in the computer's own internal language. The translation of this file to an output driver format became a separate operation and while the latter file could not be reprocessed, the former could be. Moreover, there was a real advantage in maintaining what proved to be a "generic", output-independent, version of the formatted text since typesetter driver programs could be developed more easily when such files constituted their input. These driver programs could be used to produce paper or magnetic tape in the format expected by a particular typesetting device, or, more commonly, came to be used to create spooling files from which a typesetter could be driven on line.

Shortcomings of the printout. It turns out, however, that a computer printout, even in upper and lower case, does not provide a satisfactory record for the proofreading of material to be photocomposed. The character repertoire of the customary line printer is too limited and there is no easy way to represent the many hundreds of special symbols and signs which typesetting machines have available and which readers of typeset products expect to see. While combinations of characters could be improvised to represent such symbols as the degree sign, the superior footnote call-out reference, the French accent circumflex or the Greek mu, even if the proofreader can cope with such conventions there is no assurance that the wanted characters will in fact appear and that the complex requirements of the job have been properly understood and executed.

Nor does the printout permit the proofreader to judge how successfully lines have been justified by the program unless spaceband statistics (indicating some measure of looseness or relative tightness) are also provided.

Consequently commercial typesetters found it useful to "go to type" several times so that they could proofread and correct galleys—if not pages—in a form similar to that contemplated for the final product. Because of the cost of the necessary photographic materials "soft typesetters" were developed by some vendors. This provided the capability of reviewing the formatted material on a video screen in a manner which simulated the appearance of the type itself. Obviously this required the use of video displays which could represent generic versions of such type faces as serif and sans serif, bold, roman and italic, in sizes and with character widths which were as precise as possible. Unfortunately such "soft typesetters" were generally not interactive devices. In other words, while you could see the probable results on the screen, you generally had to go back to a monospaced version in order to make changes.

7. Batch Versus "Interactive"

Batch processing of text proved to be tedious and extravagant in many cases. In the early days of such efforts, such as with the RCA PAGE-1 program which was introduced in the late 1960s, an entire book might have had to be reprocessed many times, even through to the typesetting device. Keyboarding mistakes (both "typos" and the more serious errors in input and correctness of composition commands) simply could not be avoided by the most tedious efforts at "quality control" and every time new changes were introduced it was necessary to go back to the beginning to reformat the entire document, re-running it through hyphenation and justification, as well as pagination and typesetting. The only solution available was to do the job in many small "takes" and try, somehow, to merge them together. For the most part pagination was abandoned as too difficult to achieve. Galley composition was more congenial since individual galleys could be recomposed as often as necessary, and hand make-up (paste-up) was resorted to for page assembly. Even today (1982) pagination is not common among commercial typesetters except for very straight-forward materials. In any event, batch solutions are too risky and expensive for most of the tasks the typical typesetter is called upon to cope with. There is simply too much reprocessing of long files.

One way out has been provided by the capability of "partial processing" of text through the hyphenation and justification routine. A company by the name of *Imlac,* now a subsidiary of Hazeltine, offered such a capability in the early 1970s. It is possible for the user to re-start the h&j process at any point in the text, but as the program was originally written he was obliged to continue the process from that point on to the conclusion of the "take." Imlac also pioneered in offering a display of proportionally-spaced characters in several sizes on the screen, thus simulating, to some degree, the appearance of "true type."

Another company, *Atex, Inc.*, took the concept of partial processing one step further by enabling the user to define any text block, at the video terminal level, and to process or reprocess only that block through h&j, making whatever changes in parameters were desired in order to avoid a "widow" (a paragraph ending with a single word on a line by itself) or a "hanger" (a paragraph ending with only a portion of a word by itself), or to achieve better interword spacing or meet copyfitting requirements. In the same fashion, other corrections could be introduced without affecting the balance of the job.

Due to the serial nature of formatting commands, previously alluded to, there is always the risk that some variable introduced when working with a single block of text might inadvertently be carried forward. Atex's use of "style files" helps to avoid this problem. Eight modes can be represented on the screen and each mode can stand for different stylistic conditions, having to do not only with type face and point size parameters, but line length, leading, hyphenation characteristics, justified or ragged setting and other such conditions. The style file is literally a separate file which is referenced when the composition pass is run. Style files can therefore be redefined at will without the need to access the document itself.

Unless there are specific overriding parameters embedded in the text, the mode definitions obtain for all processing runs and for instructions to the output typesetting device.

But even these "interactive" solutions are not sufficient for some requirements. The most highly interactive of all composition programs is offered by stand-alone systems or subsystems for the setting of display ads. These terminals or systems permit the user to associate with any block or element of text any parameters he desires. The text file is brought in to terminal memory, often without any markup whatever except for some indication of block endings. A block could be as short as a single stand-alone line such as "Spring Sale!" Or it might consist of a brief descriptive paragraph pertaining, for example, to the features of the product. The user has the opportunity, however, to split pre-defined blocks apart, or to combine them into one, or, having arranged them as he wishes, subsequently to freeze the relationships between the elements so that they can treated as a unit—as, for instance, moving them about the page. Moreover, subsequent strings of text which are to be formatted in the same manner can automatically be assigned the same characteristics and thus spring into position and format.

While the operator may be required to type in a few commands relating to selection of type face, all other features can be assigned by approximation. By striking an "enlarge" key the operator can cause the block to be composed in the next available larger point size, and likewise a "reduce" key will step down to successively smaller point sizes. Up and down arrows can cause the block of text to be moved in a vertical dimension within the defined ad space, and other arrows will float the text to desired horizontal locations.

While the first of these devices (the Harris 2200) was entirely keyboard-controlled, subsequent vendors provide for the use of a graphic tablet not only to indicate the desired position of text elements but also to "pick" commands, or to sketch boundaries and outlines within which text might be "flowed." This feature was first introduced by *Camex* and is now also available on products by *Raytheon, Compugraphic, Xenotron, Mycro-Tek* and *Linotype-Paul.*

While it would appear that these same techniques would be helpful for the composition of text matter other than display ads, limitations in software and hardware design inhibited the general use of such solutions. They have been successfully applied to tabular composition and to the production of business forms, but only within the last year has there been any evidence that they might be extended to applications involving the processing of substantial areas of running text, as opposed to small blocks, records or entries each of which can be readily identified and assigned its unique properties.

Real Time Composition Systems. The Bedford Computer Company, under the leadership of its founder, N. Edward Berg, managed to combine some of the features of the display ad terminal with those of more conventional text processing, in what is called the Real Time Composition System, although the name could also be used to describe a generic classification of such systems as they emerge in imitation of the Berg concept.

Features of the Berg system include the ability to show on the screen of the video terminal a simulation of "true" type styles, in different sizes and with the actual width values of the characters in the desired fonts. This is done by means of bit-map display technology, but other kinds of screen display techniques might also be applied.

The ability to define text elements for manipulation according to assigned attributes, and to see the results immediately is also a characteristic of this approach. Each defined element is able to "stand on its own" and the text may be re-arranged, as in the Atex approach, without losing its identity. Thus blocks of type can be treated much as they were in the hot metal days, when they could be picked up physically and moved about within a form—excepting that now, of course, the attributes can easily be redefined at any time.

8. When Is Batch Better?

Now that we have begun to explore the possibilities of interactive composition—a process which can be aided by the use of such exciting tools as bit-map displays, even, perhaps, the use of color monitors—graphic tablets, and software which permit on-line manipulation, we come to appreciate, however, that some tasks are handled more efficiently in a batch environment. Preference for the use of interactive solutions for the correction or modification of those proposed by batch methods has been made evident for many classes of work. This is especially true for the pagination of documents. Here interactive intervention may only be required in order to deal with certain recalcitrant situations, such as the positioning of text and graphics in mutually-beneficial juxtaposition.

On the other hand, there are many situations in which interaction is essential—even, or perhaps especially, an editorial environment. A classic example is the news magazine, in which stories are written to fit pre-assigned spaces. A similar example is the mail order catalog where copy is also carefully allocated. In such cases either the original author or the copy editor must have recourse to hyphenation and justification and he is permitted not only to change the parameters (within limits) to achieve the desired result, but also to modify the text itself for this purpose. Not even a "copy depth estimate" program, which counts characters but does not compute line endings, is sufficient for the precise fitting of text.

While some feel that interactivity is necessary for aesthetic reasons, to permit the operator to make subtle changes in relationships between particular characters or text blocks, others argue that it is indeed possible to de-skill many matters of aesthetic judgment, as may be witnessed by the extensive use of kerning tables which have been developed by type experts for individual fonts and which can be applied automatically even when the users are not aware of what the niceties of kerning imply.

9. Varieties of Pagination Approaches

Although there was a great deal of interest in pagination programs in the 1960s, when attention focused on automating the production operations of trade composition shops setcorprimarily engaged in "book work," the primary interest in the 1970s lay in newspaper editorial systems, and, to a lesser degree, similar systems for news magazines. Newspapers were not particularly interested in page make-up programs. Display ads had to be pasted up in any event, and there was an abundance of labor in the composing room production operation due to the fact of "keystroke capture" in editorial offices—at least in the United States and Canada where union restrictions gave way to the imperative of technological advance.

Today, however, concern over the adequacy of pagination solutions is receiving a great deal more attention for several reasons. First, because it now seems possible to output graphics as well as type, thus removing one element that would have had to be stripped-in in any event. Second, because new technology is pointing toward the possibility of going "direct-to-plate"—which would make paste-up impossible. Third, because an increasing volume of newspapers and magazines are being printed in more than one location, and this tends to encourage the transmission of "complete" and "perfect" pages (including graphics). Fourth, perhaps because of the prospect of a growth in "demand printing," since delivery to the home, office or library of paginated documents tailored to the needs of the individual reader could conceivably revolutionize the delivery of the printed word.

It is clear, at least to this writer, that there is no universal solution to the problems of page make-up. Paging systems are often an essential part of the editorial process and under such circumstances cannot be left entirely to non-interactive approaches. In some instances pagination is in fact a by-product of the editorial control and management of copyflow, and this should properly be the case with newspapers and many magazines.

It is unfortunate that some of those who are concerned with document preparation have a myopic view of the aesthetic and creative aspects of publishing, tending to think only of ways to get the manuscript out the door and into the hands of the reading public. The present excitement about "word processing" encourages—at least momentarily—the exacerbation of the tendency to apply simplistic solutions to the arrangement of text and graphics on a page. However, it is to be anticipated that interest will continue to grow in "going to type" from document- and word-processing systems. Many trade typesetters are making quite a business of accepting word processing input, usually via telecommunications, and also magnetic tapes supplied from main-frame document processing systems.

In some instances the output is galleys which are then pasted up as pages by supplier or customer. In other cases straight-forward pages are handled in a manner not much different from the pagination routines of word processing programs: the generation of "headers" and "footers" with fairly arbitrary page break procedures, often permitting "widows" at the top of pages, frequently not observing consistent page depth specifications, and failing to cope with footnotes, or positioning them badly.

10. Document Processing, Word Processing and Typesetting

The presentations in this book, with the exception of the contribution by this writer, whose background and experience differs significantly from most of his colleagues in this common venture, will no doubt support the conclusion that increasingly sophisticated batch solutions are becoming available and may prove to be advantageous especially in situations in which most documents conform to pre-determined specifications. Generic coding introduced by the user provides most of the information required for purposes of composition.

On the other hand, it is to be expected that input and editing terminals with bit map or similar displays capable of representing type images and areas for interactive manipulation will certainly become more practical in the future and the quality of electrographic bit-map or raster-scan output devices will be successfully combined even at the microprocessor level, so that "what you see" will be "what you get."

A final observation must also be made. Many existing document processing systems seem to this writer to be extravagant in terms of their use of computer resources and personnel. This may be tolerated and possibly encouraged in a scientific or academic environment. But the applications which emerge from this area—perhaps including some described in this book—even if they meet the aesthetic requirements of "commercial typesetting"—may not offer solutions which are practical in an economic sense. On the other hand, those developed for commercial use may also prove to be viable in a scholarly setting. Such an example is offered by the adoption by the Supreme Court of the United States of an Atex copy processing system with all of the features Atex has developed for its newspaper and national publishing accounts. Atex is of course not alone among the vendors and developers of sophisticated but "dedicated" commercial copy processing systems. The question arises as to whether such systems can become more "general-purpose" in nature without compromising their efficiency in their field of primary application and, conversely, whether more general-purpose configurations can be taught, over time, to offer many of the advantages inherent in the better dedicated systems.

DOCUMENT PREPARATION SYSTEMS
J. Nievergelt, G. Coray, J.D. Nicoud, A.C. Shaw (eds.)
© North-Holland Publishing Company, 1982

ERRORS IN DIALOG DESIGN
AND HOW TO AVOID THEM

J. Nievergelt

Institut für Informatik, ETH, CH-8092 Zurich, Switzerland

Abstract

The development of interactive command languages is repeating, with a 20-year delay, the history of programming languages: large collections of unrelated individual commands are being replaced by systematically structured modes that satisfy general principles of consistency. A survey and classification of design errors common in today's man-machine dialogs leads to concepts and design principles whose observance avoids such errors.

But the very notion of *command language* is of doubtful utility for systematizing the design of highly interactive man-machine interfaces. Observation of users of interactive systems shows that the most common difficulties experienced are expressed well by such questions as: *Where am I? What can I do here? How did I get here? Where else can I go and how do I get there?* Such questions reveal the fact that the fundamental problem of man-machine communication is how to present to the user what he cannot see directly, namely the state of the system, in such a manner that he can comprehend it at a glance. If the *output language* of a system, what the user sees or can get onto the screen easily, is rich and well structured, the command language proper, or *input language*, can be simple. Instead of emphasizing the *command part* of the man-machine interface, designers should focus their attention on the *display part*.

The questions above also provide hints about how the display of an interactive system should be structured. *Where am I?* and *What can I do here?* refer to the state of the system. A good design answers them by displaying to the user on demand his current data environment *(site)* and his current command environment *(mode)*. The last two questions refer to the past and future dialog *(trail)*. A good design makes as much of the past dialog as can be stored available to the user, to be undone (in case of error), edited and reinvoked; and it gives advice about possible extrapolations of the dialog into the future *(help)*.

Key words and phrases

interactive systems, man-machine communication, system design

Contents

1. Anecdotes, horror stories, and what we can learn from them

Recently I concatenated several files that contained sections of a report into a single file. Bitter experience has taught me that file operations on many a system are error-prone. With relief I saw the target file name appear in the directory; but when I wanted to look at the result, the editor complained: file too long! In interactive systems a text editor is the primary utility for splitting and merging files, since it allows the user to browse through the file and exploit his eyes' pattern recognition ability. Deprived of my most powerful tool, I realized that this "correct" file that could not be seen was useless. Only half in jest I said: "I bet the file will be too long to be deleted". The quickest remedy was to start from scratch, catenating as many of the original files as would fit.

So what? Today's programmer accepts as a matter of course the fact that, on the same system, an editor, a file server, a printing routine all have their own file size limits.

A few months ago, as I was editing at an "intelligent" terminal, my friend inadvertently switched the power off the minicomputer to which my terminal was attached. There was no way I could have noticed from the terminal's behavior that I was off-line, so I continued editing for half an hour before attempting to write the buffer content onto a power-off disk. Starting up the system re-initializes the terminal, so there was no practical way to save the file content that was still visible on the screen. The most efficient remedy was to scribble the major modifications onto paper and to redo them.

With foresight this system could have been designed so that the nuisance above could never happen. Why was it not done? Today's computer user routinely wastes hours with boring work just to get around trivial design flaws.

A couple of years ago a competent computer man grabbed the nearest disk pack in a hurry to run a test program. The program required a large block of contiguous disk space, so he applied a *squeeze operation* to the disk content. The drive misbehaved, the directory of my disk got destroyed. He was choking as he called late at night to announce the loss of my files. The remedy? He spent several days writing a *scavenger*, a program that searches the disk trying to identify file headers from which the file structure can be reconstructed. We spent another day "manually" pasting file fragments together, were able to reconstruct most of the old disk content that mattered, and clean up the disk as a beneficial side effect. The scavenger joined our collection of utilities.

What should he and I have done to avoid this near-disaster? I hear a sermon: "Obviously you use a scratch disk for running hardware tests and keep up-to-date backups!" True. Similar advice is given to rock climbers. But notice that we don't use a scratch record to try out a record player, and that few people keep a backup car. Now that computers are becoming consumer products, they have to start behaving accordingly. Anecdotes and horror stories such as the ones above, instead of describing the state-of-the-art, must become tales of the good old days.

The spell of an anecdote lies in the unexpected; the reliability of a system manifests itself in that only the expected happens. Suspense and reliability are incompatible: We must learn to build systems that never catch the user by surprise. The history of mature fields of endeavor teaches us how to achieve this goal: we must suffer a lot of surprises, study and classify these, develop concepts and principles that exclude the known errors, and enforce them. No other way can relegate painful surprises from everyday experience to rare accidents.

Over the past decade I have observed hundreds of users of interactive systems suffer many surprises in a variety of settings. I have analyzed these impasses, tried to reduce them to a small number of causes, and proposed design techniques to avoid them. The procedure used is common sense observation and deduction. A similar approach to developing design rules based on the analysis of human errors is described in [Nor 82]. More rigorous techniques have recently become fashionable, and the literature on the psychology of human-computer interaction has mushroomed. [Mor 81] is a good introduction to this subject. But the greatest improvements on the sad current state of man-machine dialogs can be achieved with common sense alone, without the fine-tuning of controlled experiments. The following sections are intended as a casual introduction.

2. Survey and classification of errors

All roads lead to Rome. In a thicket of superficially unrelated phenomena, all considerations about man-machine dialogs lead to two fundamental concepts: *the STATE of the system and its INTERFACE to the user.*

The *state* is concerned with everything that influences the system's reaction to user inputs. The *interface* is concerned with interaction: what the user sees on the screen, what he hears, how he inputs commands on the key board, mouse or joy stick. Today's fad is to engineer fancy interfaces: fast animation in color, sound output and voice input. This is desirable for some applications, unnecessary for others, but in any case it does not attack the main problem of man-machine communication.

> **The fundamental problem of man-machine communication is how to present to the user**
> **what he cannot see directly, namely the state of the system,**
> **in such a manner that he can comprehend it at a glance.**

So let us start with common errors of dialog design which hide vital state information from the user.

2.1 Insufficient state information

Imagine that you leave your terminal in the middle of an editing session because of an urgent phone call. When you return ten minutes later, the screen looks exactly as you left it. Even if the system state is unchanged, you may well be unable to resume work where you left off:

> D: *"What file was I editing?",* *"Is there anything useful in the text buffer?";*
>
> C: *"Am I now in search mode?",* *"What is the syntax of the FIND command?";*
>
> T: *"Has this file been updated on disk?",* *"Has it been compiled?".*

Such questions indicate that part of the state information necessary to operate this system has to be kept in the user's short term memory. When the latter is erased by a minor distraction, the user needs to query the system to determine its state. Hardly any system lets him do this systematically, at all times.

Today's systems provide state information sporadically, whenever the programmer happened to think about it. The file directory can be seen in the file server mode, but not in the editor; in order to inspect it you must exit from the editor, an operation that may have irreversible consequences. In order to see the content of the text buffer you may have to insert it into the main text. In order to find out whether you are in search mode you may have to press a few keys and observe the system's response - not always a harmless experiment.

A designer who follows the following principle avoids all the problems above:

> **The user must be able AT ALL TIMES to conveniently determine**
> **the entire STATE OF THE SYSTEM, WITHOUT CHANGING THIS STATE.**

The phrase "entire state" will become more precise in section 3, but one refinement of this notion can be explained now. In any interactive system the user operates on data (perhaps he only looks at it) by entering commands (perhaps he only answers multiple-choice questions). Thus the state of the system must include the following two major components: the *current data environment* (what data is affected by commands entered at this moment), and the *current command environment* (what commands are active). The questions above labelled D and C refer to data and command environments, respectively. The questions labelled T refer to the user's *trail*, i. e. the dialog he is conducting during a session.

A particularly dangerous version of "insufficient state information" is the deceitful presence on the screen of outdated state information. The programmer is consciously aware of the moment he has to write some information on the screen, but he forgets to erase it when it no longer describes the state of the system. The user sees 'current file is TEMP' in some corner of the screen, when in fact his current data environment is another file. The bad habit of leaving junk lie around the screen must have originated in the days of the teletype, when messages written could not be erased, but it should not be allowed to persist on today's displays.

So our answer to the question: *Is it really necessary for an interactive system to have so many commands?* is: not if the general dialog commands are shared by all the interactive utilities on the system, and the latter limit themselves to the commands that are specific to the type of data they handle. The solution to both problems of too many commands and of the Tower of Babel confusion lies in the concept of universal commands. An interactive system should have a set of about a dozen general dialog commands that are universal in several meanings of this word:

they are always active,
they are always invoked by the same key presses, and
they always have the same interpretation regardless of the type of objects currently being handled.

Commands are the ingredients of the system's input language; responses make up the system's output language. Because the user actively composes commands, but only sees or hears responses "passively", it is perhaps natural that initially the "command part" of a command language has been stressed. With terminals of limited display power as those traditionally used, it was indeed a necessity to code most of the complexity of the man-machine interface into the input part of a command language. Now that wide-bandwidth graphics terminals are becoming common, it is a mistake. The complexity of the interface is much more effectively embedded in the *response part* of a command language, and the input part should approximate as much as possible the command language with one single command, pointing. For this to become possible, a designer must impose a rich and clean structure on the output language, so that the user can easily explore the state of the system (see [XS 82] for an example).

An elementary but common violation of the duty to pay attention to the output language is omission of feedback to the user. You enter a command and wait; if the response is not instantaneous, you may start wondering: have I hit return already, or is the system waiting for me to do so and thus activate the command? is it possible that a squeeze operation takes this long? has the system crashed? Without feedback the user has no good option in this situation: if he presses return twice, the second key press may be interpreted as answer to the next system prompt; if he aborts the command he may do irreparable damage; if he decides to wait, how long should he wait?

The reason that today's dialogs provide feedback only sporadically is the same one that causes screens to be littered with outdated information. The programmer of a man-machine dialog tends to identify himself with the machine - after all, he communicates with the user via the medium computer-driven screen [Nie 82]. Thus those moments when he (or the computer) has to take the initiative are foremost in his mind, such as when he has to put a menu on the screen; but he forgets to reassure the user when it is the latter's turn to be active .

The only way to avoid leaving the user in suspense is to follow a systematic procedure of providing feedback as a default, and to suppress it only by conscious decision. Feedback should be provided as a matter of course on at least the following four levels (see also [Fol 80]):

- the key press level (usually by echoing)
- the lexical level (e.g. a parameter of type *integer* has been recognized)
- the syntactic level (e.g. a command has been recognized)
- the semantic level (e.g. a command is being processed or has been completed).

A beep that announces completion, or the continuing appearance of dots on the screen to inform the user that the system is up and working on his problem, can be amazingly reassuring. The programmer just has to place the feedback where it will be seen, usually near the user's last input, or else in a standard place on the screen to which the user has become accustomed. But this advice already belongs to our next topic, that of:

Encoding of commands and system responses

Is the "/*$ syntax" of many of today's command languages the fault of the limited character sets of early hardware or of the indolence of the programmer who wrote the command interpreter? Whatever the reason, '/•C $X $Y' is of little mnemonic value. 'Copy from .. to ..' makes everything clear, in particular the important issue whether the first or the second argument is the destination to be overwritten.

Undiplomatic and uninformative encodings of system responses are common. 'Illegal command' is one of the most frequent messages to appear on the screen. The appearance of a menu or other information that

2.2 Poor design of the interface

The interface, that is, the face that a system presents to the user, has a *physiological* and a *logical* component. The former is the traditional subject of ergonomics or human factors engineering. Many frequent violations of established ergonomic principles can be cited: rigidly fixed key boards that force the user into an unnatural position; flickering displays; excessive use of inverse video techniques that produces stark contrasts in brightness among different parts of the display; placing the display in front of a window, thus forcing the user to look into a surrounding area much brighter than the screen. The eyes tire as they continuously adapt in their sweep of the screen and its surroundings; [GV 80] discusses such issues. I will concentrate on the neglected topic of the *logical design of the man-machine interface*. This discussion is best separated into two subtopics:

- the structure of the command language, and
- the encoding of commands and responses.

Structure of the command language

A command language consists of two parts, an input language (the set of commands) and an output language (the system's responses). The former is traditionally considered to be the important part, hence the name "command language", in analogy to "programming language". We will argue that "command language" is a misnomer, that in fact the output part of the language is the important thing, but in order to mirror the development of the field we discuss the input part first. Interactive systems have a lot of commands. It is not easy to count them, since one single command with many parameters can always be traded for many simple commands. But if one counts a command with the multiplicity of the number of parameters it has, that is, with the number of distinct decisions that the user may have to make, one easily reaches a hundred. As an example, a glance at the manual of a successful interactive system for hobby computers (UCSD Pascal [AP 79]) yields the following approximate counts: *Top command level: 8 commands without parameters. Filer: 18 commands with an average of one or two parameters. Editor: 28 with an average of one or two parameters.* Even without counting 20 compiler options and an untold number of error messages that the system may throw at the user, we see that even a small system requires the user to have present in his mind many more chunks of information than he can keep in short term memory (see "The magical number seven, plus or minus two" [Mil 56]). Systems for professional use (CAD, document preparation, etc.) are even more complex.

The consequence of this complexity is that the system can only be used effectively by those who have memorized this large set of commands, not by casual users who must retain the information necessary for working in their short-term memory, which is subject to the limitation of half a dozen chunks at a time [Mil 56]. And the cost of memorizaton is high: It takes me at least a week to get to know an interactive system well enough to work at my level of capacity; if I stop using it for a month, it may take a day to regain the proficiency I had earlier.

Is it really necessary for an interactive system to have so many commands? An analysis of various interactive utilities, such as editors for different types of objects (text, diagrams, forms) yields a surprising answer: only a minority of the commands are specific to the type of objects to be manipulated by each editor; the majority of the commands have a general interpretation that is independent of whether we speak of text lines or graphic lines, paragraphs or pictures. There are *dialog control commands* such as next, back, quit that are completely object-independent; general *utility commands* such as copy, create and delete that only depend on the fact that an object can be uniquely identified, say by naming or by pointing; there are *motion commands* such as up, down, left, right that only depend on an ordering of the objects, and can be used equally well to move from line to line, file to file, or picture to picture.

It is the major shortcoming of today's interactive systems that every interactive utility introduces another set of commands necessary to conduct a general dialog, rather than limiting itself to the data-specific commands necessary to manipulate its own type of objects. This leads to the sad state of affairs that the programmer of each utility re-invents his own general dialog commands. Quit (from the current command or data environment) will always be present, but it will be named Q in one utility, E or X (for exit) in another, and be invoked by Control-C or the escape key in a third. This multiplicity of names may leave the user in doubt whether the state of the system is different after executing differently named quit commands. The casual user in particular bears the burden of this Babylonian language confusion.

tells the user just what inputs are expected at that moment is less offensive and a lot more helpful. The kindest statement possible about 'Illegal command' is that it beats a system crash - a cruel but regrettably not unusual punishment for "illegal inputs".

There are manuals of style for speaking and writing, and we need manuals of style for novice authors of man-machine dialogs. Proper expression is not just a matter of esthetics; it is also a matter of efficient use of people's time. [LWSS 80] presents the results of an experiment designed to investigate the effect of ill-chosen names and syntax on user productivity. Two groups of users ranging from novices to experts were given the same editing tasks. They also used the "same" text editor - except that the commands had different names and a slightly different syntax. Whereas the original editor conversed in phrases such as 'FIND:-5' and 'RS:/KO/,/OK/', the revised editor called the same two commands 'backward 5 lines' and 'change "KO" to "OK"', whose meaning can be guessed without a manual. As you would expect, experts as well as novices did better with the editor using meaningful names with respect to work completed and number of errors.

2.3 Ignoring the user's trail

"We have seen the enemy, and he is us!" The user is by far the most dangerous component of an interactive system - at least 90% of all mishaps that occur during operation are traceable to faulty user actions. Designers of interactive systems must accept the fact that high interactivity encourages trial-and-error behavior. Exhortations to discipline are worse than useless - they are counter-productive. A designer using a CAD system, a writer using a text processor, a programmer debugging his programs - they must concentrate on their creative task, and cannot allow a fraction of their conscious attention to be sidetracked, continuously double-checking clerical actions. A system should be foolproof enough to absorb most inaccuracies and render them harmless.

It is surprising that virtually all research on reliability and security is directed against either hardware and software failure or deliberate attack by third parties. But the majority of users of interactive systems have no one but themselves to blame when their data is suspect or has been damaged. In cleaning up one's files the most recent version of a document is thrown away and an old one kept instead. You hit **D** instead of **C** on the keyboard, so something gets deleted instead of created. You forget to label a file permanent and so it vanishes. The catalog of plausible errors is different on each system; they all have in common that, as soon as we become aware of the blunder, we gasp: "How could I possibly have done that!". We can and do, at the rate of many oversights a day.

The mechanisms built into today's systems to protect the user from his own mistakes are primitive. Are you sure? is one of the favorite questions, followed by a sporadic request to press some unusual key if the action is really serious. This double-checking is effective only against accidental key pressing, not against an erroneous state of mind. When I delete a file I'm sure that's what I want to do - though I may regret it later.

The most effective protection of the user from his own mistakes is to store as much of the past dialog as is feasible. At the very least a universal command undo must always be active that cancels the most recent command executed. The memory overhead of keeping two consecutive system states is negligible, since these two states differ little - typically by at most one file. The error-prone and time-consuming Are you sure? is unnecessary when the user can always undo the last step. Ideally undo works all the way back to the beginning of the session, but that may be too costly: in order to replay the user's trail *backwards* the system must in general store *states*, not just the *commands* entered, as many operations have no inverses (e.g. delete). A practical alternative is for the system to keep a log of commands entered and to allow the user to save the current state as a check point for future use, from which he can replay the session.

2.4 Compounding the problems

Every one of the design errors mentioned above may seem mild when considered in isolation. While reading section *2.1 Insufficient state information* you expect to face errors of that kind, and hence you recognize them. But in an unsuspecting state of mind the user is likely to take every misleading system message at face value. I remember a user walking away from a time-sharing terminal muttering "the system is down again". "It's up", I said. "No, it doesn't react to any of my commands". He had somehow gotten into the editor's insert mode, but the indication of this mode change had long ago been scrolled off the screen. *He* thought he was entering commands, whereas *the system* thought he was entering text, and that the only thing it was supposed to do was to faithfully echo his key presses, just as the terminal does in local mode.

In "Breaking the man-machine communication barrier" [HBR 81], an amusingly sad story is told of how intolerant a system can be. The user of an electronic mail system asks to see all the messages that have recently arrived from a particular sender. He types a long command: 'haeders from robertson since May 15', which contains minor syntactic errors. The system tolerates no misspelling and has no memory of the previous command line entered by the user; it rejects his attempts time and again with uninformative comments such as '?illegal message sequence'. Trial and error and help from expert users finally lead to the correct formulation: 'headers from "robertson" intersect since "May 15"'.

The barrier illustrated by the example above is caused not by any single design error, but by the cumulation of imperfections that result in the syntactically correct form of the command being intuitively less meaningful than the original faulty formulation. Several improvements should occur immediately to the skilled designer of man-machine dialogs, such as:

A casual user needs a mode that prompts him for selection of one among a few options, or for input of a single parameter; the *user control mode* exhibited in the example above, where a long command with several parameters must be entered without guidance, is only appropriate for skilled users.

In limited domains of discourse (and programs are only able to converse in very limited domains of discourse) the system can afford to be tolerant about the precise form in which a command or parameter is entered. A date, for example, should be accepted in any of the forms it is usually written. In order to avoid misunderstanding, the system should paraphrase the user's input: '11/12/81' might be acknowledged by '11. Dec. 1981' in one country, and by 'Nov 12, 1981' in another; in either case the user is likely to notice any misinterpretation and correct it.

One last admonishment: clear and concise formulation of instructions is hard, but is well worth careful thought on the part of the author of a dialog. The colloquial style that makes human communication versatile is ill-advised in man-machine dialogs because it is hardly ever backed up by the intelligence necessary to make informal conversation effective. 'Would you like an opportunity to practice?' sounds fine until you discover that the program does not know how to react to the natural reply *What do you have to offer?*

As a general rule computer dialogs should present options rather than ask questions. There are two objections to computer dialogs based on questions: A question contains little information and it invites answers that may be beyond the program's ability to understand. Do you want to exit? leaves me in doubt as to what system state will occur if I answer Y, yes, no, or what else can I do?. The instructions:

```
Press X to exit to the top command level
      R to repeat the exercise
      L for a list of other options
```

may take three times as much space on the screen, but contain six "chunks of information" instead of the single one in the original question. Whereas the question only told me that I had the option to exit, without telling me where I would end up, the menu specifies for each of three commands how it is invoked and where it brings me. *Say it, don't ask* is a useful rule for finding unambiguous ways of expressing your message.

In striving for clarity and efficiency, the author of a dialog must also resist the temptation to play cute games. I've often used a formatting program called Sally. Sally had the disconcerting habit of introducing herself with a random name. *I'm Jennifer, what can I do for you?* I now take it for granted that any time a woman's name appears on the screen I must be in the formatter. As a novice I wasted time discovering Jennifer's text formatting skills.

Our attempt at classifying errors included parts of a solution to the problem of how to avoid them, in the form of a few general principles and many isolated suggestions for improvement. There remains the task of integrating these insights into a design technique. In the following sections we sketch our approach to this problem, first with respect to the system's behavior, then to its implementation.

3. An interactive system as seen by the user

Observation of casual users at a terminal provides valuable insight into the fundamental design question of how a machine should present itself. Most of the recurring difficulties they encounter are characterized well by the following questions:

- **where am I?** (when the screen looks different from what he expected)
- **what can I do here?** (whén he is unsure about what commands are active)
- **how did I get here?** (when he suspects having pressed some wrong keys)
- **Where else can I go and how do I get there?** (when he wants to explore the system's capabilities).

We are beginning to learn that the logical design of an interactive system must allow the user to obtain a convenient answer to the questions above **at all times.** In other words, the man-machine interface must include queries about the state of the system (without changing this state), about the history of the dialog, and about possible futures. This principle is much more important for today's computerized machines, *black boxes* that show the user only as much about their inner working as the programmer decided to show, than it is for mechanical machines of the previous generation, which by visible parts, motion and noise continuously give the user a lot of state information.

In order to answer the user's basic questions in a systematic way, the designer of an interactive system must also design a simple user's **model of the system:** a structure that explains the main concepts that the user needs to understand and relates them to each other. The major concepts will certainly include many from the following list: the *types of objects* that the user has to deal with, such as files, records, pictures, lines, characters; *referencing mechanisms,* such as naming, pointing; *organizational structures* used to relate objects to each other, such as sets, sequences, hierarchies, networks; *operations* available on various objects; *views* defined on various types of objects, such as formatted or unformatted text; *commands* used to invoke operations; the *mapping of logical commands onto physical I/O devices;* the *past dialog,* how to store, edit, and replay it; the *future dialog,* or help facility.

The list is long and the design of the user's model of the system is an arduous task; but it should be possible to explain the overall structure of the model in half an hour. If the system's behavior then constantly reinforces the user's understanding of this structure, it will quickly become second nature to him. In contrast, if the system keeps surprising the user, it interferes with his memorization process and slows it down. Because questions will always arise during the learning phase, and because the right manual is rarely at the right place at the right time, an interactive system should be self-explanatory: it must explain the user's model of the system to the user, at least in the form of an on-line manual, preferably in the form of an integrated help facility that gives information about the user's current data and command environments at the press of a single key.

The user's model of the system is a *state-machine:* it has an *internal state* and an *input-output behavior.* Components of the state must include:

- the user's **data environment** (data currently accessible)
- the user's **command environment** (commands currently active).

The questions *Where am I?* and *What can I do here?* are then answered by displaying the current data and command environments, respectively [NW 80]. The user must be able to invoke this system display at all times, regardless of which applications program he is currently in, and its presentation must not change the state of the system in any way.

The system must have *universal commands,* which are active at all times. At least the state inquiry commands postulated above must be universal. In a highly integrated system many more commands can be made universal. General dialog commands that are needed in every interactive utility are taken out of the text editor, the diagram editor, the data base query language, and incorporated as universal commands into the system. The consequence on the user's view of the system is that all these utilities "talk the same language", and that in order to become proficient at using a new editor he only has to learn a small number of new commands: the data-specific commands are new, the data-independent commands remain the same.

4. Programming the man-machine interface

We have discussed the implications of the principles explained in this paper for the system's behavioral design. For a discussion of the implications for a system's internal structure I refer to other publications that present experience gained from implementing prototypes based on the ideas explained above. In any case the consequences must be discussed separately for the case of writing interactive application programs on an existing system, and for the design and implementation of an integrated interactive system. [Nie 80] *A pragmatic introductionto courseware design* is a tutorial for the first case. [XS 82] describes the goals, the design, and the implementation of an experimental interactive system that attempts to live up to all the principles stated in this article.

Most programmers have traditionally judged the quality of their programs from the point of view of machine efficiency and of internal structure. It is satisfying to observe that many have recently also become concerned with the quality of the man-machine dialog that their interactive programs conduct, as judged from the user's point of view. Well they might, for the computer user population is changing rapidly. Until recently only a small minority of computer users had the opportunity to use interactive systems. They were mostly professionals who use the computer daily: they are concerned with the inherent power of the computer for their application and get so used to its idiosyncrasies that a mysterious or even illogical man-machine interface doesn't bother them any more. An example of this situation is provided by UNIX, widely acclaimed as a model of a well-designed operationg system. [Nor 81] reaches the conclusion "the system design is elegant but the user interface is not". With the spread of low-cost single-user computers many casual and occasional users join the professionals, and for them the quality of the man-machine interface is crucial - an interactive system is only useful if the learning effort is commensurate with the brevity of the task they want to accomplish. It is for their benefit that computer professionals should start paying as much attention to their communicative skills as writers have always done.

Acknowledgments

My interest in man-machine communication was awakened while working on the PLATO project at the University of Illinois, to which I owe many insights. The experimental systems XS-0 and XS-1 served as test beds for evaluating the design techniques presented in this paper. I am indebted to my co-workers on these projects, in particular to G. Beretta, H. Burkhart, P. Fink, B. Plattner, J. Stelovsky, H. Sugaya, A. Ventura, and J.Weydert. This is a revised version of a paper presented at the 1982 International Zurich Seminar on Digital Communications, MAN-MACHINE INTERACTION, March 9-11, 1982.

References

[AP 79] *Apple Pascal Reference Manual,* APPLE COMPUTER INC., Cupertino, California, 1979.

[GV 80] E. Grandjean, and E. Vigliani (editors), *Ergonomic aspects of visual display terminals,*
Proc. Intern. Workshop Milano, March 1980, Taylor and Francis Ltd., London, 1980.

[Fol 80] J. D. Foley, *The structure of interactive command languages,*
in R. A. Guedj (ed.), Methodology of Interaction, 227-234, North Holland Publ. Co., Amsterdam 1980.

[HBR 81] P. Hayes, E. Ball, and R. Reddy, *Breaking the man-machine communication barrier,*
IEEE Computer, Vol 14, No 3, 19-30, March 1981.

[LWSS 80] H. F. Ledgard, J. A. Whiteside, W. Seymour, and A. Singer,
An experiment on human engineering of interactive software,
IEEE Trans. Software Engr., Vol 6, No 6, 602-604, Nov 1980.

[Mil 56] G. A. Miller, *The magical number seven, plus or minus two:*
Some limits on our capacity for processing information, Psych. Review, Vol 63, No 2, 81-96, March 1956.

[Mor 81] T. P. Moran (guest editor), *The psychology of human-computer interaction,*
Special Issue, ACM Computing Surveys, Vol 13, No 1, March 1981.

[NW 80] J. Nievergelt and J. Weydert, *Sites, modes, and trails: Telling the user of an interactive system where he is, what he can do, and how to get places,*
in R. A. Guedj (ed.), Methodology of Interaction, 327-338, North Holland Publ. Co., Amsterdam 1980.

[Nie 80] J. Nievergelt, *A pragmatic introduction to courseware design,*
IEEE Computer, Vol 13, No 9, 7-21, Sep 1980.

[Nie 82] J. Nievergelt, *The computer-driven screen: an emerging two-way mass communications medium,*
Educational Media International, Int. Council for Educational Media, London, 7-12, No 1, 1982.

[Nor 81] D. A. Norman, *The trouble with UNIX,* 139-150, Datamation, Nov 1981.

[Nor 82] D. A. Norman, *Steps toward a cognitive engineering: Design rules based on analysis of human errors,* Proc. Conf. on Human Factors in Computer Sysyems, Gaithersburg MD, Mar 1982.

[XS 82] G. Beretta, H. Burkhart, P. Fink, J. Nievergelt, J. Stelovsky, H. Sugaya, J. Weydert, A. Ventura, *XS-1: An integrated interactive system and its kernel,*
Proc. 6-th International Conference on Software Engineering, Tokyo, 1982.